Pathfinder Force

PATHFINDER FORCE

A HISTORY OF 8 GROUP

Gordon Musgrove

MACDONALD AND JANE'S · LONDON

First Published in 1976 by
Macdonald and Jane's Publishers Limited
Paulton House, 8 Shepherdess Walk
London N1 7LW

Printed in Great Britain by
Redwood Burn Limited
Trowbridge & Esher

ISBN 0354 01017 4

Contents

Foreword

by Air Vice-Marshal D.C.T. Bennett CB, CBE, DSO

By the number of people involved; by the duration and intensity of their efforts; by the importance of its destruction politically, strategically and tactically; and by destroying the German will to fight; the bomber offensive of the Royal Air Force was the greatest section of the British war effort. Without Pathfinders bombing was a disappointment; with them it was a great success.

The aircrews of the Pathfinder Force were not flamboyant 'glamour boys'; they worked in complete secrecy and no press or public relations officer ever came near them. They were serious, studious, meticulous – and gallant. Their contribution to victory was unique.

The tactical planning by Pathfinder Headquarters, for route-marking and target-marking, for diversional raids to draw off the German fighter aircraft, not only got our bombers on to target but also kept Bomber Command losses down to reasonable levels. Striking effectively at the heart of the Reich did more than anything else to break German morale. Destroying the heavy coastal batteries saved what would otherwise have been murderous casualties amongst our invasion barges. The ploughing up of all the French marshalling yards by Bomber Command, led by Pathfinders, deprived the powerful German army of the supplies it needed to repulse the relatively small invasion Forces which we landed. The 'buzz bombs' would have destroyed a large part of the South of England had not the enormous stocks and the launching sites been destroyed by our bombers with the necessary super-precision target-marking provided by the Pathfinder Force. Thousands of tons of high explosives opened the way for our armies in Normandy time and time again and the precision daylight marking, even in fog, stopped vital supplies to Rundstedt's Ardennes offensive and brought it to a halt.

These things were done by Pathfinders, offering their skills and their lives, that we, the British, should be free and independent. That was their target – and their only reward. This book tells their story.

Don Bennett

Dedication

On one occasion when King George VI was making an investiture in the Group, he turned to Air Commodore C.D.C. Boyce and remarked that, although he realized that outstanding bravery should be rewarded, the men he admired were those who went time after time doing their duty quietly and efficiently. These men he considered to be the backbone of the Force.

He could have been referring to F/O W.F. Keeler, one of the Pathfinder Force contingent on the Pforzheim raid. Shortly after take-off one engine feathered of its own accord, but the captain pressed on to the target and arrived on time. Many other pilots and crews undoubtedly did the same sort of thing and this is precisely what the King meant. It was not just a question of opening the throttles; corners had to be cut – more work for the navigator and the H2S set operator; higher fuel consumption and greater strain on the engines – more anxiety for the flight engineer; away from the anonymity of one aircraft in a bomber stream – more strain on the gunners until every speck of dirt on the perspex looked like a distant nightfighter; and for the captain the constant strain of flying an unbalanced aircraft, in Keeler's case for 6½ hours.

Target-marking was a team effort – each duty requiring a different skill – it was essential for Pathfinder aircraft to be over the target at a specific time in order to ensure a successful attack. As each crew was an integral part of the marking process and each crew member a vital cog in its efficiency, it follows that each individual in the Pathfinder Force was a part of its greatness. To each and every one of them I dedicate this book.

Acknowledgements

The author is indebted to the Air Historical Branch of the Ministry of Defence for granting permission to study its records to obtain the factual background so essential to this work. The staff were always willing to research into more secret documents to confirm or refute 'hearsay'. Mr G. Tibbutt, head of DRO (Air), was particularly helpful in tracing specific documents; his friendly interest was always a tonic: Mr F.S. White, the librarian at Air Minstry, proved to be a fount of knowledge, not only in his own sphere but as a 'Who's Who'.

The author gratefully acknowledges permission given by HM Stationery Office, the Imperial War Museum and RRE (Malvern) to reproduce material and photographs.

I should like also to express my gratitude to Air Vice-Marshal D.C.T. Bennett for the frank discussions we had about PFF; to Dr F.E. Jones for his help with the section on *Oboe*, and Sir Bernard Lovell in conjunction with H2S; Dr Noble Frankland for his generous loan of the map 'Mosquito Night Operations January 1943-1945'; and Mr R. Alfrey for his assistance and co-operation with maps and diagrams.

Of the many people who have helped by giving me information, lent me books, pamphlets and photographs, I should like to mention W/Cdr E.W. Anderson, Air Commodore C.D.C. Boyce, Mr A.J. Blanchard, Mr F.A.E. Crosskey, F/Lts C.R. Godfrey and G. Goddard (for their factual account of S/Ldr I.W. Bazalgette's last sortie) and Mr A.D. Walton of Keele University.

More personally I should like to thank Mike A. Garbett for his interest and help, his peerless knowledge of the Lancaster and its crews being of inestimable assistance; equally – placed second only because his name comes later in the alphabet – Howard Lees, whose intimate knowledge of the people and activities at PFF HQ filled in a vital gap in my research; in them I have found two new friends. My special thanks to my pilot, Geoffrey Parker, and to Peter Lowe for undertaking the task of reading, correcting and criticising the script; and finally to Joan, my wife, who did all the onerous and dull tasks which, although essential, would for me have been soul-destroying.

Ranks and titles in the book are those held at the time of the event, those listed in the index the highest attained. Every effort has been made to ensure accuracy.

I Genesis

Before the end of 1939 German fighters had proved they were far superior to our lightly armed bombers and consequently daylight sorties in strength were suicidal. If Bomber Command were to survive, attacks on Germany would have to be made at night even though the bombers were neither designed nor equipped for this. With the fall of France and the Low Countries the RAF had been robbed of its advanced bomber bases, and this meant longer time had to be spent over enemy territory to reach German targets. For economical as well as tactical reasons larger bombers were necessary and, to do lasting damage, bigger bombs were essential. The Course Setting Bombsight, although adequate for daylight needs, was virtually useless at night.

Poor equipment, however, was only half the story; bad navigation was the other half. The crews had not been trained for night raids, and the cloak of darkness which hid them from the fighters perversely hid the target from them. Navigating was largely a matter of map reading and relied on pinpoints, confirmed by radio bearings, or astro-navigation which was a lengthy procedure and also a highly skilled operation. Astro needed cloudless skies above, pinpointing cloudless skies below with preferably a moon to help – and there are very few nights in a year when these conditions prevail over both England and the Continent. Small wonder many aircraft got lost.

By 1941 heavy bombers were coming into the front line: Stirlings (February 10-11, 1941), Manchesters (February 24-25, 1941), Halifaxes (March 11-12, 1941). Larger aircraft meant a larger payload and bigger bomb-bays meant bigger bombs could be carried. The first 4,000-pound bomb was dropped on March 30, 1941. Progress was maintained through 1941 and continued into 1942 when the first 8,000-pounder was dropped (February 10-11, 1942) and when, exactly a month later, the Lancaster made its debut. Improved bombsights were in the pipe-line but they did not reach the squadrons until some time later.

From the beginning of 1941 to the end of June Bomber Command had dropped over 13,500 tons of bombs, more than in the whole of 1940, and a further 18,000 tons were dropped by the end of the year. Yet PRU (Photographic Reconnaissance Unit) photographs showed no appreciable increase in the damage to German industry. The Butt Report, published in August 1941, confirmed the dismal story of failure and showed that, at night, only one-third of those who claimed[1] to have bombed the target actually got within a 5-mile radius of the aiming point (A/P).

Because the build-up of Bomber Command was slow the German defences had time to organize, and although their expansion was also slow it was sufficient to keep pace with that of the bombers. Col Josef Kammhuber was put in charge of the defence. He organized an early-warning system along the northern shores backed by a searchlight belt about 20 miles in depth. The nightfighter orbited a Master searchlight until he spotted his quarry and returned to it after he had either lost the bomber or had shot it down. Intruders were never extensively used by the Germans although Kammhuber considered them to be a very profitable method of defence. Starting in June 1941 they made successful sorties over England until October when Hitler decided it was pointless shooting down bombers over England:[2] German morale could be boosted only by seeing the wrecked aircraft strewn across Germany, so the Group was posted to Sicily for daylight duties.

The Butt Report came out at the height of this intruder activity and made the crews realize that the high 'chop rate'[3] was to no purpose. Morale was at a low ebb and crews complained that they were being asked to do the impossible. They felt that Headquarters did not appreciate their difficulties and confidence in the AOC-in-C (Air Officer Commanding in Chief) was declining. In truth, it was not Sir Richard Peirse's fault. Reduction in standards of training, diversion of better trained crews to other Commands, misjudgment of operational capabilities were all sins of his seniors; he was just the whipping boy.

Early in 1942 two important events boosted the morale of the crews and started the Force on its whirlwind course.[4] The radio navigational aid Gee, first tried operationally in August 1941, was being pressed into service, and Air Chief Marshal Sir Arthur Harris took over Command at High Wycombe (Bomber Command Headquarters). Gee was easy to

---

1. In fact only 1 in 5 bombed within the 75 square miles as, on average, only 66% of those dispatched claimed to have bombed the target.

2. Most strategists consider this one of the big blunders of the war. At take-off and landing bombers were more vulnerable than at any other time during the sortie, with the possible exception of while on the actual bombing run. From 1942 the freedom from intruder attacks immeasurably cut down aircrew losses.

3. Percentage losses on operations.

4. Harris, quoting from the Bible (Hosea) during a Cinema News interview, said: 'They [the Germans] have sown the wind, and they shall reap the whirlwind.'

operate and provided the navigator with a simultaneous fix, which he could plot in less than in a minute. It was nicknamed the Goon Box because it was so easy to obtain a fix; any goon could do it. It was very accurate over England and being independent of the weather was an enormous boon to crews arriving back from a raid shot up or short of fuel. Compared with astro-fixes, radio bearings and dead-reckoning (DR) on Met forecast winds, this seemed like the ultimate, and in fact it did stand the test of time. After the war many parts of the world used Gee for civil aviation and some still do – India comes readily to mind. There were three main snags: limited range, decreasing accuracy as the range increased, and the fact that it could be jammed. It was not the complete answer but its values on this side of the North Sea more than compensated for its shortcomings.

Air Ministry, fully aware of Command's potential, were anxious to find a way of unleashing it effectively. The glowing reports given by the crews who used Gee on the August 1941 raids led the Air Staff to expect miracles, and their spring offensive was based on this optimistic assumption. During the Blitz the Germans, even with *Knickebein*[5] to help their main force, had found it advantageous to use a small force of 'fire-raisers', using incendiaries, to guide their bombers to the target. The British in their turn used the *Shaker* and *Sampson* techniques. Selected crews using Gee dropped flares in the target area and other experienced crews marked the target visually with incendiaries (*Shaker*). If the target was cloud-covered, both finders and markers dropped blindly on Gee fixes (*Sampson*). In both cases the finders attacked in waves keeping the target illuminated throughout the raid.

The illuminating technique was tried on its own on March 3-4 with an attack on the Renault works at Billancourt, near Paris. Night photographs, confirmed by a PRU sortie the next day, indicated the attack was very successful. Two attacks on the Matford works at Poissy, north-west of Paris, were successful too. So, with great hope, 211 aircraft, 82 with Gee, were sent to Essen on March 8-9. On this raid the *Shaker* technique was employed. Command said: 'The results were disappointing', and that was the understatement of the year. It was extremely difficult to drop a bomb on Essen without treading on Baron Krupp's corns, but the RAF almost achieved this. The Ruttenscheid area of Essen received most damage; but the flares were so widespread that the Germans had no clear idea which town was the actual target, and damage was reported at Duisburg, Hamborn and Oberhausen.

The next night was a repeat performance, and showed up the danger of using incendiaries as target markers. A Stirling carrying incendiaries was set on fire by flak and, as it was not the ideal load to be carrying in this

5. German radio navigational aid.

predicament, the pilot decided to jettison. Much to his surprise he found he had many friends in the area. The blaze also attracted latecomers, so Hamborn, 18 miles to the north-west of Essen, received far more concentrated attention than the target itself. Although the German gunners may have been elated with their success, Herr von Thyssen did not share their enthusiasm because his steel works were practically gutted.

Another instance of fires being bombed indiscriminately occurred on March 25 when Essen was again the target; a decoy at Rheinberg proved far more popular than the target itself. Essen was attacked eight times during March and April, and both the *Shaker* and *Sampson* techniques were tried, but the sprawling Krupp empire suffered very little damage. The best that could be said was that all the bombs had been dropped on the Ruhr, and that did not come within the most liberal limits of area bombing. More was being asked of Gee than, in the circumstances, it could provide. It did ensure that more aircraft reached the target area, but to pierce the smoke haze of the Ruhr a more accurate aid was required, and to avoid confusion an unmistakable target indicator had to be used. Outside the Ruhr its success was more marked, notably on Kiel and even Cologne, where the bend in the river helped visual identification. Lubeck on March 28-29 and four raids on Rostock between April 23 and 26 were devastatingly successful.

There were others, besides Air Ministry, who expected miracles of Gee, but Harris, ever the realist, was not one of them. When the Foreign Office suggested broadcasting a list of 20 German towns doomed for destruction,[6] he protested in no uncertain fashion: even if his force were capable of progressively destroying them, which he doubted, the weather, ever a fickle jade, would make the task impossible. Harris firmly believed that Bomber Command would be the decisive factor in the ultimate victory, but rightly judged it would be a long road with many obstacles, and that the German defences would prove the most formidable of them.

The lean years of 1939 to 1942 had not only sapped the morale of the crews, they had put in jeopardy the whole future of Bomber Command as a separate unit. The new AOC-in-C knew he must spike the big guns of the Army and Navy Chiefs of Staff, who were clamouring to get Bomber Command disbanded and the planes and crews put at their disposal to use as a tactical force. The Butt Report had given the critics some powerful ammunition and, knowing their views were gaining support in Parliament, they became more vociferous during April and May 1942; so much so that the Prime Minister minuted Harris to prepare a document on the role and work of Bomber Command.

The successes outside the Ruhr had done wonders for the morale of the

---

6. For propaganda purposes. As each town was destroyed, it was hoped the cumulative effect would make the whole German nation panic and so bring an early end to the war.

crews but little to silence the critics. A major victory against a major target was needed to achieve this. On May 30, Harris brought off a sensational coup by sending a force of '1,000' bombers to Cologne even though some were held together with string and sealing wax. It was a milestone in Bomber Command's career. To prove, to the Germans in particular and the world in general, that it was no flash in the pan, the dose was repeated two nights later at Essen, and then a third time at Bremen on June 25-26. The magical figure of 1,000 caught the imagination of the public and so the critics were silenced, and Harris was able to send a crushing reply to the Prime Minister on June 28. Officially styled a 'note', it contained 18 paragraphs and more than 2,500 words. Paragraph 17 begins: 'To sum up, Bomber Command provides our only offensive action yet pressed home directly against Germany. All our other efforts are defensive in their nature . . .' Paragraph 18 reads:

'Finally, it is apparent that an extraordinary lack of sense of proportion affects outside appreciation of the meaning, extent and results of Bomber Command operations. What shouts of victory would arise if a Commando force wrecked the entire Renault factory in a night, with a loss of seven men! What credible assumptions of an early end to the war would follow upon the destruction of a third of Cologne in an hour-and-a-half by some swift mechanized force which, with but 200 casualties, withdrew and was ready to repeat the operation 24 hours later! What acclaim would greet the virtual destruction of Rostock and the Heinkel main and subsidiary factories by a naval bombardment! All this, and far more, has been achieved by Bomber Command; yet there are many who still avert their gaze, pass by on the other side, and question whether 30 squadrons of night bombers make any worthwhile contribution to the war.'

The crews were delighted with Gee; it might be a bit 'dodgy' in the Ruhr and points east, but over this side it was 'bang on', and getting back in one piece was all part of the exercise – to them, the most important part. The enthusiasm did not reach the top. To the Air Staff it was a big disappointment; it was not the panacea they had hoped for, nor were the techniques an unqualified success. The common factor in all the outstanding successes of the spring offensive was that the target could be visually identified. There was now a growing conviction that only a target-finding force could solve the problem. The boffins had given Gee six months before the Germans could find some method of jamming it and, as the next marking and navigational aids (*Oboe* and H2S) would not be in service until the end of the year, there was some urgency to get such a force organized in order to maintain the momentum.

G/Capt S.O. Bufton was the champion of a target-finding force *per se*. Bufton's views carried a lot of weight with the Air Staff because of his extensive operational experience. From July 1940 he was successively CO of 10 Squadron, CO of 76 Squadron and Station Commander at

Pocklington until November 1941 when he became Deputy Director of Bomber Operations. He spoke both from his own personal operational flying experience and also from listening to crew de-briefing when no punches were pulled.

Harris and his Group Commanders were totally opposed to forming a *corps d'élite*. Harris was in favour of pathfinding in principle but wanted a selected squadron from each Group to fill the role. This would promote competition within the Group to become the best squadron and so take over the mantle of leader; in addition each Group could develop its own technique. A separate force, he believed, would create jealousy, make other crews feel inferior and, more than likely, make them perform in an inferior manner. Again it would be unfair to the Groups to take their best crews, and this would undoubtedly weaken Bomber Command. Bufton pointed out there were strong arguments on the other side. Jealousy would be created if one Group got equipment before another.[7] Although several techniques could be developed simultaneously when the whole force was on one target a standard technique would be an advantage. Each new navigational or target-finding aid, besides being in short supply, would need specially trained aircrews and ground personnel. As the target finders were to get the innovations first, training and supervision would be much easier if the force were concentrated under one commander. *Oboe* for example, with its total reliance on ground stations and limited planes per hour, would perpetually pose problems if divided among the Groups.

The gulf between the two was one of tactics. Harris believed that area bombing could and, in time, would win the war, and that the present methods of marking were adequate taking into consideration the capabilities of the average crew. Bufton believed that area bombing was just a transitory stage and that the present degree of concentration was totally inadequate; eventually, smaller and primarily strategic targets would have to be attacked. To this, Harris replied that if that contingency arose then the Group most suited to the role would be given the task, and by then it would have its own target finders already trained.

The argument went on through March and April 1942 and when no compromise seemed possible the Air Staff came out on the side of Bufton and ordered the new force to be formed. This was one of the rare occasions when Harris's wishes were overruled. Sir Charles Portal, Marshal of the Royal Air Force, tried to pour oil on troubled waters by affirming that the order came direct from the Air Staff and was solely their responsibility. In his letter of July 6, 1942, to the Prime Minister, Harris said: 'I have been overborne by the CAS and the Air Staff', but in his Dispatch, written later, he categorically stated that junior officers had

7. This did happen when 5 Group was equipped with Lancasters before the others.

been allowed to countermand the wishes of the Field Officer. This was entirely against accepted protocol and explains his antipathy towards the new force.[8]

Once the order had been made official Harris lost no time in announcing his choice of Commander for the new force, W/Cdr D.C.T. Bennett. Bennett's overseas posting was cancelled and he was summoned to High Wycombe. Harris explained the situation to Bennett and made no secret of his opposition to the whole idea, although he promised to support Bennett personally. Harris thought very highly of Bennett. He wrote: 'He [Bennett] was, and still is, the most efficient airman I have ever met.'[9] This assessment was not based on hearsay – Bennett, during his short-service commission in the RAF, served under Harris as a flight commander on 210 Squadron, and Harris says he helped him to get into Imperial Airways. Whilst it is always useful to have this kind of support, in Bennett's case it may not have played any real part as his qualifications were second to none. An outstanding pilot – even those who disliked him readily conceded this – he had a First Class Navigator's Licence: only six people before him had achieved this distinction. Also he had a Wireless Operator's Licence; he was probably the only pilot in the world to possess both. In addition to these qualities he employed a highly professional approach to every task he undertook. When he pioneered the London-America air service for Imperial Airways few thought it possible. By careful planning and excellent navigation he made the first trip successfully in anything but ideal conditions. Because of the strong headwinds he had to fly at 20 feet during daylight hours and at night at a mere 500 feet in order to save fuel. It was not until he was three-quarters of the way across the Atlantic that he could climb to a reasonable cruising height. He did the navigating himself and George (the automatic pilot) proved himself to be a tireless and efficient co-pilot. His wireless operator, A.J. Coster, was in constant touch with England and Canada and the crossing went without a hitch. He crossed the Canadian coast on track and on ETA. He gained further long-distance flying experience at the beginning of the war when in charge of ferrying planes from the New World to the Old Country.

Before being summoned to command Pathfinders, he had gained operational experience with 77 Squadron and later with 10 Squadron. As CO of both these, with characteristic thoroughness he studied the job of each crew member until he knew it intimately. When he interviewed new crews they were always impressed at his extensive knowledge of all aspects of operational flying. As W/Cdr E.W. Anderson said: 'Nobody who knows

8. Harris felt so strongly he refused to call it a target-finding force and christened it the Pathfinder Force.

9. Harris, 'Bomber Offensive'.

Air Vice-Marshal Bennett will deny his genius for anything to do with flying.'[10]

Like many outstanding men he could not understand why ordinary men were content to be ordinary, nor could he 'suffer fools gladly – and by his own standards there were many fools'.[11] This gave him an air of intolerance which made airmen shrug their shoulders and say: 'He may be able to do our jobs better than any one of us but he can't do better than all of us.' He was in fact shy and, off duty, covered this by a brusque manner which made him seem aloof and left him respected but not loved by his Force. Only those close to him saw the true Bennett and these to a man claim him as a friend; such friendships have endured through the years. He identified himself with the Force and any reflections on its good name he took as a personal insult. No Pathfinder could do wrong outside 8 Group – and such was Bennett's stature he would defend any member against his accuser no matter how powerful. Inside the Group it was a different story. Mistakes were not tolerated and he axed anyone who could not meet his requirements. This did not mean he let personalities sway his judgment, for he was ready, if the man was right for the job, to subjugate his own feelings to the greater good.

Technical knowledge, vitality, and thoroughness do not of themselves make a great leader, moral courage is an essential ingredient, and this quality Bennett undoubtedly possessed; in this he was like Harris. He also shared other characteristics with him – stubbornness combined with a maddening faculty for invariably being right. Diplomacy was not his long suit; he was a Ludendorff when perhaps a Hindenburg might have served Pathfinders better. But the Force needed a Ludendorff to cut through the red tape, and to overcome opposition and prejudices both to the new Force and its commander. His forthright manner and outspoken criticism made him few friends in high places, but this did not worry him, for he was in the war to beat the Hun and, like Harris, he fervently believed the bomber offensive was the quickest and surest way.

The structure of the Force was odd even for a country renowned for muddling through:

(i) Its commander was a newly promoted group captain, a rank which was not sufficiently senior to be in charge of five squadrons, so although Bennett was actually in command, on paper the Force came under the AOC-in-C Bomber Command.

(ii) The squadrons were moved to stations on which they had little more than squatters' rights.

(iii) Although the squadron personnel were under Bennett's command

---

10. Anderson, 'Pathfinder'.

11. Harris, 'Bomber Offensive'.

the permanent staff of the stations was under the control of Air Vice-Marshal J.E.A. Baldwin, AOC 3 Group.
(iv) Orders came through 3 Group HQ.
(v) The replacement of men[12] and materials, from the smallest bolt to the largest aeroplane, depended on the goodwill – of which there was none – of the Groups from which the original squadrons came. Bennett was allotted a staff of four: three officers and a corporal WAAF.[13] He set up his headquarters at Wyton, one of his selected stations: Oakington was the second station of his choice, and they each had a satellite, Graveley and Warboys.

Fortunately, a little more thought was given to the aircrews. Because they were required to complete 50 operations[14] instead of the usual 30 without a break, and also to face the extra hazard of being first on target, it was proposed to give them one step up in rank regardless of establishment. The promotion was to take place when they were considered proficient, but the seniority was to last only as long as they remained with Pathfinders. The Treasury, in the person of Sir Kingsley Wood, was opposed to this favouritism, but Harris stood firm – if the country wanted Pathfinders, they should be prepared to pay them; so the Force got its danger money.

Harris had intended to honour the Raid Leaders by giving them a special badge, and he now proposed that members of the Force should be honoured in a similar manner. When they became proficient they were to be awarded the honour temporarily, and this would entitle them to wear the 'Air Force eagle' below their ribbons. Provided they maintained that proficiency they were later awarded the badge permanently, which meant they could wear it after leaving the Pathfinder Force. There were numerous incidents of airmen being charged by the Provost Marshal's office for being incorrectly dressed and Group Commanders ordering them to take the badge down once they had left the Force. Bennett championed their cause and eventually Bomber Command issued a reminder to all Groups that the King had approved the badge and it was awarded on Air Ministry Order – even Air Vice-Marshals had to respect AMOs.[15]

All crews were volunteers and this remained the practice even after the

---

12. Ground crew and aircrew.

13. S/Ldr A. Buchan (Angus); F/Lt E.W. Anderson (Andy); F/O Barnicot (Barny); and Cpl Ralph (Sunshine), who was Bennett's personal WAAF secretary and came with him from 4 Group.

14. This was later reduced to 45, and in June 1944 a points system was introduced: 5 points for German targets and 3 points for the non-German targets, 5 points equalling one operation.

15. After the war another effort was made to ostracize the badge, but the PFF Association fought relentlessly for its serving members and won the day after a prolonged and bitter struggle.

Force became a group, and crews could be posted in direct. The nucleus, or founder members as they termed themselves, consisted of five squadrons; 156 Squadron from 1 Group; 7 Squadron from 3 Group; 35 Squadron from 4 Group; 83 Squadron from 5 Group and 109 Squadron from WIDU (Wireless Intelligence Development Unit).

Bennett's appointment was dated July 5, 1942, but owing to the wrangle over pay the crews did not assemble until August 17. Most people would have liked six weeks' summer leave in the middle of the war, but not Bennett; he more than filled his time with the affairs of his new command. He made his presence felt at TRE (Telecommunications Research Establishment) finding out about *Oboe* and more particularly H2S; he spent days discussing the ideas and proposals for TIs (Target Indicators); he visited the Group Commanders and found out that even if he was Harris's blue-eyed boy, it cut no ice with them. Harris had not exaggerated when he said they were opposed to the Force; only from Air Vice-Marshal C.R. Carr of 4 Group, his old Group, did he get the support necessary to start a venture of this nature. Nothing daunted, he set about the task with characteristic vitality and thoroughness and inspired his small band of aides to work to his impeccable standards.

Theoretically the squadrons earmarked for Pathfinders ought to have contained the crews which had been selected as Raid Leaders, but the Commanders, opposed as they were to the *corps d'élite*, would not allow all their best crews to volunteer and, with no pressure from Harris, their non-co-operation was made easier. Of those that came many could not rise to Bennett's standards and were posted back to their Group; the others, who did make the grade, knew they had the task of changing the attitude of the Main Force to the Pathfinders – from jealousy to respect. With Gee jammed, with no special navigational equipment, and with only makeshift markers, they were thrown into operations in their new role without any period of preparation or training.

Harris had told Bennett to be ready to operate immediately and operations were laid on for August 17, but were later cancelled because of the weather. On the following night, Flensburg was the target and only RAF jargon seems suitable for the description of that operation. The Pathfinders put up a terrible 'black', Met winds were 'up the creek', and cloud was 8-10/10ths making visual identification impossible. The number of Flensburgs bombed that night were almost as numerous as Schmidts in a German telephone directory. Viewed as a marking operation Flensburg was a 'flop'. All the pundits said: 'We told you so; we knew it wouldn't work,' and everyone was happy except Pathfinders.

II Pre Ruhr

The period August 1942 to March 5, 1943, covers the formation of Pathfinder techniques and the introduction of special navigational and target-marking equipment *Oboe*, H2S and Target Indicators. The techniques were evolved to suit the policy and strategy of the period within the limitations imposed by the availability of equipment and the capabilities of the Main Force. During that time policy was subject to revision: from the general Area Bombing policy of 1942 to the more specific requirements of the Casablanca Conference of January 1943. Command also had to bomb targets in Italy in support of the land offensive in North Africa.

Area Bombing was already accepted Bomber Command policy when Harris became AOC-in-C on February 22, 1942. During the Blitz on England, it was noticed that the disruption of gas, electricity and water supplies caused greater loss of man-hours than resulted from the destruction of part of a factory. As less skill was needed to bomb a town than to bomb a particular part of it – the rapidly expanding Force had not yet acquired precision – it was obviously better economics to use the area method. Also in a built-up area, there would sometimes be a bonus when an inaccurately placed stick[1] of bombs hit a vital factory. Another point, usually overlooked, was that there were many small, even one-room, factories in residential areas which were manufacturing essential parts.

By Autumn 1942 the Ministry of Economic Warfare[2] had finished its homework and was hoping to persuade Bomber Command to test its theories. If Area Bombing of industrial towns was to remain overall policy then the most fruitful area for operations was the Ruhr valley. The German economy relied to a great extent on Ruhr industries and such a concentration of towns promised a better result per ton of bombs drop-

---

1. Bombs could be released single, stick or salvo; fused or safe. The term 'stick' was used when bombs were released at close regular intervals.

2. The Ministry of Economic Warfare was an offshoot of the Joint Intelligence Committee which advised the Air Staff on German economy.

ped than could be expected anywhere else in the Reich. There was nothing brilliant in this deduction; most school children would have reached the same conclusion. Such platitudes made Harris suspicious of the Ministry's other suggestions concerning strategic targets and bottlenecks. Schweinfurt, the centre of the ball-bearing industry, was high on their list; Stuttgart, the Coventry of Germany, was considered worthwhile; and they laid stress on the advantage of attacking oil targets and transport facilities specifically, as opposed to the bonus damage on these installations, which Harris claimed to be getting with his policy. The Navy wanted large-scale attacks on the U-boat pens along the Atlantic seaboard. The Casablanca Conference listed these items and inserted the German aircraft industry as number two on its list.

The Air Staff put pressure on Harris and from time to time he did divert his force grudgingly to what he called 'panacea' targets. At this stage of the war, Harris was right. The Germans were unlikely to be short of ball-bearings;[3] it was not the moment to attack oil, because there were plenty of sources beyond the range of our bombers not even on maximum production; chaos in transport could not be created by isolated attacks.[4] Bombing the U-boat pens was a complete waste of time, men and materials, because Bomber Command did not have a bomb which could crack, let alone pierce, the concrete of the submarine pens. All these attacks did was to destroy French property and satisfy the ego of the naval hierarchy. The German aircraft industry continued to expand even through the devastating bombing of late 1944.

The RAF and the USAAF provided the only means the Allies had of attacking the heart of Germany until the end of 1944. There were those who believed that the two air forces could bring about the downfall of the Reich without the necessity of a second front. Harris was one of these but the Chiefs of Staff could not afford to gamble on this happening. The Casablanca Conference confirmed that they considered a second front was necessary. The different views on the strategy and capabilities of the two air forces had created the need for a conference, but the factions were too far apart for any compromise to be possible. What did come out of the conference was a general policy of aims, leaving the tactical methods of achieving them to the individual air forces. The aims were 'the progressive destruction and dislocation of the German military, industrial and economic system, and the undermining of the morale of the German

---

3. After the Americans attacked Schweinfurt (October 16, 1943) Albert Speer, Reich Minister of Armaments and War Production, reviewed the ball-bearing position and found that German industry, fearing that there would be a shortage, had so over-ordered that they had sufficient stocks to last them 6 to 12 months.

4. One of Speer's criticisms of British bombing was that too much time was allowed between attacks. This was said with specific reference to oil, but applied equally to transport. (Post-war interview.)

people to a point where their capacity for armed resistance would be fatally weakened.'[5] This was exactly what Harris considered he was doing; so he continued relentlessly with the single-minded purpose of bringing the Germans to their knees.

Bennett complained, with justification, that he had to operate his force in the role of Pathfinders with inferior aircraft, without special equipment and without any period of training. He used this early period to try out new techniques, until the special equipment became available a few months later, and from the experiments three types of marking emerged: Blind Groundmarking *(Parramatta),* Visual Groundmarking *(Newhaven)* and Blind Skymarking *(Wanganui)*. All PFF attacks fell into one or more of these basic categories, appropriate adjectives being used to signify a variant within the type; for example, the word *Musical* was added when *Oboe* aircraft dropped the initial markers.

Usually, when aircrew were transferred to special duties, they were sent on a course for training but Pathfinders had to learn the techniques on operations and perfect them in what normally would have been their free time. Lectures were given by senior officers explaining the duties of each trade and ways in which crew members could help one another, so working the crews up into an efficient unit. The aim was to bring to each one an awareness of his personal and special responsibility.[6] In this way crews, who individually may not have possessed above-average ability, became conscious of the need to reach and maintain high standards, and so they consistently performed better than the Main Force. Pride and prestige had inevitably to take some knocks, but prejudice against PFF was gradually broken down and this augured well for 1943.

The role of Pathfinders in the autumn of 1942 was primarily to find and illuminate the target area. Makeshift markers, 250-pound and 4,000-pound cases filled with an incendiary charge of benzole, rubber and phosphorus, were used to distinguish PFF incendiary bombs (IBs) from the Main Force incendiaries. They were effective only in the early stages of the attack but, like illuminating flares, were intended solely as a guide; Main Force crews were briefed to locate the aiming point (A/P) for themselves. In the New Year, when Target Indicators specially designed for Pathfinders were introduced, the policy was gradually changed. H2S enabled the PFF heavy squadrons to find the target more consistently; TIs to mark the aiming point distinctively; and *Oboe* was a blind bombing aid that was more accurate than visual marking. By the end of February, the Main Force was being instructed to bomb the TIs instead of trying to locate the target itself; PFF had graduated from a target-finding force into a target-marking force. This put more pressure on the crews because if

5. Casablanca Directive sent to AOC Bomber Command, February 4, 1943.
6. For the requirements of individual crew members, see Appendix X.

they were wrong the whole attack went astray.

Time spent over the target affected the number of losses caused by flak. One of the main purposes behind the '1,000-bomber' raid on Cologne was to test the effects of saturating the defences. The aim was 10 aircraft a minute although the dangers of collision and of being hit by 'friendly' bombs was increased. 'Concentration in time' did prove advantageous and the loss rate for raids of less than 35 minutes was 2.5% fewer than for those of longer duration. TIs reduced the risk of collision because the aircraft approached the target along the same track and crews did not have to mill around looking for the aiming point; time over the defended area was cut to a minimum.

The Main Force, 5 Group apart, liked being led. Besides being quicker it was easier to bomb a marker than to search for the aiming point, and crews were also pleased to be relieved of the responsibility. Attacks became more concentrated and concentration was one of the prerequisites of a successful raid.

The Pathfinder era began on August 18-19, 1942, when 31 crews of 7, 35, 83 and 156 Squadrons set out to mark Flensburg. The race was on to gain the honour of being the first Pathfinder crew to cross into enemy territory and F/Lt D.R. Greenup claimed the distinction. The target was to be marked with flares and incendiaries but contrary winds, a dark night and ground haze made accurate marking impossible. Of the 16 crews who claimed to have marked the target, some were undeniably not over Flensburg. The German radio said that bombs were dropped in the Heligoland Bight and Kiel Bay areas. It was not an auspicious start, but conditions could hardly have been worse.

Frankfurt was the next target, on August 24-25, but cloud prevented positive identification and again the attack was a failure. In all, 5 PFF aircraft were missing from this sortie, including that of W/Cdr J. Shewell, CO of 7 Squadron, and 2 crews had combats with German nightfighters. Sgt W. Longmore was attacked by 2 fighters near Fremont and, although the Wellington was extensively damaged, he made a safe landing at base; the crew was unhurt. Sgt J.E. Land, in a Stirling, was twice attacked by a Junkers Ju88 and immediately after the second attack a Focke-Wulf Fw190 came in from the port quarter. The Focke-Wulf made two further attacks and as it broke away after the third the Stirling's rear gunner, Sgt G.T. Eldridge, saw his tracer entering the fighter. It dived away steeply and the wireless operator saw it burst into flames. Seconds later Sgt F.E. Davidson saw an orange flash on the ground. The list of damage to the Stirling was almost as long as the catalogue of spare parts. For the crew the damage to the undercarriage was the most serious as this entailed a crash landing. Although the port engine cut on the approach just before touchdown, the crew was uninjured.

Kassel, on August 27-28, proved a little better, and although the target was covered with industrial haze there were a few smiling faces at debriefing. Bomber Command summary recorded fires all over the town. One large bomb, which fell in the Henschel works, caused a series of explosions which started fires in the factory area. The German nightfighters were up in strength and most crews reported seeing combats. Pathfinders lost three Wellingtons and another three aircraft were intercepted. Sgt W.P. Thomson's Wellington was attacked continuously for half-an-hour. At 03° 00E, a Messerschmitt Me110[7] attacked twice from astern, but rear gunner, Sgt W.S.G. Belton, damaged the fighter, which dived towards the sea and was not seen again. Thomson jettisoned a 500-pound bomb to get more height and speed but 20 minutes later a single-engined fighter made three attacks, one from the stern and one from each side. The front gunner was able to add his weight to the defence and this was sufficient to discourage the enemy. Belton was trying to unblock stoppages to three of his guns when an unidentified aircraft attacked from the stern; again the fighter was discouraged by accurate fire. Thomson felt as if he was the intruder in a fighter stream so, with only one gun serviceable, he decided to abandon the mission.

Two Stirlings were also in the firing line. F/Sgt A.A. Bishop, like Thomson, found the fighter stream. A minute after he had jettisoned 24 x 30-pound incendiaries because the Stirling would not climb above 9,000 feet, his rear gunner, Sgt R. Hart, reported an Me110 following from 1,000 feet below. The fighter pilot must have seen the incendiaries go down, and perhaps thinking the Stirling was in trouble shadowed the bomber for 20 minutes keeping just out of range. Tiring of the game, the Hun made three exploratory approaches, but found Hart too accurate to risk a determined attack. As he came in for the third time, Bishop turned towards the fighter and this gave Sgt S. Bernard, the mid-upper gunner, a chance to get in a long burst of fire. He hit the Me110's tailplane and the fighter dived away. Almost immediately an Fw190 came in from the starboard but concentrated fire from both gunners forced it to break away. Some 30 minutes later, the Stirling, now down to 7,000 feet, was again attacked by an Fw190 but three short bursts from the vigilant Hart were sufficient to discourage the fighter pilot.

S-Sugar of 7 Squadron was 20 miles west of Munster when it was engaged by a Ju88. F/O C.W. Gwilliam immediately jettisoned his incendiaries and Sgt J.W. Pearson, the rear gunner, opened up early to try to deter the fighter. The German pressed home the attack and evasive action gave all three gunners a chance to fire at the enemy. The Ju88 fell belly

---

7. The Messerschmitt BF110 was, during the war, incorrectly referred to as the Me110 by the Allied forces.

upward until lost to view at 2,000 feet – it was claimed as 'probably destroyed'.

The next raid on August 28-29 gave the force its first real success and, on a clear night, Nuremberg was identified and marked with special 250-pound incendiaries, Red Blob Fires, which were bombed to good effect. BCHQ telephoned Bennett to tell him that the marking was plumb on the target and of great value to the attacking force. Experienced crews said it was a better raid than the '1,000-bomber' raid on Cologne. Three PFF aircraft had inconclusive brushes with enemy fighters and another three were missing. From 175 sorties flown during the month, 16 aircraft failed to return, a loss rate which did not encourage volunteers.

September began with a 'black'. On the first of the month, Saarlouis was marked instead of Saarbrucken and the Main Force bombed the town and started some good fires. Harris chided Bennett over the error, but finished by saying that much industrial damage had been done and, although the target did not rate the attention it had received, the raid could not be classed as a failure. The following evening 201 bombers, led by 18 Pathfinders, set out for Karlsruhe. The Illuminators lit up the target area and other PFF crews dropped 250-pound IBs and Cookies (4,000-pound bombs) around the aiming point, one of the Cookies starting a fire in the dock area. The attack was a concentrated one and the target was covered with columns of smoke rising to 6,000 feet.

During September, Bennett explored the limits of the techniques so far available to Pathfinders by trying different permutations in the methods of illuminating and marking the target. In the same period, he experimented with coloured flares and Pink Pansies,[8] and introduced Primary Visual Markers. Pink Pansies were used as target markers for the first time on Dusseldorf on September 10-11. Coloured flares were also used; red to mark the west of the town and green to mark the east. The Main Force flew between the reds and greens and dropped their bombs on the Pink Pansies. A large area of fire, between the river and the aiming point, could be seen from the Dutch coast; from above, the town was obscured by a dense pall of smoke.

T – Tommy, F/O J.P. Trench's Stirling, was hit by flak over Maastricht and both port engines were put out of action, the port outer actually falling off. The wireless operator wedged himself into the nose of the aircraft and, by putting pressure on the rudder bar and control column, helped the captain to keep it on an even keel. At the Dutch coast the plane was down to 200 feet and everything movable was jettisoned into the sea. By the time the English coast was reached the Stirling had lost another 100 feet and at this point the starboard inner cut. The plane crashed in a field near Clacton and the navigator dragged out the uncon-

8. The name given to the 4,000-lb incendiary because it ignited with a distinctive pink flash.

scious pilot and wireless operator. The front gunner and the engineer dashed back into the burning plane to rescue the injured tail gunner; the petrol tanks exploded and they were killed. The mid-upper gunner, F/Sgt R.F. Jenner, eventually rescued P/O W.N. Glendenning, who suffered severe burns.

Primary Visual Markers were used in the first of two successful attacks on Bremen, when, on September 4-5, PFF was divided into three groups each with a particular role. The Illuminators were first on target with white flares; then the Primary Visual Markers following closely behind, dropped coloured flares if they identified the aiming point visually; next came the Backers-up who dropped their IBs on the coloured flares. This raid was described as the 'best to date' and the next day PRU found many fires still burning in the docks and town. Several factories in the shipyards were gutted; railway sheds and warehouses in the goods yards had been destroyed by fire and others were still burning. The second attack, on September 13-14, was far more spectacular: two Pink Pansies[9] started an enormous fire and the Main Force crews were able to exploit it, leaving two square miles in the centre of the port area ablaze.

Timing and technique were improving with each raid, but the weather was still the deciding factor; the major successes had all been on clear nights. The attacks on Duisburg, Frankfurt and Essen illustrated this point. The varied cloud and industrial haze at Duisburg on September 6-7 prevented many crews identifying the aiming point and, although one big fire and many small ones spoke of some success, the raid lacked the concentration of recent attacks. Two nights later the 8-10/10ths cloud made the task of the Pathfinders difficult and although they started fires in Frankfurt the bombing drifted to the south-west. First the woods to the south of the town were set on fire and later fires were started in Russelsheim 14 miles away. Russelsheim housed the Opel car factory and the Michelin tyre works and both these factories were damaged so the night was not completely wasted. Seven Pathfinder aircraft were intercepted but on this night the enemy came off second best. Trench was attacked by an Me109 from the starboard quarter, while a second Me109 approached from astern. The rear gunner engaged the fighter coming in from the starboard and, at point-blank range, Glendenning was certain he must have damaged it. Both fighters then broke off the encounter, and the Stirling went on to bomb the target. Back at base, Glendenning broke out in a sweat when he was shown the hole made by a cannon shell, which had missed him by less than 6 inches.

P/O Malkin, in Halifax G-George of 35 Squadron, was attacked by an Me110 on the way to the target. As the fighter approached, the front and rear lights were switched on and off; so the mid-upper gunner searched

9. A photograph showed one of them on the aiming point.

the sky in case the Me110 was a decoy. The rear gunner fired two long bursts and strikes were observed. The Halifax was hit by cannon and machine-gun fire and Malkin was wounded in the leg. He made a diving turn to starboard and this gave both gunners a chance to fire at the enemy. Tracer was seen to enter the fighter between the two engines, the Me110 drifted down and disappeared, Intercepted Traffic[10] suggested that the fighter was probably destroyed. Malkin bravely piloted the plane back to base and landed safely.

The 'elusive' Essen was the target on September 16-17 and once again it lived up to its name; although a huge explosion and large fires were reported, PRU photographs showed no substantial damage. The Wellingtons of 156 Squadron seemed to have attracted the German night-fighters' special attention. F/Sgt T.E. Case was attacked by a Ju88, but a long burst of fire from his tail gunner convinced the enemy that discretion was the better part of valour. Sgt V.J. Bastable was attacked by a single-engined fighter and he too escaped without injury. Sgt G.A. Proudfoot was not so fortunate. The crew were all positioned to drop their Illuminator flares when an Fw190 attacked from astern. Cannon fire raked the aircraft; part of the starboard aileron was shot off and fabric was ripped from the starboard wing and the mainplane. P/O R. F. Tinkler, the wireless operator, was injured in both feet. The nightfighter came in a second time to complete the kill but instead was itself shot down, flames coming from both wings. On the way home, near Emmerich, the Wellington was attacked by a single-engined fighter and as the aircraft was difficult to manoeuvre Proudfoot side-slipped down to 5,000 feet and into the protection of nearby cloud. At this stage, the port engine began to misfire and finally cut 20 miles from the English coast. Because his undercarriage was also damaged, Proudfoot had to crash-land on one engine and during the crash the flares, which the crew thought had been jettisoned, burst into flames when forced through the floor of the aircraft. The navigator, Sgt B. Couchman, was badly burnt while rescuing the injured wireless operator.

On September 19-20 Bomber Command was out in strength and two targets were attacked. The night was clear over central Germany and PFF crews were able to identify Ammer See and from this pinpoint they made an accurate DR run to Munich which they lit and marked efficiently. An innovation, route-marking, proved very successful; Ammer See, the last turning point before Munich, was marked by PFF. The flares ensured the bombers were on track at the beginning of their run up to the aiming point, and many fires were started in the target area. One terrific explosion lit up the whole town and the last aircraft reported 17 or 18 fires 'burning strongly'.

10. From home-based wireless operators monitoring the German GCI.

By contrast, the haze over Saarbrucken made visual identification of the aiming point impossible and the attack a poor one. In the news again was 156 Squadron – S/Ldr A. Ashworth was carrying flares and they ignited so, with flames and smoke coming through the floor of the plane, he ordered 'abandon aircraft' and the crew baled out. To his horror, he could not find his own parachute and so he made for open country to find somewhere to land. Incredibly the fires died out and he brought the plane back to England single-handed, landing at West Malling.

Owing to a clampdown in the weather there were no operations during the last ten days of September. The bad weather persisted until the end of the year and Bomber Command operated in strength only 25 times during October, November and December. The frustration, caused by long periods of inactivity, gnawed at the AOC-inC's patience and on more than one occasion crews had to take off and land in appalling conditions.

On the night of October 5, when Aachen was the target, most crews took off in a thunderstorm. Just after getting airborne, Halifax T – Tommy of 35 Squadron was struck by lightning, blinding the engineer, Sgt J.E. Jones. Fortunately, he recovered his sight after several days, but it was an alarming experience. 156 Squadron had a disastrous night; only 5 out of 12 aircraft detailed managed to take off and of these two crashed in England, one of the pilots being killed. A third ran into an electrical storm near the French coast. The aircraft was struck by lightning and this put the port engine out of action. F/Lt D.R. Greenup jettisoned his flares and turned for base. The defences seeing the flares and thinking they were being attacked opened fire on the Wellington. To escape the intense and accurate flak, the pilot threw the plane into a dive. The crew decided to bale out but, because of the turbulence, Greenup was unable to keep the aircraft steady enough to get out himself so he set course for England, and eventually crash-landed at Manston.

On October 13-14 the target was Kiel; in spite of ground haze and a smoke screen PFF started some good fires. They provided a beacon for the Main Force and later crews reported that the glow could be seen for 100 miles. Aircrews were very superstitious and P/O O.W. Rees might have been excused for thinking 'unlucky 13th' after being hit by flak over the target and losing his starboard engine. The petrol tanks were holed and when he landed at Sutton Bridge the gauges were reading empty. Two days later his luck was still running sour – just after bombing Cologne he was coned by searchlights and received an unholy pasting from flak. Despite the starboard and tail wheels being damaged, Rees made an excellent landing at Martlesham Heath. Three of the crew were injured, F/Sgts H.R.M. Stroud, W.G.L. Brown and Sgt G.F. Culver, the last having to have both legs amputated. The attack on Cologne was a poor one, but that was not PFF's fault. Main Force crews were as far adrift as

Bonn. Red Blob incendiaries and Pink Pansies lost their effectiveness once fires got a hold so the blaze at Cologne, started by Pathfinders, needed something to distinguish it from the many others within a 50-mile radius. Because of the cloud over Germany and inaccurately forecast winds, most crews were lost and so they reverted to type and bombed the nearest fire.

Between October 22 and November 30, Bomber Command made 11 sorties to Italy in support of the invasion of North Africa by British and American land forces. Two attacks on Genoa and one on Turin, on October 22, 23, and 24, were followed by four attacks on Genoa in the first half of November. On each occasion the weather was clear and extensive damage was inflicted. Notably on November 7-8, the raid was an outstanding success. A large number of heavy-calibre bombs were dropped which, according to the Italian radio, caused 'huge damage'. Eight large fires spread through the town and dock area, and two impressive explosions in the inner harbour were logged by most crews. Pathfinder Illuminators did an excellent job; the area was so well lit by flares and fires that buildings could actually be seen to topple.

Weather at bases was appalling and many crews were diverted. For once, life was more hazardous over England than over the target. P/O D.B Todd was going round again at Waterbeach when the aircraft mysteriously exploded and all the crew were killed.

Boozer, a new device which warned aircraft when the ground defences were taking a particular interest in them, was tried out by 7 Squadron for the first time on the Genoa raid of November 13-14. A red light came on in the wireless operator's compartment when searchlights or guns were vectoring the bomber. By receiving this early warning the pilot could take evasive action before being coned or shot up by predicted flak. Sandwiched between the four Genoa raids in November, Bomber Command made a sortie to Hamburg on the 9th-10th. A wind change which blew most aircraft south of track, severe icing and 10/10ths cloud combined to make the attack a 'complete and costly failure'. That was the bitter summary from the Oakington ORB (Operational Record Book). Of the 10 Pathfinder Stirlings which took off from Oakington, 5 returned early because of icing and 3 failed to return. In all 13 PFF crews returned early, the highest percentage ever recorded by Pathfinders.

The second half of the month followed the same pattern with four attacks on Italy and one on Germany. Turin was the Italian target and the Fiat works were singled out for special attention. On November 20-21, the total force of 233 included 54 Wellingtons – the largest number of aircraft sent to Italy during this phase. The Bomber Command report said that it was reasonable to assume that the smoke, which completely covered the target, was due to the attack and not to a smoke screen. On November 28-29, Command again mustered more than 200, although 67 of these did not see the concentrated PFF flares round the aiming point. Nor could they claim any of the credit for the fierce fires and explosions around the arsenal; they were already on their way home. The following night was even worse; only 19 Main Force crews braved the Alps. All the 16 Pathfinders – 9 Stirlings and 7 Lancasters – completed the sortie but the target needed no finding because fires were still burning from the previous attack.

Ashworth's solo flight from Saarbrucken in September and Greenup's October solo channel crossing were followed by W/Cdr B.V. Robinson's landing at Colerne without his crew after the Turin raid on November 18. The flares, which had hung up over the target, ignited as the Halifax was crossing the Alps on the return journey. Smoke poured into the aircraft and the crew were ordered to bale out. With the escape hatch open, the smoke cleared and the fires died out. For a time, pilots were not the most popular crew members, and it was feared the fashion for solo flying might spread to the Sergeants' Mess.

On November 22-23, the target was Stuttgart and although it was a bright moonlit night a thin layer of cloud and ground haze made target identification difficult for the 25 PFF crews, with the result that the weight of the attack fell to the south-west of the aiming point. Sgt R.J. Wallis's Wellington was hit by flak over Stuttgart, the rear gunner was injured in the hand and eye and the wireless operator was wounded too. They were intercepted on the way back by an Me210[11] which fired only two short cannon bursts but damaged the port tailplane, the port aileron and the hydraulic system, leaving the flaps and undercarriage unserviceable. Sgt R.H. Stewart, the gunner, in spite of his injuries and a damaged turret, kept on firing. The fighter came in so close that Stewart saw the pilot's face as he passed over the Wellington. By diving steeply to port and losing height to 3,500 feet, Wallis evaded a second attack. Sgt F.J. Walder had to help the pilot in order to keep the aircraft straight and level. Together they nursed the plane back to England and made a belly landing at Bradwell Bay.

Most of the other crews enjoyed the sortie. The route took them low over France to fox the German RDF (Radar Direction Finding) and GCI (Ground Controlled Interception). Trains were shot up, searchlights shot out, gun posts attacked and a flak ship silenced. F/Lt P.A. Mackenzie's exploits were typical. His gunners, Sgt C.M. Coghill and F/Sgt L. Fieldhouse, set a warehouse on fire; sent the workers at two factories scuttling to the shelters; and attacked two trains and two flak batteries. Flying at 200 feet, they were coned by searchlights; Mackenzie's gunners shot

11. In fact it is doubtful if it was actually an Me210. Probably all these gunner's references to Me210s were cases of misidentification – the aircraft were rarely used and the Germans considered them a failure.

them out but not before three flak guns opened up, which they dealt with as summarily as with the searchlights. The French people up and down the country came out to look at the bombers, leaving their doors wide open, ignoring the blackout rules.

On November 28 Bennett invited the other Groups to Wyton to hear their comments on the raids to date. Nos 1, 3, 4 and 6 Groups were on the whole complimentary, asking for less illumination and more groundmarking. By contrast, 5 Group wanted more illumination and no groundmarking. All were agreed that the flares were bursting too high, resulting in aircraft being silhouetted. Bennett thought that barometric fuses would solve the problem and put the suggestion to Bomber Command. The innovation of route-marking and land-marking was favourably received by all the Groups; as 5 Group made no comment this was taken to mean they could find nothing unpleasant to say.

The raid on Frankfurt on December 2-3 was a complete failure; thick haze prevented visual identification, and opinions differed as to where Frankfurt really was. F/O H. Duro had a sharp encounter with a Ju88 near Cambrai on the homeward route. It attacked from below, coming in from the port quarter, and Duro's Stirling was raked with cannon fire. The first sight the crew had of the Junkers was as it turned to attack from ahead, but apparently the pilot did not know Stirlings carried front gunners for when Sgt H.L. McBeath opened fire, he dived steeply to port and was not see again. Brief though the encounter had been, the starboard engine was put out of action and equipment in the wireless operator's compartment was extensively damaged.

The Ju88 which intercepted F/O C.A.J. Smith was not relying on surprise. It had a red light in the nose and a white light underneath in the rear. The lights were being switched on and off as if the pilot were signalling. Smith made a diving turn to port and the fighter tried to perform the same manoeuvre but overshot. The same tactics were employed when the Junkers made its second attack and, although the fighter made a tighter turn this time, it gave F/O I.C. Meickle, the mid-upper gunner, an opportunity to engage it. His accurate fire set the port engine ablaze and the plane blew up and fell in flames. As it hit the ground, there were two explosions.

On December 6-7, 9/10ths cloud over Mannheim meant that its day of reckoning was postponed but, the next night, the weather at Turin gave the crews a chance to relieve their frustration. PFF illumination was excellent and 5 Group bombing was on the mark; night photographs were plotted all round the aiming point. One 8,000-pounder exploded between the railway yards and the river and a huge blaze could be seen 60 miles away. In fact, the raid was so successful that fires were still burning 24 hours later and smoke from them hindered the second raid which was, by comparison, disappointing. The third sortie, on December 14-15,

1. Air Vice-Marshal D.C.T. Bennett with G/Capt J.E. Fauquier, CO of 405 Squadron, and the first Canadian-built Lancaster to enter service

2. (*Top*) An unmodified Stirling 1 of 7 Squadron which survived more than 40 operations. Bennett had all the defensive armour plating stripped from Pathfinder Stirlings to try to improve their performance

3. (*Middle*) Halifax TL – L bears Alec Cranswick's family crest. Cranswick was one of PFF's most highly respected pilots and was revered by all 35 Squadron crews

4. (*Bottom*) 35 Squadron Halifaxes and crews lined up for an inspection by the Prime Minister on March 3, 1943

5. (*Top Left*) S/Ldr K.H. Burns, an early Master Bomber from 97 Squadron, lost an arm when shot down over Berlin. After being repatriated he became CO of 35 Squadron and was in charge of the crews which toured America after the war

6. (*Top Right*) A/C 1 L.H. Pakenham-Walsh was a First World War pilot, being awarded the DFC and Croix de Guerre. Too old to fly in 1939 he volunteered for ground duties

7. (*Bottom*) 'Buck' Senger was a 'Yank' in the RCAF. His Stirling was severely damaged by a nightfighter when outward bound for Stuttgart on March 11, 1943 but he showed typical PFF resolution by 'pressing on' to the target

8. (*Top Left*) G/Capt J.H. Searby of 83 Squadron was the first Master Bomber; he controlled the highly successful Peenemunde attack on August 17-18, 1943

9. (*Top Right*) 'Pat' Daniels was one of the founder members of PFF, serving with 83 Squadron. Later, in November 1943, he became CO of 35 Squadron. He is seen here flouting the rules by wearing a Pathfinder Force badge on his battle dress

10. (*Bottom*) 'Tony' Davies was a long-serving member in PFF. Although he had completed a tour previously on Whitleys he did two tours in 8 Group. On at least three occasions his gunners drove off enemy nightfighters: 'Fire First' was their maxim

should never have taken place; there was continuous cloud en route and icing caused many of the crews to abandon the mission. Of six crews from 35 Squadron, only Sgt R.F. Wilkes could get sufficient height to cross the Alps, the other five Halifaxes having to turn back because of severe icing.

The weather clamped down until Christmas week when a short break between December 20 and 22 allowed Harris to get in two raids, one to Duisburg and the second to Munich. In bright moonlight and good visibility Pathfinders took off for Duisburg on the first night and dropped their flares to the north and south of the town; the Fire-Raisers did an excellent job and many fires were still burning furiously two hours after the attack. Wilkes was in the news again. While he was making his bombing run, his Halifax was hit by heavy flak and lost two engines, the port inner and the starboard outer; the DR compass became unserviceable and many electrical wires were severed. It was fortunate that the Halifax was at 18,000 feet when it was damaged as it could not maintain height on two engines. By careful handling, the Dutch coast was reached with the altimeter reading 6,300 feet and, although the North Sea was a daunting prospect on such occasions and claimed many victims, with fingers crossed they all felt they would make it. Suddenly 10 miles west of Over-Flakke, a Ju88 came in out of the moon on the port quarter firing from two fixed cannons. Sgt M.A.E. Bradford, the rear gunner, replied and the fighter dived away without scoring any hits. The Halifax was incapable of taking violent evasive action, but Wilkes turned into the attack as the Junkers came in a second time from below. The Hun misjudged his attack probably because the bomber was doing only 90 knots. For the third attack, the fighter climbed to the port quarter and closed to 300 yards without firing. Bradford hurled some invective at the German pilot, slandering his parents and exhorting him to come closer. At the same time, he discouraged him by firing a very accurate 10-second burst with all four guns, most of the bullets hitting the enemy. The Junkers fell away and was not seen again; the crew claimed it as 'damaged, probably destroyed'. A frustrated mid-upper gunner had to play a spectator's part because his turret was unserviceable. Wilkes made an excellent landing at Martlesham Heath. All through the ordeal, crew discipline was of the highest standard.

W/O H.R. Anderson was late on target and as he flew his lonely way home he must have been on every German GCI set on his flight path. He tempted fate by going three miles south of Gilze-Rigen, a nightfighter aerodrome. The inevitable Ju88 appeared on the Wellington's tail. The rear gumner opened fire first and missed and the return fire also missed. Then Anderson took violent evasive action and, although the fighter followed him down to 2,500 feet, there were still no strikes on either side. Finally, the enemy made his third attack from the stern and this time Sgt E.B.Hadden hit the Junkers and it broke off the engagement with smoke trailing from the port engine.

The following night everything looked set for a repeat performance by Bomber Command: skies were clear even as far as Wurm See, the last turning point before the run-up to Munich. However, a bank of 10/10ths low cloud over the target prevented visual identification and most PFF crews dropped their flares on a DR run from Wurm See. Fortunately, this turning point was route-marked by 83 Squadron and so, providing the Main Force crews flew a timed run from it, the attack had to be in the right place. The clear night and the deep penetration gave the German nightfighters a golden opportunity to make their presence felt. Four PFF crews were shot down and three others were attacked. Sgt T. Oakes was intercepted on the outward journey just south-east of Rheims. The first attack was from underneath and the enemy aircraft must have been in an almost vertical climb as the first hint the crew had that they were being attacked was when tracer was seen going upwards. The Lancaster was raked from nose to tail and the flares and photoflash ignited, setting fire to the mid-upper turret. F/Sgt P.E. Connell suffered second-degree burns about the face when his Mae West and parachute harness caught fire and the bomb-aimer was seriosuly wounded. Apart from the captain, who was fully occupied taking violent evasive action, the rest of the crew set about putting out the fire and throwing out the burning flares. During that five minutes, no one had any idea how many attacks the fighter made, but as the rear gunner climbed back into his turret, he saw the enemy dead astern. Although the tailplane was hit in this attack, the turret escaped damage. During the next 10 minutes, some semblance of order was regained. F/Sgt L.B. Wallace, the wireless operator, realized he too was wounded, and the rear gunner, mid-upper and flight engineer discovered their oxygen masks had been damaged during the first steep twisting dive. The bombs were jettisoned and the pilot decided to go down to 6,000 feet, where oxygen would not be a necessity, and make for base. At this point, Sgt A.D. Bouchard's voice cut across the conversation, 'Enemy fighter 600 yards astern closing fast; dive to port; go.' Although the fighter scored further hits, Bouchard's return fire was very accurate too. The enemy, who had previously had it all his own way, did not like the new odds, and broke off the attack. An unexploded cannon shell taken from the Lancaster proved to be of a new type which employed an extra detonator.

F/Lt J.F. Barron had a brush with an Me110 but it was the Messerschmitt which suffered damage and it had to break off the engagement leaving the bomber free to continue to the target. About 90 minutes later, Barron was not so fortunate; a Ju88 got his Stirling in its sights and the port wing, tailplane and the rear turret were damaged. The bomber dived to 7,000 feet but the fighter dived with it and made a second attack from the starboard, hitting the wing. By taking further evasive action and going down to 300 feet, another attack was avoided. F/Lt C.A. Hughes was also attacked: an Me109F opened fire from 800 yards but the tail gunner's second burst set it on fire and it crashed in flames. Fortunately, the crew did not relax their vigilance because 7 minutes later they were attacked by an Me110. The tail gunner, Sgt T.G. Elliott, again proved equal to the occasion and the damaged Messerschmitt sought the protection of a nearby cloud.

This was the last heavy attack of the year. PFF had flown 1,091 sorties with 50 crews lost over enemy territory. The unsuitability of the Wellingtons and Stirlings was reflected in the numbers which went missing, and their vulnerability to fighter attack and flak has been shown in the description of some of their ordeals. In all 18 Wellingtons were lost (6%) and 16 Stirling (5.4%), whereas the loss rate on Halifaxes and Lancasters was 2.5 and 3.7% respectively.

The experience gained in PFF's first four months was of great value in the New Year. Indicating the target area with long and short sticks of flares, using different coloured flares to mark the boundaries, and encircling the area with flares were just expedients and became obsolete when TIs were introduced; 250-lb incendiaries and Pink Pansies were also stop gaps; Illuminators, Backers-Up and Primary Visual Markers became part of the technique and route-markers were used on the majority of night sorties.

From August to December, 109 Squadron had logged a lot of flying hours, but none of them were against the enemy. After changing from the Wellington to the Mosquito, the *Oboe* transmitter in the aircraft started giving trouble and there was also intermittent interference which proved difficult to locate.[12] Modifications were suggested, wrangled over, and some were eventually approved. Everyone was getting hot under the collar at the delays and so, on December 20, 4 Mosquitoes were ordered to bomb Lutterade using unmodified *Oboe* equipment. Other bombing sorties were made and, on New Year's Eve, S/Ldr H.E. Bufton dropped Skymarker flares over Dusseldorf for 8 Lancasters of 83 Squadron. The Lancaster crews were briefed to drop their bombs when they had a flare in their bombsights, but 10/10ths cloud prevented assessment of the results – the first *Wanganui* of the war.

Oboe Mosquitos then carried out ten skymarking raids, eight on Essen and one each on Duisburg and Dusseldorf. Both 1 and 5 Groups took part in the experiments and the number of heavies increased from 20 of 5 Group on January 3-4, 1943, to 75 (25 of 1 Group, 50 of 5 Group) on January 23-24, when Dusseldorf was the target. Relying on the accuracy of *Oboe*, Bomber Command could now attack large towns through

12. Expanded in *Oboe*. See Appendix I.

10/10ths cloud.[13]

The first Main Force attack in January did not take place until the 14th-15th. Lorient was the target and Pathfinder crews found themselves in a double role as, after dropping their flares, they made a second run dropping incendiaries. The attacked started well but wild bombing by some of the Main Force ruined it. The following night, on Lorient again, there was 3-5/10ths drifting cloud, and the challenge seemed to bring out the best in the Main Force; most crews waited for a break in the cloud before dropping their bombs. An oil fire was started in the target area and a 1 Group Wellington 'gardening'[14] off the west coast of France could see the fires from 100 miles away.

On January 16-17, Pathfinders led the way to Berlin for the first time. Cloud persisted almost all the way and Berlin, although clear of cloud, was shrouded in haze. The night was memorable in spite of a poor attack because it was on this raid that the first authentic Target Indicators were used. Although doubt was cast on their accuracy, a distinctive red glow could be seen through the haze and this provided the Main Force with a definite target to aim at.

Dusseldorf, which had been the stage for the first *Oboe* skymarking attack, was the setting for the first *Oboe* groundmarking of the war,[15] on January 27-28. It was also the first time 109 Squadron had marked for more than a handful of the Main Force – 3 out of 5 Mosquitoes dropped red TIs and 11 out of 13 Lancasters, acting as Backers-up, dropped greens. A thin 10/10ths layer of low stratus covered the target so the 157 heavies dropped their high explosive and incdendiaries on the glow of the TIs seen through the cloud. Crews said they would not have been able to attack the target without the assistance of PFF marking.

On the night of January 30-31, H2S was used operationally for the first time. On this historic occasion, Hamburg was the target and PFF put on its finest pyrotechnic display to date. Red flares were dropped as route-markers and later green flares 16 miles from the target. H2S aircraft groundmarked the target with red TIs and the Backers-up dropped greens. To complete the display a second wave of marker crews dropped flares, red with green stars; this was a precaution in case the target was cloud-covered. The 130 Main Force heavies from 1 and 5 Groups were perhaps bewildered by the display for, although fires were reported visible from 70 miles away, the Medmenham[16] back-room boys could find

13. It is alleged that Hitler refused to believe that accurate bombing was being done from above cloud. He threatened to have the Defence chiefs and Met. officers shot for neglecting their duty and conspiring to deceive him by falsifying their reports.

14. Laying mines.

15. Webster and Frankland, in *The Strategic Air Offensive Against Germany*, overlooked this attack as they give the Hamburg raid on the night of January 30-31 as the first time when TI groundmarkers were used in conjuction with radar.

16. Central Interpretation Unit.

very little fresh damage.

Cause for celebration came appropriately during this important month when, on the 25th,[17] the Force was elevated to Group status and its commander to Air Commodore. The Air Staff wanted to put a stooge above Bennett but Harris was as good as his word and insisted Bennett should remain in charge. Group status meant a big increase in staff and orders now came direct from Bomber Command HQ and not via 3 Group. W/Cdr C.D.C. Boyce was made Senior Air Staff Officer and Bennett was at last relieved of some desk work. While never on the friendliest of terms with his SASO, Bennett knew he was the right man for the job, and they both set aside their personal feelings for the good of the Group. The AOC had more trouble finding a Senior Administrative

DELEGATION OF DUTIES AT GROUP HEADQUARTERS

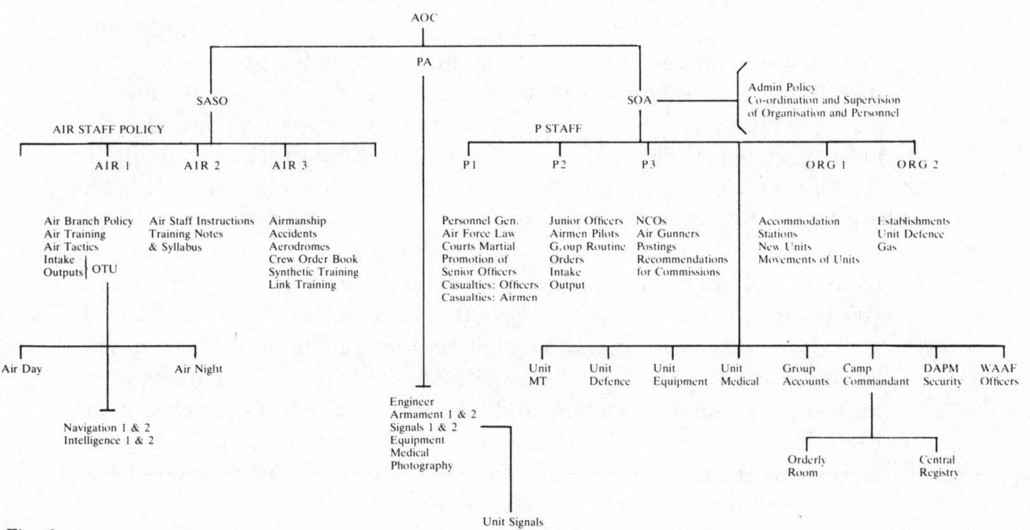

Fig. 1.

Officer to meet his requirements. S/Ldr H.McC. White was the fourth in line and he lasted the course. Officers who remained with the Group throughout its wartime career were S/Ldr W.T.R. Shepherd (Group Intelligence Officer), Dr J.C. McGown (Senior Medical Officer), W/Cdr C.F. Sarsby (Engineering Group Officer), S/Ldr W. Rathbone (Group Armaments Officer) and S/Ldr H.W. Lees (Group Photography Officer). There were two civilians attached to Group HQ: M.J. Thomas (Senior

---

17. With effect from January 13.

Met Officer) and J. Jukes from ORS (Operational Research Section). The junior positions at HQ were filled by tour-expired officers, and these were changed at frequent intervals so Bennett always had men with the latest operational experience at his elbow. He says: 'I had at HQPFF a band of hard-working types determined, in a practical way, to get the war won.'[18]

The new Air Commodore made plans immediately to convert 156 Squadron to Lancasters. He set up a maintenance depot at Wyton for Lancasters, and later one at Upwood for Mosquitoes. Bennett says: 'The serviceability of Pathfinder aircraft, in spite of the high damage rate, was as high, I believe, as any ever achieved in the Air Force.'[19] Coastal Command boasted that they inaugurated planned maintenance, but Bennett's genius for organization had pointed the way.

In contrast to the previous months, the weather in February was very good, particularly for the time of year, and the Main Force operated on 16 nights. Italy and the Navy's 'panacea' targets accounted for all but 4 of the attacks. On 5 nights the target was totally obscured by cloud, but with their new equipment PFF was able to mark the aiming point blindly and the Main Force bombed on their skymarker flares. The first of 4 attacks on Wilhelmshaven on February 11-12 was by far the best and also the most spectacular. The night saw PFF prepared for every eventuality. If the sky was less than 5/10ths cloud-covered, the H2S aircraft were briefed to drop only their flares initially and then to try to identify the target visually (*Newhaven*); if 5-8/10ths, then they were to groundmark blindly on H2S (*Parramatta*); if more than 8/10ths, to drop skymarkers (*Wanganui*). In fact the target was 10/10ths cloud-covered, so the H2S aircraft kept the target marked with flares for 15 minutes. At 2006 hours, crews reported a gigantic explosion. The flash lit up the sky and remained for nearly 10 minutes as a huge red glow visible for 60 miles. Subsequent PRU photographs revealed that the naval arsenal and ammunition dump at Mariensiel had been hit and totally destroyed, leaving an area of 120 acres round the depot completely devastated.

By comparison, when 160 Main Force crews set out to attack Wilhelmshaven on February 18-19 in clear sky and with excellent visibility, they were able to map-read their way to the target from the Fresians. The bombing was well concentrated around very accurate markers and S/Ldr D.A.J. McClure brought back a photograph showing his TIs falling on the aiming point. The following night, at Wilhelmshaven again, H2S operators mistook a new housing estate to the north of the town for the target. It was then discovered that the target maps were so out of date they did not show this suburban area nor any of the recent developments.

---

18. Bennett, 'Pathfinder'.
19. Bennett, 'Pathfinder'.

Maps of other towns were studied and most of these too needed revising.

Of the three raids on Cologne in February the *Wanganui* attack on the 14th-15th was by far the best, when 8 Halifaxes and 10 Stirlings were responsible for the skymarking. The same night crews from 83 and 156 Squadrons dropped TIs visually on Milan for 145 Lancasters of 1 and 5 Groups who started concentrated fires in the town which could be seen from 100 miles.

The first of three sorties to Lorient on February 7-8, was undoubtedly the best. The Illuminators dropped their flares accurately and these enabled the Visual Markers to identify and groundmark the aiming point. The attack was in two waves, the first dropping incendiaries and the second stoking the fires with H.E. Huge fires and smoke to 7,000 feet was Command's summary of the raid. Crews spoke highly of PFF marking and illuminating. Four enormous explosions stood out in spite of the inferno below. The decoy fire site was clearly recognized and, as one crew put it, was poorly patronized.

The month ended in a blaze of glory. The blaze was St Nazaire and much of the glory went to Pathfinders. All 5 Pathfinder squadrons were operating; 2 out of 4 *Oboe* Mosquitoes dropped greens and these were well backed by the heavy contingent. The A/P was marked continually for 34 minutes and the Main Force crews took full advantage of the TIs. One crew described the target area as a 'bubbling mass of red fire', and one explosion sent up a thick column of black smoke which gradually enveloped the town.

Only two crews were lost in January, but this was not entirely due to the fact that Dame Fortune was smiling on Pathfinders. Four of the 8 Bomber Command sorties were to France, where the defences were non-existent by Ruhr standards, and for the two attacks on Berlin, the Wellingtons and Stirlings were given a stand-down. In February, the losses rose to five but the sorties more than trebled so the percentage was down on January. No 156 Squadron was now operating in Lancasters and this helped the figures. The interceptions too were down and many of them were just probes by the enemy – the fighter made a pass at the bomber without firing, or just fired one burst and broke away. The German nightfighters were being increased in strength, and no doubt the new crews had been told there were plenty of rear gunners who slept on the way back from the target and that, until they had acquired some experience, it was safer to search for these crews rather than take on a wideawake gunner. As with the bombers, so it was with the nightfighters: more crews were shot down during their first five sorties than at any other stage.

Two attacks do not come into this category. P/O V.S. Moore was returning from a sortie to Hamburg on February 3 when he was attacked from below by an Me210. Moore was flying straight and level at the time because the navigator was taking an astro-fix[20] and the wireless operator was getting a simultaneous loop bearing. It was dark below with broken cloud, ideal conditions for the nightfighter to make a sneak attack. The fighter opened up from 700 yards with a long and accurate burst of cannon and machine-gun fire which raked the Lancaster from nose to tail and wounded Sgt J.T. Page, the bomb-aimer, in the foot. Crew discipline was excellent; the flares and TIs, which had not been dropped at the target because of the 10/10ths cloud, were jettisoned and P/O R.G. Luck, the rear gunner, went into action immediately, at the same time instructing Moore to make a diving turn to starboard. The enemy, seeing the flares and TIs burst, probably thought the Lancaster was on fire and so did not waste time on a dead duck. He broke away and the 'lame duck' limped back to base on three engines – the starboard inner having been set on fire – and Moore made a good landing in spite of a severely damaged tailplane.

On February 2, W/Cdr T.G. Mahaddie had just released his flares over Cologne when he was attacked by an Me110. The intercom in the Stirling was not working and the pilot did not know of the attack until red tracer and cannon shells were ripping into the bomber. Why the rear gunner did not use the visual intercom which was fitted for such an emergency was never explained. True he was in every kind of trouble: the rear turret was unserviceable and only one gun was firing, and that had to be operated manually. In the heat of the fray he shouted his instructions. The Stirling was out of control down to 9,000 feet and this probably saved the crew as, once again, the fighter did not stay around to count the pieces. The wireless operator, P/O I.J. Edwards, was severely injured and the mid-upper gunner, F/Sgt R.C. Pointer, slightly.

In December 1942 Bennett had readily agreed to allow one of his stations to be equipped with FIDO[21] and on February 18 the AOC went to Graveley to make the first test: despite a cross-wind he made a successful landing between the burners.

March began with a particularly good attack on Berlin. The H2S Halifaxes and Stirlings were out in strength, and 16 Lancasters from 83 and 156 Squadrons helped with the marking. Route-markers were dropped at 53° 51N 11° 59E as well as warning flares, 12 miles from the target, to bring the 274 Main Force crews over the TIs. The PFF timing was excellent and the reds were well backed with greens, although the main weight of the attack fell to the south-west of the Big City.[22] Fires could be seen from 100 miles and, much to everyone's delight, the defences were less active than usual. PRU photographs showed 22 acres of fire devasta-

20. Finding one's position by the stars.
21. Fog clearance. See Glossary.
22. Berlin.

tion in and around the Templehof marshalling yards; Telefunken Blaupunt-Werke and Askania Werke were severely damaged as well as the MAN and Daimler-Benz works. The fire-fighting services were unable to contain the fires, which spread rapidly fanned by a strong wind. Unter den Linden and Friedrichstrasse, the Oxford Street of Berlin, were still burning three days later. An unfortunate aspect of this raid was that the H2S screens had been saturated with responses over Berlin so that pinpointing on the PPI (Planned Position Indicator) had been impossible.

On March 3-4, at Hamburg, most of the Blind Markers dropped their TIs on the wrong bend in the river and these were backed up by other PFF crews. The Main Force followed PFF and so the weight of the attack fell on Harburg to the west of the town. The bombing force of 382 aircraft could not be blamed for this unprofitable night's work; rockets from PFF HQ went to all 8 Group stations, first for the bad blind marking, and secondly to the Backers-up who had little excuse for backing the wrong TIs as the night was clear and visibility good. Backers-up were supposed to bomb the estimated MPI (Mean Point of Impact) of all the TIs and had they done this the weight of the attack would have been much nearer the aiming point.

But the most outstanding 'black' of this period was put up by the Air Staff with the approval of the War Cabinet. Just after the introduction of H2S and *Oboe*, Harris was ordered to attack the submarine pens at Lorient and St Nazaire.[23] It was a gross misdirection of the Main Force and the Air Staff were made to realize this when the Battle of the Ruhr got into its stride.

---

23. Directive, Bottomley to Harris, January 14, 1943.

III Battle of the Ruhr

The Battle of the Ruhr began on March 5 and continued until July 14, 1943. For tactical reasons the attacks were not confined to the Ruhr area, but of the 47 major sorties all but 6 of the targets were inside the Reich. During the early stages of the battle advantage was taken of the long nights to make deeper penetrations into Germany. By attacking Kiel, Stettin and Berlin in the north-east and Stuttgart, Munich and Nuremberg in the south, Harris prevented the Germans from reinforcing the Ruhr defences. Led by Pathfinders, Bomber Command began its offensive in earnest and, as success followed success, the people of the Ruhr came to be regarded by their fellow countrymen as heroes on the level of those fighting with the VIth Army in Stalingrad.

The order of priorities laid down at Casablanca was altered during the period and from April 6 the main bomber effort was relieved of the unprofitable task of bombing submarine bases.[1] Amendments to the Casablanca decisions were contained in the Pointblank directive which was sent to Harris on June 10. The new plan called for a 'Combined Bomber Offensive' against the German aircraft industry – the RAF was to follow up the USAAF daylight attacks with night raids on the same targets. It was a good idea but unrealistic tactically because the weather over Germany could not be expected to remain constant; nor were similar conditions necessarily desirable for day and night forces. The state of the moon and the short summer nights were limiting factors for Bomber Command but did not affect the USAAF.

The Americans, who had ignored the warnings of Harris and Churchill that daylight bombing without fighter cover was suicidal, found that the combined fire power of their formations was not sufficient to ward off repeated fighter attacks. Long flights over Germany gave the fighters time to make inroads into the formations and losses became prohibitive. They were in a cleft stick; the plants had to be destroyed to prevent heavy

1. Letter, Bottomley to Harris, April 6, 1943.

losses, but to attack them involved deep penetration into German territory and heavy losses had to be endured.

The Battle of the Ruhr opened on March 5 with an attack on Essen. Harris showed his powers of leadership by choosing this target for the opening gambit. He knew that a successful raid against Essen would provide an effective boost for PFF; all Bomber Command's plans depended on the new Group being accepted as leaders. To date Essen, shrouded in industrial haze, had not been successfully bombed and even the '1,000 bomber' raid of 1942 had done little damage.

The 407 Main Force and 35 PFF crews on the Battle Order were determined to put an end to this immunity and the hopes of everyone connected with the operational side of Bomber Command were flying with them. The raid was planned as a *Musical Parramatta* and on the night 5 out of 8 Mosquitoes dropped red TIs and 22 PFF heavies backed up with greens. Pathfinders also dropped land-markers, yellow TIs, 15 miles from the target, so that all crews could attack from a datum point to avoid collisions. Zero hour was at 2100 hours; the first Mosquito marked at Z-2 as planned[2] and the last Backer-up dropped at Z+38 exactly on schedule.[3] The Main Force was divided into three waves, all aircraft to bomb within a 40-minute period. Halifaxes of 1, 4 and 6 Groups made up the first wave and they soon had some good fires going, an enormous explosion early in the attack helping to spread them. The Stirlings and Wellingtons of the second wave had no doubt the attack was in the right place because the *Oboe* reds were falling plumb in the middle of the inferno below. The all-Lancaster final wave kept the pot boiling and their HE bombs made fire-fighting almost impossible.

At debriefing, crews commented enthusiastically on the intensity and size of the closely grouped fires and they praised the technique and accuracy of PFF. PRU photographs showed devastation throughout the Krupp factories, 53 separate workshops being damaged, some of them completely gutted; fire damage was extensive. Bomber Command lost only 14 aircraft. Why it wasn't 15 seemed like a miracle. F/O F.J. Garvey had a ciné-camera on board to photograph the raid and he decided to make two runs across the target, dropping his Cookie on the second run. Immediately the 4,000-pounder was released it was hit by flak and exploded; the plane was lifted 500 feet vertically. The whole aircraft, in particular the bomb-bay, was riddled with shell splinters and pieces of bomb casing, and the plane was set on fire. The bomb-aimer had the presence of mind to jettison the photoflashes, which were in the bomb-

2. Webster and Frankland say the Mosquito was 2 minutes early – this is incorrect.

3. The sceptical may be surprised to learn that PFF heavies carried clocks in the bomb-bays, which recorded the time the bombs were released.

bay, before they could do any harm. The whole crew remained calm and the fire was extinguished in 5 minutes. At base, the souvenir-hunters had a field day; the filler plug from the Cookie was taken out of the mainplane and the arming pistol out of one of the engine nacelles. Pieces of the bomb were everywhere, the tailplane was dented and the port inner propeller tip bent. Altogether, it was a remarkable escape.

Nuremberg was the target on March 8-9 and the initial red TIs were dropped blindly by H2S aircraft of 7 and 35 Squadrons. The reds were too scattered for the Backers-up to get a good concentration of greens. Each group of markers had its advocates and many fires were started. The MAN factory, making diesel engines for submarines, was one of the early callers for the fire brigade, but the fires were so intense they could only aim at containing them. Other 'medieval buildings' which the Germans claimed the RAF had destroyed included the Siemen Schuckert electrical works, an aluminium and a chemical works and four engineering plants. The marshalling yards, repair shops and the adjacent railway administration buildings also received direct hits. The damage was so extensive that the people were told to repair their own houses and also to help their neighbours. On Saturday and Sunday, they had to 'volunteer' to help clear up the town centre.

It was obviously good tactics for the German nightfighters to make as many interceptions as possible when the bombers were outward bound. F/O G.F. Lambert was on track for Nuremberg and had not gained operational height when he was intercepted by a Ju88. The enemy came in from the starboard quarter below and got in a long burst before the rear gunner, Sgt J. Knight, spotted him. Lambert put the Halifax into a corkscrew dive but not before the Junkers fired a second time. As soon as Knight returned the enemy's fire the fighter broke away. He had achieved his object: with the port inner propeller damaged and oil tank pierced, 2 feet of the port flap shot away, the port bomb-door shot off and the rear turret out of action, the sortie was abandoned and Lambert set course for base.

The Sergeants' Mess produced its intrepid lone flier in the shape of Sgt D.R. Spangton.[4] He was the mid-upper gunner in a Stirling of 7 Squadron. The rest of the crew baled out over the English Channel but Spangton did not hear the order and sat there oblivious of the fact that the plane was flying itself. It was not until it had crossed the English coast that he discovered his predicament. He baled out very smartly and was the only one of the crew to survive.

The value of route-marking was demonstrated on the night of March 10-11 when Munich was the target. Although the forecast winds were awry, the route-markers at Metz served to pull the Main Force back on

---

4. See Chapter II, Pages 19 and 20

track and those at Ammer See gave both PFF and the bombers an accurate DR run to Munich, which was shrouded in haze. The attack opened late, but from the scarcity of bombing on the first TIs it was obvious most of the Main Force was late too. Judging by the violent reaction of German radio, the raid must have been a success. They claimed the raid was directed against monuments of art. The monuments included two car factories making munitions, a wagon works and a gas works. Exactly a week after Essen's first real taste of war Bomber Command put on a repeat performance. Crews reported a rectangular mass of flames with smoke rising to 15,000 feet and the damage, covering 400 acres, most of it in the Krupp empire, was even greater than on March 5.

The essential difference between the two attacks on Essen and the attacks on Nuremberg and Munich lay, not in the comparison of the amount of damage done, but between the degrees of concentration obtained with *Oboe* and H2S. The relative concentrations achieved reflected the capabilities of the marking devices. In *Oboe* the human element was reduced to a minimum. Radar instruments at two ground stations continually measured aircraft position and automatically relayed the information to the crew in a recognizable manner, which enabled them to make an accurate run to the target and release their bombs when they were over the aiming point. H2S was not a precision device in the *Oboe* sense of the word. It was designed as a navigational aid for use beyond Gee range with the added guarantee that bombs would never be dropped in open country. Its use by Pathfinders in a target-marking role was an expedient necessitated by *Oboe*'s limited range. Because towns appeared as areas of brightness on the screen it was impossible, except on rare occasions, to pinpoint within the town limits. The course (aircraft heading) and time from a recognizable position to the aiming point had to be calculated so accuracy depended on the skill of the operator. Equally important, *Oboe* Mosquitoes enjoyed comparative immunity from flak and fighters whereas the H2S marker aircraft were continually harassed, particularly over the target.

Lack of precision combined with poor serviceability,[5] and the fact that only two flights of aircraft were fitted with the device, made it necessary to group the Blind Marker crews at the beginning of the raid to get a reasonable concentration of markers. The problem was aggravated because half the sets were in Stirlings, and this type's lack of speed flexibility resulted in poor timing when forecast winds were wrong. It became the job of the Backers-up to keep the target marked throughout the duration of H2S attacks. As there were several groups of Primary Markers on the ground at the same time, the bomb-aimer had to estimate

5. During the first few months, only 55% were serviceable on arrival in the target area.

the MPI of all the markers and mark that position with contrasting TIs.[6] To make the calculation was difficult enough, but to have to do it in a moving aircraft in the middle of a flak barrage and all the time keep the indefinite point in mind was well nigh impossible. Small wonder the TIs were not tightly grouped. Errors were perpetuated because later Backers-up did not have the Primary Markers as a guide. By comparison backing-up *Oboe* groundmarkers was simple. Mosquito crews were briefed to mark at regular intervals so there was usually only one salvo of *Oboe* TIs burning; the Backers-up consequently did not have any complicated assessment to make.

Incendiaries were dropped on Baden-Baden as route-markers and the fires were then backed up with more incendiaries – they provided a beacon to keep crews from straying over Karlsruhe or Strasbourg on their way to Stuttgart on March 11-12. Daylight reconnaissance showed that the weight of the attack had been to the south-east of Stuttgart. As this was the wooded area of the town, the fires reported by crews, were probably the woods alight.

Bomber Command rarely operated on three successive nights. Fatigue slowed the reflexes and decreased efficiency; the odds against survival were high enough without loading the dice. Harris, however, broke all the unwritten laws and laid on operations on four consecutive nights from March 26-29. For the *Musical Wanganui* on Duisburg on the first night, *Oboe* Mosquitoes were scheduled to drop release-point flares. Because of equipment failure only four crews marked and this left a big gap in the middle where there were no marker flares. As a result the attack became scattered, most crews having to rely on the old stand-by DR. Shortage of markers was also the main reason for lack of success the following night when Berlin was the target. With six early returns, 7 Squadron must take a good percentage of the blame. In this raid Halifaxes of 35 Squadron dropped land-markers 16 miles short of the capital and, because of varying cloud density over the target, both groundmarkers and *Wanganui* flares were dropped; despite the hostility of the natives, both types were accurately placed.

Next day all PFF crews who had not operated on both previous nights found themselves on orders. A highly successful attack on St Nazaire on a clear night rivalled the earlier raid of March 22-23 in spite of a smoke screen which tended to obscure the TIs.

On March 29-30, Bomber Command was up in strength again. A force of 329 heavies made the long trip to Berlin while a further 157 crews

6. Cambridge University made a simulation machine to train crews to assess MPI. The average radial error of untrained crews was 354 yards; this was reduced by training to 194 yards.

made the comparatively short run to Bochum, where, although 7 out of 8 Mosquitoes dropped flares for a *Musical Wanganui*, the raid was assessed as disappointing and PRU confirmed this.

For the Berlin attack route-marker flares were dropped over Muggel See so that the Main Force could make a timed run to the target. The marking was good, although there was a tendancy to err to the south and south-east of the aiming point. The attack was the best to date on Berlin, but Pathfinders thought the Main Force were 'a little shy' and that with more effort it could have been a resounding success. The forecast winds were wrong and many crews, miles off track, did not bother to go to the datum point, Muggel See, for the timed run as briefed. Others, probably using the wrong wind, bombed well short of the markers.

Blind Marker, Blind Illuminator and Primary Visual Marker aircraft were always exposed to the enemy ground defences because they operated over the defended areas in small numbers. Although Bennett sent Supporters,[7] crews under training, to help saturate the defences they were little more than a token of concern. Until *Window*[8] was introduced, like Shakespeare's Wolsey they felt 'naked to mine enemies'. This was particularly true of Berlin where the defences were so extensive that they could not be saturated.

Two marker crews of 35 Squadron were coned over Berlin on March 28-29 and felt the weight of the defences. F/Lt H.B. McDonald, who had been treated roughly by a nightfighter when leaving Cologne on February 28, had to use his skill this time to evade the ground defences. He had just dropped his flares when he was coned by 30 searchlights and was down to 10,000 feet before he had eluded them and the predicted flak. When he was clear of the target he climbed back to 15,000 feet because it was always useful to have some height to play with and there would be other crews at that height. The route took him near Bremen and he got too close to the gun belt south of the town. First the predicted heavy flak opened up and then the searchlights switched on. Blinded by the glare he could not read his compass and wandered over the centre of the town, where the gunners vented their spleen on him for disturbing their game of cards. Again he threw the Halifax out of the sky and pulled out at 1,000 feet. When he was clear of Bremen he climbed to 3,000 feet. This was just as well because the Hun had another surprise for him. Just off Terschelling he flew over a flak-ship moored there to give a welcome to the 'gardeners'. The Germans had had a frustrating night because there had been no mine-laying in that area, so the Halifax was the first aircraft they had seen. They gave him the full VIP treatment – with a red carpet of flak – and one burst threw the aircraft on its back. It stalled and McDonald pulled it out of the spin at 1,000 feet. The English coast was a welcome sight and the

8. See Glossary.

7. See Appendix X for crew duties.

Halifax landed safely at Coltishall with only 10 gallons of petrol left, if the gauges were to be believed.

For F/Lt Rees, it was lightning striking three times in the same place. Over Kiel, in October, his starboard outer engine and petrol tanks were holed. Two days later, at Cologne, it was the same story. This time the Germans tried to make sure he did not get back. After dropping his TIs he was coned and hit by predicted heavy flak. The starboard inner engine was put out of action; the starboard outer and port inner were hit; the whole aircraft was riddled with shrapnel and the petrol tanks were holed. Although the aircraft was gradually losing height, he flew the 325 miles to the Dutch coast without further mishap, safely by-passing Bremen. There remained only the North Sea, but it claimed no victims that night. He crossed the English coast north of Great Yarmouth, and Coltishall welcomed another 35 Squadron Halifax.

The third attack on Essen on April 3-4 was a mixed *Parramatta* and *Wanganui* and the 348-strong Main Force consisted of Halifaxes and Lancasters. In the event the target was clear and, after everyone had got over the surprise of seeing both sky and groundmarkers, the Backers-up and the bombers did an excellent job, achieving a higher concentration than on the two earlier occasions. Several large explosions with fires getting a good hold provided a long night's work for the Essen fire brigade and Baron Krupp's fire-fighting force had its hands more than full. According to crew reports the defences were even more hostile than usual, but that was probably because there were no Stirlings and Wellingtons below to take the stick. One crew of 83 Squadron said the searchlights could best be described as 10/10ths.

Wanganui attacks could not hope to achieve the same concentration as *Parramatta* or *Newhaven* attacks. The flares were bound to drift in the wind and accuracy could not be expected when the bomb-aimer was sighting along the equivalent of a moving backsight on to an independently moving foresight and at an unseen target. However, the technique did allow Bomber Command to operate on nights when British bases were clear and cloud over Germany prevented the target being seen, with the assurance that the bombs would not be scattered far and wide over the Reich. The morale of the people rather than the town beneath the cloud was the real target. The attacks were designed to make them realize that over *Festung Europa* there was now no adequate roof.

Nor was skymarking always successful as a standby; the weather often had the last word. At Kiel, on April 4, both marker flares and TIs were bursting in cloud – the high wind would in any case have made the flares very unreliable. The force of more than 500 bombers had to drop its bombs by DR. It was the same story at Duisburg on April 8 when the flares quickly disappeared into 10/10ths cloud. The only indication crews had that they were over the target was the flak, which came up thick and fast, but that was no criterion in Happy Valley. The next night a small force of Lancasters found the target still cloud-covered but, although the majority bombed on the release-point flares, reconnaissance photographs showed very little damage in the town from these attacks. This too had been the case after the skymarking raid of March. Duisburg, with its wide open spaces between built-up areas, was not a suitable *Wanganui* target.

By contrast Essen made a good target for this type of attack: Krupps was at the centre of the town and the people dependent on the works for their livelihood. The fourth and fifth attacks on the towns were *Musical Wanganui*. Over 300 bombers took part in the raid on April 30, and on May 27 more than 500. Pathfinders dropped route-marker flares on both occasions to give the Main Force a datum point from which they could make a timed run should skymarkers not be visible when they reached the target. Considerable damage was caused at Krupp's plant and around the town, but compared with the havoc of the groundmarking raids it served only to show the limitations of *Wanganui* even when *Oboe* was marking.

Concentrating all the H2S Blind Markers into a limited period at the beginning of a raid brought a new problem: more crews were required for the role of Backer-up. On a raid of average duration it was estimated that at least 20 crews were needed to get a good concentration of TIs and then keep the target continually marked. At this time more aircraft were being fitted with H2S, which increased the number of Blind Markers available for each raid. A modified *Newhaven* technique was to be tried at the first opportunity and this required at least 5 senior crews to mark the aiming point visually, another 35 marker crews, either Blind Marking and Illuminating or Backing-up, and as many Supporters as possible. The Air Staff decided PFF must be strengthened and accordingly on April 15 the stations at Oakington,[9] Bourn and Gransden Lodge were transferred to 8 Group; two days later 97 Squadron moved from Woodhall Spa (5 Group) to Bourn and, on April 19, 405 Squadron moved from Leeming (6 Group) to Gransden Lodge. The two squadrons were a welcome addition to the group and Bennett felt that, when they had been 'whipped into shape', he would be able to cope with attacks of reasonable duration without fear of having to thin out the marking. In addition to the new squadrons, 1409 (Met) Flight was formed at Oakington on April 1, so Bomber Command could now obtain its own Met information at first hand.

In an effort to tighten up the attacks beyond *Oboe* range, Bennett called on his Primary Visual Markers to work in conjunction with H2S

---

9. 7 Squadron had been operating from Oakington since August 1943 as a lodger unit, the station being controlled by 3 Group.

aircraft. This modified form of *Newhaven* used the H2S aircraft to mark the target blindly with TIs and then drop illuminating flares so that the Primary Visual Markers, aided by the TIs and flares, could then locate the aiming point visually and mark it with contrasting TIs. PFF carried out its first official *Newhaven* attack on April 14-15 when 462 crews set out for Stuttgart. The target was clear; the reds of the Blind Marker Illuminators went down 2 or 3 miles north-north-east of the aiming point and the first bombing started in this area. Main Force crews were instructed to ignore the reds and were given the option of identifying the aiming point for themselves or of bombing the MPI of all the greens. As the Primary Visual Markers claimed to have identified the aiming point and marked it with greens, the unsatisfactory bombing must have been a result either of bad briefing, mistaken identity or gross undershooting.

The Main Force seemed reluctant to go into the town and when a green TI[10] fell in the suburb of Bad Cannstatt further to the north the attack switched to this area. Although the bomb-aimers should have been looking for the largest concentration of TIs there was always a tendency to bomb the nearest one. As at Nuremberg and Munich in March the raid caused useful damage because Bad Cannstatt was the main industrial area of Stuttgart. Crews had difficulty in landing because the fog was thickening by the minute, but there were no casualties in 8 Group. Another *Newhaven* attack on April 16-17, on Mannheim, was also a success and the force of 251 heavies started some good fires helped by two explosions. Four A/P photographs were brought back by 7 Squadron. The Supporters enjoyed themselves: they shot up four trains, attacked an aerodrome, a barracks, gun positions, two factories and a warehouse.

On April 20-21, 425 crews made the long haul to Stettin and Rostock. They were briefed to remain low as long as possible over the sea because 11 Mosquitoes of 2 Group were making a diversionary attack on Berlin. Visibility was excellent and this third *Newhaven* attack of the month was by far the best. All 6 Primary Visual Markers had marked by Z+5, and helped by the accuracy of 10 Blind Marker Illuminators, had placed their TIs near the aiming point. Backers-up maintained the marking and this kept the bombing in the same area. The famous Pommersdorf-Milch chemical works was completely wiped out; scores of industrial buildings covering 100 acres were devastated and fires were started in the ship-building yards and naval bases. PRU reported 24 fires still burning 34 hours later. The 86 Stirlings sent to Rostock had to contend with an effective smoke screen which prevented them seeing their main objective, the Heinkel works.

The Mosquito diversion was only partially successful although one was intercepted over the capital and another was missing. Weather suitable

---

10. Nineteen Backers-up were also dropping greens but this one was probably a stray.

for *Newhaven* attacks was unfortunately also ideal for nightfighters, and April 20-21 was no exception. In all, 43 interceptions were made, of which 17 were on the outward route and 17 more over the target. Three Pathfinders had combats. F/O B.F. Smith's gunners, F/O S. Hayes and Sgt L.J. Jones, damaged the Ju88 which attacked them, and accurate fire from F/Sgt H. Plant, F/Sgt L.A. Rickenson's rear gunner, drove off 2 Ju88s which intercepted them before either of the fighters had a chance to fire. F/O S. Baker was 20 miles north of Stettin when the mid-upper gunner, F/Sgt C. Thornhill, saw an Me109 going in the opposite direction. The fighter pilot spotted the Stirling, made a steep turn, put the Messerschmitt in a shallow dive to gain speed and made his attack from underneath and astern. The rear gunner, F/Sgt J.E. Robbins, followed the manoeuvre closely and warned Baker to be ready to dive to port. Before the enemy was set Robbins opened fire and shouted 'Go, go, go' to his pilot. The Messerschmitt broke away and climbed giving Robbins a second chance; he raked the fighter with a long burst setting it on fire. Both gunners and the wireless operator saw it hit the ground still burning.

On that night flying low as far as Denmark was a costly tactic. By chance the route took the bombers across a German convoy and the flak ships had a field day. Their firing alerted the coastal defences and they too took their toll. Of the 31 aircraft missing, more than half were shot down in this area and 52 more were damaged by flak. One of the unlucky ones was Sgt J.R. Petrie-Andrews. A shell burst in the nose of the Halifax, which at the time was flying at 1,000 feet, wounding the navigator and the wireless operator. The DR compass, the bombsight, the ASI (Airspeed Indicator) and the intercom was rendered unserviceable. In spite of the damage to the aircraft, and with two vital members of the crew wounded, they continued to the target and completed their mission.

There were two attacks in April which can be classed only as failures. On the 10th-11th, at Frankfurt, some crews claimed to have bombed through 10/10ths cloud on the glow of TIs, others on the glow of fires; but it was anyone's guess which were TIs, decoys, fires or dummy fires, or indeed, which part of Frankfurt was underneath the bombs. At the same time as the 251 bombers were making their excellent *Newhaven* attack on Mannheim on April 16-17, a further 327 aircraft were carrying out an abortive raid on the Skoda works at Pilsen. Pathfinders have usually been blamed for this fiasco, but too little attention has been paid by their accusers to the briefing details. Because of the difficult nature of the target all crews were briefed to identify the target for themselves. The TIs dropped by PFF were not target-markers; they were intended as a guide for the run up to the aiming point which lay beyond them. After dropping their groundmarkers, PFF crews then released illuminating flares to help the Main Force crews make their visual identification. Without doubt, many crews mistook Dobrany for the Skoda works and the Dobrany asylum for one of the factory buildings. Pilsen was swarming with nightfighters which may have accounted for some of the itchy bombing fingers, and 36 bombers were shot down from this force as well as 17 on the Mannheim raid. In addition to the aircraft missing on the Pilsen attack, 57 more were damaged. The barracks at Dobrany received a direct hit and 200 German soldiers were killed, but this in no way compensated for the loss of 250 aircrew.

On May 13-14, PFF marked the same target for 120 Lancasters of 5 Group. The aiming point was again the Skoda works on the edge of the town and practically all the bombs fell within 3 miles of it. The weight of the attack, however, fell in open fields. If the aiming point had been in the centre of the town this would have been classed an excellent raid. Harris had repeatedly pointed out the risk of failure when attacking a target on the edge of a town and the point could not have been brought home more forcibly even if he had planned it to demonstrate his convictions.

Both 97 and 405 Squadrons operated with the group for the first time on April 26-27, when PFF laid the foundations for what should have been a successful attack on Duisburg. Crews at de-briefing reported seeing fires from 100 miles away, and others, over the town towards the end of the raid, said the town was covered with a pall of smoke. Daylight reconnaissance told a different story; the town had escaped once again and most of the damage was spread over a wide area to the north-east. The attack was a *Musical Parramatta* and if a steady supply of *Oboe* TIs could not keep the bombing near the aiming point, then it was either a case of gross undershooting or a return to the bad old days when any fire was good enough.

Although Duisburg was the largest inland port in Europe and its heavy industries and rolling mills were high-priority targets, the fact that more sorties were flown to it than to any other target during the Battle of the Ruhr suggests an attention in excess of its importance. The plain truth was that the four raids, totalling more than 1,500 sorties, had done very little lasting damage. On May 12-13, to try to redress the balance, Harris sent a force of 572 aircraft, carrying a record weight of bombs, 1,559 tons.[11] By the end of the attack Duisburg knew from experience what cities like Essen had suffered. *Oboe* reds were accurately backed by greens – S/Ldr K.H. Burns brought back an A/P photograph – and over 85% of the crews, who claimed to have bombed the target, were within 3 miles of the aiming point and 80% of the TIs were plotted within 2 miles. As the raid progressed fires gained a hold throughout the target area and these could be seen from the Dutch coast. PRU photographs showed acres of damage in the port area and the old town was completely gutted. Four of von

11. Previous highest, Cologne 'Millennium', 1,516 tons. Now 572 aircraft carried a greater load.

Thyssen's steel plants were among the many industrial targets showing fresh damage; many warehouses round the docks, the marshalling yards and main railway station were destroyed by fire; a boat yard, building barges, was burnt out.

The first attack on Dortmund took place on May 4-5. *Oboe* crews, marking with greens,[12] placed their TIs accurately and their timing was good. The reds, dropped by the Backers-up, tended to undershoot and this accentuated the normal creepback. Useful damage was done in the centre of the old town and in the dock area, but the decoy fire site to the north-east attracted too much attention; 300 craters were counted in the vicinity. Fewer than half of the 596 bombers were within 3 miles of the aiming point. Meanwhile the weather over England had deteriorated and many crews had to be diverted. Crashes at Wyton and Warboys which blocked the runways made the situation worse for Pathfinder crews. One plane crashed at Chatteris and another at Culverton, both crews having baled out because of shortage of petrol. F/Sgt J.A. Cobb crashed into a tree at Graveley and, except for the rear gunner, Sgt J.H. Robertson, all the crew were killed. Sgt A. Reilly of 97 Squadron was diverted to Waterbeach, where he overshot the end of the runway and crashed into a Stirling. Reilly was killed and three of his crew were injured.

The growing respect for the German nightfighters was reflected by the ten-day stand-down during the full-moon period. It did not mean a slack time for PFF crews; an intensive training programme was laid on and most nights crews were marking for *Bullseyes*.[13] By May 23, PFF were pleased to get back to the serious business of bombing the Germans into submission. Harris called for a maximum effort: 826 aircraft were on the battle order, the largest number on a single target during the Battle of the Ruhr, and 8 Group celebrated by sending more than 100 aircraft on one sortie for the first time. Eight out of 11 Mosquito crews marked Dortmund for this huge force and the Backers-up were right on the ball. There was no cloud, but ground haze prevented visual identification of the aiming point and the value of TIs combined with the new Blind Bombing aids was manifest.

The order of the day called for the best 250 crews from all the groups to make up the first wave. They were instructed to bomb TIs and, if none were visible, they were to go round again and wait until the next salvo was dropped. From 53 photographs plotted in this wave 24 showed bombing errors of less than a mile. The attack completely eclipsed that of May 4-5 and set a new high level. It was exceptionally severe and highly concentrated; no district and few industries escaped damage. Hoesch, one of the

12. To distinguish their TIs from a small PFF attack on Rheine.

13. *Bullseyes* were simulated operational sorties for Operational Training Units and Heavy Conversion Units.

largest steel works in Germany, was out of production for some time – 48 buildings in the complex were affected. Dortmund was virtually eliminated in the two attacks.

Sgt R.H. Willis, on his first sortie as a captain, was attacked by a fighter over the target and he, the navigator and the rear gunner were wounded. It was an instance where Bennett's requirement that pilots should have a rudimentary knowledge of navigation was vindicated for Willis was able to bring the plane back to England by following the navigator's flight plan, using the stars as a guide. F/O M. Sattler was attacked by a nightfighter after leaving the target. Both gunners identified it as a Dornier Do217 but were certain it had RAF roundels and British camouflage. The Halifax took violent evasive action, but the German pilot, knowing he had hit the bomber and trying for the kill, made 7 or 8 attacks. Suddenly the Dornier broke away, one engine in flames, and it later crashed into the ground where it continued to burn. F/O W.R.W. Anderson, the mid-upper gunner, was wounded four times in the left arm but kept on firing. The fighter left his mark on the aircraft too. The DR and P.4 compasses were put out of action, the petrol tanks pierced, a bomb-carrier shot away and the right aileron damaged. Sattler landed the aircraft safely at Middle Wallop.

Although Bomber Command operated in strength on only seven nights during May – the good weather coincided with the full-moon period – 4,432 sorties were flown against Ruhr towns and they 'received a bombardment on an entirely different level of accuracy'[14] because the attacks were marked by Pathfinders. Duisburg, Bochum and then Dortmund were devastated, each raid excelling over the previous one, until the historian feels like a film publicity agent seeking fresh superlatives to describe the latest success.

On May 29-30 a force of 719 aircraft attacked Wuppertal-Barmen; it was the outstanding raid of the month and probably of the Battle of the Ruhr because of the enormous damage inflicted on a target only 2 miles long and barely a mile wide: 90% of that area was devastated. The attack was a triumph for the Backers-up for, although the *Oboe* Mosquito reds were accurate, failure of their special equipment left two long intervals when no reds were dropped. The Backers-up, crews from 83 and 156 Squadrons, operating in Lancaster 'Y' aircraft[15] for the first time, kept the aiming point marked throughout these periods and achieved a concentration never before accomplished and rarely afterwards surpassed. Of the 611 crews who claimed to have bombed the target, 78% brought back photographic proof. Some credit must go to the bombers in the first wave, who dropped incendiaries, because the fires they started were well

14. *Bomber Command Quarterly Review.*
15. Code name for aircraft carrying H2S.

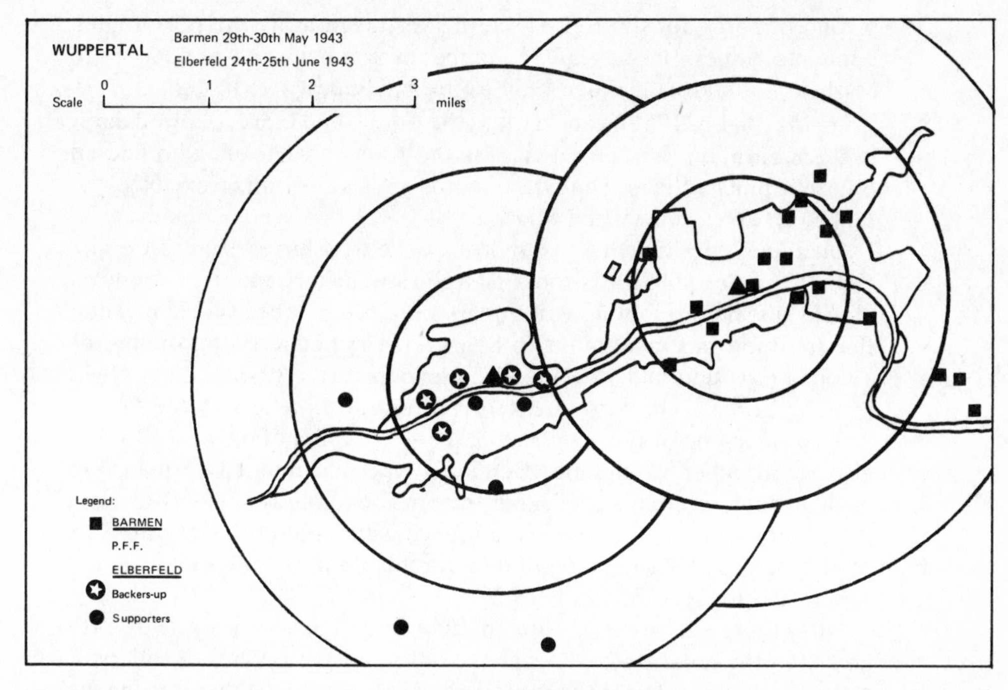

Map 1 Bomb plot maps were made from photographs taken by the aircraft. The camera shutter used a delay equal to the estimated time of bomb fall. As the position of *Oboe* TIs could be calculated by the ground station, *Oboe* Mosquitoes did not usually carry cameras. At Wuppertal *Oboe* Mosquitoes dropped the Primary markers.

grouped round the markers and so helped to get the attack off to a good start. It was a Saturday night and many of the city's officials were in the country for the weekend; the fact that there was a shortage of people with authority to give essential orders caused great confusion. Fires raged all through Sunday and fire-fighting appliances were called from all the neighbouring towns.

The only losses in the group were 4 aircraft from 35 Squadron. Command's losses were 33 and, of these, the nightfighters claimed the majority. The Me110s of NJG1 (*Nacht Jaqdqeschwader*), the oldest German nightfighter group, pursued the returning bombers far out over the North Sea and caught many crews literally napping. Bomber Command claimed 7 nightfighters were shot down; it might well have been 8. Sgt D.A. Routen had just left the target when he was intercepted by an Me110. The fighter came in from the port quarter below and closed to 350 yards before firing. This gave Routen time to corkscrew to port and the enemy's fire went underneath the Stirling. Both gunners returned the fire and missed, but when the Messerschmitt tried the same manoeuvre from the starboard quarter the rear gunner, Sgt G. Woodcock, did not let the second opportunity slip by. As the fighter dived away the port engine burst into flames. Because of the number of fires below it was not seen to crash so it could be claimed only as 'probably destroyed'.

On May 6, Lord Trenchard visited the Group and there followed, later in the month, on the 26th, a visit by the King and Queen, who had an informal lunch (that's what the records say) at Wyton. Next day, the Duke of Gloucester visited Marham.

On June 1, 105 and 139 Squadrons were transferred from 2 Group. Both these Mosquito squadrons had a glorious history and their low-level attacks just before joining Pathfinders were often done as a team. Their fine tradition was maintained in 8 Group, 105 Squadron becoming the second *Oboe* unit and 139 Squadron leaders of the LNSF (Light Night Striking Force). The introduction of Mosquito bombers to the Group proved to be one of the significant events of 1943, not only for PFF but also for Bomber Command. Bennett's foresight and 139 Squadron's brilliant achievements added a new dimension to the Bomber Offensive. At first their raids were of mere nuisance value, but during the next six months they established a reputation for adaptability, culminating in the role of Pathfinders for the LNSF.[16]

Dusseldorf was the target for the first raid of June on the 10th-11th and, after the stand-down through the full-moon period, Harris called for a maximum effort. It was the second of two attacks on the town during the Battle of the Ruhr, the earlier raid having been on May 25-26. Neither of the attacks was up to standard and only one-third of the combined total of 1,542 bombers dropped their load within 3 miles of the aiming point. These two attacks illustrate the difference the weather made to the chances of success. In May, 9/10ths cloud at 18,000-20,000 feet and another layer at 8,000 feet made backing-up almost impossible. The *Oboe* reds went down on time yet it was 16 minutes before they were backed-up, most PFF crews making two or three runs. The Main Force was not as conscientious as Pathfinders with the result that bombs were scattered over a wide area, some incendiaries being as far as 12 miles from the target. The enemy enjoyed himself with his new toy, decoy TIs which, in conjunction with decoy fires, were quite popular. Conditions were ideal for exploiting the gullibility of the Main Force. The raid illustrated the pressures on PFF crews, for the rest of the force could drop their bombs through cloud, get a photograph of it, and no one could tell how far from the aiming point the bombs were dropped. On the other hand there were 700 crews ready and willing to report stray TIs.

On June 11-12, the land-markers and the first *Oboe* reds were very accurate; one Main Force bomber in the first wave had a photograph showing TIs on the aiming point. All went well until Z+25 when a

---

16. Expanded in Chapter VIII.

Mosquito crew inadvertently dropped a salvo of reds 14 miles north-east of Dusseldorf. Unfortunately some idiot backed them up, giving 50 bombers a justifiable excuse for attacking them. A cross-wind much stronger than forecast accounted for some inaccurate bombing, but the wind was a two-edged sword for it helped to spread the fires which swept through the town unchecked, and some were still burning a week later. The fires wrought havoc; 130 acres in the town centre, and altogether 1,000 acres lay waste.

Krefeld on June 21-22 was an interesting raid and an excellent example of a *Musical Parramatta*. It was the first night 'K' *Oboe*[17] took the limelight and the Directors showed a certain lack of confidence in their new star. A team of 10 Mosquitoes with 2 reserves was laid on to groundmark the target with red TIs. The normal Mosquito load in these circumstances was 3 TI reds and one LB (Long Burning) TI red. On this occasion 4 aircraft were carrying 2 TI red, 1 LBTI red and 1 TI red with a 5-minute delay – this meant it did not ignite until 5 minutes after hitting the ground. It was a precaution to cover any gaps in the sequence due to failure of the special equipment. As a further safeguard, in case there were no *Musical* pyrotechnics, 31 H2S 'stand-ins' were detailed to drop yellow TIs so that the audience of more than 700 bombers, who were braving flak and fighters to witness the display, would not be entirely disappointed. The 37 Backers-up were briefed to aim their greens at the reds or yellows. The curtain was due to rise at 0130 hours, with an *Oboe* prologue at 0127. The second *Oboe* solo was scheduled for 0131 and thereafter at 6-minute intervals until 0219 hours. The 'stand-ins' were divided into 2 groups, 18 at 0132 and 13 at 0157 hours, and were allowed to take the stage only if there were no reds dropped. The show was planned with audience participation divided into 6 waves: specially selected Lancaster crews, followed by Wellingtons, then Stirlings, 2 groups of Halifaxes and finally Lancasters. Two pairs of ground stations were 'working' the *Oboe* crews and one pair had a successful evening.

First Pair	Schedule	0127,	0137,	0149,	0201,	0213
	Actual	0127,	0137,	0148,	0159,	0209

The second pair suffered because the first aircraft was 3 minutes late and the third had to return to base because of engine failure.

Second Pair	Schedule	0131,	0143,	0155,	0207,	0219
	Actual	0134,	0148,		0226,	0239

The absence of interference enabled the crews to make very accurate runs. All but one of the 37 Backers-up dropped their greens and all bombed with a red in their bombsights. Audience participation was wholehearted and 619 crews claimed to have bombed on TIs; from photographic evidence 75% were within 3 miles of the A/P. The people

17. See *Oboe*, Appendix I.

of Krefeld were unaware that history was being made and would have been too preoccupied to appreciate the fact had they known. The town, not including the suburbs, covered 11,000 acres and the following day 9,000 were in ruins. The fires were so concentrated that the fire services were unable to contain them and the intense heat caused a firestorm which swept through the town – a portent of what was to happen in Hamburg 5 weeks later.

Of the 42 aircraft missing 12 were from 8 Group and they were all 'Y' aircraft. There was nothing sinister in this but they were all senior crews and 6 of them were from the stand-in marker crews acting as insurance against complete *Oboe* failure. Although in this instance Bennett was ordered to send the crews, the incident highlighted one of the AOC's constant problems: to detail too few marker crews was to risk a failure; to detail too many was to expose more senior crews than necessary to danger.

Nightfighters were up in force and, aided by the moon, they made more than a hundred interceptions: some 30 bombers were shot down and 27 others reported combats. Only two Pathfinder crews were intercepted and both escaped by taking evasive action. A third was fired on by another Lancaster. Sgt D.H. Milne was forced to ditch his aircraft 30 miles off Cromer. On the outward journey, just south of Rotterdam, the Halifax was hit by flak and the starboard outer was put out of action. The aircraft handled reasonably well so Milne decided to press on to the target. He bombed at 19,000 feet and on the homeward route gradually lost height to the Dutch coast. Almost immediately after crossing it at 14,000 feet the port inner cut and a distress signal was sent. As they approached the English coast the starboard inner cut and Milne decided to ditch. The sea was calm and a successful ditching was made north of the Cross Sands lighthouse at 0300 hours. The dinghy was launched and everyone clambered aboard. When they heard aircraft approaching they fired their Very pistol and two Mustangs circled them until Coastal Command had fixed their position. Then with a waggle of wings the Mustangs flew off and shortly afterwards two Walruses of 278 Squadron rescued them.

Cologne did not come into the firing line until late in the Battle, then four attacks were launched in the space of three weeks. In all, 16 H2S Pathfinder Halifaxes and Lancasters were detailed to drop skymarkers for a force of 42 heavies from 8 Group and 150 Lancasters from 1 and 5 Groups on June 16-17. Due to unserviceability of special equipment the attack opened late and few markers were released; most crews bombed on ETA. On June 28-29 the weather at the target (Cologne) was uncertain so Bennett laid on a mixed *Musical Parramatta* and *Wanganui* and Main Force crews were briefed to bomb on ETA if no markers were visible. As a result of technical faults only 6 out of 11 Mosquitoes dropped their *Wanganui* flares and groundmarkers. The TIs quickly disappeared into the 10/10ths cloud and it was impossible to back them up, the cloud being too thick even for the glow to be seen. Because of the failure of the first 2 Mosquitoes, markers did not go down until 0147 (Z+7) and they in turn were followed up at only irregular intervals; consequently the majority of the force bombed on ETA. Fortunately, a large number waited patiently for the flares and so a useful attack was delivered in spite of the unfavourable conditions.

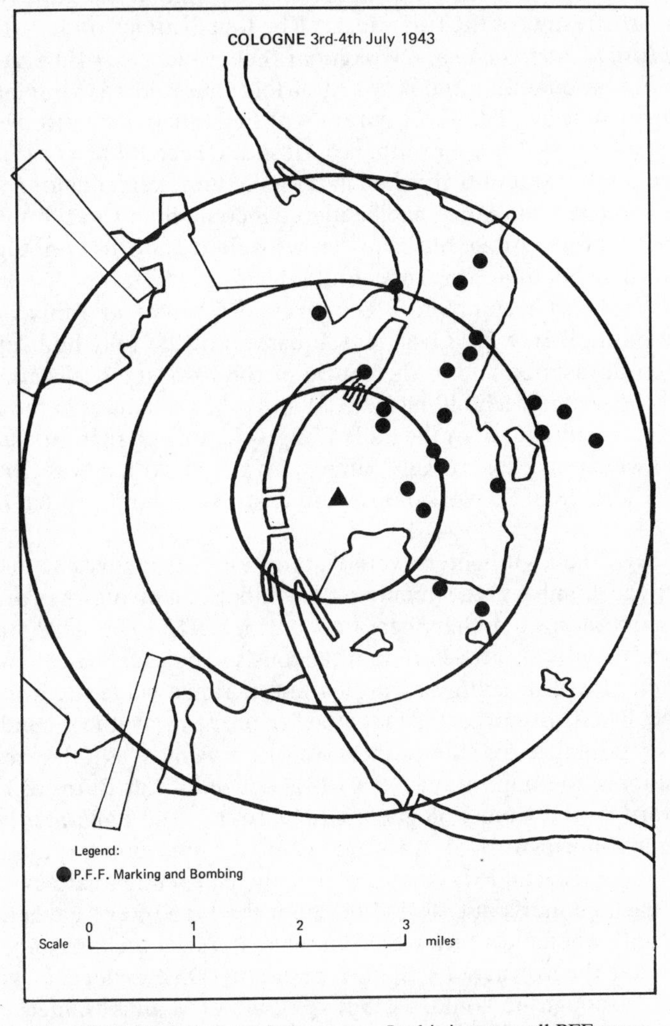

Map 2 Not all aircraft carried cameras. In this instance all PFF crews carrying cameras were within 3 miles of the aiming point and these included some of the Backers-up. Primary marking was carried out by *Oboe* Mosquitoes.

For the sortie on July 3-4 the aiming point was moved to the east bank of the Rhine where most of the factories were located. Again the attack was planned as a mixed *Musical Parramatta* and *Wanganui* but the skies were clear and the TIs could be seen. Only 7 out of 13 *Oboe* crews 'coped',[18] but the Backers-up did an excellent job and kept the target marked throughout the attack. Of the force of 665 bombers, 65% dropped their bombs within 3 miles of the aiming point. Daylight reconnaissance on July 4 showed devastation on both banks of the river although, as there had been no PRU cover of the previous raid, it was impossible to separate the results of the two attacks. The fourth attack on July 8-9 was also a *Musical Parramatta* and *Wanganui*. The cloud was 9/10ths at 8,000 feet with some cumulo-nimbus to 17,000 feet. The raid was a miniature of the one on June 28. The short duration of the attack, with just over 300 heavies, meant that not more than 6 Mosquitoes could be controlled in the time. Only 3 out of 6 attacked and the first markers did not go down until Z+5. The Main Force had been told it could bomb on ETA if there were no markers visible, but many crews waited and PRU photographs showed their bombing was concentrated.

Harris asked for complete PRU cover of Cologne and this was not completed until July 25. Over three-quarters of the fully built-up area had been devastated and in the centre of the town the destruction was worse, with scarcely a building free of battle scars. Damage in the industrial area, mostly caused by the raid of July 3-4, affected some 80 factories many of which were extensively damaged. Typical of them was Gottfried Hagen where 28 of 35 workshops were destroyed and the other 7 damaged.

Although the nightfighters were faster, more manoeuvrable and outgunned the bombers, the number of combats involving two or more fighters operating together increased during 1943. The extraordinary thing was they rarely attacked simultaneously. The usual pattern was for one to employ distracting tactics just out of range while the other one attacked. Then, as soon as the first attacker broke away, the second came in quickly hoping to find the gunners confused. Almost as if they realized the quality of the opposition, 3 Fw190s engaged S/Ldr Burns as he was homeward bound from Cologne on June 16-17. The Lancaster was 18 miles north-north-west of Antwerp when the mid-upper gunner, Sgt E.H. Skinner, saw an Fw190 on the port quarter ready to attack. It was part of each gunner's duty to tell the pilot the type of evasive action he wanted and, when the attack was from the rear, it was the tail gunner who usually gave the instructions. Skinner shouted: 'Dive to port, go, go, go,' because, although he could see Sgt G. Lambert's guns trained on the fighter, no orders had been given to the skipper. As soon as Lambert's

18. A successful attack using *Oboe* was known as a 'cope'.

guns opened up Skinner searched the sky to make sure the enemy was alone and sighted a second Focke-Wulf lining up in the same position. Ordering Burns to continue the evasive action he engaged the fighter himself because Lambert's turret had been put out of action. When the fighter came within the arc of Lambert's guns, he began firing and this allowed Skinner to break off and search just in time to see a third Fw190 coming in to attack, supported by one of the other two firing from out of range.

Why the Germans did not continue the combat no one in the bomber knew or cared. They had enough troubles of their own – the port inner tank was badly holed, the fuselage on fire and the cockpit full of smoke and flames. Then the bomb-doors fell open. This probably saved the aircraft as petrol had been leaking into the bomb-bay and if it too had caught fire the crew would have had little chance of escape. The fire inside the aircraft was extinguished and in due course some semblance of order reappeared. Burns had just settled back on course when Sgt J. Keddie reported an Me110 making a frontal attack. Keddie fired from 600 yards and the Messerschmitt broke away without firing. The landing lights at Bourn were a welcome sight and this was one night when they all laced their hot coffee with their after-operations rum ration.

Turrets were fitted with 'panic buttons' which operated lights on the pilot's instrument panel and instructed him which way the gunner wanted to turn. They were fitted against the possibility of intercom failure.[19] Lambert ought to have signalled to the pilot, and the crew were undoubtedly saved by Skinner's vigilance. Keddie, on the other hand, proved a point which was constantly emphasized in the Group: fire first, fire early – it needs courage to attack through a hail of bullets, however inaccurately aimed.

P/O N.A. Cobb was in deep trouble long before he reached the target (Dusseldorf) on June 11-12. About 12 miles north-east of Aachen tracer came pouring towards the Halifax from 800 yards on the port quarter and both gunners were wounded. A small fire developed between the port engines and the rear turret was badly damaged although still serviceable. The gunners did not see the enemy but as the flight engineer was telling them about a single-engined fighter passing underneath F/Sgt N.T. Williams, the rear gunner, cut him short because a twin-engined fighter was attacking from the starboard quarter below. Williams got in a quick burst, the enemy immediately stopped firing and seconds later exploded. A third attack came from astern; Williams was just regaining his night

---

19. Mahaddie's gunner had failed to use them at Cologne with near-fatal results (page 30. It was difficult if not almost impossible to remain cool with cannon shells and tracer pouring towards you and perhaps the gunners did not realize they were not being heard. The drill should have been to press the appropriate button and confirm the instructions verbally. No doubt many crews did this but virtue is seldom noted.

vision, after the flash made by his first victim, when he saw a single-engined fighter bearing down on him. He opened fire at 400 yards and bits started to break off the enemy plane as it continued to fly towards him. Although Williams fired about 500 rounds into the fighter it came on relentlessly as if the pilot was intent on ramming the Halifax, until, when only 20 yards away, it suddenly nose-dived. It seemed to be disintegrating as it disappeared into cloud apparently out of control. Cobb jettisoned his bombs and made for base getting every ounce of speed he could out of the Halifax. F/Sgt T.H. Smith, the mid-upper gunner, was grazed on the head in the first skirmish and remembered nothing after that. Williams had 7 bullet wounds in the right leg and one in the stomach. In spite of his wounds he insisted on remaining at his post until they crossed the English coast. The immediate award of the GCM can rarely have been more deserved.[20]

Harris did not confine the attacks on the Ruhr to the large towns and more than 4,000 sorties were flown to relatively smaller ones. Three attacks were made on Bochum, two each on Gelsenkirchen and Wuppertal and there were single attacks on Oberhausen and Mulheim. The raids on Bochum and Gelsenkirchen caused useful damage but the vagaries of the weather and interference on *Oboe* saved the towns from devastation comparable to that at Oberhausen and Wuppertal. The *Musical Wanganui* on Oberhausen (June 14-15) was an outstanding success. *Oboe* Mosquitoes dropped red tracking flares 24 miles from the target and greens at 12½ miles. The release-point flares were red with green stars. Of 203 bombers, 146 claimed to have attacked the target and the glow of the fires through 10/10ths stratus could be seen for 50 miles, subsequent PRU photographs showing complete devastation in the centre of the town. It was absolute vindication for this type of attack. Webster and Frankland[21] seem reluctant to give *Oboe* the credit for this raid and point out that some of the damage could have been caused when Duisburg and Mulheim were attacked. This was undoubtedly true but these raids could hardly have been responsible for the devastation in the town centre, nor does this interpretation take into account the howls of protest from the German press and radio immediately following the raid of June 14-15.

The attack on Mulheim referred to by Webster and Frankland took place on June 22-23 and crews were compelled to bomb on the glow of TIs because of the 10/10ths stratus covering the target. As the centre of the town and the adjacent steel works were severely damaged, there is no reason to suppose that the bombing extended to Oberhausen. The second attack on Wuppertal (June 24-25), this time on the Elberfeld district, should have been as good as the raid on Barmen already described. The

---

20. Williams had already been awarded a DFM and Bar when serving with 10 Squadron.

21. *The Strategic Air Offensive Against Germany.*

marking and backing-up were of a high order but there was a pronounced creepback from the bombers and many incendiaries were miles short of the aiming point. By attacking second-class targets, the inhabitants of all the smaller towns were kept in a state of fearful anticipation that made them clamour for protection. Yet, in spite of the loss of life and extensive damage to property, the morale of the people did not crack and clever propaganda hardened their resolve. A riddle, put round for this purpose, asked: 'What is a coward?' 'Someone from the Ruhr who volunteers for the Eastern Front.'

From the beginning of the year, 7 and 35 Squadrons had done all the H2S marking and illuminating. The courage of the crews was outstanding. In outdated aircraft, they faced the defences of the largest cities where there were four or five times as many flak batteries as planes in the target area. They pressed on in the face of heavy losses, many of them being senior crews. For example, 7 Squadron lost its three flight commanders during one week in June. W/Cdr R.G. Barrell, B Flight commander, was on his sixtieth trip and most of his crew were also finishing their second tour. The two squadrons did get some respite when Mosquitoes did the initial marking but they spearheaded all the attacks to Germany beyond *Oboe* range.

May saw the new Lancasters, with an H2S cupola instead of the ventral turret, coming off the line and crews from 83 and 156 Squadrons were training in them by the middle of the month. Small attacks on Bocholt, Rheine and Munster were carried out by 8 Group to enable new set operators to get operational experience before undertaking Blind Marking duties. Sufficient crews were trained by the middle of June to allow Bennett to take 7 Squadron out of the line to re-equip with Lancasters. The attack on Munster on June 11-12 served a dual purpose. Besides giving experience to H2S crews, many senior crews were on duty testing a new three-colour technique to improve *Newhaven* attacks. Bennett left the 85 crews in no doubt of what was expected from them and, in the event, the raid was a resounding success, the night photographs showing excellent concentration. PRU cover confirmed that the amount of damage was outstanding considering the smallness of the force. It was a fine example of the cumulative damage from concentrated bombing.

The last attack of the Battle of the Ruhr was on July 13-14 when 374 crews set off for Aachen. Because of a stronger tail-wind than forecast, most crews were milling round the target area waiting for PFF, with the result that the majority bombed within a minute of the first TIs igniting. It was a spectacular sight. The incendiaries burst almost simultaneously throughout the town and the whole area lit up as if someone had tripped a master switch. Although 35 Squadron dropped route-markers and carried out their backing-up duties, it is doubtful if more than a handful of crews saw their greens. The report said that more than half the town was devastated, which was hardly surprising, for no ARP service could possibly have coped with the number of fires started in so short a time. A vast area of fire was blazing merrily the following day and prevented PRU from getting cover photographs.

There were four interesting raids outside the Ruhr during June and July. On June 19, when 290 crews set off to bomb the Schneider works at Le Creusot, 26 PFF crews later went on to Montchanin where they were joined by 26 Main Force crews for an attack on the transformer station. At Le Creusot only flares were dropped; the Main Force was briefed to identify the target for itself. Crews were to make two runs over the target to shorten the sticks of bombs because the target was so small. The Main Force, more used to bombing TIs, found it difficult to pinpoint through the glare and smoke of the flares and they found accurate bomb-aiming almost impossible. Much damage was done to the Schneider works and to Breuil steel works nearby. All the plotted photographs were within 3 miles but the target was so small that only 21% of the bombs fell within the factory boundaries. At Montchanin the Markers and Illuminators mistook the Henrie Paul iron and bronze works for the transformer station and most crews bombed on the TIs. There were some who bragged they knew the markers were in the wrong place, but as there were no bombs dropped on the transformer station they did not make good use of their knowledge.

Bomber Command paid a second visit to east-central France when 35 Squadron did the marking for a small force of 125 heavies on July 15-16. The target was the Peugeot works at Montbeliard. It was a bright moonlit night with clear visibility and the target was only lightly defended, yet the attack developed to the south-east of the aiming point, a large proportion of the bombs were wasted, and the works were not written off as they ought to have been. The pall of smoke which blotted out the whole of the target area did not make bombing easy for later crews and this undoubtedly caused some of the spread.

On June 20-21, four crews of 97 Squadron went 'slumming'. Setting out from Scampton, they spearheaded an attack on the Zeppelin works at Friedrichshafen on Lake Constance for 56 Lancasters of 5 Group. The attack was controlled by the Deputy Master Bomber (the Master Bomber had engine trouble) and he ordered all crews to climb 5,000 feet because the flak was heavier than anticipated. This meant that no one had a correct target wind and it may have accounted for some of the not-too-accurate bombing. F/Lt J. Sauvage got his TIs within 200 yards of the aiming point, and the Deputy ordered crews to bomb them. The controller undoubtedly helped crews who bombed the TIs but could do little to help those who did a DR run from a pinpoint on the coast because the TIs had gone out before they had bombed. The Lancasters waited until all crews had bombed and then went on to North Africa, completely deceiving the

11. (*Top Right*) 'Hamish' Mahaddie's Stirling, shot up over Cologne on February 6, 1943, had 174 bullet and cannon shell holes in her. Lack of protective armament resulted in the wireless operator being seriously injured

12. (*Middle*) The fates were unkind to S/Ldr D. B. Everett. Having flown his Lancaster back from Mersburg-Leuna, on January 15, 1945, without the rear turret and later, on February 7-8, having had part of an engine shot away whilst on Long Stop duties over Goch, he was eventually shot down over Hemmingstedt-Heide on March 7-8, 1945. This photograph shows his turret-less Lancaster

13. (*Bottom*) Julian Sale had to crash-land his blazing Halifax at Graveley on December 21, 1943 because the mid-upper gunner's parachute had been burned. Both pilot and gunner escaped before the aircraft exploded

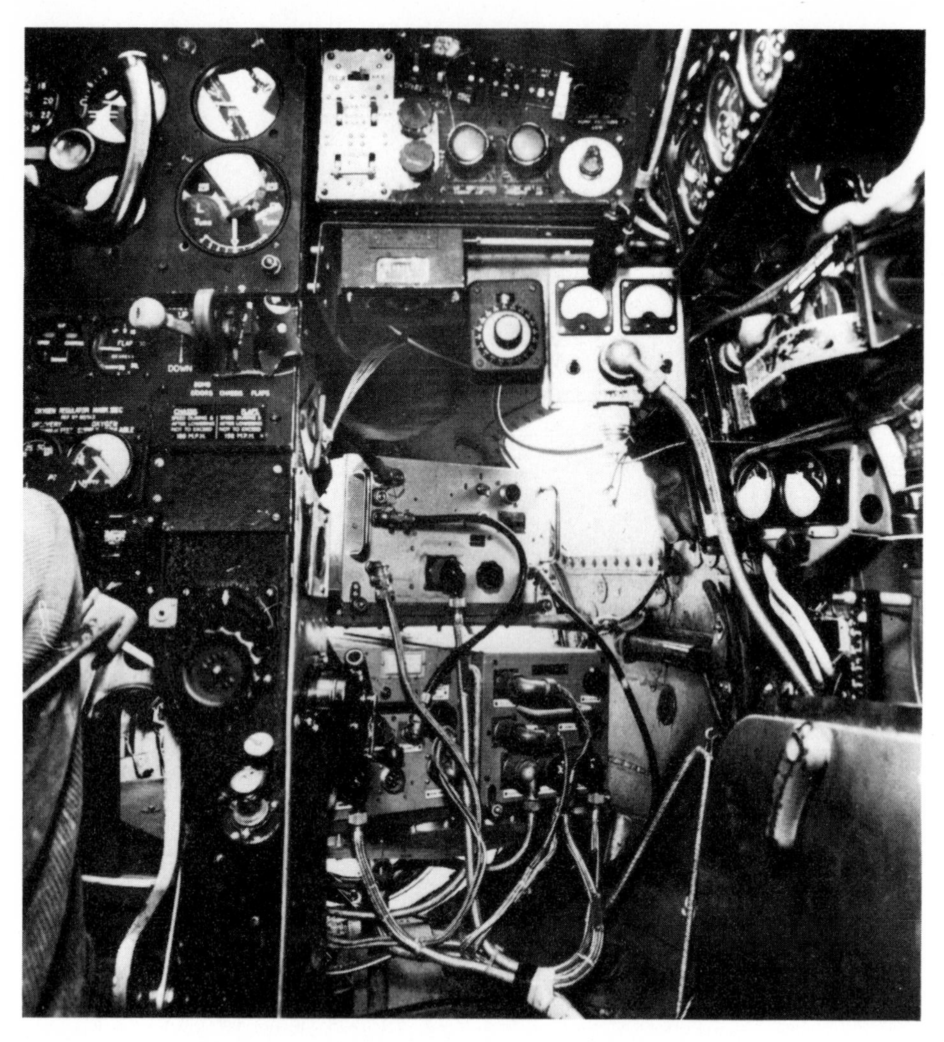

14. *Oboe* equipment in the nose of a Mosquito

15. (*Top*) *Oboe* Ground Control was carried out in the confined space of a caravan. This photograph shows a Ground Controller looking over the heads of his WAAF assistants. In the early days the Controller did the manipulation but subsequently it was realised that he had better control when supervising

16. (*Bottom*) Targets and routes already pinned up by 0930 on the large map which covered one wall of the Operations Room at PFFHQ. Air Vice-Marshal D.C.T. Bennett (centre) listening to the Met man (Mr M.J. Thomas) outlining the weather prospects for the evening

17. (*Top*) Site of the famous Leipzig Fair Ground blasted in the *Wanganui* raid of December 3-4, 1943

18. (*Bottom*) During the Battle of Berlin many high priority factories were extensively damaged. This photograph shows widespread damage in the Askania works. The whitened areas show where whole buildings have been literally pulverised

19. Shipping held up in the Kiel Canal after the dawn mining operation by Mosquitoes of 8 Group on May 13, 1944. The canal was completely closed for seven days.

20, 21 & 22. Three stages in the breaching of the sea wall at West Kapelle on the island of Walcheren, October 3, 1944. 20 (*Above*) at 1257 hours (Zero-3) TIs grouped in the target area. 21 (*Top Opposite*) during the fifth wave, on target at 1400 hours, the water began to seep through and a breach in the wall apppeared. 22 (*Bottom Opposite*) the last three waves widened the breach and, at the end of the attack, the sea was rushing through a gap of more than 100 yards, completely flooding the town

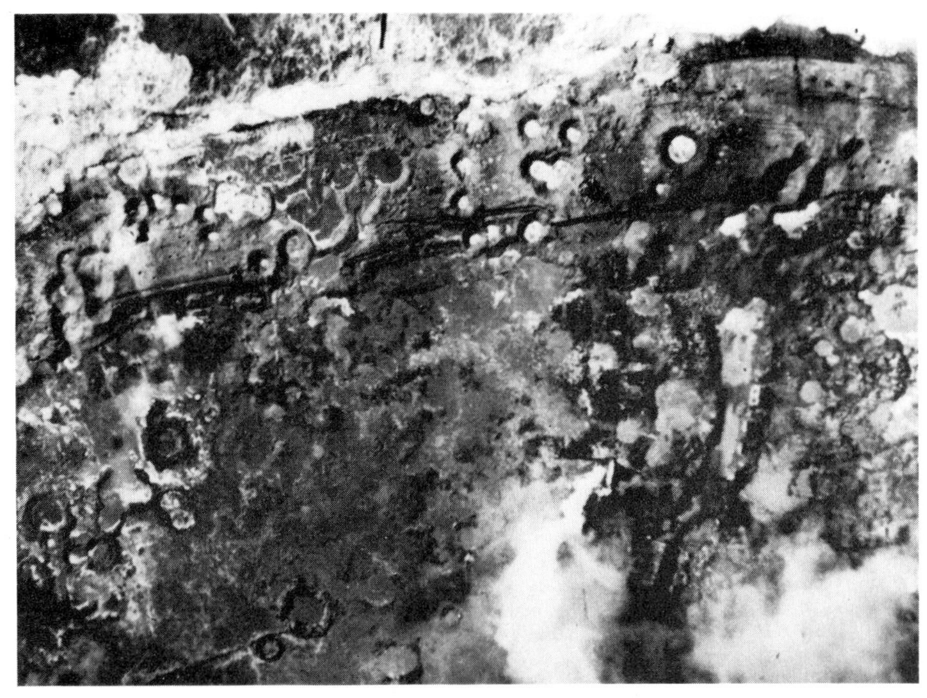

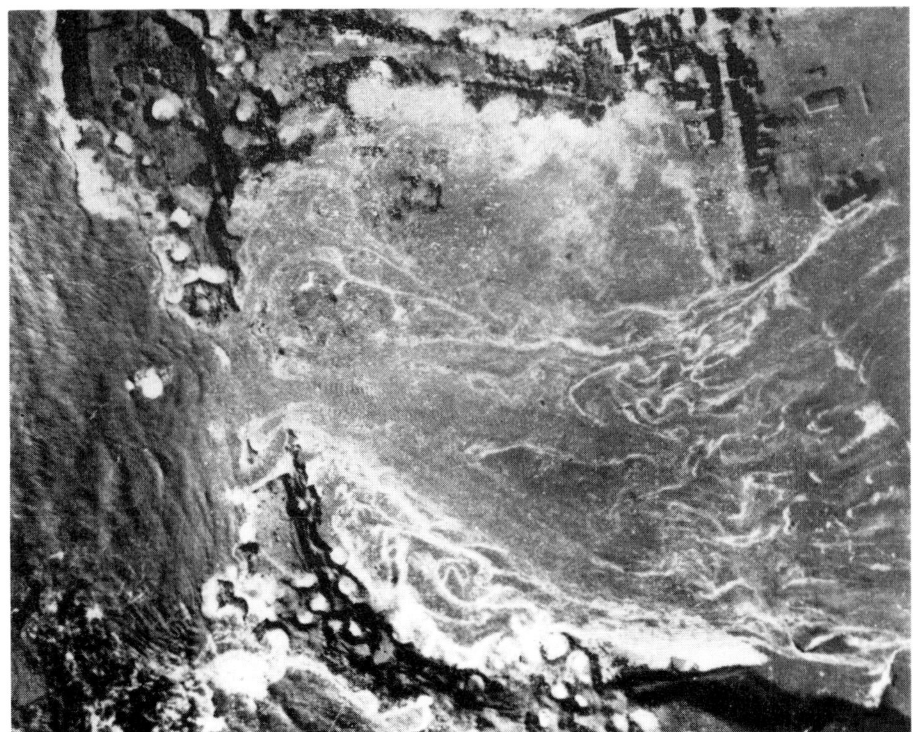

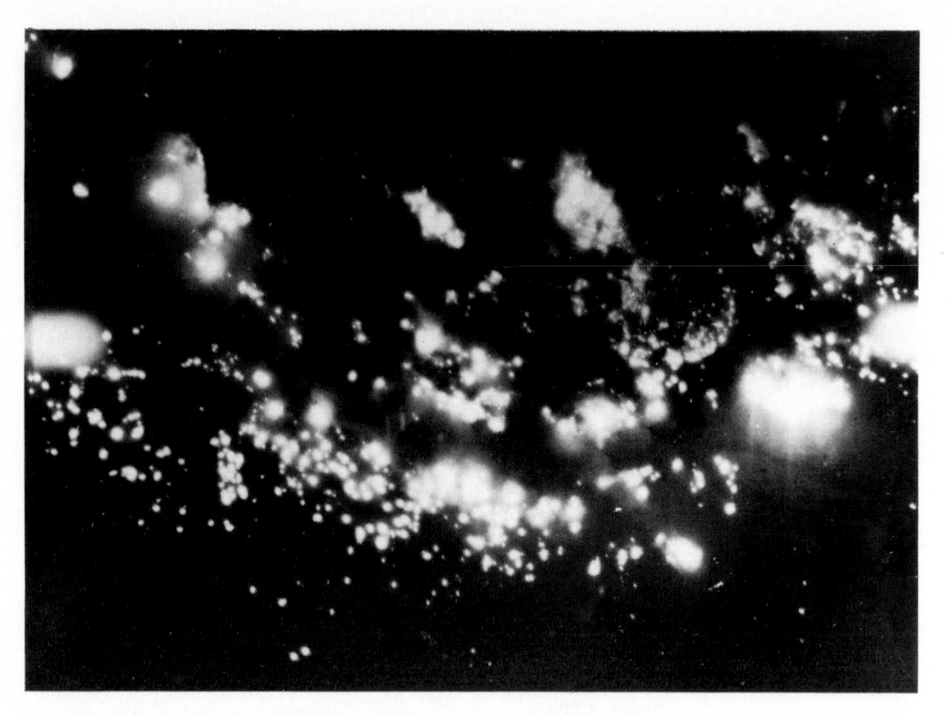

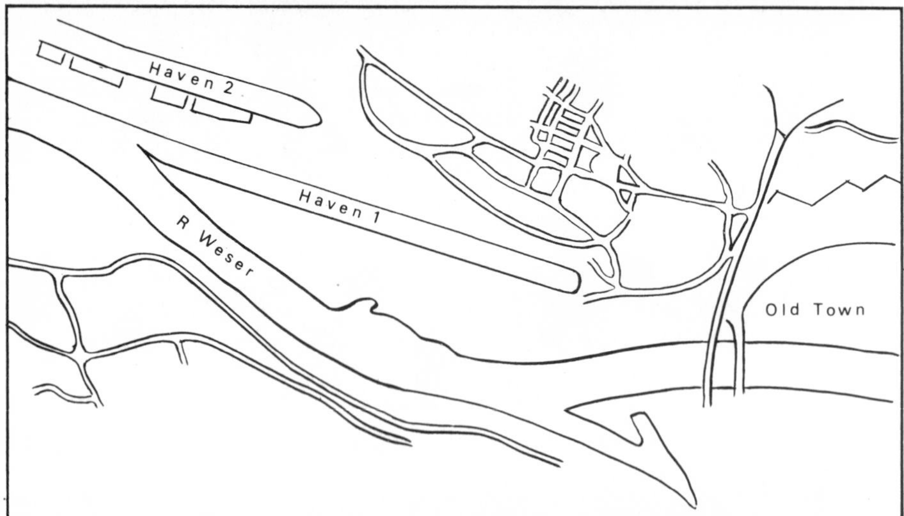

23. (*Top*) F/Lt Briggs, of 1409 Flight, took this night photograph of the fires during the raid on Bremen (August 13-19, 1944). The outline of the river can be seen clearly

24. A ground plan covering the same area

nightfighters who were poised to intercept them on the return route. The Marker crews were badly mauled by flak over the target and only 2 of the 4 were able to make the return trip, when La Spezia was bombed. The 5 Group Lancasters escaped any serious damage.

At dusk on July 12 a total of 224 Lancasters took off for the long trip to Turin. Cloud over France was welcome cover but many crews experienced icing and 16 turned back before crossing the Alps. Once across, the route was clear to the target and the turning point at Lake Annecy was marked by PFF. The attack started to the south-west of the aiming point but spread backward towards it and this is where the main fires were. A large explosion with thick black smoke rising in a column indicated someone had 'struck oil'. Incendiaries were scattered all round the town; although crews liked dropping their bombs on fires, it was a curious fact that if they were given a load of incendiaries they seemed to want to start a war of their own. Some PFF crews marked late but over half the Main Force were so late that the last TIs had burnt out before they arrived. PRU over Turin the following day reported 50 fires still burning, extensive damage to the Fiat works and a deplorable spread to the north of the town, probably caused by decoy TIs.

Because there were so few hours of darkness available on this July night, the return route was from the Alps to the west coast of France, skirting the Brest peninsula and up the western approaches – a round trip of 1,600 miles. The homeward flight offered two Pathfinder crews extra excitement. F/O M.R. Chick sighted two U-boats off St Nazaire and shot them up for the hell of it, passing their position to Group: Coastal Command sent out a Beaufighter which sank one of them. P/O W.J. Senger, at 2,000 feet, was looking for the English coast when land appeared exactly on ETA. To get a pinpoint he made an orbit. Most of the German garrison at Brest were rubbing the sleep from their eyes when the plane appeared over the town. Few of them had ever seen a Lancaster and certainly not at 2,000 feet, but they quickly recovered from the shock and it was then Senger's turn to get a surprise. The flak opened up, and Senger used what little height he had and full bore to get away as fast as possible. When he landed at Thruxton he had been airborne for 11 hours. In retrospect it was all worthwhile – it made a good story: 'There we were at 2,000 feet . . .'

IV Battle of Hamburg

The Battle of Hamburg was the name given to Bomber Command attacks during the period from July 24 to November 18, 1943. There were 32 major attacks on 18 German towns. Hanover, Mannheim and Kassel were left in ruins but the outstanding success occurred during the first 10 days of the battle when Hamburg was raided 4 times by Bomber Command and twice by the USAAF. Altogether, Bomber Command dropped more than 7,000 tons of HE and incendiaries on the city and it was not until September 1944 that any comparable damage was achieved.

Window, used for the first time at Hamburg on July 24, completely disrupted the German defence system: searchlights and radar-controlled guns were unable to pick out individual aircraft and similarly the German GCI was useless within the *Windowed* area. To counteract its effect the newly formed *Jagdgeschwader* 300, the *Wild Boars*, were strengthened and they were directed to the target by radio. Col J. Kammhuber, who was in charge of the German night defences, ordered all the *Tame Boars* to use the *Wild Boar* tactics when *Window* interfered with their normal procedure. Over the target the *Wild Boars* acted in conjunction with the searchlights and the flak was limited in height so they could attack the bombers without the risk of being shot down by their own defences. In an effort to cut down losses, the British used two new airborne jamming devices, *Cigar* and *Tinsel*, and *Corona* broadcasting false information to the *Wild Boars,* but as a last resort the fighters had the PFF flares and markers as a guide. Bennett introduced spoof raids to draw the fighters away from the main target, a tactic that succeeded on a number of occasions, but by the end of the period, when longer nights meant that Berlin could be attacked in strength, it was clear that the loss rate was going to be comparable to the Ruhr attacks of 1941-2.

Pointblank was still the avowed policy, but little was done to make it a combined offensive. The British losses were increasing but not on the same scale as those of the Americans, who lost 88 crews between October 10 and 15. Then on October 16 they made a sortie to Schweinfurt and the German fighters harassed them from the moment their fighter escort left.

From 291 aircraft dispatched 60 failed to return and a further 138 were damaged, 17 severely – 68% of the force. The fact had to be faced that, without a long-range fighter escort, deep penetration in daylight was suicidal. At this point the Americans retired from the scene to regroup and remuster.

Hamburg's ten-day ordeal began on July 24 when 791 aircraft were sent to attack the town. The route took the bombers out to sea and north of the target. The southerly track to the aiming point continued through the town to avoid collisions and in the hope that crews would not drop their load until they were over the centre of the city. *Zephyrs*[1] were broadcast, so all crews would have a good target wind. The plan was for a *Newhaven* attack, but in case the Primary Visual Markers could not identify the aiming point Blind Markers would drop yellow TIs. The Backers-up were briefed to drop on the Primary Visual Markers' reds or, failing this, on the MPI of the H2S yellows. The first bombs were concentrated round the markers and soon fires were taking hold, the four main areas of fire being to the north of the city. Recenterers[2] were used for the first time and marked throughout the raid to try to keep the attack concentrated, but they had little effect and even the track through the town did not prevent the Main Force bombing fires, or worse, the fringe of them, causing creepback. It was a devastating attack, even if not on the aiming point, and ground detail was soon obliterated by thick black smoke; it did not, however, hide the raging fires nor an enormous explosion which was seen from 100 miles away. Crews reported the searchlights were 'clueless' and the flak, although daunting in its intensity, was aimless. The *Tame Boars* were helpless and their ground controllers unable to give them directions. Only 12 aircraft were missing and the toil of pushing *Window* out of the flare chute became a labour of love. A cloud of smoke hung over the city the following morning, and the hot summer sun did nothing to disperse the gloom. The Americans put in two short raids on the Sunday and Monday mornings and spread the damage to the port area. A feeling of despondency was creeping through the city as the people realized these attacks had all the earmarks of a prolonged ordeal. Six Mosquitoes over the town on Sunday night and 4 more on Monday sent the townsfolk back to the shelters; crews reported that fires were still burning. Harris had warned those taking part in the first raid that the destruction of the

1. Selected crews relayed the winds they had found to HQ; these were averaged and broadcast to all crews. Bombs followed the path of the aircraft heading at the moment of release. The greatest bombing errors were caused by aircraft on the wrong heading. Accurate concentrated bombing was achieved by all aircraft using the same target wind.

2. Re-marked the aiming point usually with a two-second overshoot as opposed to Backers-up who marked the MPI sometimes with a two-second overshoot.

port could not be achieved in one night, and had the inhabitants known the code name for the attacks was 'Gomorrah' more would have packed their bags and fled from the town.

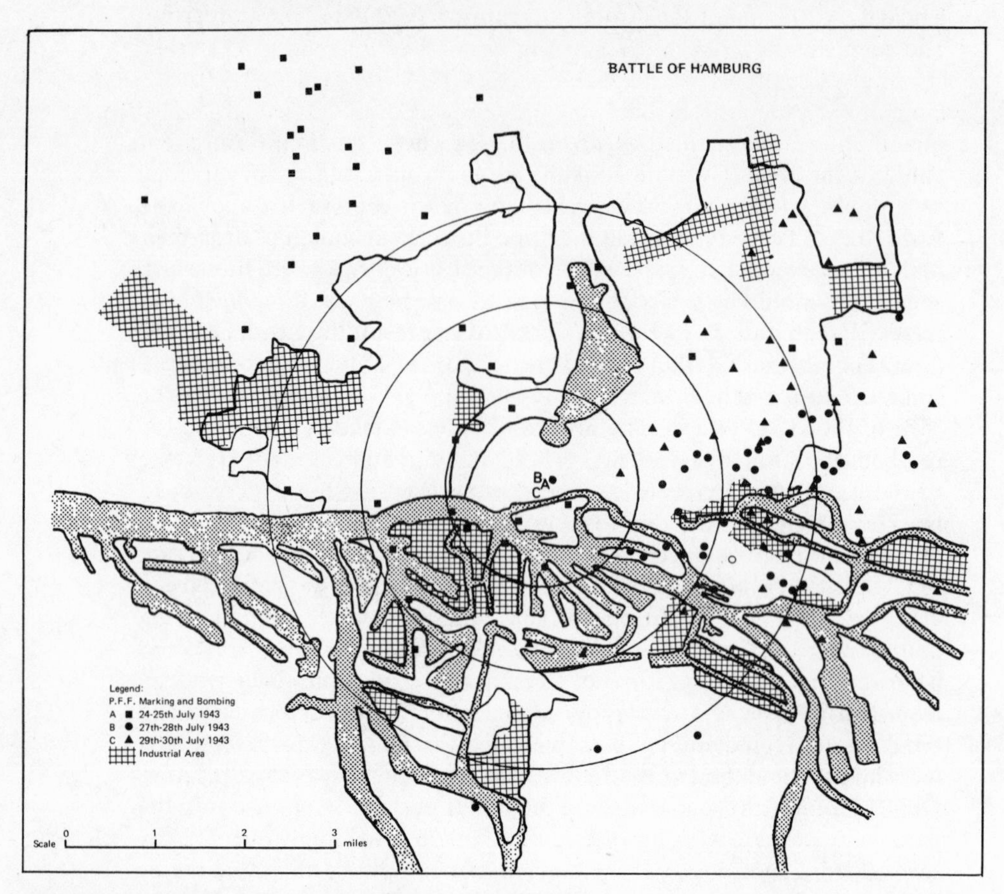

Map 3 These three bomb plots illustrate the essential difference between *Oboe* marking and Visual or H2S marking. Here Visual (A) and H2S (B & C) were responsible for the Primary markers. After they burnt out the MPI tended to creep back along the line of approach. *Oboe* TIs would have been reinforced at regular intervals thus eliminating the errors caused by a changing MPI.

A total of 787 bombers took part in the second major attacks on July 27-28. The raid was planned as a *Parramatta* because on July 25 the Blind Markers had found the port easy to identify on their H2S screens. The turning point on the promontory north-west of Fridskop, 60 miles from Hamburg, was marked and backed-up throughout the attack. Blind Markers using H2S dropped yellow TIs on the town and also released sticks of flares to help the Backers-up. The yellow groundmarkers were to the east of the aiming point and this is where the attack developed.

Although fires were still burning from the previous raids, it was the new fires that attracted the majority of the bombers. The whole area soon became a mass of concentrated fire. A line of warehouses, estimated to be a mile long, was ablaze and the glow could be seen from 140 miles away. The smoke haze, which hung over the town at the beginning of the raid became a cloud and at 20,000 feet it looked like a huge cumulus with the familiar anvil shape at the top, where light winds at 23,000 feet gradually spread it. As one of the crews from 83 Squadron said: 'It was a most unholy sight lit up by the raging fires.' The new fires joining with the old ones produced such intense heat in the narrow streets of the dock area that it created a huge vacuum. Winds, rushing in to fill the vacuum, reached hurricane strength and caused a firestorm: trees were uprooted and flaming timbers, carried on the wind like straws, spread the fires: the cycle was repeated starting further storms. As a result the Reich Defence Commissioner asked for a voluntary evacuation of women and children and thousands left.

Window was used again on this raid and it helped to keep the flak damage down, but the nightfighters were up in strength and there were signs that they had devised a method to counteract jamming. Only 17 aircraft were missing, a remarkably low loss rate. The following night 4 Mosquitoes of 139 Squadron over the city found an embarrassing number of fires to bomb.

On July 29-30, when the third major attack took place, 3 Mosquitoes went ahead of the Pathfinders and *Windowed* the target. Minutes later the yellow TIs of the Blind Markers were cascading down followed by the inevitable greens. Out of a force of 777 aircraft, 691 claimed to have attacked the target and the Germans considered this the most effective raid. Their reports stated: 'Compared with the number of planes and the bombs dropped, this was the heaviest attack, and it was chiefly on those parts of the town which had not been affected until now. The port was severely hit and the remaining part of the thickly populated district of Barmbeck was completely destroyed by fire. Damage was gigantic.' Crews reported that the heat from the fires could be felt in the aircraft. Once again firestorms were created and the President of the Hamburg police reported: 'Numbers jumped into the canals and waterways and remained swimming or standing up to their necks in water for hours until the heat should die down.' The number of bombers shot down rose to 30, an indication that the technique of relaying a running commentary of the raid to the *Wild Boars* was successful.

The fourth night attack of the series by a force of 700 bombers took place on August 2-3. This time the weather took a hand. Harris knew there were large cumulo-nimbus over the North Sea travelling towards Hamburg, but he hoped his force would get in and out before the clouds reached the port. Everyone was waiting for a 'scrub' but as take-off time approached no red Very cartridges were fired, and some Pathfinders took off in a storm. The weather deteriorated as the force moved eastward and cloud thickened to 9-10/10ths. A bank of cumulo-nimbus covered the enemy coast and there was a particularly active one with base 10,000 feet and tops rising to 25,000 feet at 53° 00N 04°00E, the last turning point before the run-up to the target. Pilots were faced with the perilous choice of severe icing and electrical storms or flak at 9,000 feet. Most crews challenged the elements. It was awe-inspiring to see the corposant glowing all round a plane making it look as if it was on fire, or to watch the sparks arc from one prop to another leaving the eerie halo of St Elmo's fire round the blades.

The weather made a mockery of the plan of attack. PFF did mark, although few crews saw the markers; 405 Squadron was operating in a Blind Marker role for the first time, but the conditions were so appalling that even this keen squadron could not overcome them: only 5 crews managed to reach the target, 3 bombed alternative targets, 3 were compelled to jettison their loads and 3 were missing. Hamburg itself was in the middle of a thunderstorm: lightning and the roll of thunder mingled with the flashes and sounds of bombs exploding. Most crews were bombing on DR and that made it more terrifying for the people below as bombs appeared to be dropping everywhere. In spite of the bad weather the German nightfighters were up in strength, and again the number missing was 30, although the weather undoubtedly claimed some victims.

The destruction wreaked in the 'Gomorrah' raids dwarfed anything that had gone before: 74% of the city was destroyed. With gas, electricity and water supplies seriously affected and little food in the town, the survivors were totally demoralized and they wandered around dazedly looking at the destruction on all sides. It was two months before any semblance of normality returned to the port.

If the people of Hamburg got little rest between July 24 and August 2 neither did Bomber Command crews. As well as the 4 raids on Hamburg 2 attacks were made on the Ruhr, and both were highly successful. To celebrate Mussolini's downfall on July 25, 16 *Oboe* Mosquitoes, 2 acting as reserves, dropped red fireworks on Essen; 33 PFF heavies backed-up the reds with greens. In spite of the inevitable Ruhr haze and a thin layer of strato-cumulus the TIs were clearly visible and the 560 Main Force crews lit a gigantic bonfire as their contribution. *Oboe* now had 3 pairs of ground stations and it was the first time all of them had been used on one raid. The result was that red TIs were burning for almost the whole attack. This undoubtedly helped to keep the bombing concentrated; numerous explosions were reported and fires were still burning furiously 12 hours later. In 50 minutes the force inflicted more damage on the town than in all the previous attacks put together. In the Krupp works alone, 110 of the 190 workshops suffered damage and many were completely gutted. In 13 of the 28 departments production ceased entirely for weeks, and in the other 15 the output figures never exceeded 50% of their previous peak. The next morning, when Dr Gustav Krupp saw the smouldering ruins of his empire, he fell down in a fit from which he had not recovered sufficiently to take his place among the war criminals at their trial in 1947. The surrounding districts were in the same plight, the fire services being inundated with calls; more than 500 separate fires were reported. Absenteeism at Krupps during the week following the raid had a marked effect on production as well as retarding repair work. 'One of the most impressive sights I have ever seen,' was General F.L. Anderson's[3] summary. The general was a passenger with F/Lt F.J. Garvey and many a pulse at Wyton steadied when 'Q' made a safe return.

The second Ruhr target was Remscheid and the sortie took place on July 30-31 between the third and fourth attacks on Hamburg. Continuous *Oboe* marking was acheived for the first time and 191 out of 228 crews bombed within 3 miles of the aiming point. Devastation throughout the town was severe and the centre was flattened. The fires were completely out of control and 24 hours later the fire services had made little impression on them. Again a comparatively small force had wreaked havoc with an attack concentrated in space and time.

During the first ten days of using *Window* the attackers had a comparatively easy ride and celebrated their new-found immunity by delivering 5 devastating attacks on the Fatherland. However, each succeeding attack showed that the German defences were adapting themselves and adopting new tactics, and the losses began to mount, mainly because of the increased successes of the nightfighters. On July 29, the Germans anticipated the attack would be on Hamburg, and their new running-commentary method of directing the fighters was used to good effect. The number of interceptions rose sharply and more than 90 incidents were reported. The 'cat's-eyes' fighters were easier to lose than the *Tame Boars*, providing evasive action was taken early enough. So the danger zone became the target area where aircraft could be either coned or silhouetted by the searchlights, and this is where the *Wild Boars* operated most effectively.

F/Sgt P.R. Raggett was intercepted *en route* to Hamburg on July 29 by an unidentified twin-engined fighter. The enemy opened fire and the rear gunner replied with a 5-second burst. By diving to port and losing 2,000 feet the Halifax evaded a second attack. The fighter must have been a *Tame Boar* because the bomber's *Monica* picked it up at 1,000 yards. Although the Halifax was hit in the mainplane and the No 4 petrol tank was holed, Raggett went on to the target. While on the bombing run he was coned by searchlights and it was fortunate that neither Sgt D.S. Wood

3. Later became Deputy for Operations to General Spaatz.

nor Sgt P.H. Palmer, the gunners, were fire-watching because an Me110 came in from the port quarter. Raggett made a steep diving turn to port and Wood put in 3 short but effective bursts. The fighter crossed from port to starboard but Wood's aim had been true. The Messerschmitt burst into flames and was seen to strike the ground by the bomb-aimer, F/O S.A. Baldwin.

The same night over Hamburg W/O J. Finding's Lancaster was coned by 20 to 30 searchlights and was hit by flak fired into the cone. Suddenly the flak stopped and almost immediately tracer was seen coming from astern and slightly to port. Because of the dazzling effect of the searchlights the enemy was not seen until he had closed to 250 yards. The mid-upper gunner, Sgt J.A.P. Logan, protected from some of the glare by the Lancaster's mainplane, was the first to spot it, and he shouted: 'Me109, dive to port, go, go, go,' and opened fire. When Sgt C.R.B. Everard added his weight to the defence the Messerschmitt broke away, climbing hard to port. Logan kept on firing and the fighter was sufficiently discouraged from making a second attack. The co-operation between the ground defences and the fighter were excellent; the flak had stopped as the fighter came in to attack and the searchlights kept the bomber coned throughout the combat. The Lancaster was held altogether for 5 minutes by the searchlights which were switched off shortly after the Me109 broke away.

On the night of August 2-3, to add to the bombers' problems, the nightfighters were up in numbers in spite of the appalling weather. Baker, now a flight lieutenant, was over Westermunde when Thornhill, his mid-upper gunner, reported an exhaust glow 400 feet below and 350 feet astern on the starboard side. Thornhill fired a short burst and ordered a dive to starboard while Robbins, although he could not see anything to shoot at, fired along the mid-upper's tracer. When the fighter broke away to port above it was identified as an Me210. A second attack was made from the starboard and both gunners observed strikes on the enemy. Baker then made for cloud but as he came out of it the fighter was waiting and the German, not realizing the quality of the opposition, had the temerity to close to 200 yards. Both gunners again scored hits; the enemy suddenly stopped firing and dived away to starboard. A red ball of fire was seen in the cloud below and seconds later a red explosion. Lancaster G-George, although showing a few scars on the tailplane caused by cannon fire, proudly boasted another bomb painted on the side to mark the completion of another sortie, but this bomb was adorned with a small swastika to signify an enemy fighter had been destroyed.

After the fourth attack on Hamburg Bomber Command turned its attention to Italy and because these attacks coincided with the full-moon period there was no lull in activities as in previous months. On July 27 President Roosevelt had offered the Italians honourable terms if they capitulated and General Dwight Eisenhower followed up with threats of heavy bombing if they did not. Bomber Command had to implement these threats and the enormous havoc caused in the main Italian cities by the 10-day Blitz was a vital factor in persuading the government to negotiate an armistice. The raids began on August 7 when Milan, Turin and Genoa were successfully bombed. At Milan after 3 more attacks between August 12 and 15 almost half of the fully built-up area was in ruins, and fire damage around the central station and the Scalo Farino goods yards was widespread. Important factories like Alfa Romeo, Isotta Fraschini, Pirelli and the Breda works were among the factories partially destroyed. The ORS report stated that 239 industrial plants were affected, 19 destroyed and 7 almost completely devastated.

After 2 more raids on August 12 and 16 Turin too realized that Eisenhower's threats were no idle boast. The town centre had escaped extensive damage because the weight of the attacks had fallen on the industrial sector to the north and north-east. The Fiat works, the town's largest concern, was seriously damaged and 8 buildings had gaping holes in the roofs caused by HE and fires. The Royal Arsenal, 3 railway stations and nearby warehouses all received direct hits.

The famous attack of August 17, 1943, on the German experimental station at Peenemunde was a landmark in PFF history as important as the Essen raid of March 5. Parallel development of V-1 and V-2 rockets had reached a critical stage and it was imperative to halt the progress of both projects. Normal area-attack methods were unsuitable because it was required to destroy specific buildings, so the attack was divided into 3 waves on 3 different aiming points, PFF shifting the markers by applying a false wind to their bombsights.[4] Red Spot Fire TIs were used for the first time. Although they made a smaller area of fire than candle TIs, they could be placed with greater accuracy, burnt more brilliantly and lasted for 10 minutes. Ultimately success or failure depended on the human element and, as had been shown in the 'Dams raid', encouragement and advice from a leader could tip the scales. W/Cdr J.H. Searby was made MC for the raid, the first time a Master Bomber had been used with the Main Force in strength,[5] and the tenacious and intrepid manner in which he performed the difficult and dangerous role was to a great extent

4. When describing *Zephyrs* (footnote page 57), it was pointed out that the aircraft heading at the time of bomb release was the most important single factor in bombing accuracy. Several aircraft at the same height and airspeed and with the same false (incorrect) wind on their bombsights using the same datum point (group of markers) to drop their bombs (TIs) would hit the same point on the ground. The false wind required to mark a second A/P could be calculated on the ground and given to crews at briefing. Provided the original markers were in the correct place the A/P could be shifted accurately *ad infinitum*. Later, in 1944, 5 Group 'invented' this method which became known as 'off-set marking'.

5. Searby had had a dress rehearsal at Turin on August 7.

responsible for the success of the operation.

Until briefing time the target was 'most secret' and only the squadron COs knew the routes and details; the armourers were not told the bomb load until after lunch. All 3 aiming points were successfully marked although there was some confusion as earlier TIs were still burning when later aircraft arrived; but the raid was an unqualified success with 571 out

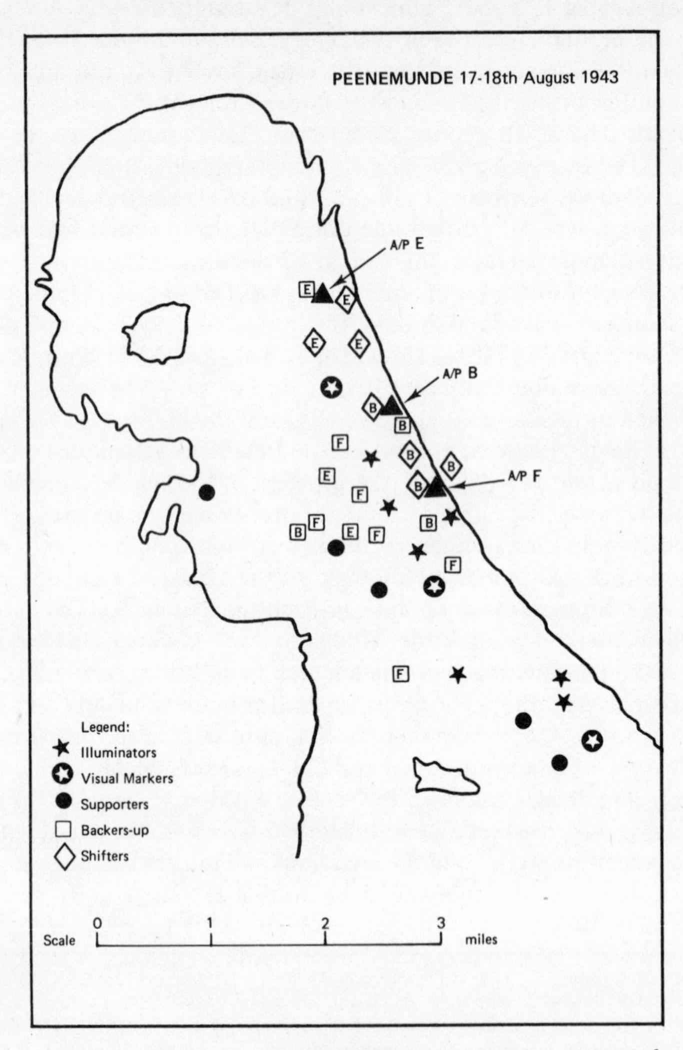

Map 4 The chief snag with using Shifters was that the accuracy of subsequent marking depended entirely on the accuracy of the initial markers – errors being perpetuated. A/P F was the first to be marked. The tendency for the concentration to be south of the A/P is reflected at A/P B. The relative position of the Shifter TIs to A/P E is almost identical to those on A/P B, which clearly illustrates the point.

of 597 in the force making good their attack. The Main Force used the Berlin sea route outwards and 8 Mosquitoes of 139 Squadron, using the same route, continued on to Berlin dropping *Window* and carrying out a successful spoof attack on the capital. The German nightfighter force assembled over the Big City waiting for the expected attack. When the German controllers realized their mistake they called up fighters from as far away as the southern Ruhr and they managed to intercept the last wave on the return journey. Visibility was excellent, so that crews could see the fighters clearly miles away as they approached from all directions; some though, were using *Schrage Musik*[6] for the first time and this enabled them to attack from below without being seen. In all, 41 planes were shot down, which was a small price if the importance of the target was taken into account. For General Hans Jeschonnek, chief of the *Luftwaffe* general staff, the destruction of Peenemunde was the last straw – the following morning he committed suicide. Threats of retaliation by 'secret weapons' remained as blood-curdling as before but they became less specific regarding the launching date. Although the move from Peenemunde had actually begun before the raid, it was speeded up as a result and caused a serious loss of efficiency which greatly hampered the German missile programme.

On August 23 Harris sent a large force to the Big City. This was the first attack on Berlin since the end of March and Bomber Command hoped that now the H2S crews had gained experience they would be able to pinpoint within the city limits. It was a vain hope, for the attack developed miles west of the aiming point. Still, the Backers-up achieved a good concentration of TIs and as the weather over the capital was clear they were visible for miles. The majority of the 575 bombers from a force of 719 who claimed to have attacked the target bombed with a TI in their bombsight. Large fires enveloped the markers and many crews reported a series of explosions which lit the sky with flames leaping to a great height. Decoy fires were lit but were so insignificant in comparison with the main conflagration that they were completely ignored. It was impossible to guess at the number of searchlights operating for the total effect was almost to turn night into day. Nightfighters were up in great numbers and there were combats everywhere. Crews missing numbered 56 but the bombers shot down 11 nightfighters.

W/Cdr K.H. Burns was the Master Bomber on the raid, but few crews claimed to have heard him; they were too busy evading flak, searchlights or fighters to worry about his instructions. One exception was W/Cdr W.H. Shaw who was listening out when he was attacked by a fighter and so did not hear his mid-upper gunner's directions. The wing commander,

---

6. German name for two cannons fixed to slant upward from a platform on a nightfighter, so that the pilot could fly straight and level below the bomber and attack without being seen.

whose great desire was to bring back an A/P photograph, had flown straight and level over the target on earlier sorties, but lack of success had convinced him this method paid no dividends and, considering the dangers involved, he had abandoned the stratagem. Fortunately he had gone to the other extreme and because the fighter could not cope with his violent evasive action it veered off to find easier game. Once again, the visual intercom was not used, although in this instance the gunners had some excuse because they could hear each other but were unaware their captain was listening to the Master Bomber.

The Germans had been dropping flares and also groundmarking near isolated bombers, but on August 30-31 over Berlin they used a new tactic: :ares were dropped in lanes to mark the bombers' route in and out of the target and the fighters flew in the lanes looking for their prey. This idea combined with searchlight co-operation over the target had a bad psychological effect on many crews. The target area had never been the place to hang around, but now many bomb loads were dropped early, some with gross undershoots. Berlin was a long way from base when the winds were nothing like the forecast ones, and this night there was cloud along the route to the target, but it was sufficiently broken over Berlin for the TIs to be seen provided the bombers flew over the city. The Main Force could not be blamed for the fact that all the bombing was south of the aiming point, for the TIs were to the south, but most of the bombing was 8 to 30 miles short and there were no TIs that far away. Fighter flares, fighters and the cloud, which prevented the markers being seen from a distance, all contributed to making this one of the worst raids since the introduction of TIs.

Some 42 combats took place in the target area and one of the victims was W/Cdr J.K. Burns. The wing commander was only a few minutes from the target when an Fw190 made a head-on attack, setting the whole of the port wing on fire. Burns, realizing the plane was doomed, ordered everyone to bale out. The bomb-aimer, wanted to jettison the bombs but his skipper said: 'No, leave 'em be and I'll aim the kite where they'll do some good.' With the crew away he trimmed the Lancaster nose down, unstrapped his harness and was just taking off his helmet when the bombs exploded, blowing the aircraft to pieces. Three-and-a-half hours later, he recovered consciousness and found himself lying under some pine trees. As the numbness started to leave his body, he felt pain in his right ankle and foot, and moving his right arm to feel the ankle discovered the hand and half the forearm were missing. He could scarcely believe his eyes; there was no pain in the arm and in fact it felt normal. He realized he must get help for he was getting weak from loss of blood and a feeling of lassitude was creeping over him. As he got up, he was amazed to find that the ripcord of his parachute had not been pulled and there was so little of it open, it could have cut down his falling speed only fractionally. He was too bemused to work it out. Staggering across some fields, he fell down exhausted near a signal box by a suburban station. As well as losing his forearm and pints of blood, the doctors found one lung had collapsed because of the blast. From the red weal round his neck, they deduced that the intercom cord, by half strangling him, had prevented the other lung collapsing. The story has a wry epilogue. The Germans treated him well and when he was fit enough he was moved to *Dulag Luft*, where he complained of pains in his back – it was discovered that he had broken it when he fell. When the prison Commandant enquired of the doctors why they had not found the break, he was told the X-ray facilities at the hospital had been destroyed by the RAF.

The third attack on September 3-4 was Bomber Command's last sortie to the capital before the Battle of Berlin started on November 18-19. Of 316 Lancasters, 295 did some concentrated bombing on the north-western industrial districts of Charlottenburg and Wedding, which had not been bombed before, and many important factories, previously undamaged, were hit. PFF put up 81 Lancasters, 55 Markers and 26 Supporters. The Group also sent 4 Mosquitoes acting in a new role dropping fighter fiares in lanes some distance from the Main Force track to confuse the nightfighters. If judged by the amount of damage inflicted on the enemy the raid was an outstanding success, but as the aiming point was in the north-eastern sector, the whole raid was an undershoot and therefore technically a failure. The problem of blitzing Berlin had not as yet been solved, nor was the loss-rate very encouraging for the future; in the 3 raids Bomber Command had flown 1,647 sorties and 123 aircraft were missing, 7.5%.

If the German controllers correctly guessed the target early, PFF was in serious trouble; this is reflected in the number of interceptions reported by the Group, and by the number of aircraft missing. On August 23, 11 crews were missing from 117 detailed, 4 crews had combats and another was shot down by an intruder. Two Station Commanders were among the missing: G/Capt B.V. Robinson of Graveley and G/Capt. A.H. Willetts of Oakington. Station Commanders were limited in the number of times they could operate each month and it speaks highly of them that they did not choose the easy sorties.

Loss of an engine presented the pilot with a difficult problem and naturally each reacted differently.[7] Mechanical defects predictably had a

7. W/Cdr J.E. Fauquier, the keen Canadian Commanding Officer of 405 Squadron, was somewhat of a martinet on the subject. A PFF crew on probation – no names no pack drill – returned early from an operation on 3 engines and the wing commander refused to give them permission to land. He ordered them back to their original squadron telling them they were unsuitable for Pathfinders. By contrast, W/Cdr W.G. Lockhart, CO of 692 Squadron, on the way to Berlin in a Mosquito, lost an engine but continued the sortie on one and bombed the capital.

bad psychological effect, probably because the trouble increased slowly and created tension. F/O J.L. Wright's starboard inner had been overheating for most of the outward journey and by the time he had reached the outskirts of Berlin, he was compelled to feather it. The Lancaster immediately began to lose height so he jettisoned his bombs, retaining his TIs. This happened to be close to the decoy fire site near Potsdam where a Ju88 was orbiting waiting for someone to be attracted to the fire. P/O K.A. Crankshaw, the rear gunner, spotted it on the port quarter below and ordered a dive to starboard, which must have surprised the enemy because most crews turned towards the fighter. Wright's reactions were so quick and violent that P/O R.C. Reynolds, the mid-upper, was thrown out of his seat and on to the floor of the bomber. Two long bursts of accurate machine-gun fire from Crankshaw were more than enough for the enemy and, as the Junkers broke away, flames were seen coming from the starboard wing; a few seconds later an explosion was seen on the ground.

F/Sgt T.G. Stevens was on his bombing run when his Lancaster received a direct hit by flak which damaged the port wing and set one of the starboard engines on fire. The navigator, Sgt A.C. Clegg, and the mid-upper gunner, Sgt I.R. Wright, were wounded by shrapnel: Clegg in the head, the shoulder, the left arm and leg. There were many instances of German pilots braving their own flak to engage a bomber and Stevens was the victim of one of them. It was all so sudden that the fighter was not identified beyond the fact that it was twin-engined. Sgt V.E. Altree, the tail gunner, shouted: 'Starboard quarter level 150 yards,' and then silence. Wright, in spite of severe wounds in both feet, swung his turret and saw tracer striking the Lancaster's tailplane. It must have been during this attack that Altree was killed. Wright followed the fighter as it moved from port to starboard and he saw his tracer strike in the cockpit area. The fighter broke away and was claimed as 'damaged', but, if the German survived, he too could claim he had damaged the bomber and set the port engine on fire. The Lancaster was extensively damaged and two Merlins were not equal to the task of maintaining height. Everything possible, including ammunition, was jettisoned to lighten the aircraft. Stevens, keeping the nose pointed westward, stuck grimly to the controls begrudging every inch of height, knowing that more than 500 miles, much of it over enemy territory, stretched between the crew and sanctuary.

After 1½ hours Sgt T. Stocks, the wireless operator, gave the good news that he had obtained a fix. The wireless had been damaged and the sending key broken; Stocks had mended the set and fashioned a new key. Next he revived Clegg, who plotted a course for base. For 4½ hours Clegg fought off unconsciousness, as Stocks supplied him with fixes until, shortly before 0600 hours, the Lancaster crossed the English coast. Stevens, wanting to get the wounded to hospital as quickly as possible, landed at Attlebridge so ending a nightmare flight lasting 9 hours 50 minutes.

Although gunners were warned against relaxing vigilance until the aircraft was back in dispersal, the sight of the English coast after a 7½-hour flight had a soporific effect; it was like coming into a warm room with an open fire after trudging for hours through a snowstorm. The fire that greeted Sgt C.S. Chatham was entirely different: it consisted of white tracer and cannon shells. Intruders were operating over East Anglia at this stage of the war either as bombers attacking airfields,[8] or as fighters waiting for the unwary, who, in this instance, was even sporting navigation lights. The fighter, coming in from the starboard bow and below, made only one attack. The first fire started in the nose of the Lancaster, then the starboard inner burst into flames, and when they spread to the starboard wing Chatham ordered 'abandon aircraft'. Everyone baled out except the mid-upper gunner who had probably been killed by the fighter. His body was found in the burnt-out plane which crashed 3½ miles north of Marham.

An extra degree of tension among the crew during the sortie following a combat was only natural and as F/O J. L. Wright approached Berlin on August 30, the adrenalin was flowing rapidly. Although everything went without a hitch over the target a feeling of apprehension persisted. Even T-Tommy seemed to feel the need to get away as quickly as possible as it searched its 4 engines for additional power. Suddenly, there was the click of a microphone switch and everyone tensed, then, cutting through the rattle of machine-gun fire, Reynolds shouted: 'Twin-engined fighter, starboard quarter, up.' Crankshaw swung his turret into line and opened fire. The fighter turned over on its back and went into a steep dive and shortly afterwards the crew saw an explosion on the ground. They were too experienced to relax their vigilance but the tension was gone.

On September 3-4, F/O J.C.H. Davies was 30 miles east of Egmund, outward bound for Berlin, when he was intercepted by an Me109. The enemy opened up at 400 yards and Sgt W.G. Trotter, the rear gunner, replied with a continuous burst as the Messerschmitt closed to 100 yards before falling away in flames. The crew are confident Trotter shot it down because, although they did not actually see it hit the ground, it was still burning and obviously out of control when it disappeared into cloud.

P/O D.A. Routen did see the Me210 which attacked his Lancaster hit the ground and burst into flame – in fact he was a mere 2,000 feet above it when it happened. Coned over the target by approximately 40 searchlights Routen had lost height to 15,000 feet, trying to escape the

8. Bennett was so infuriated because his stations were being attacked – in fact it was an honour – that he ordered Station Commanders to supervise personally the defences during alerts. 'Get out on to the runways . . .' was the command.

limelight, when F/Sgt G. Woodcock, the tail gunner, saw a Messerschmitt climbing to attack and he warned the skipper. By now the aircraft was held by only two searchlights and, as the enemy opened up, Routen turned hard to starboard and dived. The fighter pilot followed the Lancaster down but the combined fire-power of Woodcock and F/Sgt J. Kanelakos, the mid-upper, sent the Me210 into a spin and it hurtled past them and crashed. Routen pulled out of the dive at 2,000 feet and, at this stage of the raid, it may have been the safest height to be.

The same night three crews of 97 Squadron were intercepted, two over the target and one on the homeward journey. F/O W. Riches had just dropped his bombs and closed the bomb-doors when Sgt F.C. Nordoff, the rear gunner, yelled: 'Go to port, Skipper.' Riches did a diving turn to port, the enemy broke away underneath and luckily for the crew did not make a second attack. Nordoff's vigilance saved the crew but he lost his life; the rear turret was riddled with holes and the tailplane and fuselage severely damaged.

As 2nd Lt J.E. Russell swung his Lancaster on course for base he saw a twin-engined aircraft on the starboard bow. He told the mid-upper, Sgt E.W. Bark, to look out for it but got the reply: 'Sorry Skipper, I have one in my sights on the port quarter and another behind him queueing up. He's coming in, Skipper, dive to port, go, go, go.' Bark's fire was more accurate than the enemy's and he saw his tracer enter the nose of the fighter, which broke away and was not seen again. Seconds later the sky seemed to light up as F/Sgt R.H. Marston, the rear gunner, shouted: 'Corkscrew, corkscrew.' A second fighter was attacking from the port quarter and 50 to 60 searchlights were trying to help it. Marston opened up at 500 yards but the fighter pilot pressed home the attack and scored hits on the Lancaster; however, he too had no stomach for a second encounter.

There was so much fighter activity along the return route that F/Lt D.I. Jones had the whole crew except the navigator on the alert looking for anything that moved. As the rear gunner, F/Sgt J.R. Burke, swung his turret, searching, he saw a Ju88 on the starboard quarter ready to attack. 'Corkscrew, corkscrew starboard.' Jones obeyed the order instantly, a quick reflex action which probably saved the Lancaster for, judging by the tracer, the Junker's fire just missed the bomber. Both gunners replied with long bursts and saw their tracer enter the fighter which turned over and dived through the cloud. They claimed it as 'damaged probably destroyed'.

Between the first and second raids on Berlin, Bomber Command made two other sorties to the Reich, Nuremberg on August 27-28, and Munchen Gladbach on August 30-31. Some 674 aircraft were on the detail to Nuremberg including the PFF contingent. All Pathfinder 'Y' aircraft with serviceable H2S dropped a 1,000-pound bomb on Heilbronn to test their equipment before going to their marking duties at Nuremberg. The marking was good although the Backers-up tended to bomb a little short. But the real offenders were the route planners at Bomber Command HQ. The approach from the south-east resulted in many bombs falling outside the town area when creepback became pronounced. Recenterers and a Master Bomber tried to halt this tendency, but only 24 % of the force claimed to have heard the MC's instructions. Two crews of 83 Squadron were in trouble over the target. P/O R. King, a Visual Marker, came down to 14,000 feet to try to get a pinpoint but at that height he was at the mercy of the flak and his hydraulics were damaged. Back at Wyton he could get only one wheel to lock so he had to make a crash landing. S/Ldr N.F. Hildyard, needing only one more sortie after this to complete his second tour, had a sharp reminder that the Fates were no sentimentalists: he was coned on the run up and hit by flak before he could escape from the searchlights. Jettisoning his HE he went round again and successfully dropped his TIs.

The raid on Munchen Gladbach was in two parts, with Command planning a 2-minute gap after 22 minutes while PFF changed the aiming point to the adjoining town of Rheydt. The switch to the second aiming point was carried out smoothly and both targets were continuously marked. Some crews, probably blown south of track by the strong tail-wind, said they bombed on ETA because there were no TIs burning, but they were plotted some 15 miles south of the target. Fire damage was extensive in both towns, with the heaviest destruction in the central areas. Many factories were completely demolished. Damage to railway property, the marshalling yards at Rheydt in particular, was especially significant because the towns were important traffic centres; photographs taken a week later showed conditions that still appeared chaotic.

On September 5, although cloud over France varied from 5-10/10ths, skies cleared just before Mannheim making conditions ideal for a *Newhaven* attack and Pathfinders were able to put on a classic display. Route-marker flares were dropped by 9 Blind Markers and 10 Backers-up 5 miles due south of Luxemburg and from this point the Main Force made a direct run to the target. Pathfinders were routed over Kaiserslautern 34 miles due west of Mannheim – and from there they were to make an accurately timed run to the aiming point which, for tactical reasons, was set at the eastern edge of the town centre. The Blind Marker Illuminators were carrying TI reds and 4 x 4 bundles of flares; the first bundle was to be dropped 10 seconds before the TIs, the second with the TIs, the third 6 seconds after that and the fourth 6 seconds later: no reds were to be dropped after Z-4 but flares could be dropped at the Captain's discretion. Primary Visual Markers were briefed to mark the aiming point with a mixed load of yellows and greens if they identified it visually; no yellows to be dropped after Z+3. Zero hour was 2300 hours and the

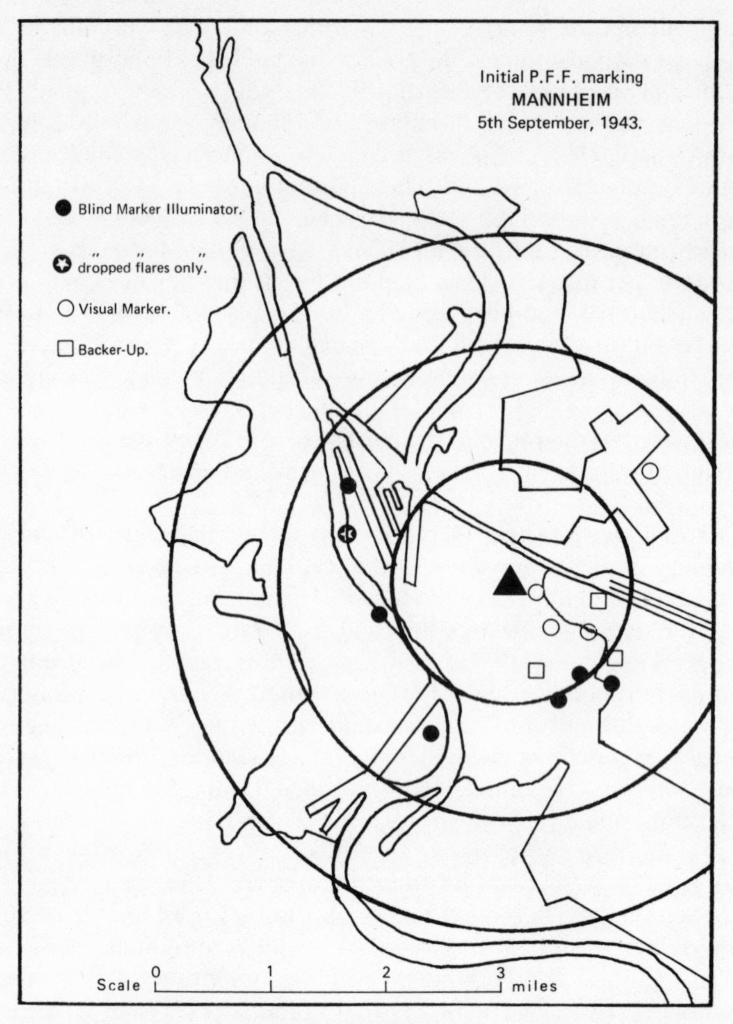

Map 5 The accuracy of the Primary Visual Markers carrying cameras is clear, three of them being less than 1 mile from the A/P. The first three Backers-up surrounded their greens and yellows with greens giving the first wave of Main Force crews a pool of green fire with a yellow centre as an unmistakable target to aim at.

attack was scheduled to last 40 minutes. Because Kaiserslautern was difficult to pick up on the H2S screen, only 10 out of 24 Blind Marker Illuminators had marked by Z-4. Six more dropped flares later but retained their TIs; all were well positioned. Of the 7 Visual Markers, 6 (guided by the reds and helped by the flares) were able to identify the aiming point positively and they duly marked. One of them, S/Ldr A.S. Johnson, said he could identify the actual house were his TIs burst.

Backers-up were briefed to drop their greens on the yellows or, if no yellows were down, on the MPI of all the greens with a 2-second overshoot; and failing this on the MPI of the reds with a 2-second overshoot; the first Backers-up to drop between Z+1 and Z+5. They started on time. Within a few minutes PFF had an excellent concentration of TIs within 1½ miles of the aiming point, an unmistakable bullseye for the 530 Main Force crews.

Bomber Command had made its plans carefully: the Main Force was divided into six waves, the first comprising 33 PFF Supporters reinforced by 71 picked crews from the other Groups in order to get the attack off to a good start. By 2311 hours, 111 crews had bombed and incendiary fires were springing up all over Mannheim with an overspill into Ludwigshafen – an area of 4 x 3 miles. The tactics of marking the eastern edge of the town now began to pay off because the inevitable creepback made certain the centre got its share of the bombing. To prevent the creepback from becoming excessive, 7 Recenterers were briefed to mark blindly, one every 3 minutes from Z+12 if their H2S was serviceable, otherwise to revert to Backers-up. In fact, 5 Recenterers dropped their greens and 28 out of 35 Backers-up kept the target marked throughout the duration of the attack. HE bombs of the later waves caused the smaller fires to join together creating an uncontrollable blaze. In all, 380 out of 512 crews bombed within a 3-mile radius of the aiming point and fewer than 10% were plotted outside the main area. Fires were burning two days later and, when PRU got photographic cover, it showed 1,000 acres of devastation in Mannheim. The main station and three suburban stations were gutted and Ludwigshafen's main station was partly destroyed. Adjacent storehouses and sheds were burnt out and warehouses in the dock area were still ablaze three days later. Many priority munition targets were damaged: Heinrich Lanz and Joseph Vogele, making tanks and military tractors, were extensively damaged, no building in either factory escaping. The chemical factory of Rashig & Sulzer was also severely damaged. The only important factory to escape was I.G. Farbenindustrie situated on the outskirts of the town.

The Mannheim attack on September 23-24 was aimed at the northern districts which had received only isolated damage in the previous raid. The weather was ideal for *Newhaven* and the Primary Visual Markers were again on the ball. Out of 556 crews, 473 attacked and the weight was in the right place. The damage to I.G. Farbenindustrie was so severe that the whole factory was at a standstill the following day. The devastation caused by the two raids was sufficient for Harris to decide that another large attack would be unnecessary for some time.

The previous night the destruction of Hanover had begun. Visibility was good over the target and the last turning point, Steinhuder Meer,[9]

9. Frog Lake as it was known in PFF because of its shape on H2S screens.

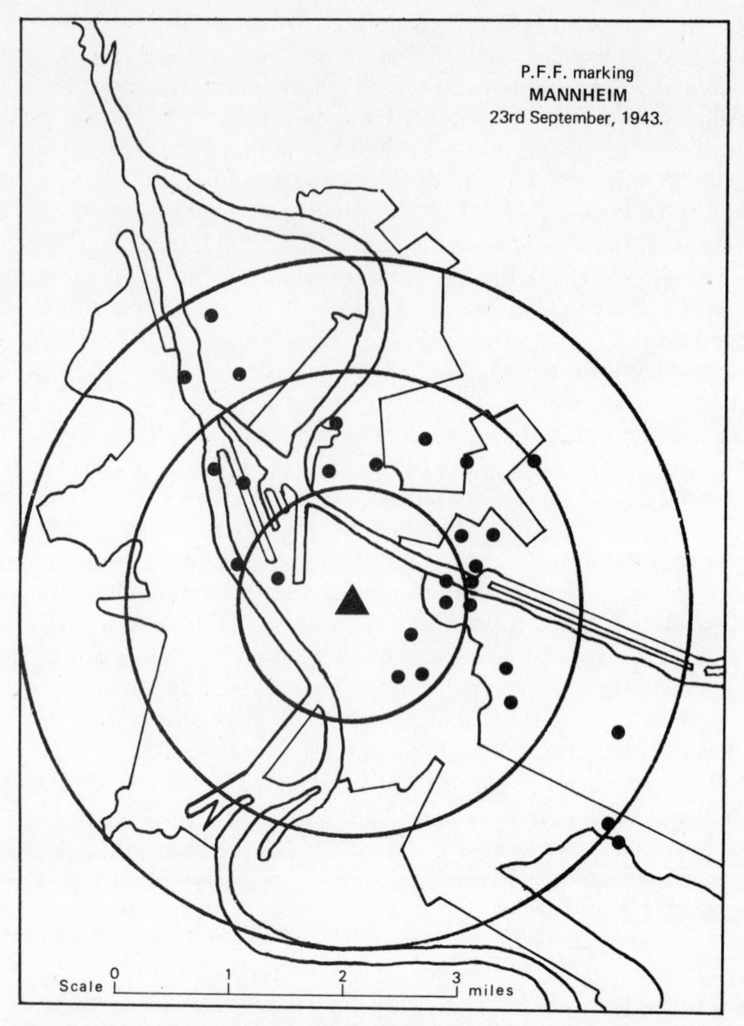

Map 6 Another fine crop of photographs, more than 78% being within 2 miles of the A/P.

was pinpointed visually. PFF was briefed to make a timed run to the aiming point from this position. Winds were 20-25 m.p.h. stronger than forecast and, although many navigators had found the correct wind, few of them used it. The result of using the Met wind instead of their target wind was an overshoot of 2 miles. Most Blind Marker Illuminators overshot and their red markers and flares attracted those Backers-up who had committed the same sin. The 716-strong Main Force, coming in south of track, saw this concentration first and started some good fires in the south-east districts of Hanover, completely ignoring the yellow TIs of the

Visual Markers, well placed around the aiming point. From the practical point of view the attack was a resounding success. Fires were burning next morning and 56 factories had been hit. Much damage was done to railway installations and the line to Hildesheim was closed, a four-track railway

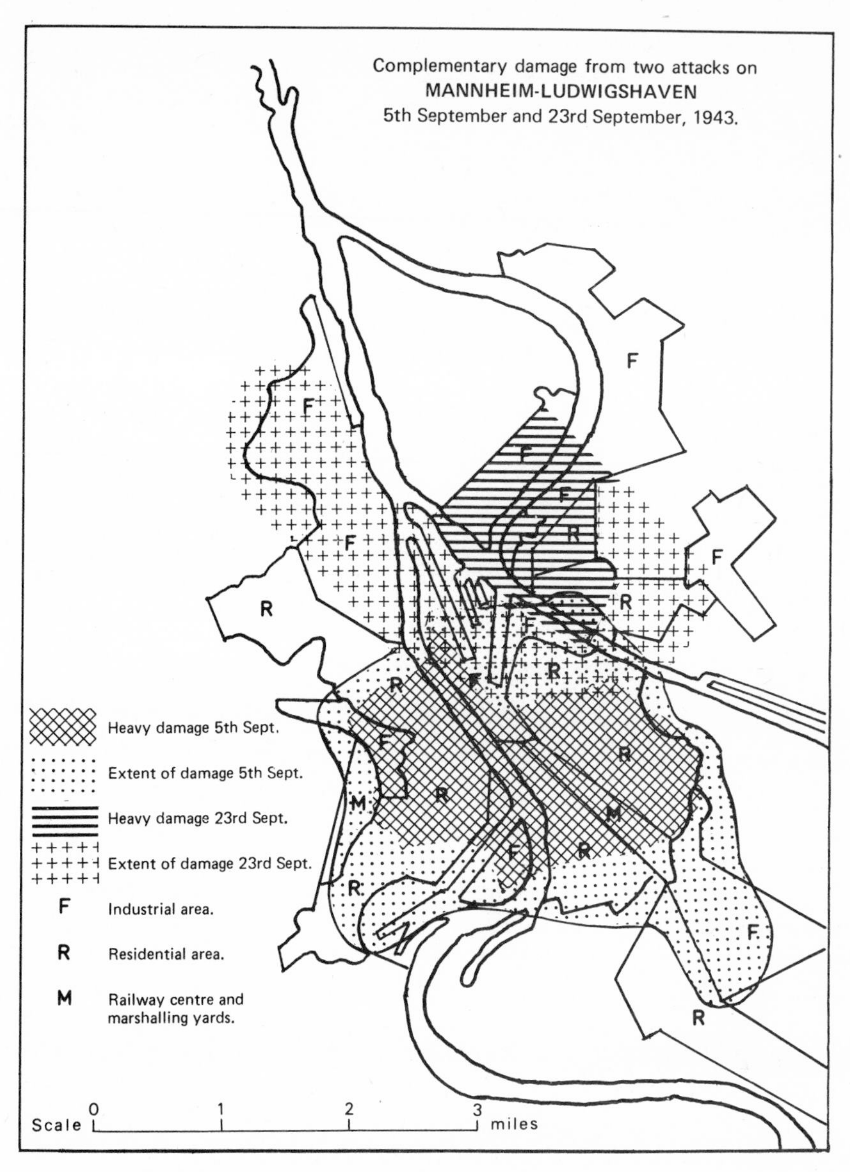

Map 7 This damage map shows clearly how the two raids complemented each other. It also illustrates that lacking the excuse of stray TIs even the 'fringe merchants' were prepared to drop their loads within acceptable limits.

bridge, after receiving a direct hit, having collapsed onto the tracks below.

For the second attack on September 27-28, the aiming point and the datum point were the same as the previous raid and it was a clear night. The only thing different was the wind. Again many PFF navigators used the Met wind and this time the attack developed 5 miles north of the aiming point. Some 582 out of 613 Main Force crews did the most concentrated piece of bombing of 1943: over an area of 15 square miles they achieved the remarkable figure of 130 tons per square mile. The Brink district of Hanover was completely flattened. The Supporters were the only people from 8 group to come out with credit, their blind bombing being infinitely better than that of the Blind Markers. Nobody dared whisper the word Hanover within 25 miles of PFF HQ at Huntingdon.

A *Musical Parramatta* to Bochun on September 29 provided a morale booster for PFF. The Mosquito reds were very accurate and, although the concentrated greens of the Backers-up encouraged the Main Force to drop their 1,000 tons of HE and incendiary bombs on the centre of the town with devastating results, a feeling of tension remained among the 8 Group heavies.

Briefing on October 8 was a very serious affair in the Group. Hanover was the target, and PFF crews got the impression that anyone who did not bring back an A/P photograph was for the high jump. Once again the weather was on the side of the attackers, the TIs went down in the right place, and three crews of 83 Squadron brought back A/P photographs. The last turning point was 20 miles 005° from Hanover and this brought the Main Force over the correctly placed TIs first. The attack was concentrated into 10 minutes, achieving a peak concentration of 44 aircraft per minute so most crews had bombed before the initial markers had burnt out. The force of just under 500 bombers tore out the centre of the town. Day cover showed a large area of devastation, and fires were still burning fiercely with a volume of smoke that proved they were out of control. They were still burning three days later and hardly a building of importance within 2 square miles of the city centre escaped damage. After the three attacks Hanover was going to be a liability to the German war effort for some time. The Commander-in-Chief Bomber Command signalled to all crews: 'The last attack on Hanover was an outstanding success for us and another major catastrophe for Germany. Good show! A few more like this and the Boche will break.' The Gods, as at Hamburg, considered the town had taken enough punishment: when crews arrived over Hanover on October 18-19, the target was cloud-covered and the final attack caused only scattered damage.

A remarkable feature of this period was the success the Germans had with their decoy TIs. They were quick to realize that, with a Main Force briefed to bomb groundmarkers, decoy TIs would always attract some attention, particularly if they were combined with decoy fires or a smoke

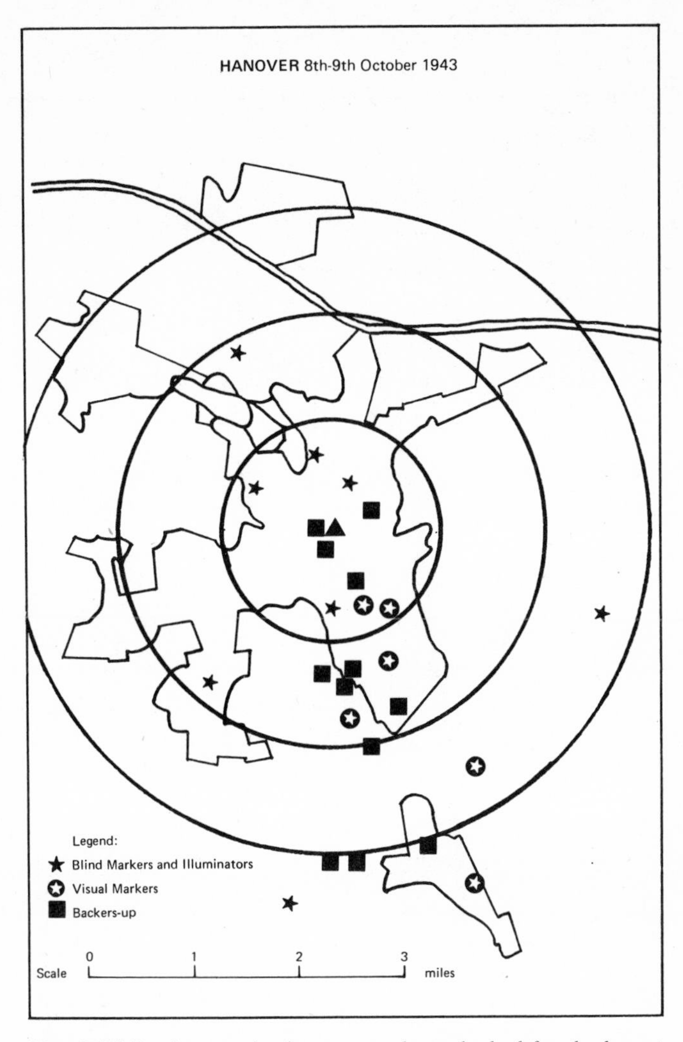

Map 8 Whilst the conscientious crews always looked for the largest concentration of TIs there were many who bombed the first cluster they saw. On this night the track, approaching the city from the north, took the crews directly over a corridor of green fire pockmarked with circles of yellow. As this concentration was south of the A/P, normal creepback ensured that the part of the city to the north of the target received its quota of bombs.

screen. It was easy to sit back comfortably at base and say that decoys didn't burn as brightly as genuine TIs; they didn't burst and cascade in the same manner; they were not grouped in clusters and the navigator's ETA target would prove they were decoys. Bennett inisisted it was either bad briefing or bad navigating. While this may have been true, it ignored the

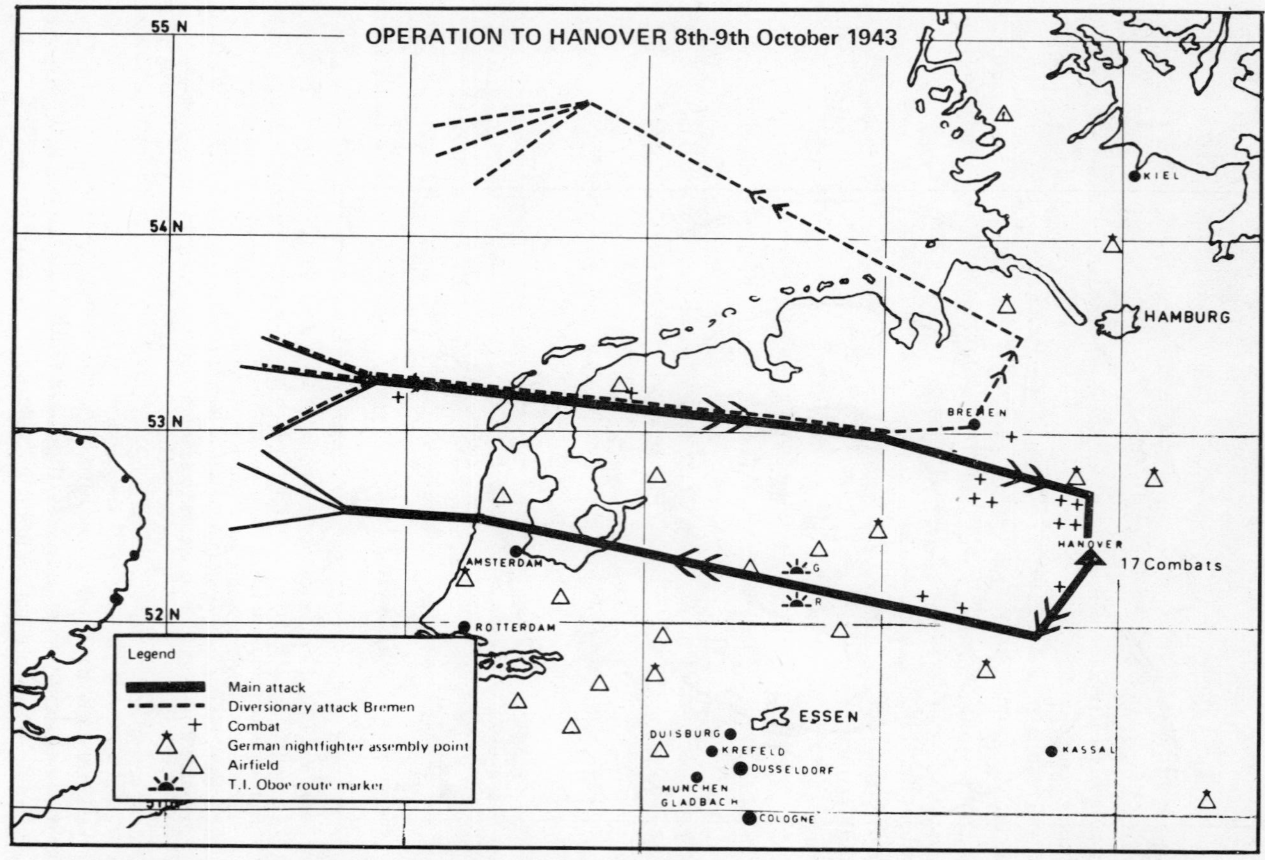

Map 9 A spoof attack on Bremen by 25 PFF heavies drew some of the fighters away from the Main Force. Extensive *Windowing* from 8°E by this force made the German controllers uncertain which was the main target. At Hanover there were only 17 combats in the target area and 3 on the return route. *Oboe* Mosquitoes dropped green TIs to the north of track and reds to the south. They served a dual purpose: in addition to pulling the wayward back on track, the navigator could take a running fix on them and so find a wind.

fact that there would always be crews who did not pay attention at briefing, and that there were bad navigators who did not have either a good target wind or an accurate ETA nor were they conversant with the Pathfinder technique of adding time to allow for various types of evasive action. Many crews made a bee-line for the first TIs they saw, dropped their load and were away as quickly as possible.

During March and April there had been sporadic reports of pyrotechnics being fired from the ground and, once the rumour got around, the sightings became quite common. The first raid when decoys had a marked effect on results was at Bochum on May 13-14. The Main Force was instructed to bomb *Oboe* reds in preference to the greens of the Backers-up. The raid got off to a good start but technical failures resulted in a gap in the sequence of *Oboe* markers and the Germans exploited it to the extent that 27% of the Main Force claimed to have bombed red TIs at times when no reds were burning. This figure can be reduced marginally; some allowance might be made because of bad interrogation, bad log-keeping and inexperienced bomb-aimers mistaking fires for TIs but, in the majority of the incidents when photographs were available, the aircraft were plotted miles from the target. On the raid at Turin on July 12-13 the Main Force was late on target and the TIs had burnt out; yet 31% of the bombers claimed to have bombed TIs. Most of the damage was a long way north of the aiming point so the majority of them must have been deceived. October was the worst month: in six of the nine major raids the Germans succeeded in diverting between 12% (Stuttgart, 7th-8th) and 33% (Kassel, 22nd-23rd) of the bombing effort.

Experiments with different types of TIs and with a timed run from a datum point had limited success – the only real solution, as in the case of creepback and haphazard bombing of fires, was to make each crew realize they were risking their lives for nothing if they wasted their bombs.

Exasperation at Wyton caused by the 'Powers that Be', who from time to time could not decide on the target for the night, is reflected in the Squadron ORB for October 1. Crews were on standby all morning. Eventually the call came through for 13 crews on Stuttgart. Armourers were in the process of bombing-up when the call was changed to two UT[10] crews on Hagen. At this stage the flight sergeant armourer disappeared smartly for lunch leaving his ancestry to be questioned out of earshot. The last stage of de-bombing was taking place when, at 1500 hours, Stuttgart was 'on' again. By 1600 hours, when most of the aircraft had been bombed-up, the target was switched back to Hagen. 'On regaining their sanity the armourers de-bombed again and visited the chapel for prayers.'[11]

---

10. Under training.
11. 83 Squadron ORB.

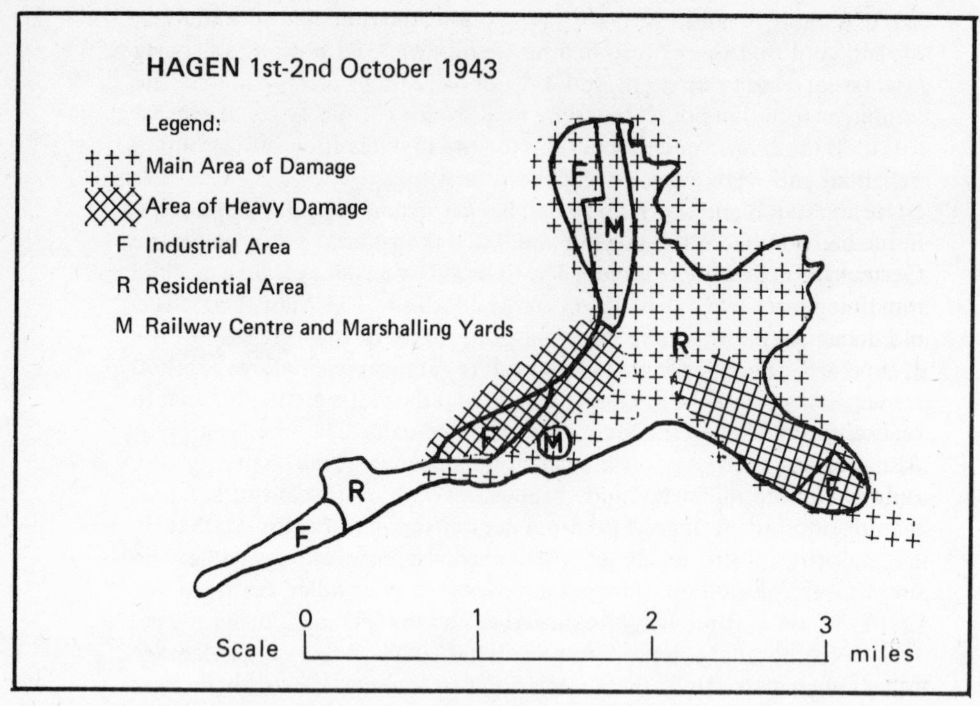

Map 10 The accuracy of *Oboe* enabled a mere 200 bombers to inflict heavy damage on this small but important target.

The first of two attacks on Kassel during that month took place on October 3. It was planned as a *Newhaven* but no red TIs were dropped as the light from the flares was reflected in the ground haze and the Visual Markers could not see through the glare. Conditions were ideal for decoys because, in the haze, the glow from them looked authentic and 26% of the 467 Main Force crews were deceived. In Kassel, 17 factories were seriously affected, three of them high-priority targets, but most of the bombs fell outside the town area as the decoys spread the attack to the north-west. Ihringshausen, 3 miles to the north, was the site of one of the largest ammunition depots in Germany; here, at 2206 hours, someone dropped his load into the depot causing a very large explosion. The 'fire bugs' joined in and 10 minutes later, after another enormous explosion, a column of fire shot into the air, attracting more bombers. When the dust had settled 84 buildings had been destroyed by fire or blast and the whole area was pockmarked with huge craters, one being 300 feet in diameter.

If the 26% bombing decoy TIs on this raid could blame the haze, the 33% who bombed decoy reds during the second attack on October 23 had no such excuse. From the Pathfinder standpoint the *Newhaven* marking was technically better than that of September 5 at Mannheim. Blind marking and illuminating was excellent, and 8 out of 9 Visual Markers identified the aiming point. All were plotted within a mile radius; the Backers-up were almost as accurate and the Supporters showed that future marking would be in good hands.

Although the route to the target was cloud-covered and many crews experienced severe icing, most of them arrived on time. The first Main Force crews all bombed reds and it was estimated that one-third of the Force had bombed by Z+4 when the last red went out. At this point, the Germans got busy with their decoys and succeeded in luring half the remaining force away from the target. With the attack scarcely 5 minutes old, incendiary fires were springing up within an area of 5 square miles around the aiming point and, 10 minutes later, 12 square miles were ablaze. There was utter devastation in the centre of the town and factories on both sides of the river were on fire. All three Henschel factories were damaged and their local rival, Wegmann, ceased to be a rival. The main railway station, rail shops, marshalling yards, two goods depots and the transit sheds were a heap of smoking debris; it was easier to raze what was left standing and start again. PRU reported that the fires were still burning seven days later with no ground detail discernible on the photographs because of smoke haze. Lt Gen E. Heinemann, OC Flying Bombs, said that this raid did as much to delay the launching of the V-Is as any other single factor.

Bomber Command's attacks on Munich, Frankfurt and Stuttgart between October 2 and 8 followed daylight attacks by the USAAF, but the combined offensive was short-lived because on October 16 the Americans were dealt their knockout punch by the German Air Force.

The attack on Munich on September 6 had taken place in conditions of 8-10/10ths cloud and, although PFF dropped emergency *Wanganui* flares, most crews made a DR run from Wurm See and bombing was scattered over a wide area. Now, following two daylight attacks on September 26 and October 2, by the USAAF based in North Africa, 294 Lancasters of 1, 5 and 8 Groups set out in the evening of October 2 to attack the city. Five Primary Visual Markers dropped TIs, but only two were on the aiming point, the other three being south of the target. *Zephyrs* were being used so crews should have had a reasonably accurate target wind. The southerly TIs were seen first and most of 1 Group bombed in this area achieving a reasonable concentration, but as the attack developed it spread back 15 miles from the aiming point. This was chiefly the fault of 5 Group whose pet theory was that a DR run from a point outside the town was more accurate than bombing TIs. It had proved unsound at Friedrichshafen on June 20; on that occasion they said that they could not see the datum point, and had no target wind. This night neither excuse was available for Wurm See was practically clear of cloud and they had the broadcast winds. Yet they achieved an average of only one in 26 within 3 miles of the aiming point. Those in 5 Group who did bomb TIs got infinitely better results. PRU cover from all attacks showed severe but scattered damage through the town, principally by fire.

The attack on Frankfurt was successful in spite of decoy fires and decoy TIs to the south-east of the town. It was another success for PFF with Blind Marker Illuminators all within 3 miles of the aiming point and the 4 Primary Visual Markers inside 1½ miles. Backers-up maintained the marking although most of the damage was done while the reds were burning. Incendiary fires, started in the initial stage, were confined to an area of 3 x 1½ miles. The most spectacular ones were in the dock area, ¾ mile to the east of the aiming point, where most of the warehouses were gutted by fires, which lasted for three days. Dockland railway yards, station buildings, marshalling yards and other business and residential property were extensively damaged by HE and fire.

On the night of October 7, Stuttgart was protected by a layer of 10/10ths cloud and no visual identification was possible. Most crews bombed on the glow of two groups of TIs 5 miles apart, each having its partisans, and the glow of fires could be seen in both areas.

The fact that the fighters got credit for most of the losses tends to obscure the very real danger from flak, probably because the effect of flak damage was often delayed. It was nevertheless the undoubted cause of many planes crashing on the homeward journey. The story of F/Lt. J.R. Wood is a good example. On October 4 he lost an engine over Frankfurt after being coned for nearly 5 minutes and repeatedly hit by flak. Nearing the enemy coast a second engine cut and crossing the Channel he lost a third. The fourth cut as he was attempting a single-engined landing at Biggin Hill – inevitably the Halifax crashed, four of the crew being injured.

During this period Bennett extended the idea of diversionary sorties. The Pathfinder attack on Munster on June 11 had been laid on for experimental marking purposes but it was noticed that the raid attracted more nightfighters than the diversions carried out by 139 Squadron Mosquitoes. The first official spoof raid was on September 22-23 on Oldenburg, when 29 PFF crews *Windowed* and marked the town, 139 Squadron acting as Backers-up. In addition to the damage done to the town, the subterfuge was successful; only 24 (3.7%) of the force on Hanover were missing.

The following night, when the Main Force was on Mannheim, a small force from 8 Group made an excellent attack on Darmstadt, but the nightfighters were not to be drawn. The controllers were confused, issuing conflicting instructions, but Darmstadt was too close to Mannheim and from 20,000 feet it was obvious which was the major attack. Again on September 27-28, although the controllers were deceived and sent fighters to the spoof target Brunswick, many switched to Hanover when they saw the fires developing there; 33 bombers (5.4%) were shot down. When heads were counted S/Ldr L.E. Logan was missing from the Brunswick raid, but was later reported as a PoW. The Squadron Leader had been shot down earlier in the war and had escaped.

The idea was extended on October 4-5 when 36 crews of 1 Group were detailed to assist PFF for a spoof raid on Ludwigshafen. If anyone was fooled, it was the crews from 1 Group: PFF marking was not up to standard, and the Pathfinder Narrative said: 'A considerable amount of bombing took place around worms (*sic*) several miles to the north.' Even with a captial 'W', the marking had little to be proud of. However, the German reaction was slow and the main attack on Frankfurt had started before the controllers had made up their minds; meanwhile the nightfighters flew to the largest fires.

On October 7 only 4 aircraft were missing from a force of 309 bombers claiming to have attacked Stuttgart. As the weather made the attack scattered it was fortunate the losses were low. Bad weather in southern Germany grounded most of the nightfighters and the few that did get off the ground were sent to Munich, the target for 8 Mosquitoes of 139 Squadron. The Germans took the diversionary attack by 18 PFF heavies on Friedrichshafen seriously; they lit smoke screens to protect the port from visual identification. The spoof idea obviously had merit and, later, when 100 Group radar jamming was developed, the operations became so complicated that they read more like science fiction novels than actual sorties.

After the last attack on Italy in August, Harris found it difficult to find worthwhile targets for his force during the full-moon period. On September 15 a force of 374 bombers, mainly Halifaxes and Stirlings, attacked the Dunlop rubber factory at Montlucon. A novelty was provided for the first 4 Visual Markers who had to identify and mark the target by moonlight. Later another 4 Visual Markers supplemented their TIs with the aid of the more conventional flares. However, 7-8/10ths cumulus cloud rising to 10,000 feet made the bombing run difficult. It was a controlled *Newhaven* and the Master Bomber, W/Cdr D.F.E.C. Deane, suggested that crews should come below cloud base, which he gave as 4,000 feet. Many crews took his advice and were able to confirm the accuracy of the TIs. All 26 buildings were hit, 12 of them destroyed, ten others seriously damaged and the main rubber store was still burning furiously the following day.

The next night the force went to Modane on the French-Italian border near the entrance of the Mont Cenis tunnel. This and a second raid on November 10 followed similar patterns. Both were overshoots, Visual Markers mistaking the main station and sidings for the marshalling yards. On both occasions the main area of damage was around the station with the normal creepback causing damage to the yards and the tracks leading into the tunnel. It was a new experience for marker crews to locate a target with mountains rising on either side to 11,000 feet and the noise of the HE exploding, echoing and re-echoing down the valley was most alarming.

On November 12, a total of 100 Main Force Halifaxes and 6 Supporters from 35 Squadron, led by 18 Halifaxes and 10 Lancasters of PFF, attacked Cannes. It was a *Newhaven* attack and the marker crews dropped their TIs from 5,000 feet achieving an excellent concentration. Although the marshalling yards escaped extensive damage, railway repair shops were damaged by blast and many craters were concentrated within the station yards. An aircraft factory received several direct hits as well as the main hangar on the aerodrome; and a small industrial plant in the vicinity was destroyed. F/O J.R. Petrie-Andrews, with one engine unserviceable, pressed on to the target and after bombing decided a winter in the Mediterranean was preferable to a cold Nazi PoW camp, so he ditched his Halifax near Sardinia and the crew was rescued after spending some hours in a dinghy.

On November 17 Bomber Command gave all groups a stand-down, but Bennett sent out a signal that Pathfinders might be required. The Boffins had complained that H2S was never used as a blind-bombing device and so Bennett suggested to Harris that PFF should be allowed to carry out a bombing attack using it. Harris chose Ludwigshafen and 83 'Y' aircraft duly set out on their novel mission. The laugh was on the enemy who, hearing the approaching bombers and seeing no TIs, proceeded to light a smoke screen and to fire off decoy reds. It was a successful raid. Fires were started in the target area and two explosions in quick succession were reported.

The spoof attack on Bonn by 4 Mosquitoes of 139 Squadron was also a success. The German controllers were deceived and the Ludwigshafen heavies saw condensation trails of fighters crossing their track as they rushed to defend Bonn. This was the last raid before the assault on Berlin. Great hopes rested on the new Mk III H2S which during the past weeks had been arriving on the squadrons.

V Battle of Berlin

The Battle of Berlin began on November 18, 1943, and the series of raids may be said to have ended with Nuremberg on Mar 30-31 1944, although the officially designated end of the battle was the sixteenth raid on Berlin of March 24. Between November 18 and Mar 30-31, 16 of the 35 major attacks (9, 111 out of 20, 224 sorties) were made on the Big City. The battle was intended to be the climax of the bomber offensive for Harris had written to Churchill on November 3: 'We can wreck Berlin from end to end if the USAAF will come in on it. It will cost between 400-500 aircraft. It will cost Germany the war.'

Harris grossly underestimated the weight of bombs required to destroy Berlin and even Field-Marshal Erhard Milch's figure, 25 attacks, might have been too few. Hamburg became a disaster area after four attacks at a cost of 7,000 tons of bombs: in the first four raids on Berlin, Bomber Command dropped the same tonnage but the capital absorbed the damage. Because of its location it was possible to crowd the Hamburg raids into 10 days, while the 16 attacks on Berlin had to be spread over four months; and, as buildings could be shored up in the intervals between raids, the cumulative damage was less. The law of diminishing returns applied as the number of raids increased and devastated areas acted as fire breaks. It is doubtful whether a city as large as Berlin could be completely destroyed other than by atomic bombs. The surprising thing is that a shrewd commander like Harris thought he could destroy a town 27½ times as large as Hamburg with only 4 times the number of attacks.

There were other contributory factors. The battle was a bitter struggle and the British crews were not conditioned for one: by grossly underestimating the Germans' resilience – 'reeling' after the Ruhr, 'staggering' after Hamburg, 'tottering' after Hanover – Command had given the impression the war was almost over. Tactically, because of the longer nights, this was the only feasible time of year for making regular deep penetrations, physically and psychologically it was the worst. Long hours at sub-zero temperatures dulled the brain, reflexes were slowed and mistakes made. Frostbite was common even among pilots and navigators;

with the cabin that cold, conditions elsewhere in the aircraft had to be experienced to be believed. Most nights there was cloud somewhere on the route: fly through it and get iced up;[1] fly round it and get off track into the sights of the nightfighters waiting for the stragglers; fly below and be greeted with a hail of light flak. Crews often reached the target to find it 10/10ths cloud-covered: more than 2,650 sorites were flown in the first six Berlin raids and fewer than 400 crews reported seeing TIs on the ground. To make matters worse, between November 1943 and February 1944, PRU made 37 attempts to get cover of the raids, but were successful only on two occasions, so no one knew the extent of the damage.

To gain height and a little reserve of speed some crews dropped their *Cookie* over the North Sea, literally throwing away one of their most lethal bombs. Pathfinders reported this, for discarded *Cookies* could be spotted – they invariably exploded even when dropped 'safe' – and Bennett, although by now forbidden to operate, went up himself and verified the reports, but Harris refused to listen.

Bennett said the force 'baulked at the jump' as they had at Essen in 1942, and to some extent he was right; certainly the conditions were similar. Berlin proved as difficult to mark as Essen had before the advent of *Oboe*. Definition over Berlin with the new Mk III H2S, which had been rushed into service for the battle, was very little better than with Mk II and many experienced operators preferred the sets they were used to. Persistent cloud over the target made bombing difficult and sky markers could never be as accurate as groundmarkers because they drifted in the wind. Pathfinders dropped route-markers to guide the wayward bombers but many considered the cure to be worse than the disease: they may have been 'light-houses' for the Main Force, as Harris once described them, but they were also 'beacons' for the German nightfighters.

By intercepting stragglers, off-track or late on target, the nightfighters had forced Bomber Command to hide the individual aircraft by concentrating the bomber stream. Now, by feeding the fighters into it, they used the concentration to gain their ends. The Main Force was being equipped with H2S and, whilst the device could not be jammed, the emissions could be plotted and no amount of *Window* could disguise the route. The nightfighters were equipped with radar devices to home on to *Monica*, *Fishpond* and H2S, and although aircraft using them seemed no more vulnerable they undoubtedly helped the fighters to filter into the stream.

In the Battle of Berlin there was no loss of morale as at Essen in 1942; it was more a loss of face. Webster and Frankland drew the wrong conclusion from Bennett's letter to Harris. He did not say there was a decline in morale of the crews, nor indeed did he think there was. He blamed those group commanders who had pressed for an increase in the all-up weight

1. Icing reduced the aircraft's performance; turrets and guns froze.

25. A PRU photograph taken subsequently showing the extent of the damage

26 (*Top Left*) Four TIs, the Mosquitoe's maximum load, on their way down to mark Coulon Villiers on August 1, 1944

27. (*Top Right*) The Mk. XIV Bombsight computer whose inner workings turned an ordinary bombsight into a lethal weapon

28. (*Bottom*) The Moquito bomb bay

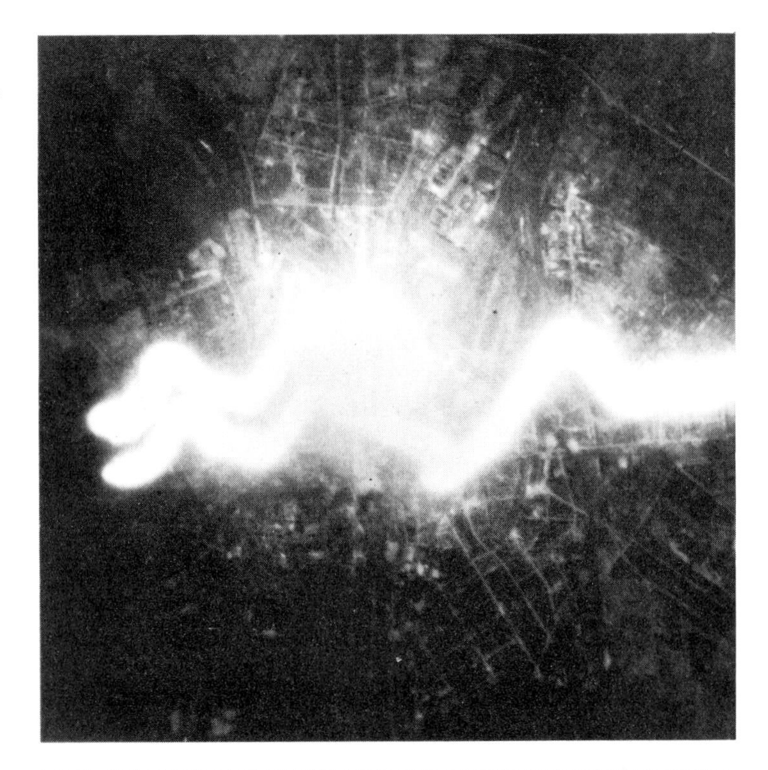

29. The highest night photograph ever taken. Osnabruck from 36,000 feet, taken by F/Lt J.W. Jordan

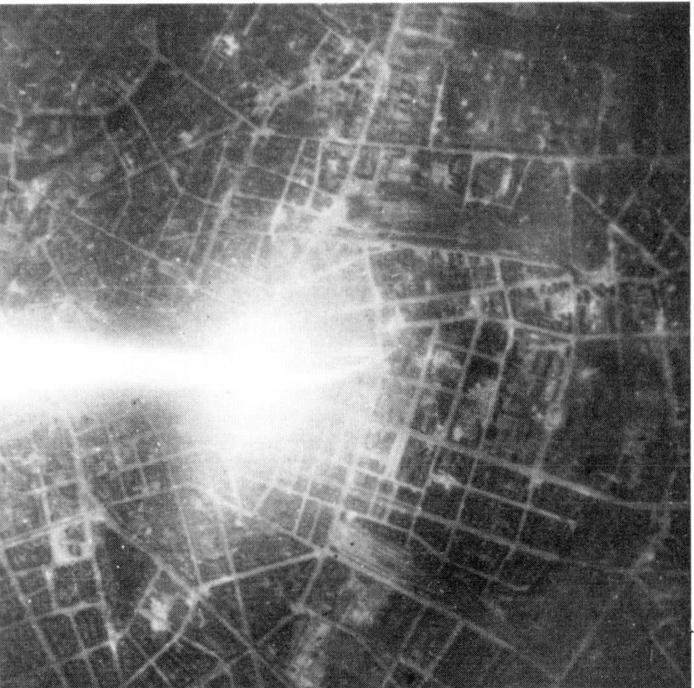

30. A night photograph of Berlin taken from a Mosquito

31 & 32. The King and Queen took a deep interest in Pathfinders and visited the Group on several occasions. Invariably the visits were informal: officers and airmen on parade wore battle dress

of the Lancaster. Without operational experience they had no conception of what a sortie to the Big City entailed. If there was one time in an operational tour when the crew felt they needed the best the aircraft could offer, it was on a sortie to Berlin. Crews could get neither height nor performance with the new all-up weight, and, although performance was improved by getting rid of bombs either over the North Sea or Germany, psychologically the damage was already done. Pilots had lost confidence in their aircraft, and crews, who elsewhere would not have hesitated to go over the centre of the town became 'fringe merchants'.

The excuse that they could not see through cloud was also absurd: they did not have to. Pathfinders dropped skymarker flares throughout the attacks and the 'Berlin Method' ensured a plentiful supply. Although there was no danger of being coned when the target was cloud-covered the Germans illuminated the cloud with searchlights to aid *Wild Boars* watching for the silhouettes of bombers in the glow. Flak batteries put up an excellent defence, some of them trying to shoot out the flares, others making a barrage around them at operational height. It was a daunting prospect, when to bomb the flares meant flying through a wall of flak with every second over the target increasing the risk of interception. The 'negligible amount of bombing on the markers' referred to by Bennett mainly concerned *Wanganui* attacks from which crews could bring back unplottable photographs of cloud. Webster and Frankland's criticism that the markers were inaccurate and scattered is not supported by ORS reports and they also failed to point out that PFF were bringing back photographs showing where they dropped their markers.

S/Ldr H. W. Lees, 8 Group's photographic leader, devised a method of mounting 35mm cameras which could be swung into position to photograph the H2S screens at set times and places. As well as confirming the aircraft's position, navigation officers were able to assess the quality of the picture and advise inexperienced operators how to improve their standards. PPI photographs of the target and points *en route* were also used at briefing to show the operators what to expect to see on their screens. If the writers of *The Strategic Air Offensive Against Germany* did not realize the efficacy of this, the USAAF did. They used Pathfinder H2S photographs of Berlin in a pamphlet issued to their H2X operators when, in March 1944, they joined the battle against Berlin.

The battle opened on November 18 with 398 out of 440 Lancasters on Berlin. The attack was a poor one: H2S was serviceable in only eleven of the Blind Marker aircraft and the skymarker flares quickly disappeared into cloud. Four days later 764 bombers, carrying 2,464 tons of HE and IBs, took off just after dark; 40 Stirlings took part in the attack, their last sortie to Berlin. An all-time 8 Group record of 121 Pathfinders to the Big City was overshadowed by the great excitement at Gransden Lodge where 'Q' of 405 Squadron was scheduled to take off on her maiden

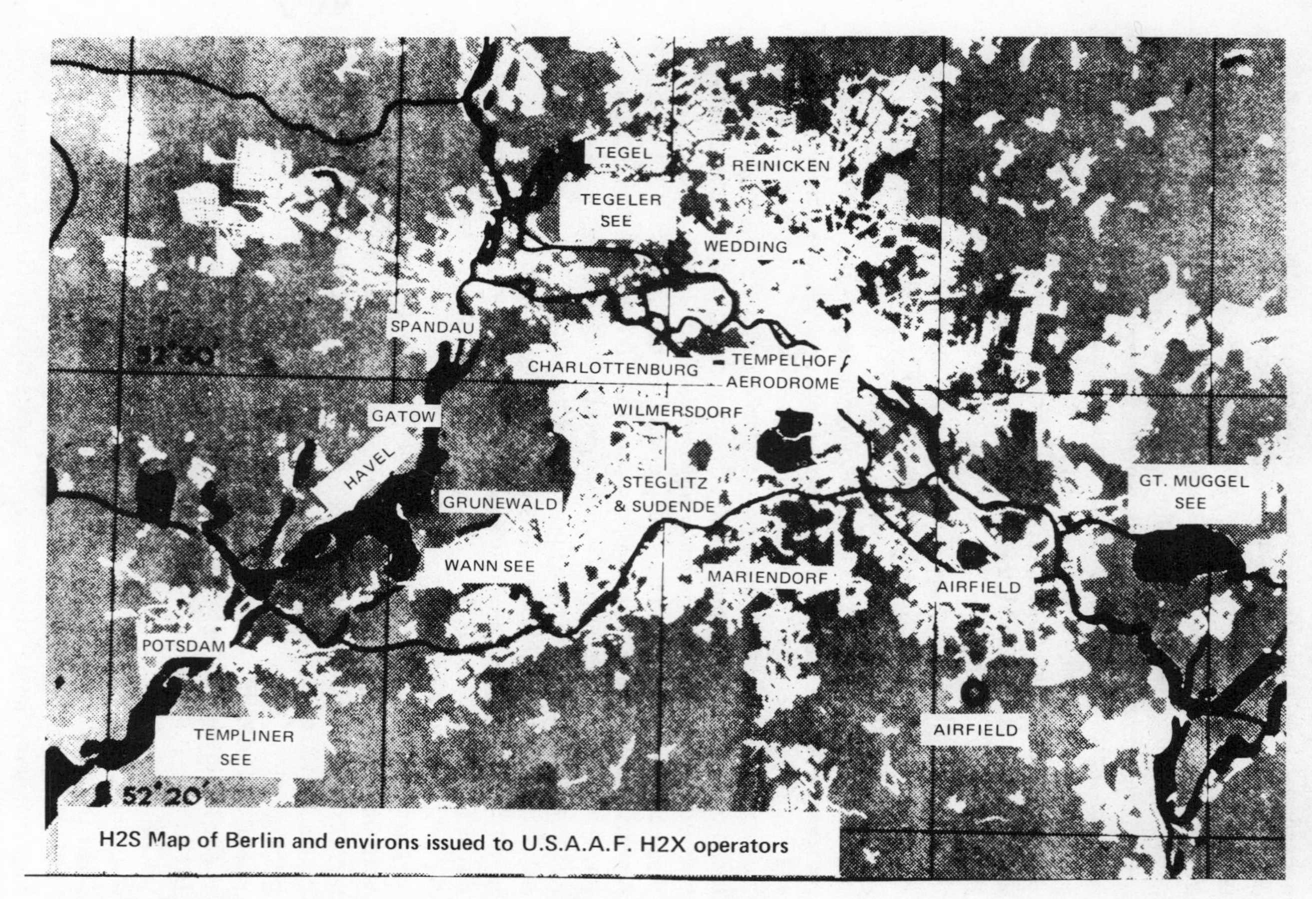

Map 11 This map was on the cover page of a booklet compiled for the USAAF H2X operators. The succeeding pages had larger P.P.I. photographs of Berlin, all taken by Pathfinders, showing the salient features of selected districts and approaches.

sortie. Christened 'The Ruhr Express', she was the first Canadian-built Lancaster to go into service. The Canadian press was there to report on her success story but unfortunately she was one of 68 aircraft forced to return early.

Meanwhile, at Berlin, Pathfinders' timing was good, but although TIs as well as *Wanganui* flares were dropped, few crews saw the ground-markers because of 10/10ths cloud. However, continuous marking was achieved and many crews bombed the glow of TIs seen through cloud. More than 1,000 tons of IBs were dropped starting large fires which could be seen from 100 miles away.

When 303 out of 383 bombers attacked the following night, PFF achieved and maintained a good concentration of TIs and *Wanganui* flares but the eleven areas of fire, still burning, were too big a temptation for many Main Force crews who bombed them willy-nilly, ignoring the skymarkers. The fourth attack by 443 Lancasters on November 29 was one of the most damaging. Crews arrived over the target in cloudless skies and the sprawling city lay beneath them, with fires still smouldering from the attack of November 23. The rare sight of TIs burning on the ground was a tonic for the Main Force. The Backers-up were agreed on the MPI so a very concentrated attack developed with very little stray bombing. Night photographs were plentiful, and showed an area of damage six miles north-west of the city, plumb in the middle of the industrial districts. Many high-priority targets were severely damaged. Typical of them was Rheinmetal Borsig making tanks, torpedoes, bombs, shells and fuses, where 45% of the factory was in ruins when the fires eventually died out. Red multi-flash TIs were used for the first time as route-markers but they did not stand out as clearly as normal TIs.

Just before 1700 hours at Wyton, when all crews were standing by to take off, F/O H.R. Hyde's Lancaster -K blew up: several people including three of the crew were killed. In spite of the severe shock all the crews took off with the exception of S/Ldr A.H.J. Sambridge who was on the next pan. Although none of his crew was injured, they were affected by the blast and were wisely 'scrubbed' by the Squadron CO. The following day the AOC sent a message to 83 Squadron praising all crews for carrying out their mission.

Because Bomber Command's Lancaster squadrons put up near-maximum efforts on the four Berlin raids, it was left chiefly to the Halifax and Stirling squadrons to supply aircraft for other attacks. They were, though, all marred by cloud. Harris frequently used Mannheim as a diversionary target and 405 bombers attacked the town on November 18 when the Lancasters went to Berlin, but cloud prevented the Visual Markers from identifying the aiming point and consequently bombing was scattered. The germans used a smoke screen and fired decoy reds, and 118 crews reported seeing red TIs when no reds were dropped. The

German controllers sent the fighters to Mannheim and F/LT A.C. Harding's crew on their last sortie was one of 23 missing from the raid.

Although some Pathfinder crews had been carrying *Wanganui* flares in case the target was cloud-covered, the policy was changed for Berlin. PFF dropped both types of markers, irrespective of conditions over the target, and this became known as the 'Berlin Method'.[2] The Main Force was briefed to bomb TIs when visible and only attack the *Wanganui* flares as a last resort.

Because of the appalling weather in December only six major attacks took place; four on Berlin and one each on Leipzig and Frankfurt. On December 2, the early call was for 650 heavies on Berlin but, because of bad weather at bases, the number was reduced to 440, all Lancasters except for 15 Halifaxes of 35 Squadron. Berlin was well endowed with decoy fire sites and the biggest was at Nauen 15 miles west of the capital: built like a city, it extended for 9 miles. During the Battle of Berlin, as soon as the first markers were dropped, decoy TIs were fired into the Nauen fire site, searchlights formed a cone in the vicinity and shells were fired into the cone, bomb flashes were simulated and small fires started. In the meantime, the Berlin ground defences remained more or less quiet. If this activity did not draw the first wave of bombers then other decoy sites would open up. All this effort was wasted on December 2 because of the northerly winds and the 8/10ths cloud.

Met had said their winds were unreliable and they were right:

	Base to 4°	*4-10°*	*Target*
Forecast	270°/40	210°/60	270°/25
Actual	160°/50	180°/20	355°/25[3]

The winds along the outward route had been more southerly than forecast and although some 'Y' aircraft navigators had calculated the correct target wind it was so different from their previous wind and the forecast one, many of them did not use it. Bad map reading compounded the error, many bomb-aimers committing the cardinal sin of reading from map to ground. The route was Stendal, Rathenow and Nauen with a DR run from Rathenow to the aiming point using Nauen as a checkpoint for direction and groundspeed. Most crews tracked over Genthin, Brandenburg and Potsdam believing they were on track and arrived over Berlin 15 miles south of the aiming point. Although the attack started on time and near the aiming point, it drifted south-south-east as crews bombed the nearest markers, and, in fairness to the Main Force, they were more plentiful than the accurate ones further north. Nightfighters were in their

2. Made official at a meeting on December 20.

3. Berlin meteorological charts showed the wind at 500 mbs. (18,500 feet) to be stronger, 355°/35.

glory for the bombers left the target 15 miles south of track and the winds blew them further south. Many crews wandered over the Ruhr and those who had the skill and luck to survive the ordeal were able to confirm its reputation as the best defended area in the world. They were handed on from one searchlight cone to the next and, all the time, heavy and light flak guns were shooting into the cones. Seven Pathfinder crews were among the 40 aircraft missing, one of them a Mosquito.

The following night one of the most spectacular attacks of the war took place. The early call was for crews on Berlin but later the target was switched to Leipzig. The outward Berlin route was used as far as 52° 25N 12° 22E and then turned south to Leipzig with a southerly return route. From the last turning point 6 Mosquitoes of 139 Squadron and 4 of 627 Squadron[4] *Windowed* the route to Berlin and then dropped TIs over the capital, completely deceiving the German controllers, who sent the *Wild Boars* to Berlin. The first interception took place just off the Dutch coast and many were made as the bombers approached the last turning point, 12 being reported in this area. From there to Leipzig only three aircraft reported combats at a time when the nightfighters were expected to take their biggest toll. From a force of 527 bombers only 23 were missing and 3 nightfighters had been destroyed. The target was covered by 10/10ths stratus at 5,000-6,000 feet, but from Z−2 to Z+14 PFF put down a continuous stream of *Wanganui* flares which did not drift too quickly because winds were light over the target (20-25 m.p.h.). Crews had been briefed to make their bombing runs on 182° magnetic with zero wind on their bombsights if the attack was *Wanganui*. The last wave on target reported fires burning furiously in an area of 2 square miles with thick black smoke rising to 12,000 feet. Some 10 hours later, a PRU aircraft reported a dense smoke cloud covering the whole town. It was not until a fortnight later that photographs were obtained and the damage could be assessed. Nearly 30% of Leipzig lay in ruins: the area of greatest devastation was around the imposing new railway station which itself miraculously escaped serious damage. Both gas-works were severely damaged, gas-holders were blown out and adjacent buildings completely flattened. Southward lay the site of the World's Fair, 564 acres of permanent exhibition buildings converted to factories for war production, in particular for assembling Junkers aircraft. Every building showed some damage and seventeen of the largest, covering over 100 acres, were among those listed as seriously damaged or destroyed. The largest hall, which boasted an unsupported roof span of 321 feet, lay shattered and open to the elements. One ORS report said the attack missed the western industrial areas; some people were hard to please. Bennett said: 'Crews taking part

4. Formed at Oakington, November 12, 1943.

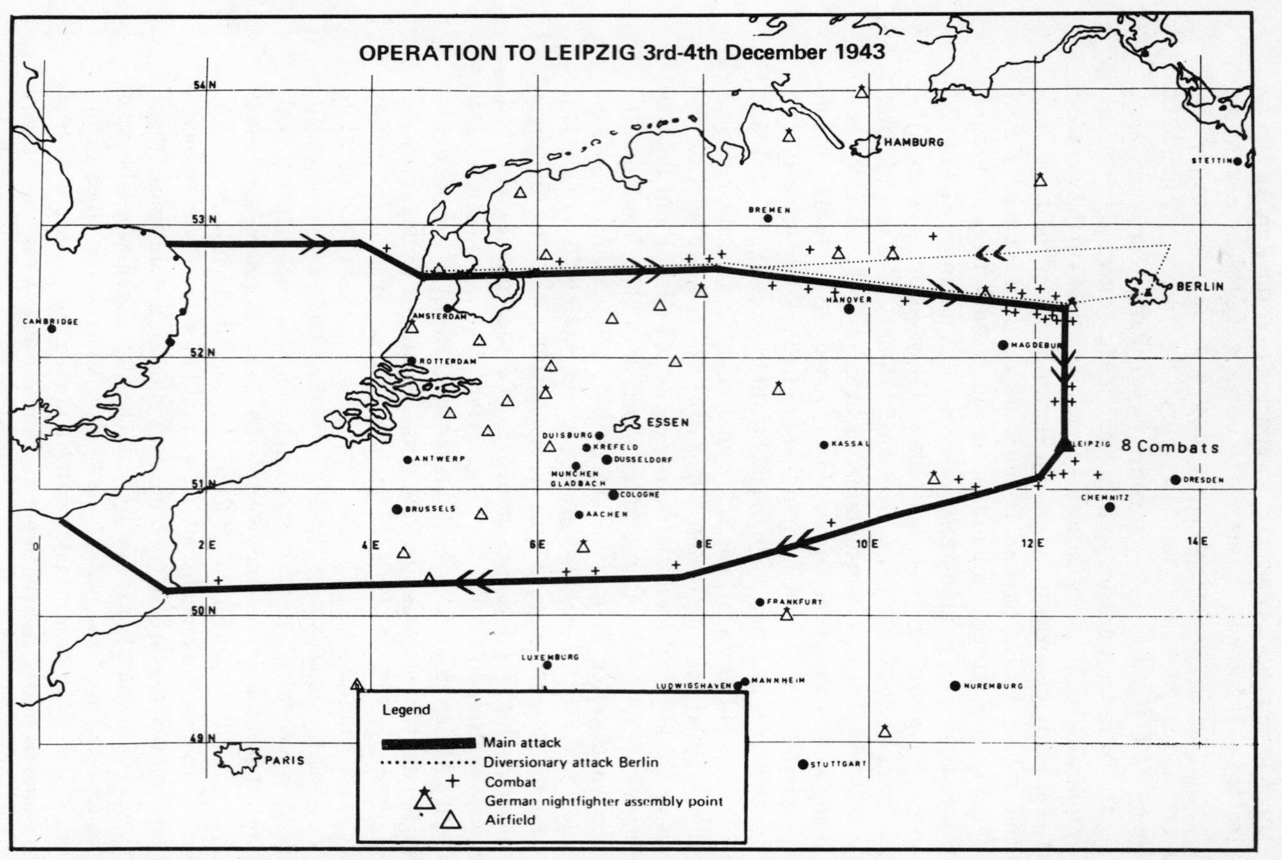

Map 12 A fine example of a successful Mosquito spoof on Berlin. The map shows clearly how the interceptions increased as the bombers penetrated deeper into the Reich. The 11 combats plotted near the last turning point was a portent of what would have happened had the bombers not turned south. There were only 8 combats in the target area which was surprisingly few; however 7, just after leaving the target, probably means that the nightfighters over Berlin made a mad dash to Leipzig. The pursuit petered out as they became low on fuel resulting in a peaceful trip for the remainder of the sortie for all but 5 of the force.

in this raid deserve their name Pathfinders. Timing excellent, marking good, and results satisfactory.'

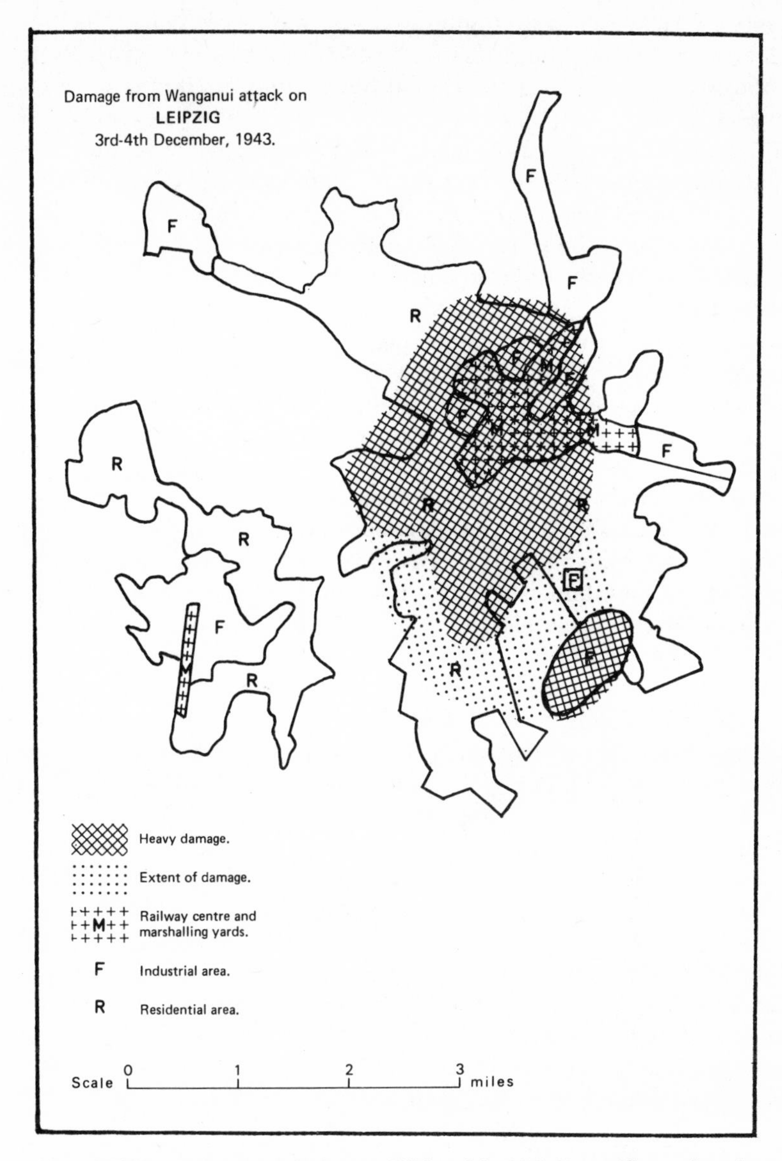

Map 13 This map shows clearly the capabilities of the Main Force. The track took the bombers over the centre of the town; the 10/10ths cloud allowed each crew to think they were not the cynosure of every German gunner's eyes; the absence of aerial combat undoubtedly helped; and, very important, a steady supply of accurately placed *Wanganui* flares allowed them to bomb without waiting or deviating.

From December 3-16 it was left to the Mosquitoes to keep the sirens sounding: Hamborn, Leverkusen, Krefeld, Duisburg, Essen, Dusseldorf and Bochum were all bombed by *Oboe* aircraft and 139 Squadron bombed Osnabruck and Bonn, some of their crews using GH. On December 16, 482 Lancasters and 10 Mosquitoes set out for Berlin. Cloud was 10/10ths over the capital but Pathfinders laid down a good concentration of *Wanganui* flares. The Main Force bombing was not up to the standard achieved at Leipzig, but the force had to contend with nightfighters and vastly stronger ground defences. The German wireless spoke of heavy damage, thus confirming reports made by experienced crews. The fighters had a successful night and pursued the bombers from the Dutch coast to the target and back to the coast again. Before the force reached Hanover 10 Lancasters were shot down and, taking this into consideration, the total of 25 missing, although 6.2% of the force, was remarkably low. Five nightfighters were shot down, and F/Lt L.C. Kingsbury on only his second Pathfinder operation claimed one of them. He was intercepted by an Fw190 just north of Brunswick, the fighter attacking from the starboard quarter down and opening fire at 350 yards. Kingsbury made a diving turn to starboard and the cannon shells went sailing over the Lancaster. This manoevre left the Focke-Wulf exposed to Kingsbury's gunners, F/O E.G. Bedwell and Sgt E. Parr, and, at point-blank range, their bullets tore into it setting it on fire. Diving, seemingly out of control, it disappeared into the 10/10ths cloud below.

Harris had gambled on the force getting back before the weather clamped down. At take-off, visibility was 2,500 yards and cloud base 1,200 feet with tops at 5,000 feet. This was hazardous enough but on return conditions had worsened: cloud base was 500 feet and getting lower by the minute. PFF lost 12 aircraft over England with 50 aircrew killed and 12 injured, 3 dying later; 6 aircraft were lost over Germany; more than 100 casualties in one night.[5] It was the same story throughout East Anglia and 14 aircraft of 1 Group crashed. Trouble began early in 8 Group when F/Sgt Watkins, on a training flight, crashed onto the Earith-to-Sutton road. The Lancaster burst into flames and the crew was killed with the exception of the rear gunner, Sgt Dalton. At Bourn conditions were appalling. Two crews of 97 Squadron baled out and they were the lucky ones. Three crashed at base, only Sgts P.H. Mack and L.N. Laver survived. A fourth crew from the squadron crashed at Graveley with only one survivor, the mid-upper gunner, W/O J. Benlow.

5.

Squadron	*No. of Crews*	*Missing*	*Crashed*	*Landed away*
83	14		1	2
156	21	1	1	
7	27	4		5
405	14		3	5
97	21	1	5	2 baled out

At Gransden Lodge conditions were almost as bad. Only 6 out of 14 crews from 405 Squadron were able to land there. The others were sent to Graveley, where it was thought that FIDO would disperse some of the cloud, but it was a vain hope and the search for somewhere to land continued. Marham managed to get five down, two of 7 Squadron and three of 405 Squadron, a fourth aircraft of 405 Squadron crashing nearby with only two survivors, the captain, F/O E.B. Drew, receiving severe injuries. The sole survivor of two other crashes near Graveley was W/O S.H. Nutting, who was returning from his 45th sortie completing his second tour. The next day there was a numbness at Bourn and Gransden Lodge. Everyone moved about as if waiting for someone to wake them from a nightmare.

On the night of December 20-21 a force of more than 600 Halifaxes and Lancasters set out for Frankfurt. The raid was planned as a *Newhaven* but 6-8/10ths strato-cumulus prevented visual identification and so the Visual Markers retained their TIs. The Main Force bomb-aimers were looking for their red TIs, but it was the Germans who supplied them. The Hensenstamm decoy fire site to the south-east of the city was lit and red decoy TIs were fired in the vicinity with the result that the main weight of the attack fell 5 miles from the city centre: most of the damage in the town was caused by creepback, which for once was a blessing.

S/Ldr J. Sale, a Primary Visual Marker, made five attempts to identify the aiming point, flying lower each time. On the last run at 5,000 feet he was still in cloud, so he dropped his bombs and retained his TIs. Back at Graveley, when circling the airfield prior to landing, a TI exploded setting the rear turret and one wing on fire and filling the Halifax with smoke and fumes. Sale turned away from the aerodrome, climbed at full throttle to 2,000 feet and ordered the crew to bale out; then, trimming the aircraft before baling out himself, he looked up to find an embarrassed mid-upper gunner F/Lt.R. L. Lamb holding out his badly burned parachute. Jeopardizing his own safety, Sale asked base for a priority landing. The Halifax roared along the runway with everything blazing and Sale pulled up as far away from the buildings as possible. Lamb and Sale were practically out of the aircraft by the time it stopped and were making a 200-metre dash in flying kit which would have made Jesse Owens look like a tortoise. They flung themselves flat on their faces as the Halifax exploded and then, when the dust had settled, clambered to their feet unhurt.

The Frankfurt force was harassed continuously by the nightfighters who were not deceived by the spoof raid on Mannheim. F/O D.W. Field, who had skillfully survived an alarming collision with a Lancaster on November 26 when the elevators, fin and rudder were damaged, was in trouble again on December 20. His Lancaster was attacked and the hydraulic system extensively damaged and, because the bomb-doors would not open and both turrets were unserviceable, he turned for home.

Later when the defenceless Lancaster was attacked again the port inner engine was hit – the enemy was lost by evasive action. Without serviceable flaps and with the undercarriage jammed he thought a crash landing at base with a full bomb-load would be too dangerous so he ordered the crew to bale out. The rear gunner, W/O R.B. Smith, was killed through being knocked unconscious by the tailplane before he had pulled his ripcord.

P/O G.P.R. Bond was intercepted three times. Just after leaving the target F/Sgt R. Underwood, the rear gunner, opened up on an Fw190 with a 3-second burst and it proved to be an adequate deterrent. At 2002 hours the mid-upper gunner, P/O C.H. Moon, tried the same treatment with a Ju88, but the pilot was made of sterner stuff and returned the fire, wounding Moon in the lung and right shoulder as well as holing the port outer petrol tank, which broke away underneath. A minute later the enemy approached from astern and at 400 yards Underwood fired a 5-second burst, hitting the Junkers and forcing the pilot to break away without firing. The enemy came in from the port quarter for his third attack and opened up out of range. Firing continuously he hit the starboard outer, and set it on fire; the starboard tyre was punctured and another shell buckled the rear wheel. As the Lancaster dived to port Underwood scored more hits. Two of his guns had stoppages, and with no firing coming from the mid-upper turret the Hun must have thought it safe to attack from astern. This time his fire passed under the Lancaster as Bond pulled the aircraft up in a corkscrew and, when Underwood ordered 'Dive starboard' and fired at the Junkers, it broke away and disappeared. Ten minutes later an unidentified twin-engined aircraft approached but by now Underwood had cleared the stoppages and with the four guns blazing, he drove off the enemy who dived away without firing. Bond nursed the crippled Lancaster back to base and made a masterly landing in spite of the burst tyre and buckled wheel. Moon, who was immediately rushed to hospital, recovered after a protracted convalescence.

Interceptions on the Mannheim raid were few yet F/Lt R.G.F. Stewart was attacked twice. Homeward bound just south of Coblenz F/Sgt D.A. Mills, the mid-upper gunner, spotted a Ju88 and ordered Stewart to corkscrew. The Junkers came in from the port and although the rear gunner, F/Lt C.F. Horner, called 'Turn to port,' it was not soon enough to prevent his turret being hit and put out of action. Four minutes later when the enemy came round again Mills got in a 3-second burst before his guns jammed. Two minutes later the fighter attacked from dead astern, scoring more hits on the turret, hitting the starboard nacelle and bursting the starboard tyre. The fourth attack, which was also from astern, caused further damage on the starboard side. Although hit and on fire, the Lancaster was by no means crippled: the only reasonable explanation why the fighter pilot broke off the attack was that he had run out of ammunition. The Lancaster had completed another 50 miles on its westward route when Mills sighted an Me109 coming in to attack. His fire did not stop the Messerschmitt from closing and the Lancaster was holed by incendiary bullets which started a fire underneath the mid-upper turret. The Messerschmitt made another attack but was driven off by the mid-upper gunner before doing any further damage. The crew quickly got the fire under control and later Stewart proved he too could make a safe landing with a burst tyre.

On December 21, daylight photographs were obtained of Berlin for the first time since the Battle opened. Damage, though widespread was severe. Eight square miles of devastation in the centre of the city, as far as Charlottenburg in the north-west and Wilmersdorf in the south-west, was caused chiefly by fire. Most of the industrial damage was in the Tegel and Reinickendorf area where over ninety factories, many of them high-priority targets, were damaged to varying degrees of severity, and many commercial premises were blasted or burnt out. Although photographic cover was incomplete it revealed devastation of more than 3,200 acres with over 2,500 in the fully built-up area.

A mixed force of 709 Lancasters and Halifaxes took off at dusk to attack Berlin on December 29 and no one was surprised to find the target cloud-covered. The force did some excellent bombing on a well concentrated and plentiful supply of skymarkers and the glow of fires could be seen for 200 miles; crews late over target reported the smoke to 16,000 feet. The German 'Transocean Report' said the raid did considerable damage in the thickly populated part of the town. The LNSF carried out spoof raids on Magdeburg and Leipzig and the controllers sent nightfighters first to the one and then to the other. Flak accounted for most of the 18 missing aircraft.

F/Sgt A.R. McQuade of 405 Squadron was hit by flak during his bombing run. Most of the damage was in the nose of the Lancaster and the bomb-aimer had a lucky escape. The starboard outer engine had to be feathered immediately and the port inner was also hit. The starboard outer powered the H2S so the navigator had lost his chief navigational aid, and the aircraft wandered over Bremen. McQuade had been forced to descend after leaving the target because the air-pressure bottle had been damaged and at the lower height the Lancaster, now at the mercy of light as well as heavy flak, was hit again. Then just after leaving Bremen the port inner failed and the aircraft began to lose height. At the enemy coast it was down to 8,000 feet so McQuade decided to make directly for Woodbridge[6] where, after making the North Sea crossing without mis-

6. Woodbridge, Manston and Carnaby were coastal airfields specially designed to handle aircraft in difficulties, and their staff had the training and experience for dealing with emergencies.

hap, he arrived with enough height for a good approach and a safe landing.

The main effort against the German capital during the second half of the Battle of Berlin was in January when, in six attacks, Bomber Command dispatched 3,324 aircraft and dropped 13,594 tons of HE and incendiaries. The target was never clear of cloud but, using the Berlin Method, there was always a good supply of skymarkers and crews bombed on the glow of TIs when the cloud was not too thick.

The first major attack was on January 20-21 when 679 out of 769 claimed to have bombed the target. The best concentration of *Wanganui* flares, which included a TI Floater for the first time, was early in the raid before the Main Force arrived in strength. Over 1,200 tons of IBs were dropped and Mosquitoes, over the target the following night, reported that fires were still burning in the centre of the city.

On January 28 six LNSF Mosquitoes dropped *Window* and bombed the city at 2225 hours forcing the Berliners to the shelters. Four-and-a-half hours later, the sirens sounded again and few dared to stay abed. Those who went to the shelters were wise because this was the best attack of the month and probably the best to date on Berlin; it was certainly the most concentrated. Bennett's idea of reducing the number of Primary Markers and increasing the number of Backers-up prevented the mistake of January 20 being repeated. PFF timing was excellent and a fine concentration of markers was maintained and evenly distributed throughout the attack. Gaps in the cloud allowed some crews to bomb on TIs, a rare luxury at Berlin. Many explosions were reported and one at 0314 hours was described by many crews as the most impressive they had ever seen; it lasted for 45 seconds and was triggered by a blue flash. Fires were spreading and gaining a hold over an area of five square miles, but once again the extent of the damage was conjecture for PRU were able to report only 10/10ths cloud.

The activities of the evening were typical of Bomber Command's attacks during the month. Three-and-a-half hours before the Main Force took off for Berlin *Oboe* Mosquitoes began a two-and-a-half hour seige on German nightfighter aerodromes in the Low Countries. In addition 63 Stirlings laid mines in Kiel harbour. They flew the Berlin track to get the fighters airborne and the ruse was successful. TIs and flares were dropped by 4 Halifaxes of 35 Squadron at 54°52N 10°24E and the Stirlings made timed runs to their dropping zones from this datum point. LNSF Mosquitoes attacked Hanover at 0215 hours, *Windowing* the route and bombing the target. In addition to the 6 Mosquitoes which had attacked Berlin at 2225 hours, another 6 attacked at 0312 hours, *Windowing* the route in and out for the Main Force. They dropped false fighter flares and 40 miles south-west of Berlin, spoof route-markers. The various diversions gave the German nightfighters a busy night but did not quench their lust for

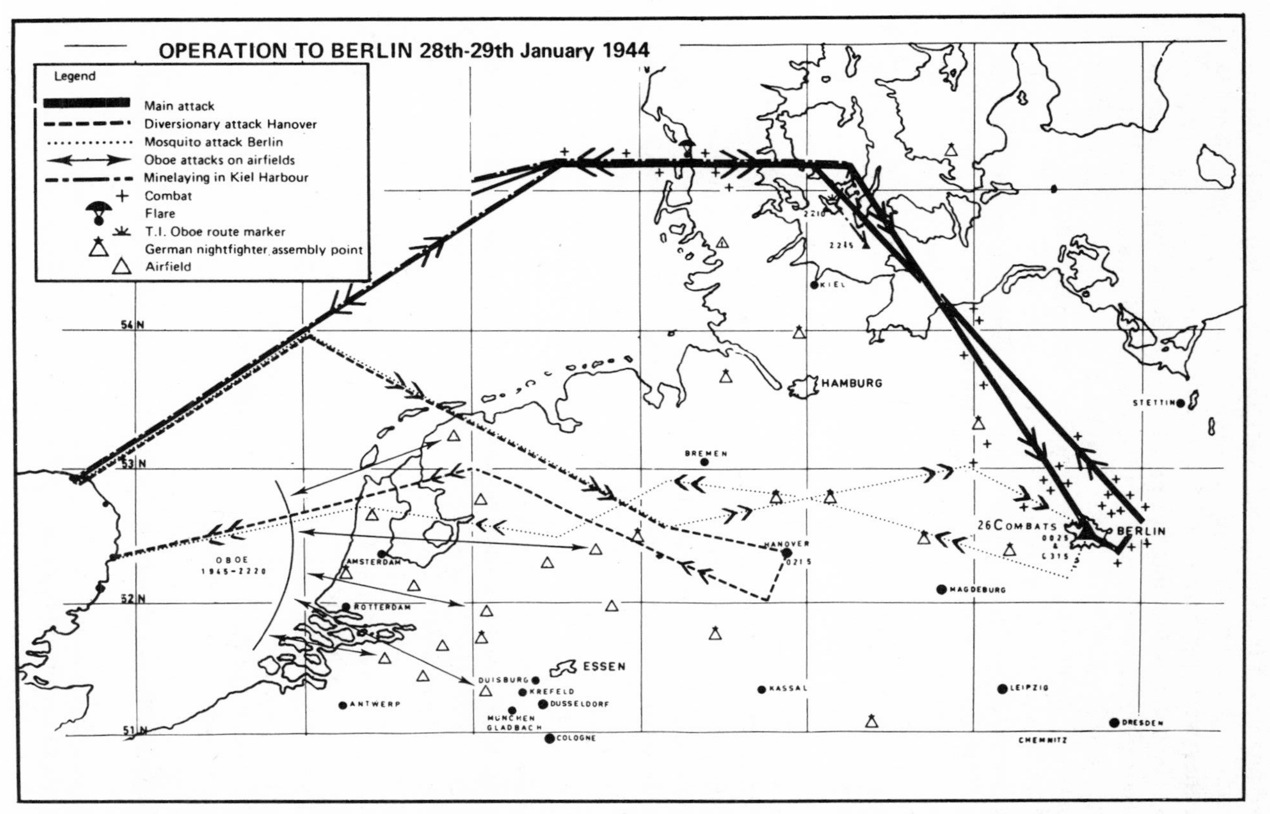

Map 14 In spite of all the spoofing, the German nightfighters were not to be denied. They gamely rose for the second time and took their toll of the bombers. Goering's boast that no bombs would fall on the German capital had long since been proved 'idle' but the defences, ground and air, seemed to possess an extra venom when Berlin was under siege. Crews could always expect a 'hot' reception at Nuremberg and Munich too. Happy Valley, where, by the time the tail of the aircraft was clear of one battery the nose was in range of the next, did not seem to be so spiteful. Perhaps the thought that, 'If Hans doesn't Fritz will', diluted some of the venom. Bremen, where the enthusiastic naval cadets manned some of the guns, was not the place where the bomb-aimer anachronistically said, 'Hang about'.

battle: 12 bombers were shot down before reaching the target; 6 over the target where 27 combats took place, and 3 more shortly after leaving it.

In common with the other groups Pathfinder losses were higher during the Battle of Berlin but, because only senior crews were assigned marking roles, they were constantly on orders and inevitably many were shot down. There can be nothing but praise for crews who flew consistently into the centre of Berlin to drop their markers accurately. In January losses reached a peak of 7.4%: 67 crews were missing, 60 others had combats and many aircraft were seriously damaged by flak.

W/O T.B. Macauley was compelled to make an early return on January 1 after his Lancaster had been severely damaged in three attacks by a Ju88. F/Sgt R.L. Jones and F/Sgt C.S. Goodman having repulsed the Junkers twice, set its starboard engine on fire during the third attack and the fighter fell away in flames.

F/O A.F. Abbott had a theory that if you got an enemy aircraft on the end of your trace, held it there and let it fly up to the centre you would certainly shoot it down. Abbott's pilot, F/O J.C.H. Davies, was weaving his Lancaster back from Berlin on the night of January 2-3 when it was intercepted by an Me110. The fighter was sporting a white light in the nose and it was on this that Abbott trained his guns. Telling Davies to dive to port, he opened fire as the enemy aircraft moved from the port bow to the starboard and tested out his theory. The Messerschmitt burst into flames and exploded and the delighted Abbott shouted: 'It works! It works!'

On January 28-29 two squadron leaders from 7 Squadron were in the news. S/Ldr P.K.W. Patrick was attacked three times, but when the fighter came in too close W/O J.H.Smith and Sgt W.S. Bremner shot it down. S/Ldr F. Curtis was just starting his bombing run when a Ju88 attacked from 600 yards. Both gunners fired and tracer was seen to enter the fighter which throttled back out of range. Curtis continued the run and, just after he had dropped his markers, the enemy closed to 500 yards hoping to catch the gunners fire-watching. He was quickly disillusioned and after taking more punishment he broke away without firing. Two minutes later, an Me110 attacked from the starboard quarter down but an immediate corkscrew to starboard saved the Lancaster, the tracer passing underneath the port wing. F/Sgt H.R. Mackay, with a quick burst, hit the Messerschmitt in the cockpit area. While still in the target area a second Me110 attacked from the port quarter and Curtis, diving to port, had the satisfaction of seeing the tracer miss again. Mackay's fire followed the fighter as it broke away to port. On the way home, the Lancaster was intercepted by yet another Me110 but Mackay opened fire and the Messerschmitt climbed to port and a safer climate without firing. Excellent crew co-operation saved the Lancaster from damage and, by firing early and accurately, the gunners discouraged the fighters from pressing home their attacks.

F/Lt R.V. Jones was over Berlin on January 30-31, when his Halifax was attacked by a Ju88. The rear gunner, F/Sgt G. Carrell, ordered a dive to port and opened fire. The Junkers came round again very quickly and Carrell yelled: 'Keep diving,' and opened fire again. The enemy made a third attack from the same quarter and this time Carrell hit the Junkers, setting the starboard engine on fire. Two minutes later the Halifax was intercepted by an Me210, which made six attacks, but Carrell's accuracy kept it from getting in close to the bomber. On one of the attacks, Carrell saw his tracer hit the Messerschmitt and smoke was pouring from its port engine when it finally broke off the combat.

The same night, F/O D.E. Biden's Lancaster was hit by flak during the bombing run; the port wing was holed and the aircraft was set on fire. A piece of shrapnel hit Sgt E.A. Wilkinson in the right arm but fortunately the wound was not serious. Almost immediately afterwards Sgt. G.L. Lanney, the rear gunner, sighted an Me110 astern and below and ordered a dive to port, but no evasive action was taken because the crew was hectically trying to put out the blaze. Lanney engaged the fighter and, although he hit the Messerschmitt, the enemy pressed home his attack damaging the port engine. As this engine powered the rear turret Sgt S.E. Hiskanen, the mid-upper, took over the defence for the second attack which came this time from the port quarter. Hiskanen ordered a corkscrew port and fired a 3-second burst hitting the Messerschmitt but, as in the previous attack, the German came in close and the hydraulics were hit thus putting both turrets out of action. The next attack was from the starboard quarter and Biden made a corkscrew to starboard avoiding further damage. Fearfully the crew waited for a fourth attack, but it never materialised and a course was set for base. F/O H.R. Farb, the navigator and W/O A.L. Weaver, the wireless operator, were wounded during the action, but they continued with their duties. The English coast was crossed near Winterton and Biden made directly for Coltishall where, as the undercarriage was unserviceable, he made a crash landing.

As well as the six attacks on Berlin in January, Bomber Command made three sorties in strength to Stettin, Brunswick and Magdeburg. They were planned as *Newhaven* attacks but the skies were clear only at Stettin. Primary Visual Markers at this time were marking the target with yellow TIs but, as they did not stand out as clearly as the reds of the Blind Markers or the greens of the Backers-up, the Main Force tended to ignore the yellows and bomb the less accurate reds or greens. Also, at Frankfurt on December 20, crews had bombed hooded flares in mistake for yellow TIs. At Stettin on January 5 the colour scheme was changed: Visual Markers dropped the more conspicuous reds and Blind Marker Illuminators and Backers-up dropped greens.

Mosquitoes of 139 and 627 Squadrons, by *Windowing* their route and marking Berlin, made the Germans think it was the main target and the controllers accordingly assembled their fighter force over the capital. Before they realized their mistake, the Main Force was bombing Stettin. There were some interceptions over the port later in the attack but only one Lancaster was intercepted on the outward route and only five other heavies on the homeward journey. The new-colour *Newhaven* was successful: there were many impressive fires, and damage to and around the main railway station was extensive. PRU photographs showed a mile-wide strip of destruction throughout the length of the town from north-east to south-west.

On January 14-15, a force of 498 Lancasters set out for the first attack in strength on Brunswick. The German controllers picked up the force shortly after leaving the English coast: spoof raids by Mosquitoes on Berlin and Magdeburg were unsuccessful and the fighters were kept on leash until the heavies reached 09°00E. Of the 30 aircraft missing 11 were Pathfinder crews. A strong force of nightfighters made interceptions between Bremen and Hamburg and of 8 Pathfinders who had combats in this area, only 2 survived.

S/Ldr W. Riches was intercepted by an Me110, which approached from dead astern. At 600 yards, F/Lt W.M. Booth, the rear gunner, ordered corkscrew to port and opened fire. When the Messerschmitt closed to 400 yards both gunners fired long bursts and they saw their tracer strike the fighter in the nose and fuselage. The fighter pilot seemed to throttle back in an attempt to follow the Lancaster's corkscrew and, as he had not yet opened fire it looked as if he intended to ram the bomber, so Booth ordered an immediate dive to port. With the Messerschmitt now less than 100 yards away, the gunners kept up a continuous fire until it burst into flames and dived away steeply into cloud. Although they did not actually see the crash they were certain they had destroyed it.

In the target area, 3 Pathfinders were attacked and 2 of them were shot down. The survivor, F/Sgt S.W.G. Neighbour, had two combats with Me109s, the Lancaster being damaged in both attacks, while Sgt F.R. Morton sat in his rear turret with frozen guns, a helpless spectator. The first attack was the more frightening for him because the Messerschmitt lined up dead astern and opened fire from 250 yards. The crew's fighter drill required the pilot to go into a corkscrew if the fighter indicator buttons were used: F/Sgt R.E. Whitehead, the mid-upper pressed the starboard indicator and immediately opened fire but the enemy skilfully followed the corkscrew and hit the Lancaster damaging the starboard inner engine, the starboard wheel was punctured and the mainplane hit. Whitehead's accurate fire forced the enemy to dive away apparently out of control. The Lancaster's mainplane was hit again when another Me109 attacked from the port quarter, Whitehead was once more equal to the occasion and claimed he destroyed it too.

The fighters followed along the homeward route and three PFF Lancasters were intercepted. P/O H.C. Williams and F/O O.C. Snell had only weak opposition and their gunners kept the fighters at bay, but the advantage the nightfighters had over the bomber in fire power was clearly demonstrated when Riches was attacked again, for his gunners, who earlier that evening had distinguished themselves, were powerless against an Me210 which fired a rocket from well beyond the range of their guns. It burst 10 yards astern of the Lancaster putting both turrets out of action and damaging the fin and rudder. The fighter, still out of range, opened up with cannon and machine-gun fire, hitting the starboard outer engine, the starboard inner propeller and flap, and the starboard tyre was holed. A second attack from the port quarter damaged that side of the aicraft: the port inner propeller, the elevator and the hydraulics were hit. During this attack, as well as the fuselage and mainplane, the cockpit was damaged and Riches was wounded in the leg. Booth had the last word: with only one gun firing and operating his turret by hand he succeeded in hitting the Messerschmitt, forcing the enemy to break off the attack. Riches, in spite of his wound and a very badly damaged Lancaster, made a successful landing at base.

At Magdeburg on January 21-22 stronger winds than those forecast caused some crews to arrive early over the target. Bennett had been opposed to giving H2S to the Main Force and, although this was unrealistic, they behaved as he had predicted. Twenty-seven crews thought they were as good as PFF and bombed without waiting for markers, 11 of them on H2S and the others visually or on ETA. The result was disastrous. When the Primary Visual Markers arrived they were unable to identify the aiming point partly because of the glare from the incendiaries dropped before zero hour. The Germans, knowing no markers had been dropped, fired decoy reds backing them with greens to simulate a *Newhaven* attack. The greens of the Blind Markers, all in the target area, looked less imposing than the concentration achieved by the enemy and most crews bombed the decoys: 40% of the 648 crews attacking reported seeing red TIs. Naturally, with the Germans doing the marking, the bulk of the bombs were miles from the target. The weight of the attack was to the south and east of the aiming point and some crews (not Pathfinders) had photographs of fields. The Germans must be admired for their excellent defence of the town, in particular for one of the finest pyrotechnic simulations ever produced. A very convincing combination of greens and reds had achieved the desired result. PFF with nine crews missing and nine more being intercepted, were not unnaturally furious; what could have been a good attack turned out to be a fiasco.

Three crews from 35 Squadron were lost and four more were intercepted. F/Sgt E.C. Gregory's gunners, F/Sgts E.J. Stuart and F.R. Nuthall, damaged a Ju88 which made four attacks, but by excellent defence – good evasive action and accurate fire – the Halifax escaped undamaged. W/O D.A. Wagar, P/O G.S.P. Honey's rear gunner, damaged an Me210, while in F/Lt R.T. Fitzgerald's case a warning on *Monica* enabled him to take evasive action.

F/O K.A. Petch was on his bombing run when the flight engineer, Sgt R. Cederbraun, watching from the astrodome,[7] reported a fighter at 1,000 yards on the starboard quarter flying along a lane of fighter flares. Cederbraun lost the fighter in the glare and cannon shells ripped through the rear turret and fuselage before P/O J. Napier, the rear gunner, had spotted it. Napier shouted: 'Dive starboard! Dive!', following up with a vividly unprintable description of the fighter pilot who had wounded him. The mid-upper, F/Sgt J. Shirley, swung his turret to the rear and opened up on an Me210 less than 100 yards away. The fighter pilot raked the underside of the Halifax; the jamming equipment blew up in the wireless operator's face, the H2S retired from active service and the port inner handed in its cards. The ammunition tracks were set on fire by a phosphorous shell and bullets were exploding and flying everywhere. However the combat manoeuvre was effective and the fighter was lost. Petch jettisoned the bombs in the target area and set a direct course for England, landing at Woodbridge. Napier sustained a compound fracture of the right leg just above the ankle; severe lacerations on his face were a result of the perspex turret being completely shattered by the hail of bullets.

A visit by the King and Queen to Warboys, Graveley and Gransden Lodge on February 8 broke the monotony of a sixteen-day enforced rest by the heavy squadrons because of the weather and the full moon. However the enemy got little peace because the LNSF attacked Berlin three times and Brunswick and Hanover twice; *Oboe* Mosquitoes kept the Ruhr towns awake, in some instances supported by the LNSF. Predictably on February 15 the target for the Main Force was Berlin and Bomber Command put up 891 Lancasters and Halifaxes, including 121 from 8 Group, equalling the largest force sent to the capital but carrying the heaviest load of bombs (2,642 tons). Unfortunately the target was 10/10ths cloud-covered and they had to bomb the *Wanganui* flares which were dropped regularly throughout the 20-minute attack except for a 2-minute gap from Z+12 to Z+14. Over 85% of the force claimed to have bombed the target and only 42 bombers were missing. Mosquitoes over Berlin later reported large areas of fire with smoke penetrating the cloud and rising to a height of 20,000 feet.

Siemen & Halske, one of the most important industrial targets in Berlin, was extensively damaged in this raid and many buildings were gutted. When PRU obtained photographic cover on February 19, it

7. Wireless operators usually stood watch in the astrodome in the target area but Petch was carrying special jamming equipment operated by the wireless operator.

showed over 46 acres of devastation in the huge complex of Siemens factories; only the Krupp works at Essen was worse hit. Daimler-Benz was one of the four other factories severely damaged in this raid. Many industrial buildings had been completely destroyed and hundreds showed fire and bomb damage. A further 400 acres of built-up area had been laid waste.

F/Sgt K.P.C. Doyle was intercepted before reaching the target. His rear gunner, Sgt G.C.C. Smith, saw a fighter switching its navigation lights on and off and waggling its wings and, as it drew nearer, identified it as an Me110. Believing it was a decoy Sgt A.C. Clarke, the mid-upper, searched for the second fighter. There were few gunners in Bomber Command who had not heard of this tactic but apparently Doyle's gunners had not heard of the Germans' latest variation: the fighter used the old distracting tactics but, instead of veering away, came in and attacked while the second fighter, knowing just when the attack was to take place, was able to time his attack to make the bomber's evasive action ineffective. The Messerschmitt closed rapidly and opened fire. Smith shouted: 'Corkscrew port! Go! Go! Go!' and returned the enemy's fire. The second fighter, an Fw190, also astern but below, opened up too soon and his tracer was seen to pass underneath. Cannon fire had put both turrets out of action and Smith and Clarke were wounded. Smith was hit in the right ankle – his leg had to be amputated later – Clarke had a compound fracture of the left leg. The gunners had some consolation for they destroyed the Me110 which exploded in the air. Smith manned his guns until the aircraft had landed safely and was awarded the GCM for his courage.

S/Ldr K.G. Davies was intercepted three times. His gunners, F/Sgt A. Grange and Sgt R. Child, shot down a Ju88 which attacked them on the outward route and were called into action again just as the Lancaster was leaving the target. This was a brief encounter, the enemy breaking away as soon as the gunners opened up. Some 90 minutes later Grange reported a Ju88 astern 600 yards away. Both gunners fired and Davies made a corkscrew to port which failed to shake off the Junkers so he followed the manoeuvre with a dive to starboard. The fighter re-appeared on the starboard quarter and again it was lost by evasive action. Next it was seen to be attacking from the port beam. This time Davies did an orbit to port but, as if it were attached to the Lancaster by a piece of elastic, the fighter made its final attack from the starboard beam. Davies orbited to starboard, losing height, until he was in cloud. Although the rest of the sortie went without incident the feeling of apprehension remained until the aircraft was on the dispersal pan and the crew had their feet on the ground.

During February there was a genuine bid to get a combined bomber offensive. The Americans were making an all-out effort to destroy the

German Air Force on the ground and in the air. By attacking air-frame factories the Americans compelled the *Luftwaffe* to try to break up their formations; this gave the P-51 fighters an opportunity to show their superiority. The destruction of the GAF was now as important to Bomber Command as to the USAAF and unusually good weather between February 19 and 25 allowed Leipzig, Schweinfurt and Augsburg to be attacked by both forces.

The increased loss rate in January forced Harris to employ new tactics and perhaps even to change his strategy. Mosquito diversions were no longer effective:[8] a much larger effort was required to deceive the controllers on a scale for which the Mosquito force was inadequate at this time. A variety of new ideas were tried and often several were employed the same evening. Such tactics comprised:

(i) Mining around the German and Baltic ports.
(ii) *Bullseyes* with the OTUs and HCUs flying the North Sea leg of the Berlin route.
(iii) Making a two-pronged attack with a gap of at least 2 hours between the phases.
(iv) Using a southerly route to the target.
(v) The number of route-markers was reduced and the use of H2S, *Fishpond* and *Monica* was limited because the nightfighters were homing on to the radiations.
(vi) Crews flying low over the North Sea to avoid being picked up on the German radar screen.

As Harris was the sole arbiter in the matter of target selection and gave no reasons for the choice, it can only be conjecture to aver that the nightfighters, mainly grouped in northern Europe, forced him to change his strategy and attack towns in southern Germany, but attack southern Germany was what he did.

The two-pronged attack proved to be the most successful. First used at Schweinfurt on February 24 in conjunction with a *Bullseye*, mining operations and a spoof attack on Kiel by 8 Group Mosquitoes, it resulted in only 33 bombers being lost from a force of 734. This attack, which followed an American daylight sortie, caused considerable damage but was marred by gross undershooting. Backers-up were partly to blame, some of them bombed short of the Primary Markers; the Main Force then compounded the error. This happened in both phases. There were markers burning in the target area throughout both attacks but the Main Force bombed the first TIs they saw and these were the undershoots well short of the aiming points.

On February 25-26 at Augsburg the two-phase method was used for

8. Mosquito diversions were successful only on the night of January 5.

the second time and with even greater success: from a force of 594 bombers losses were as low as 21. The first phase used the southerly route and, because OTUs had taken this route when dropping leaflets over France, little notice was taken of the bombers as they swept southwards. Attacks on the airfields in the Low Countries by *Oboe* Mosquitoes and a large force of 'gardeners' approaching Holland persuaded the controllers to hold the nightfighters in this area.

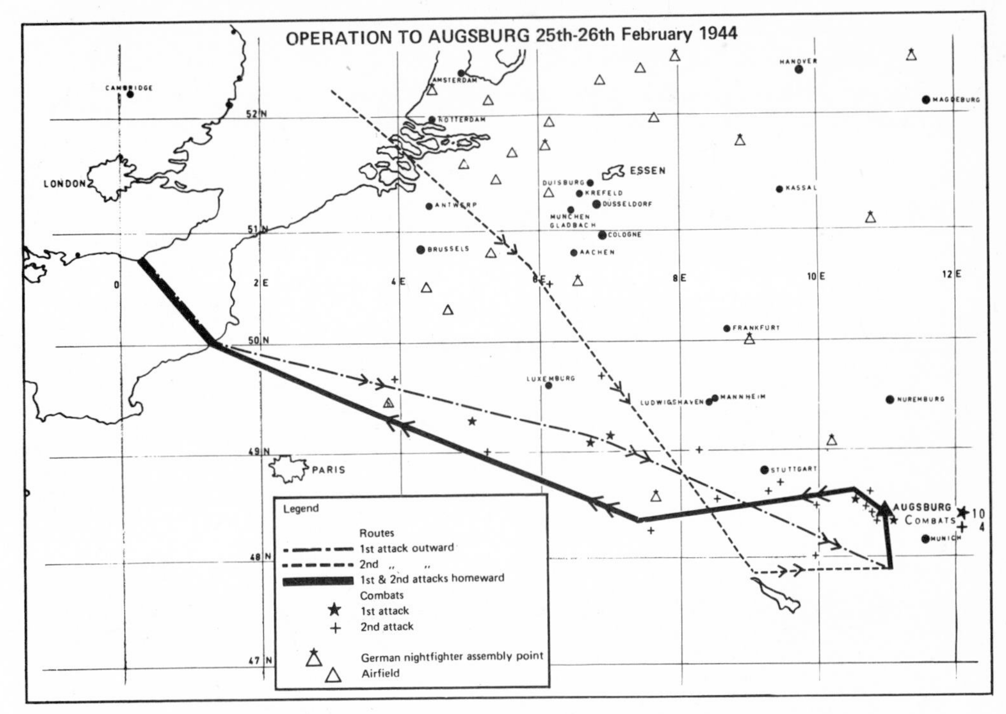

Map 15 Overture sorties by *Oboe* Mosquitoes, and a large force of 'gardeners' along the Dutch coast, not illustrated on this combat map, kept the fighters in the north during the first phase. They were hectically refuelling when the second phase swept over the Lowlands.

The raid was planned as a *Newhaven*. With the aid of flares and help from the snow-covered ground the Primary Visual Markers readily identified the aiming point. This time the Backers-up, newly roasted by the squadron commanders, were right on the ball. Concentrated marking left the Main Force with little excuse to bomb anywhere but the target area. Scarcity of fighters and, compared with Berlin, the small amount of flak were contributory factors in encouraging them to make sure they would not have to visit this target for a very long time. When the second phase arrived at 0115 hours TIs were superfluous; smoke was rising to 15,000 feet and the outlines of the town were clearly visible in the raging fires.

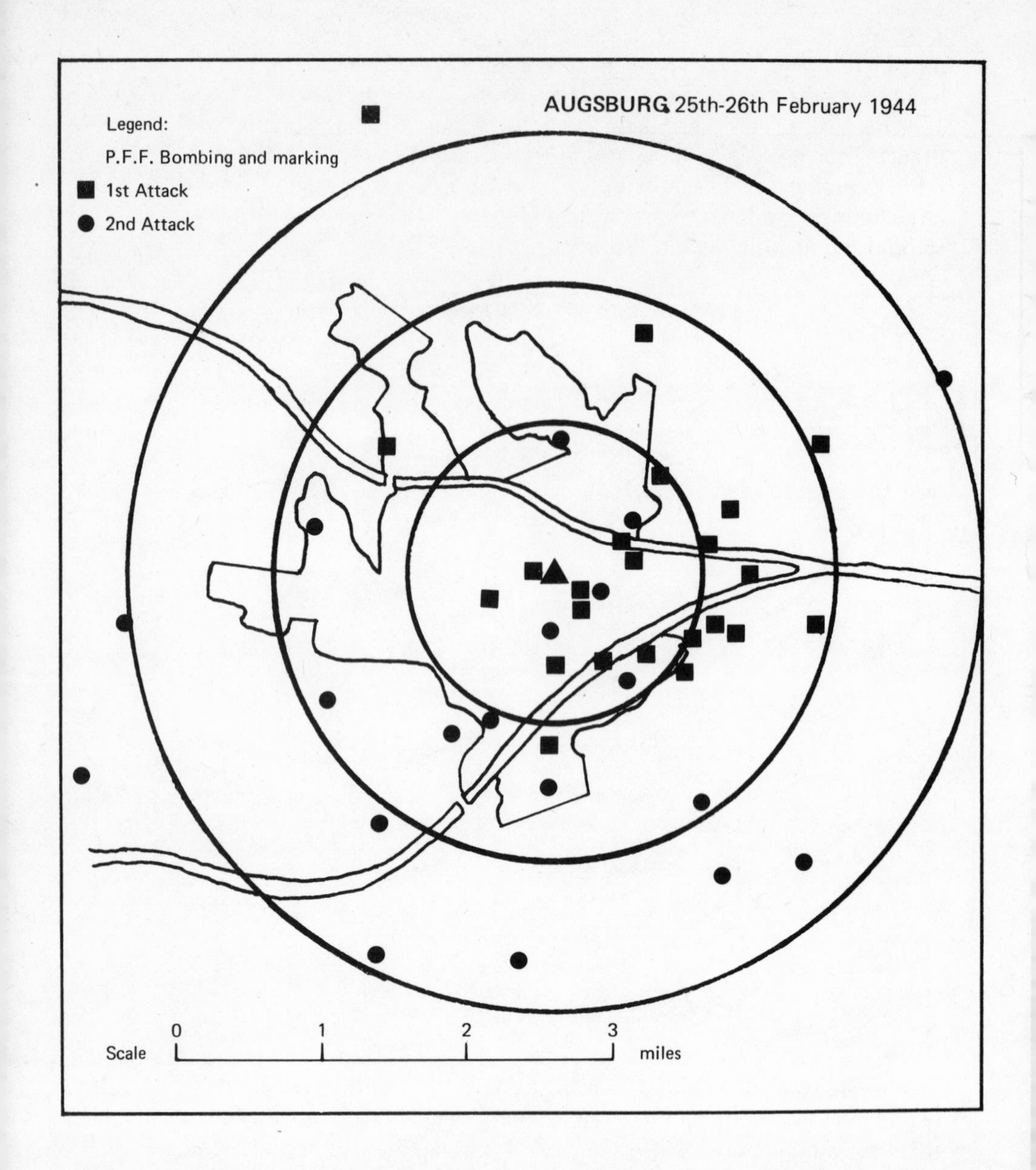

Map 16 In the first wave, and discounting crew X at 11o'clock, who would undoubtedly have been given extra training duties, 50% of the photographs were within a mile of the aiming point, the others virtually within a 2-mile radius. The Bomb Plot also shows the difference in concentration between *Newhaven* (1st Phase) and *Parramatta* (2nd Phase).

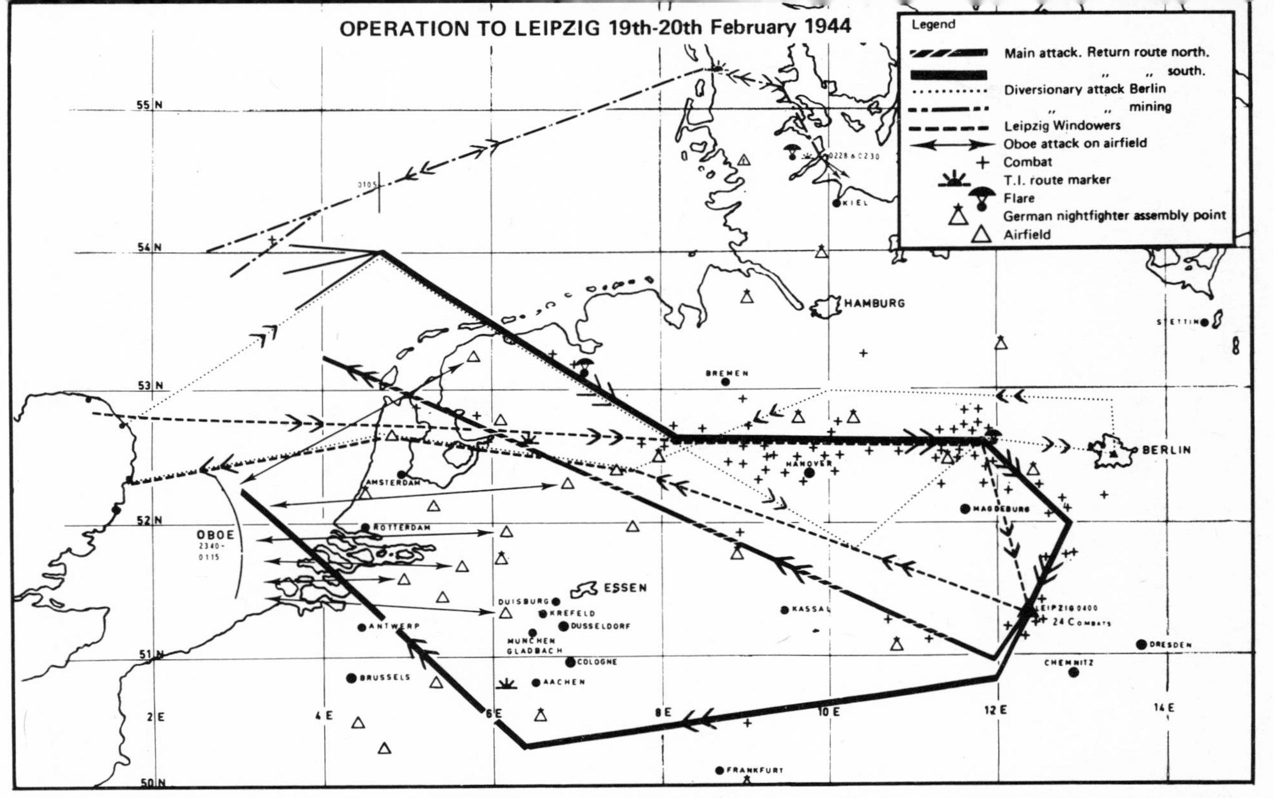

Map 17 If Leipzig was a name you wanted in your log book the time to have gone was December 3, 1943. (see Map 12). This night everything went awry. The 'gardeners' with flares and T.Is. to guide them had a trouble-free evening. They did get the German nightfighters airborne but the controllers called them back when the *Overture* attacks began on the airfields. Roaring back they met the Main Force head on. An excellent LNSF simulated attack on Berlin brought limited relief because most of the fighters pursued the bombers to the target. The pursuit petered out as the bombers split for the homeward journey: brows were mopped and logs became legible. *Oboe* land-markers to the west of Aachen guided southerly crews away from the Ruhr, while those north of track in Holland prevented crews from wandering over the defences in the Netherlands.

Those who enjoyed bombing fires were in their glory. There was also a compact group of markers, dropped by the Blind Markers and Backers-up on this phase, for the more fastidious to bomb. Mosquitoes of 8 Group, on the target an hour later, reported a solid mass of fires. Everyone knew the raid was one of the best ever carried out by Bomber Command. Photographs, obtained three weeks later, confirmed the glowing crew reports. The ancient city was devastated – it was almost impossible to find a building without fire or bomb damage – and the fires had spread into the modern industrial areas north and east of the town. Here too the damage was extensive and severe.

Sometimes the new tactics went awry as happened on February 19. 'Gardeners' went in first and got the fighters airborne but *Oboe* Mosquitoes sent to bomb their Dutch airfields drew them back to defend their bases. The Main Force on its way to Leipzig met the returning fighters just after crossing the coast. Of the 848 bombers 73 (8.6%) were shot down, for the fighters, not having wasted time in finding the bomber stream, were able to follow them with their usual persistency and without fear of running out of fuel. In all, 155 interceptions were reported and 58 crews had combats. The target was covered by thick cloud but the attack was concentrated at the beginning when the *Wanganui* flares were plentiful. Later it became more scattered but fires were still burning fiercely the next day and they acted as beacons for the 8th Air Force when they made their daylight attack.

F/Lt G.H.F. Carter had an eventful operational career before becoming a PoW. On February 13, 1943, thirteen crews from his squadron set out for Lorient, Carter on his thirteenth sortie. The Halifax was shot down by flak but Carter parachuted to safety and 'walked back'. At Graveley, he crewed up with S/Ldr J. Sale who had also evaded capture after being shot down. On December 20, 1943, he was flying with Sale when a TI exploded and he had to take the silk again.[9] On February 19, 1944, Sale's Halifax, outward-bound for Leipzig, was intercepted by a Ju88. The Junkers came in from below and riddled the aircraft with cannon and machine-gun fire wounding Sale and setting the port overload tank on fire. Sale ordered 'abandon aircraft' and the crew jumped; the Halifax went into a spin but Sale managed to get out somehow. Unhappily his wounds proved fatal and he died on March 20. F/Lt R.L. Lamb and W/O G.M. Cross, who were also in his crew on December 20, survived with Carter and spent the rest of the war as PoWs.

During March, changes in the Group saw 35 Squadron re-equipped with Lancasters in place of their Halifaxes and all heavy squadrons reduced to two flights. This change necessitated the formation of two new squadrons, 582 and 635 Squadrons. To accommodate the change the

9. Reported earlier.

Group had already acquired three new stations, Upwood, Downham Market and Little Staughton, while Marham went non-operational to have new runways constructed.[10]

Operations were laid on every night in 8 Group but bad weather caused 14 cancellations and on three nights even the Mosquitoes were grounded. Seven major attacks on five German towns brought the Battle of Berlin to a close.

The gunners gave a good account of themselves that month; 45 combats were reported but no bombers were seriously damaged. On 29 occasions the enemy was driven off before opening fire, three fighters were destroyed and another six damaged. The first success was on March 18-19: F/Lt S. Evans was still in the target area (Frankfurt) when the rear gunner, F/Sgt T.J. Hirst, ordered: 'Corkscrew starboard,' and, as he opened fire, continued, 'Me110 astern down,' to direct the mid-upper, F/Sgt G.W. Brockway, who was swinging his turret to get a bead on the fighter. Hirst hit the Messerschmitt and the fighter pilot side-slipped away directly into the sights of Brockway, and again side-slipped out of danger underneath the bomber. However, the Lancaster's evasive action gave Brockway another chance and, as his tracer arced into the Messerschmitt, it dived away steeply. Hirst saw a bronze-coloured explosion on the ground.

The Me110 which attacked P/O R.W. Beveridge's Lancaster, homeward-bound from Frankfurt on March 22-23, began by dropping red flares on the starboard quarter. The mid-upper and the wireless operator searched for a second fighter while F/O J. Allison, the rear gunner, engaged the Messerschmitt. As soon as he opened fire the fighter broke away and jettisoned the remaining flares. If it was a ruse to make the gunners think the fighter was in difficulties it failed because, as soon as the Me110 turned to attack, Allison opened fire. At 200 yards he gave the Messerschmitt a long burst and it broke in two. Less than a minute later the crew saw an explosion on the ground.

F/Lt R.K. Eggins had dropped his TIs on the Big City on March 24 and was still east of Potsdam when the wireless operator, P/O J.W. Patterson, saw an Me109 on the port quarter up crossing to starboard. The rear gunner, P/O F.A. Marden, opened the firing when it was dead astern and saw his tracer hit the Messerschmitt. It dived away. Hardly had the gunfire stopped when the mid-upper, P/O G.J. Pursely, shouted, 'Dive starboard, Skipper!' as an Fw190 came in from the starboard quarter. Both gunners engaged the fighter and when the Focke-Wulf was hit the pilot broke away, then circled and came in from the port. Eggins dived to

---

10. 156 Squadron moved to Upwood; 635 Squadron was formed at Downham Market; 582 Squadron formed at Little Staughton; 105 Squadron moved from Marham to Bourn and 109 Squadron moved to Little Staughton.

port when ordered, both gunners fired and hit it again. As the Fw190 dived away Pursely lost sight of it but Marden was able to follow it down. Black smoke poured out of the engine then it burst into flames and was later seen to crash.

The first of the two March attacks on Stuttgart took place on the 1st-2nd. The TIs and *Wanganui* flares quickly disappeared into 10/10ths cloud and, due to its thickness, no reflections were seen. The raid was scattered but PRU photographs showed some useful damage. The target was again cloud-covered for the second attack on Mar 14-15, the winds were stronger than forecast and most crews were 3-15 minutes late on target, and this included Pathfinders. The best concentration of sky-marker flares was to the south-west of the target, but because the marker crews did not arrive at regular intervals there was no continuity in the marking and so the raid was scattered. Sheer weight of bombs, 2,735 tons, over half of them IBs, carried by 863 aircraft, was responsible for the two large fires and many smaller ones reported by returning crews.

Tremendous damage was caused at Frankfurt in two devastating attacks on March 18-19 and 22-23. Some 6,240 tons of bombs were dropped in the two raids and the *Bomber Command Quarterly Review* says the second raid was, 'one of the most successful attacks ever made'. The townspeople were so shattered after the first attack that there was a mass exodus from the town as soon as the sirens sounded on March 22. The attacks were *Newhavens* and the Primary Visual Markers were accurate on both occasions. The marking for the first attack was excellent and all the Main Force crews were enthusiastic about the concentration.

The second attack highlighted the important role played by the Supporters and the first wave of bombers: they started large fires around accurately placed markers in the centre of the town, and it was the fires that attracted most of the bombers so the less accurate markers to the south-west received little attention although the attack tended to spread in that direction. A total of 1,662 bombers were engaged in the two attacks and only 55 were missing, a loss rate of 3.3%.

On March 26-27, between the last Berlin raid and the notorious attack on Nuremberg, more than 700 bombers attacked Essen. For this *Musical Parramatta*, 16 out of 22 *Oboe* Mosquitoes dropped TI reds and achieved an excellent concentration. For once the 10/10ths cloud favoured the bombers: searchlights were powerless; flak although intense, was of necessity in barrage form while the cloud was thin enough for the glow of the reds to be seen. Twenty-four buildings at Krupps were damaged; a colliery at Prosper was ravaged by fire; much of the repair work in the centre of Essen and at Krupps was demolished and the southern districts of the town, which had escaped damage in previous attacks, were extensively damaged. An attack on the marshalling yards at Courtrai and a spoof attack on Hanover by Mosquitoes confused the nightfighter con-

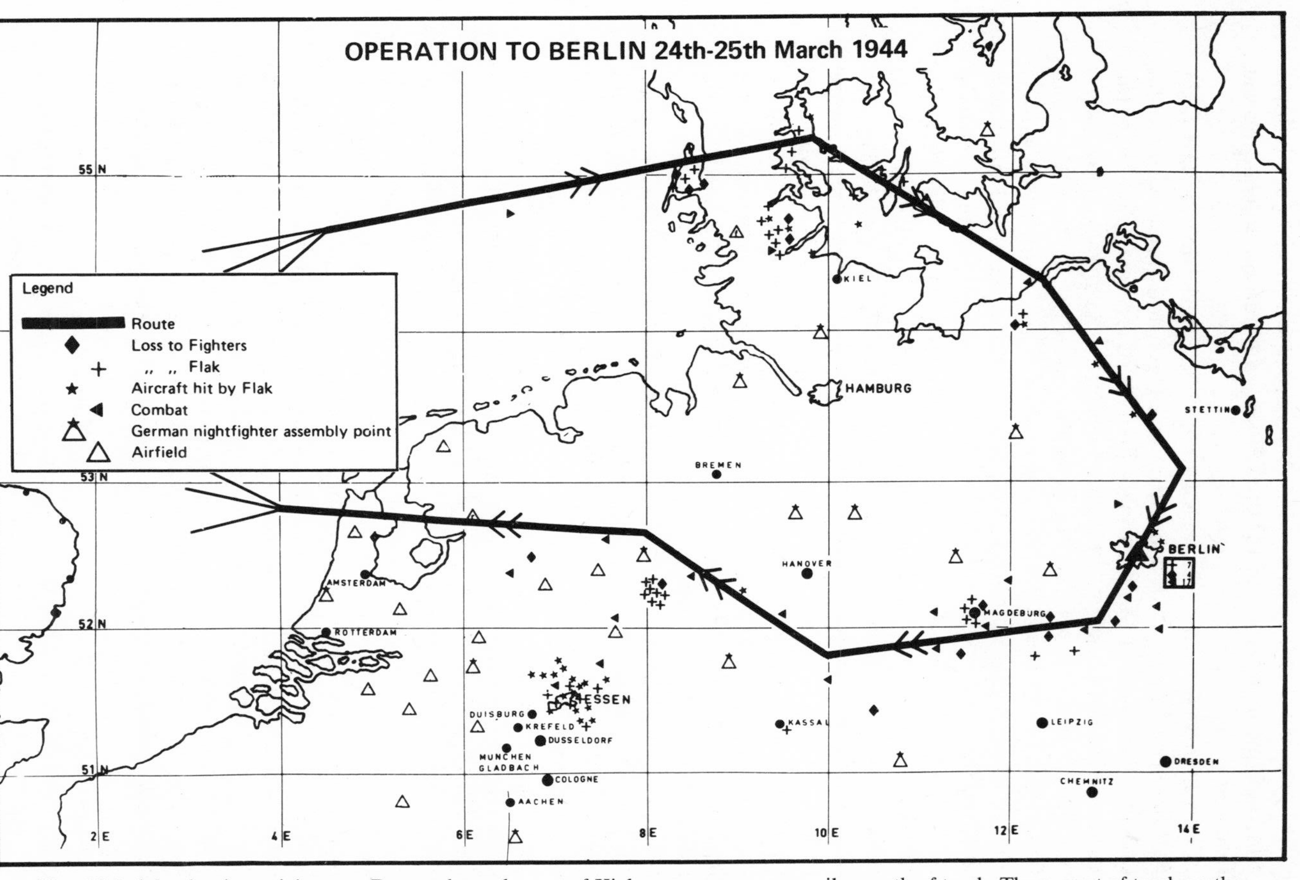

Map 18 Judging by the activity over Denmark north-west of Kiel, many crews were miles south of track. Those west of track on the second and third legs nullified the 'route-planners' hopes that the Germans might think Stettin was the target. With a 60 miles wide loose echelon formation of bombers charging back to England the Germans must have thought this was a new tactic. Osnabruck was ready and waiting, claiming 8 victims. The thought of returning from a sortie to Berlin via Essen and Happy Valley brings beads of sweat to the brow 30 years later.

trollers so the Main Force was already leaving Essen before it was intercepted and then only by a small force kept in reserve near Bonn. Nine aircraft were missing from the Essen raid and none from that on Courtrai.

Two nights earlier 822 heavies had attacked Berlin for the last time. Pathfinders achieved a fair concentration of reds and greens with a slight overshoot because of winds stronger than those forecast. Cloud over the target varied between 2-9/10ths and crews, who saw the groundmarkers, bombed in the target area. Others, who chased the drifting *Wanganui* flares, spread the attack further and further to the south-west. A PRU aircraft over Berlin on March 25 reported that fires were still burning in the Steglitz district. Most navigators were 'clueless' regarding the winds, and aircraft were blown miles off track. The searchlight and flak batteries thought it was Christmas all over again as aircraft, unprotected by *Window*, wandered into their sights. Six were shot down over Sylt on the outward journey and others strayed over Flensburg; more than 17 were shot down by flak on the outward route. Leipzig, Magdeburg, Munster, Osnabruck and finally the Ruhr, 60 miles off track, all claimed victims on the return journey. At least 50 bombers fell to flak and the nightfighters had picked off at least 17. Altogether 72 bombers were missing from the raid, 9.2%.

On March 30-31, a force of 795 bombers (110 from PFF) set out for Nuremberg, and 94 of them (11 from PFF) were shot down. Bennett, who usually had some say in the route chosen, claims he was overruled on this occasion and certainly the choice still puzzles students of Bomber Command tactics. From the east coast of England they flew directly to Charleroi, their first turning point, from there they turned and flew due east for 250 miles. Thirty years later no one has yet given a reason for this extraordinary change of tactics and, without a death-bed confession, it is doubtful if the world will ever know. What makes this direct approach even more incomprehensible is that the track skirted two well known fighter beacons and yet, apart from an LNSF spoof on Kassel, no diversionary attacks were planned to draw the fighters away. The weather played its part for, although broken cloud was forecast over the Continent, the sky was actually clear for most of the route, which undoubtedly helped the nightfighters. Even more helpful were the condensation trails extending backward for miles. At least 50 bombers were shot down before the target was reached; eight Pathfinders were intercepted on this leg although none of their aircraft suffered any serious damage. The only evidence that bombs were dropped on Nuremberg came from the German radio gloating over their success; none of the plotted photographs was in the target area. Schweinfurt was bombed by 34 aircraft although no markers were dropped on the town. Nor is this surprising, for evasive action invariably took the aircraft off track and, in this case, unexpected winds left little hope of regaining it. From the evidence of H2S photographs, Pathfinders dropped their TIs; TI floater and *Wanganui* flares to the east of the target area, but the TIs were not seen because of 10/10ths cloud. As winds were stronger than those forecast, bombing on *Wanganui* flares would in any case have been wide of the aiming point. Crew reports were so pessimistic that Harris did not even ask for PRU cover.

VI Overlord

Few of the Top Brass had thought the war could be won without a second front. Allied grand strategy had catered for it. Churchill and Roosevelt had promised Russia it would be opened as soon as possible and General Dwight Eisenhower had been appointed Supreme Allied Commander for *Overlord* in December 1943. Churchill was opposed to the *Overlord* bombing policy, and in this he had the support of most of the War Ministers, because they considered the raids would make enemies of the people who could help the Allies after the invasion. Churchill even went to President Roosevelt to seek his support, but he said that it was pointless appointing a Supreme Commander if he were not in supreme command. In the end Eisenhower was forced to point out that there was no difference in essence between bombing French railways and bombing Lorient and St. Nazaire which had been done with Churchill's approval.

Harris had had the opportunity in 1943 and early 1944 to fulfill his boast; now *Overlord*'s needs were urgent. Bomber Command crews were behind Harris to the death, which for them was the ever-increasing prospect – while proud to have Berlin in their log books, they were pleased for any diversion. However, PFF and the Main Force found the diversion more exacting than was expected. Pathfinder techniques had been geared to area bombing and the capabilities of the Main Force, but 'within three miles' was not acceptable on the new targets because many of them were less than a square mile in area. New methods of marking were required and higher standards of bomb-aiming were essential: it was a whole new war. That both these requirements were met is to the eternal credit of the crews.

Pointblank was still the overall policy but it was subservient to the requirements of *Overlord*. On April 14, Bomber Command came under Eisenhower's 'direction'; the word was carefully chosen after months of argument.[1] Harris had to divert his force when and as required by the

1. The political arguments and jockeying for position and power are beyond the scope of this book and are dealt with in depth by Webster and Frankland in *The Strategic Air Offensive Against Germany*.

Supreme Commander; otherwise he was free to carry on with his area policy.

With the advent of the P-51D Merlin Mustang the USAAF was able to operate deep into Germany with fighter cover. By attacking aircraft factories it compelled the German Air Force to defend itself and, by its victories, broke the back of the *Luftwaffe*.[2] Shortly after D-Day Bomber Command turned to daylight attacks over northern France and later, when the British fighters were based on the Continent, they accompanied the bombers to targets in Germany. British bombers were the most economical: they carried a greater load and, by dropping larger bombs, they caused more devastation. Now, because the force could bomb with precision by day or night and in condition of 10/10ths cloud, Bomber Command became the most versatile.

Although officially Bomber Command did not come under the direction of Eisenhower until April 14, the requirements of *Overlord* had been sent to Harris long before. In January, Harris had conceded the inevitability of a second front but claimed that Bomber Command could best aid the invading forces by continuing with area attacks. He maintained that his force was incapable of precision bombing but the Air Staff would not be convinced without operational proof, believing the Air Chief Marshal's views were unduly influenced by his convictions. On March 4, they issued a directive ordering him to attack selected communication centres, ammunition dumps and airfields 'to obtain experience of the effects'. Once the die was cast, Harris threw himself wholeheartedly into the task just as if it was his own pet theory. He chose seven marshalling yards from the list of targets: Trappes, Aulnoye, Le Mans, Amiens, Courtrai, Laon and Vaire. By the end of March, all seven had been attacked (Le Mans and Amiens twice). Although in some instances the bombing had not achieved the required concentration, there was sufficient evidence that, given the right conditions and locality, Bomber Command could achieve great precision.

The Allied Commanders were certain the German counter-invasion plan must rely on bringing reinforcements into the battle area by rail. The Transportation Plan, by creating chaos on the railway, would at least prevent them doing this quickly. The alternative, attacking oil installations, was discussed with that of communications at a meeting on March 25. Attacks on oil could be effective as a long-term policy but they would be of no immediate assistance to the invasion army because the Germans at that time had plenty of reserves. The Transportation Plan, however, might create chaos behind the lines and so Eisenhower backed it. Bomber Command was allocated 37 of the 80 targets and by D-Day all of them were damaged to the extent that no further sorties were thought necessary.

---

2. Not numerically; in quality and experience.

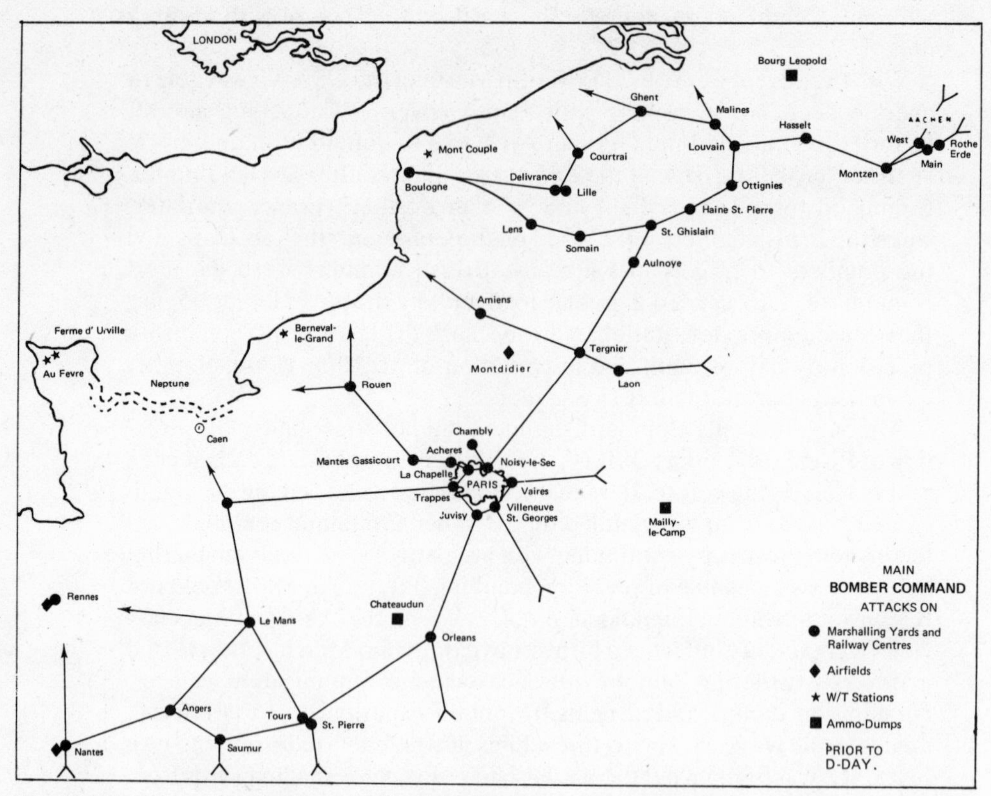

Map 19 Although the French railways radiate form Paris the close network in Belgium and France feeding the coast from the important centre of Aachen demanded equal priority. The attention accorded this area also helped to create the myth that the landing would be made in the Calais-Boulogne area. The importance attached to the destruction of the W/T stations at Au Fevre, Berneval-le-Grand, Ferme d'Urville and Mont Couple is patent.

April saw further changes in the Group; 83, 97 and 627 Squadrons were 'detached' to 5 Group for PFF duties. This was in accordance with the new policy of giving each group individuality,[3] in particular 3 and 5 Groups, but when Command operated as a unit it was still Pathfinders who led and marked the target. The loss of 83 and 97 Squadrons put a severe strain on the other heavy squadrons. Bennett's Lancaster force was reduced to three-quarter strength at a time when the number of sorties and, more significantly, the number of targets to be marked increased dramatically. Indeed 8 Group flew 13,966 sorties between April 1 and September 30, 1944, only 583 fewer than from August 1942

3. In truth it was a return to the old policy of 1939-42 with tighter control from High Wycombe.

33. (*Top*) S/Ldr H. Lees's 'lash-up' showing a 35mm camera in position to photograph the PPI

34. (*Bottom*) H2S radar equipment

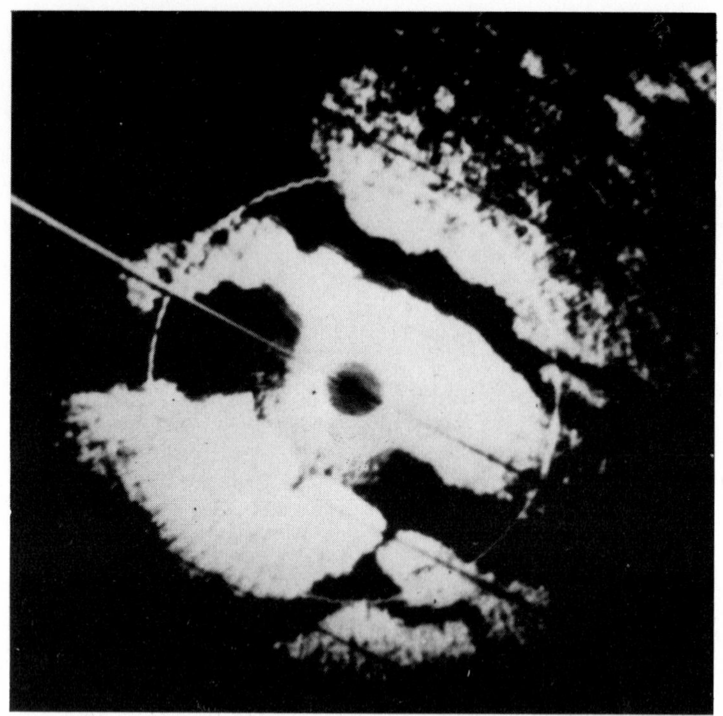

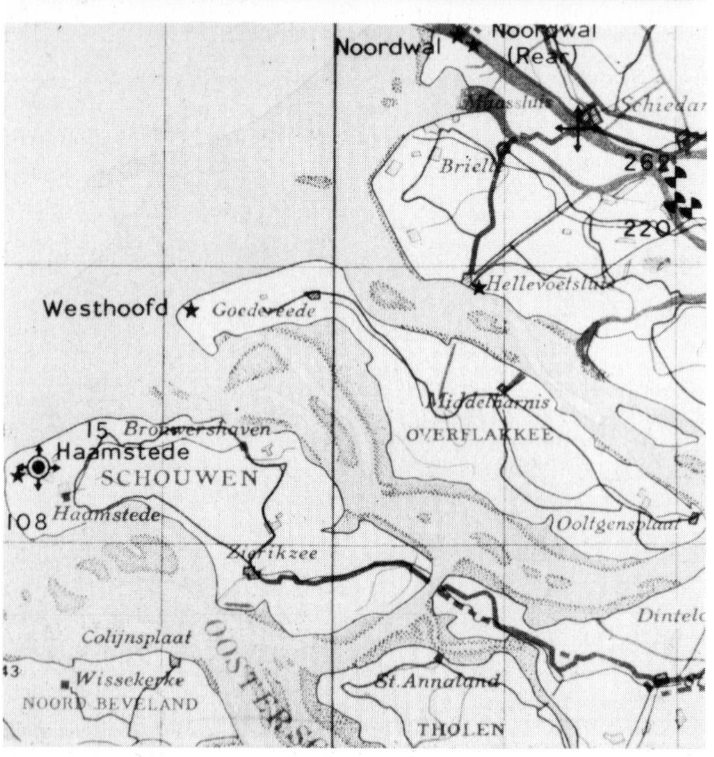

35 & 36. PPI display of Overflakkee. Coastlines came out clearly on the screen. *Below*, a map of the area shows how closely the two were correlated

37. This PPI display shows the approach to Berlin from the west between Potsdam and Spandau. The stretch of water Havel, Wann See and Templiner See show up clearly right of centre

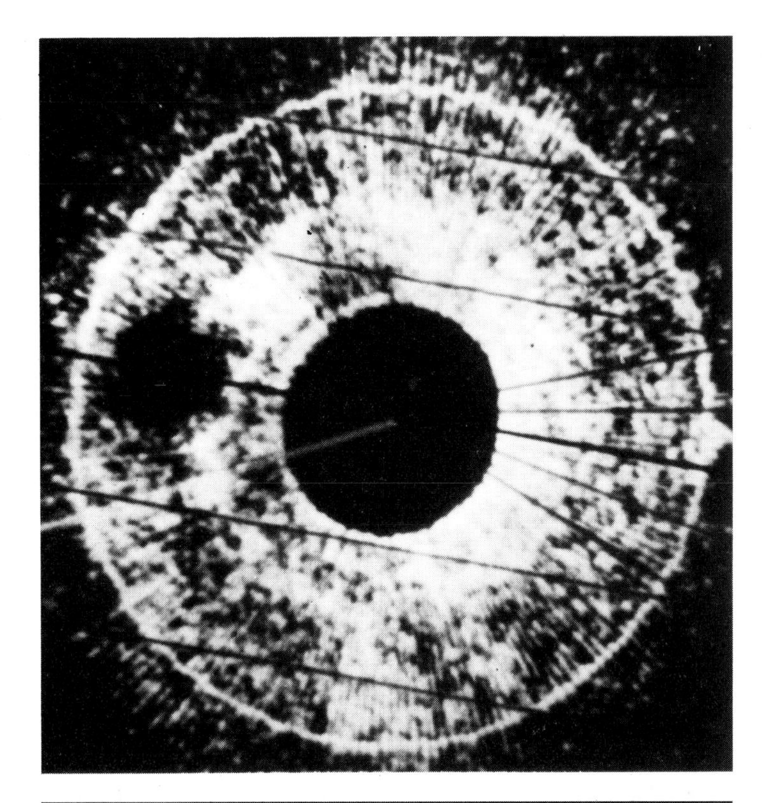

38. Dummer See, left of centre, in north-west Germany was a valuable pin-point for bomber crews

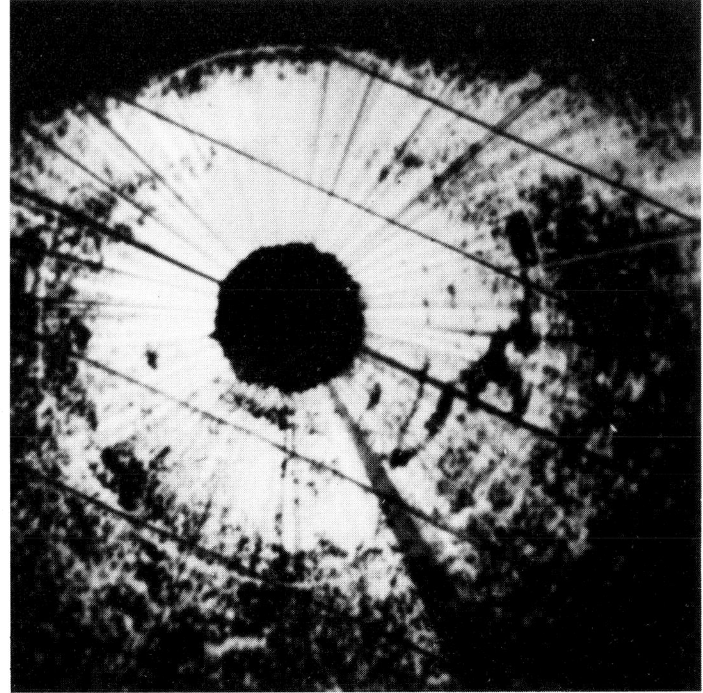

39. (*Top*) Whilst there are only two known Lancaster 'Centenarians' many 8 Group Mosquitoes completed more than 100 sorties. GB-F (LR 503), one of the most famous, was credited with 213 sorties. Seen here with Geoffrey de Havilland, F/Lt M. Briggs and F/O J. Baker shortly before their fateful flight to Canada

40. (*Bottom*) The virgin ML 914, photographed before being baptized with RAF roundels and squadron letters GB-N, was purchased with money donated by Nigeria. Heroine of 148 sorties – 16 with the author – she marked Homburg for Bomber Command's first daylight sortie to the Ruhr in strength on August 27, 1944

to March 31, 1944. *Oboe* aircraft marked for more than 500 Bomber Command attacks and on more than 400 of these the heavy PFF squadrons took part.

The few failures were mainly caused by bad weather conditions and many of the successes were in spite of them. Because of Pathfinders, Bomber Command alone of the three air forces was able to operate in bad weather and, through the courage of Master Bombers, many seemingly impossible raids were successfully carried out; by their skilful direction they taught the Main Force how to bomb TIs and so achieve concentration. It was this tutelage that made the later attacks on the Reich so devastating.

MARSHALLING YARDS The first eleven raids on the railway marshalling yards were all *Musical Parramattas* and, of the nine targets attacked, Trappes, Le Mans, Amiens, Vaire and Lille were estimated to have been effectively destroyed. At Vaire, on March 29-30, two ammunition trains in the centre of the marshalling yards blew up, killing 1,270 German troops and severing the mainline tracks. Bombing was more concentrated in the southern half of the yards where the sidings were cut in more than 100 places.

The 'back-room boys' had calculated how many hits would be required to destroy the yards effectively – calculations were made for each yard – and how many bombs would have to be dropped to obtain the number of hits. In general, the results did not reach expectations. For example, two attacks had to be made on Amiens and Le Mans before the required level of damage was achieved. The weather had played its part but in some instances the markers were not tightly grouped and, on one occasion, a salvo of TIs with a gross error had been bombed. It was thought that perhaps with someone to guide the Main Force results might have been better and the error avoided.

On April 10, when four rail centres were marked by *Oboe*, at Aulnoye, two senior Pathfinder crews were sent to assess the *Oboe* greens and then mark the aiming points with reds. In the event the markers were accurate and, according to the ORS report, 315 bombs were expected to hit the target and 287 did, 91%. An amplified version of the Aulnoye attack was used when Rouen, Tergnier and Noisy-le-Sec were attacked on April 18-19; a Master Bomber and Deputy were in attendance and were part of the marking force; *Oboe* TIs were used as proximity markers; Illuminators dropped flares around them; and Visual Markers, if they then identified the aiming point, marked it with contrasting TIs. Backers-up kept the target marked for the duration of the attack and the Master Bomber directed the Main Force. This type of attack was called *Musical Newhaven* or Controlled Visual.

At Rouen the attack was divided into two phases, the first phase attacking the southern end of the marshalling yards. Only one Mosquito marked but the Illuminators following closely behind dropped their flares over the green TIs enabling two of the three Visual Markers to identify the actual aiming point and mark it by zero hour with large salvoes of reds and greens. Backing-up started promptly at zero hour and was maintained throughout the phase. The second phase followed the same pattern and by zero hour all three Visual Markers had identified and dropped their TIs in a compact group around the northerly aiming point; the backing-up too was prompt and continuous. In general, the bombing was good but there was some undershooting: the close grouping of the markers, the exhortations of the Master Bombers, the lack of defences and the knowledge that these targets required most accurate bomb-aiming made such carelessness inexcusable. Had the bombs, which unfortunately fell on the town, been dropped in the target area a second attack might not have been necessary.

The bombing by the Halifax crews on Tergnier was appalling: the initial marking was good, but the Backers-up were short and, although the Master Bomber, W/Cdr J.F. Barron, ordered the Main Force to overshoot these markers, they in turn bombed short. The creepback extended 1½ miles and many bombs fell on the town. By contrast at Noisy-le-Sec, although some crews did undershoot, the main weight of the attack was around the compact group of TIs and the hits were 29% greater than expected.

Controlled *Oboe* was another variant. In this type of attack *Oboe* Mosquitoes dropped different coloured TIs before zero hour and a Master Bomber, having selected the most accurate ones, gave directions to the Main Force. The Master and Deputy carried TIs and flares; sometimes the marking force was augmented by Backers-up, but subsidiary marking was carried out only at the Master Bomber's discretion.

Two controlled *Oboe* attacks on the night of April 30 on the marshalling yards at Somain and Acheres suffice to show how the presence of a Master Bomber contributed to the success of the sorties. At Somain the *Oboe* markers were inaccurate and at Acheres they were late. Although W/Cdr P.K.W. Patrick ordered the 110 Halifax crews on Somain to wait until he had marked the aiming point, only 40 obeyed his instructions and it was they who did the damage. Master Bombers were briefed to be over the target by Z−6 and S/Ldr E.K. Cresswell, realizing that the Mosquitoes were late, used the time to make a visual identification and mark the aiming point at Acheres. When the *Oboe* TIs went down they too were accurate and Cresswell had no difficulty directing the 100 Halifax crews, who turned in a fine piece of concentrated bombing. The results were excellent, the ORS saying they had exceeded the expected hits by 48%.

Although the losses were not heavy on most of these raids many experienced crews from 8 Group were among the missing, including several Master Bombers and Deputies. W/Cdr A.G.S. Coussens, OC 635 Squadron, having controlled the northern attack at Laon on April 22-23, was one of four Pathfinders who failed to return that night. F/Lt J.W. Perry, also on the northern A/P, was surprised by a Ju88 just before releasing his bombs. The Junkers made only one assault, raking the Lancaster with cannon and machine-gun fire. The rear gunner, Sgt J.R. McCrea, was killed instantly. A fire started near the H2S and wireless operator's compartment; the DR compass, IFF and intercom were rendered unserviceable and the elevators and rudder damaged.

The Deputy, S/Ldr E.M. Blenkinsop, was among the 15 crews who failed to return from Montzen on April 27 and over Le Mans, on May 11, the Master Bomber, W/Cdr J.F. Barron, and his Deputy, S/Ldr J.M. Dennis, were shot down. At Trappes on June 2 four crews survived combats: S/Ldr H.W.A. Trilsbach's gunners damaged an Me210 and F/Lt G.P.A. Yates's gunners shot down the Ju88 which attacked them. On June 7-8, Bomber Command attacked the Paris marshalling yards and at one of these, Versailles Matelot, the Deputy, S/Ldr C.G. Hopton was shot down. An aircraft, which was thought to have been the Squadron Leader's was seen to crash with TIs exploding following air-to-air firing south of the target. Close by at Juvisy, W/Cdr C.M. Dunnicliffe and F/Lt H.J. Sexton were engaged by fighters. Sexton's gunners, F/Sgt E.W. Platts and F/Sgt G.W. Wright, drove off the Me110 which attacked them, but the Lancaster was extensively damaged and Sexton used the long runways at Manston to make an emergency landing.

Low cloud on June 11 gave the ground defences an opportunity to demonstrate their skill. At Tours, the Master Bomber, F/Lt W. Taggert, brought the Main Force below cloud and most crews made their bombing runs at 2,000 feet; four crews of 405 Squadron were hit and P/O C.H. Fisher's H2S set operator was wounded in the leg. The same night, F/Lt S. Smith, the Master Bomber at Nantes, found similar conditions and in his turn ordered the crews to come below cloud. Although the marshalling yards were not strongly defended the light flak batteries gave a good account of themselves, shooting down the Deputy, F/Lt C.J.K. Ash. They almost claimed a second victim, F/Lt H.M. Johnson and his crew. When Johnson broke cloud at 2,000 feet the target was directly below him so he turned to starboard intending to go round again to bomb. A light flak battery opened up and scored direct hits on the tail of the Lancaster. The rear turret was on fire with ammunition exploding and the elevator trimming tabs locked in a downward position leaving the aircraft in a shallow dive. The captain ordered 'abandon aircraft' but the intercom was unserviceable. He jettisoned the bombs 'safe' and, by exerting all his strength, managed to move the control column. The aircraft started to climb steeply. By gestures and shouting he repeated the order to bale out and the navigator, flight engineer, bomb-aimer and mid-upper all jumped from the front hatch. The rear gunner F/Sgt J.K. Ledgerwood, came forward and indicated that his parachute was in the rear turret which had fallen off. Johnson decided to try flying the Lancaster back to England and P/O R.T. Padden, the wireless operator, elected to stay and help. While the wireless operator and rear gunner were extinguishing the flames Johnson experimented with methods of controlling the aircraft and found that by varying the degrees of flap, he could control climb and glide, and by using the ailerons he could change direction. Padden sent out distress signals, plotted the fixes sent from England on the navigator's chart and gave the pilot alterations of course. Ledgerwood, although suffering from burns, manned the mid-upper turret. With Padden helping his captain to control the Lancaster they made a safe landing at Warmwell in Dorset.

At this time, 5 Group were operating their own design of *Controlled Visual* for which the preliminaries were broadly the same as 8 Group's, proximity markers and a flare force. 5 Group then sent in a Mosquito to mark the aiming point with Spot Fire TIs from a low level and these were backed up immediately, the whole attack being controlled from the same low level. Although such marking was on the average more accurate, this was not the sole reason for 5 Group's success: equally important was the fact that selected crews found a target wind, which was broadcast to the bombing force. 5 Group had often criticised Bennett's marking methods and now their new found freedom gave the crews an opportunity to prove that they could do better or die in the attempt. Some of their raids were outstanding but they had to pay the price: the loss rate in their Mosquito force was 1.538%; in *Oboe* Mosquitoes a mere 0.113% and the disparity in the heavy marker squadrons was 3.14% to 1.67%. The bomber force too suffered when there were 'hitches in the marking procedure' as Webster and Frankland put it in their appraisal of the method. On May 4 at Mailly-le-Camp 15% of the 346 crews were shot down and again at Lille, on the 10th, 13.5% were missing. These crews were not intercepted *en route*, they were waiting over the target for permission to bomb. These were not isolated cases.

Whereas crews bombing 8 Group markers were merely doing a job and were probably jealous of Pathfinders, 5 Group were bombing their own markers and seeking to prove themselves and this gave them the edge. An example of their desire to impress was the Juvisy raid on April 18. There is no denying that they demolished the target and incidently property in the vicinity but, it was estimated that 124 crews would be sufficient to destroy the yards, 5 Group sent 199.

Another hazard, if the TIs went out or were obliterated, it was almost impossible to remark the target; so they introduced 'Offset' marking.[4] A point away from the target was marked and selected crews worked out a false wind which all bomb-aimers used and whilst aiming at the TIs the bombs hit the target.

Webster and Frankland are wrong when they say that the accuracy of the markers was paramount.[5] A compact group of markers was an advantage but a good Master Bomber, combined with a cooperative bomber force, was far more effective. Their example at Brunswick on 22 April clearly illustrates the point: the accuracy of the groundmarkers was indisputable, the difficulty was to get 5 Group to bomb them.

5 Group attacks were always at the mercy of the weather and their main successes were when the target was clear. The argument is purely academic, ten months later, when 5 Group had recovered from their initial burst of fanaticism, ORS had Controlled *Oboe* attacks top of the accuracy league. Of far greater importance was that, long before D-Day the railway targets were damaged sufficiently to prevent the Germans rushing troops to the invasion area by rail; in fact from the beachheads in an arc of 300 miles radius there was complete chaos.

D-DAY PREPARATIONS The Transportation Plan was only part of the D-Day preparations, for the coastal defence guns had to be put out of action, W/T and radar stations had to be silenced, airfields in the area had to be made unserviceable and ammunition and petrol dumps destroyed. For every coastal or W/T station attacked in the *Neptune*[6] area, two outside it had to be attacked to keep the enemy from identifying the actual landing zone.

The attacks on military camps and ammunition and petrol dumps played only a small part in Bomber Command's build-up to the invasion. The military depots at Mailly-le-Camp, deep in France, and Bourg Leopold in Belgium were destroyed. Bourg Leopold was attacked twice in May, by 100 Halifaxes on the 11th and 300 Halifaxes and Lancasters of 4 and 6 Groups on the 27th. An *Oboe* TI on the aiming point set the standard for the second attack.

The Allied Air Forces had a list of almost 100 airfields which could profitably be attacked, but they did not figure high in Bomber Command's priorities. In May, small forces from 105 and 109 Squadrons bombed the airfields at Caen, Orly and Courtrai and marked Montdidier, Nantes and Rennes for the Main Force. The raid of May 3 on Montdidier was a family affair, 4 out of 8 Mosquitoes dropping preliminary markers

4. The technique was a modification of the method used by Pathfinders to change the A/Ps, at Peenemunde in August 1943.

5. The strategic Air Offensive against Germany.

6. Code name for Normandy invasion area.

for 84 Pathfinder heavies. One salvo of greens was on the tarmac in front of the hangers and the Master Bomber directed the attack on to them. S/Ldr J.M. Dennis and F/Lt H.C. Williams, the Deputy, were enthusiastic in their praise of the very concentrated bombing. The target was left covered with smoke and dust and a petrol explosion started a fierce fire. The attack was scheduled to take only 3 minutes. Bennett had four crews on the carpet, three for being 6 minutes late; the fourth, who was 11 minutes late, had the ignominy of having his aircraft letter[7] revealed in the monthly report. There were also caustic remarks about one or two crews who bombed a stray TI some 2,000 yards away: 'We should at least be able to expect the PFF not to be guilty of this stupid waste of bombs.'

S/Ldr E.K. Cresswell controlled an excellent raid at Nantes on May 7. The aiming point was between airfield buildings and a small adjoining factory. Cresswell and his able Deputy, S/Ldr E.J. Chidgey, put down a compact group of markers and, although the bomber force was fewer than 100, their bombing created so much smoke that 14 crews of 156 Squadron, briefed to bomb the factory visually, were forced to bomb the markers. The fires could be seen from 50 miles and there were six impressive explosions after the bombing stopped.

Rennes airfield, one of the most important bases in north-west France, was marked by 3 out of 5 Mosquitoes for an 8 Group attack on the 27th. One of the *Musical* markers was on the aiming point and crews could identify individual buildings, which was just as well because 35 Squadron said they did not hear the Master Bomber and No 405 reported a woman's voice jamming the VHF. Bombing was very concentrated, everyone taking careful aim. The whole area was covered with smoke and dust and the main hangars were ablaze. Impressive explosions were caused by the ammunition dump receiving a direct hit at 0145 hours: sadly this coincided with the moment the Deputy, S/Ldr H.W.B. Heney, was reinforcing the TIs and the Lancaster exploded, killing the crew.

There were 66 radar and W/T stations between Dunkirk and Brest, 42 of them, including six long-range radio stations, were destroyed before D-Day. Another 15 were unserviceable with the result that there was no radar cover on the Channel coast. Bomber Command was only concerned with four: Au Fevre, Berneval-le-Grand, Mont Couple and Ferme D'Urville. On May 19-20, at Mont Couple, both Mosquitoes failed to mark but the 'Y' aircraft, making a DR run from Cap Gris Nez, put down a compact group of markers for 100 Halifax bombers. The W/T station was made up of more than 60 transmitters, and after a second attack on May 31 they were almost wiped out. The same night the radar jammer at

7. Squadrons were allocated code letters which were painted on the left-hand side of the RAF roundels on the fuselage; each aircraft was also given an identifying letter which was painted on the right-hand side.

Au Fevre was put out of action and Berneval-le-Grand suffered a similar fate on June 2. The previous night Ferme D'Urville had been accurately marked, but cloud and haze had made bombing very difficult. The station, the headquarters of German Signals Intelligence Service in north-west France, overlooked the landing beaches and its destruction was therefore of vital importance. On June 3, 3 out of 4 *Oboe* Mosquitoes put down a concentrated group of markers and 99 Lancasters of 5 Group cleared the site; there was not a single mast left standing and all the HQ buildings had been completely flattened.

Coastal batteries from the Brest peninsular to the Scheldt were attacked and unfinished sites were included to discourage the enemy from completing the work and this was often successful. In all, 3,258 sorties were flown during the campaign which opened with an attack on St Valery-en-Caux on May 7, a month before D-Day; 50 attacks were made on 28 batteries, most of them being heavily damaged by the beginning of June. All the targets were marked by *Oboe* Mosquitoes and for the majority a Master Bomber and Deputy were in attendance. As a final bluff from June 2 to 4, ten batteries were attacked and, with one exception, all were in the Calais area.

Briefing in 8 Group on June 5 did not take place until 1815 hours but rumour was rife because it was a maximum effort. Although the word invasion was never mentioned, the stress laid on the importance of destroying the targets, the closeness of the batteries and 1,136 aircraft on battle orders made everyone think the Big Show was on. As briefing continued, speculation changed to almost certainty: no aircraft was to fly below 6,500 feet; no IFF (Identification Friend or Foe) was to be used outward or inward; no bombs were to be jettisoned in the English Channel; they had to be dropped either 'safe' over France or in the North Sea.

Operation *Flashlamp* called for 100 bombers on each of ten coastal batteries in the *Neptune* area.[8] The attacks were *Musical Parramattas* and all the aiming points were successfully marked. Harris claimed that the batteries were silenced with a single exception and that had only one gun firing. There is no actual proof that the guns were out of action because, although some were undoubtedly damaged and others destroyed, many of the batteries remained in enemy hands and certainly operated later. In one instance, where the battery was captured by the Allies, the German gunners were so dazed and shocked after the bombing they were incapable of fighting and this, probably more than any other reason, was why the guns were 'silent'.

Most of the Command were up the following night attacking railway

8. La Pernelle. Fontenay, St Martin-de-Varreville, Maisy, Pointe-du-Hoc, Longues, Mont Fleury, Ouistreham, Merville-Franceville and Houlgate.

yards and choke points just behind the enemy lines to seal off the battle zone from reinforcements of men and materials, and that was the pattern for the remainder of the week: the only crews with anything except railway lines in their bombsights were the 380 crews who attacked the airfields at Flers, Laval, Le Mans and Rennes on June 9.

Rennes was 8 Group's target and S/Ldr Cresswell, the Master Bomber, ordered Pathfinder crews to come below the cloud which he gave as 'basement six'.[9] Cresswell and his Deputy, F/Lt G.F. Lambert, guided by the Mosquito markers, had already dropped yellow TIs on the aiming point. Everything pointed to a successful attack; the target was covered in smoke and it was hoped the explosions were German fighters.

The heavy seas, which did so much damage to the Mulberry harbours, also drove a light force of enemy shipping into Le Havre. Its presence near the supply lines of men and materials crossing the Channel made its destruction vital and a cry for help, the first of many, went out to High Wycombe. On the evening of June 14, a force of 300 bombers in two waves carried out a devastating assault on the port. The attacks were Controlled *Oboe* attacks and the aircrews set about their task of destruction as if it were their own lives that depended on success. When the first phase arrived over the port at 2200 hours, the dock area was plainly visible in the evening light and the closely grouped groundmarkers pinpointed the target. Some 22 Lancasters of 617 Squadron each carrying a Tallboy[10] went in to blast holes in the concrete shelters.

When the second wave arrived, 2½ hours later, the maritime railway station was ablaze and fires were taking hold in the docks. The Master Bomber, F/Lt A.L.J. Craig, had put down yellow TIs, but they were quickly obliterated by Main Force bombs and the cycle of fires and explosions was repeated. Everyone was enthusiastic about the attacks and results measured up to expectations: 14 E-boats, 3 R-boats, 3 torpedo boats and 15 auxiliary vessels were destroyed and more than 1,000 marines killed. A similar raid on Boulogne the following day accounted for 7 R-boats, 6 mine sweepers, 3 depot ships and 9 auxiliary craft.

FLYING BOMBS Britain had been warned in 1939 that the Germans were developing rockets and agents named Peenemunde as the experimental station. One said that the launching sites were to be situated in the north of France and photographic reconnaissance showed concrete structures being erected in the Cherbourg peninsula and in the Pas de Calais. Peenemunde was attacked by Bomber Command (August 17, 1943) and the USAAF attacked Watten, one of the Pas de Calais sites, on August 27

---

9. Meaning the cloud base was 6,000 feet.

10. 12,000-pound bomb.

and September 7. They wreaked such havoc that it was easier to start afresh somewhere else than to try to repair the damage. After the connection between the French constructions had been definitely linked with 'V' weapons in December 1943, American and British air forces reopened their attacks on the sites. *Oboe* Mosquitoes were used extensively to mark for the RAF and they also led daylight formations with 2nd TAF Mosquitoes. The outcome of all this attention was to make the Germans realize that the sites were very vulnerable to air attack so they built modified sites which were smaller and more easily erected. The first of the new sites had been spotted at Belhamelin in the Cherbourg peninsula on April 27, 1944, but the air forces were too busy with *Overlord* to be diverted. When the first flying bomb exploded at Swanscombe near Gravesend at 0418 hours on Wednesday, June 13, V-1s became second in importance only to the absolute needs of *Overlord*.

As most of the sites were only lightly defended and fighters had few opportunities to intercept the bombers, losses were relatively low, but on June 23-24, when five V-1 sites were attacked, the German controllers, realizing all the activity was to be in the Pas de Calais area, sent the fighters westward. At 0025 hours, F/Lt B.G. Frow, Deputy Master Bomber on L'Hey, saw a Lancaster ahead of him being attacked by a Ju88. The bomb-aimer, F/O K. Milligan, was manning the front turret so Frow ordered him to fire and the mid-upper, W/O O.G. Erasmus, swung his turret and added his weight. The enemy, caught in a cross-fire, dived away. Five minutes later F/Lt E. Wharton, the rear gunner, saw an unidentified fighter coming in to attack and opened fire immediately. His aim was so true the combat was over in seconds; the fighter, hit in the starboard engine, dived away steeply towards the cloud and exploded.

The gunners, feverishly trying to clear stoppages, did not see an Me210 which came in from below, so Frow's first warning of the attack came when cannon shells ripped through the mainplane; the tailplane, fin and rudder were also damaged. Before the enemy could attack a second time Wharton and Erasmus had their guns working and a surprised German pilot had to dive for safety as machine-gun fire tore into the Messerschmitt. Frow set course for Woodbridge where he landed safely.

P/O G.A. Marsden was crossing the enemy coast between Dunkirk and Calais when his Lancaster was raked from stem to stern by cannon fire: the port petrol tank was holed, the booster pump shot away, the H2S blew up, the bomb-doors and fuselage were damaged, both turrets were put out of action and the gunners, Sgts H.J.W. Furner and N.A. Farley, seriously wounded. The fighter was lost by evasive action, which was just as well, because it was doubtful if the Lancaster could have survived a second onslaught. S/Ldr B.F.H. Ingram, the Master Bomber on Coubronne, was one of five Pathfinders missing from the night's sorties: he was heard directing the attack so it was presumed he was shot down after leaving the target.

On June 29, the attack at Siracourt was planned as a Controlled *Oboe* and when the Master Bomber, F/Lt S.E.C. Clarke, went below cloud to assess the TIs he was shot down by flak and some impatient crews from 1 Group, seeing the airfield near St Pol, started to attack it. F/Lt Frow, the Deputy, realizing something was wrong, took command and directed the bombers on to the correct target. Five days later at St Martin L'Hortier it was Frow's turn to be hit by flak; he flew too close to Neufchatel and one burst of light flak damaged an engine. However, he completed his duties as Master Bomber before returning to base where he made a safe landing on three engines.

When northern France was 10/10ths cloud-covered *Oboe* Mosquitoes and *Oboe*-equipped Lancasters led small formations of bombers, the formations dropping their bombs on a signal from the leading aircraft. Three different methods were used:

(i) Crews released when they saw the bombs dropping from the aircraft in front.

(ii) For larger formations later crews waited 2 seconds before releasing.

(iii) The leader fired a Smoke Puff and crews released when the aircraft came level with it.

The first in the series was flown by 109 Squadron in conjunction with 156 Squadron: W/Cdr K.J. Somerville and F/Lt H.A. Scott of 109 Squadron, flying with F/Lt H.F. Morrish and his crew in an *Oboe* Lancaster, led 6 Lancasters, also from 156 Squadron, to Nucourt on July 15; S/Ldr D.H.S. Kay and F/Lt W.L. Reinhart of 109 Squadron, in a Mosquito, acted as reserve. Three formations were flown to the same target in the afternoon: W/Cdr G.F. Grant, CO of 109 Squadron, flying a second *Oboe* Lancaster, led crews from 582 Squadron and two pairs of Mosquitoes from 105 Squadron led 6 Lancasters from each of 156 and 35 Squadrons. All made successful runs, but 35 Squadron were taken by surprise when S/Ldr J.D.G. Bishop dived away because of PD (precision device) failure. The Lancaster crews, not understanding the vagaries of *Oboe*, began to follow him, but F/Lt L.J. Holland took over the lead quickly and efficiently and order was restored. As the crews became more proficient, the numbers were increased and the formations became tighter. This method of bombing gave the highest density achieved by Bomber Command; 7.44% per acre, as opposed to its nearest rival, visual bombing, 4.18%.

Trossy St Maximin, a V-1 storage depot close to the main one at St Leu d'Esserent, had been attacked by strong forces of Lancasters on the Wednesday and Thursday so, when 61 Lancasters from 8 Group approached on Friday, August 4, the defences were primed for action. Of 14 crews from 635 Squadron, eight were damaged by flak and two were shot down. The Master Bomber, W/Cdr D.W.S. Clark, had his starboard elevator damaged and the whole of the fuselage peppered by flak; and his Deputy, F/Lt R.W. Beveridge, was shot down. F/Lt F.W. Healey saw Beveridge hit by flak as he made a run across the target to assess the markers dropped by 4 out of 5 *Oboe* Mosquitoes; the Lancaster burst into flames and nose-dived into the ground. In clear skies, Clark found no difficulty in identifying the aiming point and directing the attack using *Oboe* markers as a guide. The bombing force, all from PFF obeyed the instructions: dust and smoke quickly enveloped the TIs and those who had not bombed were told to aim at the centre of the smoke – most crews logged an enormous explosion towards the end of the raid.

S/Ldr I.W. Bazalgette[11] was nearing the target when his Lancaster was engaged by heavy flak in barrage form. Both the starboard engines were put out of action, the starboard mainplane and fuselage were set on fire and his bomb-aimer, F/Lt I.A. Hibbert, seriously wounded. The Squadron Leader pressed on to the target while the crew tried to put out the fires. Immediately the bombs left the aircraft it went into a spin, but by expert airmanship and using all his strength, Bazalgette managed to regain control. The fire in the starboard mainplane had never gone out completely and the dive seemed to fan the flames. The crippled aircraft struggled on for 30 miles and then the port engine seized. Bazalgette ordered 'abandon aircraft' but the crew, concerned over the wounded Hibbert, and the mid-upper, F/Sgt V.V.R. Leeder, who had been overcome by fumes, were reluctant to leave. The skipper assured them he would try to crash-land the aircraft so they baled out from 1,000 feet.

The people from the village of Senantes saw the burning Lancaster approaching, then saw it veer away as if the pilot was making sure it did not crash on them. Using all his skill, Bazalgette made a superb landing in a field. All to no avail, for the Lancaster exploded almost immediately and he and his two commrades were killed. Everybody in the village turned out to honour the gallant airman, and the Mayor wrote a letter of sympathy to his mother. When his crew arrived back in England the whole story was pieced together and Bazalgette was awarded the Victoria Cross.

The attacks on the flying-bomb storage depots like Trossy St Maximin and the three larger ones at Nucourt, St Leu d'Esserent and Rilly la Montagne, probably did more to stem the flow of V-1s than the attacks on the launching pads. Bomber Command made three attacks on Nucourt and two on St Leu d'Esserent. Altogether 44,335 tons of bombs were dropped on the sites and the depots, but, in truth, the bombing proved to be only a deterrent – although 25 sites were completely destroyed, there

11. The citation for his VC says he was the Master Bomber. This is incorrect: the recommendation said he had been a Master Bomber on several occasions and this was misinterpreted in the citation. The fact that he was not the Master Bomber on this occasion in no way detracts from his valour; it underlines his continued devotion to duty.

was no respite until the ground forces overran the Pas de Calais at the end of August.

Marquise Mimoyecques was repeatedly attacked by Bomber Command, yet little useful damage was done to the huge concrete constructions until 617 Squadron dropped 12,000-pounders on them, and even so it would not have prevented the Germans from using the site. With such a glorious name it was fitting that some mystery should surround its real purpose, which was not known until after it fell into Allied hands. Initially associated with flying bombs, it was in fact an underground 6-inch, multi-barrel, long-range gun battery. The guns, which were never used, were designed to fire shells with collapsible fins which came into position when the shells left the barrel, giving them more stability and greater accuracy even at extreme range; the muzzle velocity was almost 5,000 feet per second.

It would be ungracious not to mention both the 2nd TAF's and the USAAF 's part in the battle against the 'V' weapons and, in particular, the attacks by the Americans on the larger sites, the storage depots and the special fuel plant at Fallersleben. By making 'V' weapons second in priority only to the needs of Allied ground forces, Eisenhower, too, showed his concern was genuine.

CHAOS CONTINUED Even after the bridgehead had been established and the Allies had forced their way out of the *Neptune* area, the attacks on the marshalling yards continued. In June PFF marked 32 rail centres and 13 strategic choke points.

At Douai on June 14, German fighters intercepted the bombers and the Master Bomber, F/Lt J.H. Hewitt, was shot down over the target. F/O G.S. Magee had just dropped his bombs when he was attacked by an Me410; the fighter pilot made three assaults on the Lancaster but his aim did not match his enthusiasm. F/Lt G.P.A. Yates was intercepted on his way to Metz on June 28 but it was the Fw190 which was shot down in flames, exploding on the ground.

On July 4, when 100 Main Force bombers did some concentrated bombing at Villeneuve St George, a famous Pathfinder, S/Ldr A.P. Cranswick, lost his life after marking the target. He had to go down to 8,000 feet to get below the cloud, to give himself a clear run to the aiming point. The light from flares silhouetted the Lancaster against the cloud background and just after releasing his TIs the aircraft was hit by flak. Flames swept the length of the bomber and Cranswick ordered everybody out, but only F/Sgt W.R. Horner escaped from the flying inferno. Another Backer-up, S/Ldr G.F. Lambert, was also shot down in flames.

Fire was the major agent of destruction of aircraft shot down by the enemy, whether from the ground or by fighters. A severely damaged aircraft often got its crew back to England even if it had to be written off later. This was the significant difference between Cranswick's death and F/Lt R.G. Williams's survival. At Vaires on July 12, flak gunners scored a direct hit on Williams's Lancaster; both starboard engines were put out of action and the instrument panel was shattered, the H2S was hit and the undercarriage locked down. To add to his problems a 500-lb bomb with a long-delay fuse hung-up. Williams made a valiant effort to get back to base but flying an aircraft without instruments and with the power all on one side was a big strain physically and mentally and the flare path at Rivenhall proved too big a temptation.

In all, 12 marshalling yards were attacked in July and seven in August. The last raids in this series took place on August 18-19 when Connantre and Ghent/Terneuzen were the targets. At Connantre an *Oboe* red in the marshalling yard set the standard for the attack and illuminating flares enabled all aircraft to see the aiming point. A train had to be halted just outside the yards and its progress was very doubtful for some time. At Ghent/Terneuzen markers and bombing were well concentrated and several explosions were reported. The tempo of the Allied advance made Eisenhower realize that the Transportation Plan had outlived its usefulness, for further bombing would hinder the Allies more than the retreating Germans.

Bomber Command's part in the destruction of enemy airfields was a small one. After the four attacks on June 9 there followed only three in July, but in August, when the ground forces were breaking out of the bridgehead, 23 sorties were made against 12 airfields in France, Belgium and Holland, the largest effort being on August 15.

Tuesday, August 15, was a gorgeous summer day and Harris sent more than 700 bombers to attack seven airfields in the Low Countries,[12] the accompanying Spitfires being aptly described as a 'fighter parasol'. Pathfinder crews map-reading their way to the targets indulged their navigators with a plethora of pinpoints. All the aiming points were efficiently marked by the Controlled Visual method and, with the exception of St Trond where the Main Force was late, the Master Bombers had no problems: crews treated the operations as a bomb-aiming exhibition.

In September, the main assault took place on the 3rd, when 500 bombers were sent to the Low Countries to cover the push across the Pas de Calais. Venlo, Eindhoven, Gilze Rigen and Soesterberg were attacked, the same excellence in marking and bombing being achieved. The German gunners at Venlo, however, proved very unfriendly; they damaged S/Ldr A.J.L. Craig's Lancaster putting both starboard engines out of action. The Squadron Leader beat a hasty retreat to Woodbridge, keeping

---

12. Eindhoven, Soesterberg, Volkel, Brussels-Melsbroek, St Trond, Tirlemont Gossoncourt, Le Culot.

his crew occupied jettisoning everything that was movable, in order to maintain height. Craig was the Master Bomber so he handed over to F/Lt F. Wilson, who in turn was hit. Although one engine seized and the bomb-doors jammed open, Wilson stayed and controlled the attack, his gunners taking every opportunity to fire on the flak batteries.

GROUND SUPPORT The first request for Bomber Command to help Allied troops in a purely tactical manner came on June 30. A large concentration of enemy tanks had been massed at a cross roads on the western side of Villers Bocage preparatory to an attack later in the day. To give this support 254 heavies and 10 Mosquitoes set out on Bomber Command's largest daylight operation to date. The attack was by Controlled *Oboe* and, although there was little cloud in the target area, the Master Bomber, S/Ldr B.W. MacMillan, brought the Main Force down to 4,000 feet to make certain they could see the TIs clearly. He marshalled his force in exemplary fashion giving fresh instructions as each group of markers was dropped. The target, roughly the size of Wembley Stadium, was demolished. F/O D.Tidy, of 105 Squadron, who waited in the target area until the dust and smoke had cleared, reported that the five roads were plainly visible but at the junction it looked as if an enormous excavation had taken place.

Harris said that Bomber Command was capable of putting down a barrage equal to 4,000 guns; what was required to be proved was that it could be done without endangering Allied troops. The test came on July 7, when 2,363 tons of HE were dropped on Caen by 457 Halifaxes and Lancasters in the space of 38 minutes, with Allied troops only 2,000 yards away. British and Canadian troops had launched a strong attack on the city but were encountering extremely stiff opposition from the enemy entrenched in the northern suburbs. Bomber Command's task was to blast these strong-points. W/Cdr S.B. Daniels was in charge of the Controlled *Oboe* attacks and, although clouds of dust and smoke soon obscured ground detail, the flow of markers was continuous throughout both phases and under Daniels's guidance the Main Force turned in a fine piece of concentrated bombing. Spectacular explosions were commonplace and, by the time the bombers left, the German defence positions were a mass of rubble. British troops did not advance until the following morning yet they found the German troops dazed and bewildered with little or no will to resist – the after-effects of the bombardment.

At dawn on July 18 five aiming points at Colombelles, Mondeville, Sannerville, Manneville and Cagny were bombed and British forces finally broke through the ring of armour pinning them down at Caen. More than 5,000 tons of HE were dropped by Bomber Command and 349 medium bombers of AEAF dropped fragmentation bombs.

Pathfinders provided Master Bombers on all the aiming points but, because of complete failure at one of the ground stations, only four were marked by *Oboe* Mosquitoes. S/Ldr Cresswell and S/Ldr Chidgey were Master and Deputy at Manneville where, despite the *Musical* failure, a very successful attack was made. Chidgey put down accurate yellows which were efficiently backed-up and under Cresswell's guidance the Main Force bombing was highly concentrated. At Cagny, where 30 crews of 3 Group joined 71 from Pathfinders, everyone spoke with enthusiasm of the excellent concentration of bombing and a huge pall of smoke glowing red at the base confirmed the reports. All 16 crews from 7 Squadron had A/P photographs.

Cloud down to 2,000 feet in the Caumont area on July 30 marred Bomber Command's fourth foray in support of the ground forces. *Oboe* Mosquitoes marked six aiming points but only two were destroyed. On three of them the Master Bombers had been ordered not to attack below 3,000 feet while at a fourth, although the glow of TIs could be seen, the Master Bomber deemed it unwise to attack because of the proximity of Allied troops.

Zero hour for Operation *Totalize* was 2300 hours on August 7 when PFF marked the first of five strong-points set up by the Germans to delay the Allied advance until they regrouped further south. Accuracy in timing, marking and bombing were required because Allied troops, who had retreated 2,000 yards, planned to move into May-sur-Orne and La Hogue as the bombers attacked Fontenay-le-Marmion, Sequeville and Mare de Magne. Allied ground forces were briefed to fire red star shells and Bofors tracer shells over the targets and searchlights were supposed to cone the target areas.

There were 200 bombers detailed for each aiming point with only a ten-minute interval between the waves and the concentration seemed to be beyond the capabilities of the Main Force. At La Hogue, Fontenay-le-Marmion and Sequeville the Master Bombers had to call off the attacks because the TIs had burnt out before the full complement had bombed, but they had no complaints about the bombing which was very accurate. They did remark on the lack of support from the ground forces, which ranged from negligible to nil. At May-sur-Orne, S/Ldr T.E. Ison, the Master Bomber, needed all the support he could get as 4 Group crews were in one of their truculent moods, but there were no tracers or searchlights and only a few star shells were fired. When Ison warned the crews they were undershooting, several captains cut in with unprintable remarks and, as the bombing did not improve, he called off the attack.

On the last aiming point at Mare de Magne W/Cdr B.W. McMillan reported that ground co-operation was excellent. It was 8 Group's target and, as would be expected, the bombing was very concentrated: 100 Lancasters from 3 Group and 60 Halifaxes from 4 Group contributed to a very fine attack. The troops were able to pass through the gap without meeting any organized resistance and almost without loss.

Cloud conditions made the task of S/Ldr Frow very difficult on August 12-13 when a mixed force of 175 Lancasters, Halifaxes and Stirlings attacked the road junction north of Falaise. Specialist Visual Bomb-aimers, men with extensive Primary Visual Marker experience, were being carried by Marker crews for attacks requiring the utmost precision: their duties were to pinpoint the target and advise which markers to back up. Because F/Lt P.H. Crutchley performed his duty so proficiently that night there was always a plentiful supply of closely grouped ground-markers and this allowed Frow to concentrate on giving directions to the bombing force and they in turn followed his instructions. He was able to report several large explosions followed by fires, a mushroom of smoke billowing through the cloud tops as pointers to a very successful attack.

The USAAF had hit some of their own troops at St Lo on July 25 but to date, even under the appalling conditions of July 30, there had been no casualties from British bombs. Perhaps everyone was getting *blasé:* 4 Group's attitude and the ground force's mediocre effort to help the bombers on August 7 point to this conclusion but – what in hindsight seems to have been inevitable – tragically some Canadian troops were hit during Operation *Tractable* on August 14. There was a series of contributory factors which combined to make the error plausible but neither singly nor collectively did they make it excusable.[13] The army wanted the most northerly targets attacked first and, although it was pointed out that smoke might spread to the other targets, they said they would take the risk. The route took the bombers over Allied troops and when they saw the bomb-doors open they panicked and started firing yellow smoke flares and lit celanese strips[14] which looked like TIs and some crews bombed them. To make matters worse an impuslive army officer leapt into an Auster and flew up and down the lines firing off red Very cartridges which merely added more realism from the marking angle. But there was no mitigation. It was a daylight attack in clear weather, crews being briefed to make a timed run from the coast and in no circumstances to bomb before ETA; it was a good Gee area; there was no opposition; and the Master Bombers were directing them on to the correct TIs.

There were seven A/Ps and all were marked *Musically* at intervals of 18 minutes. Two strong points at Quesnay were attacked at 1400 and 1418 hours, the Master Bombers, W/Cdr H.A. Morrison and W/Cdr W.T. Brooks, warning crews of the dangers of undershooting particularly when

---

13. Guilty crews, where known, were court-martialled. In the enquiry all Master Bombers were completely exonerated.

14. This was normal practice with ground support aircraft but somewhere between Army HQ, High Wycombe and the Groups the information got lost.

the TIs became obscured by smoke and dust. The attack then moved on to Saumont St Quentin, this being the PFF target, augmented by 60 of 4 Group. The Deputy, F/Lt P.G. McCarthy, dropped yellows on the A/P and S/Ldr A.J.L. Craig ordered crews to bomb them. After five minutes of highly concentrated bombing they became obscured by dust and smoke and from 1441 to 1449 hours, 13 Halifaxes from 4 Group and 1 Lancaster from 8 Group[15] dropped their bombs on St Aignan, well short of the A/P, hitting our troops. Craig took immediate action preventing more crews from committing the same error.

Bons Tassilly was the most southerly A/P and W/Cdr T.L. Bingham-Hall had no trouble with the 100 crews from 6 Group. However, between 1514 and 1518 hours, 14 out of 120 crews also from 6 Group bombed St Aignan instead of the road junction between Aisy and Poigny, where once again the Deputy, F/O H.G.E. Hemsworth, had marked with yellows. The Master Bomber, W/Cdr D.M. Walbourn, seeing the undershooting, blistered the Main Force, told them he would re-mark the target ordering them to watch closely where his TIs cascaded, but in the meantime 23 impatient crews had bombed a quarry near Le Mesnil where Allied armoured vehicles were stationed.

W/Cdr S. Baker, the Master Bomber on Fontaine-le-Pin ordered the crews in his wave to come down to 3,000 feet so they could see the accurately placed TIs. In spite of this precaution, between 1532 and 1539 hours, 26 crews of 1 Group also dropped bombs in the quarry. The other 74 bombers flattened the village.

On the last strong point, the Aisy, Ussy and Potigny road junction, bombing was well concentrated but soon the dust and smoke obliterated the TIs and, as the whole area was covered with drifting dust and smoke cloud, F/Lt J. Ford ordered crews to 'abandon mission'. The main objective had been achieved, the way was clear for the first Canadians to advance into Falaise.

COASTAL FORTRESSES The bombing of the coastal batteries, the wrecking of the transport systems, the close army support, even the destruction of the wireless stations undoubtedly saved thousands of soldiers' lives. It would be impossible even to guess how many but the Battle of the Fortresses gives a clear indication how air power made life easier for the man on the ground. The Allies, anticipating the Germans would blow up the port installations to render them useless to the invaders, by-passed the main ports and pushed on towards Brussels and Paris, leaving a token force to stop them breaking out and harassing from the rear or cutting the supply

15. The captain stated there was a fault in the bombing mechanism; the bombs fell when the bomb-doors were opened.

lines. With but one exception, Brest, it was left to the RAF to bomb them into submission. Le Havre was perhaps the most rewarding and Walcheren the most spectacular. The USAAF combined with Bomber Command in the attacks on Brest and the assaults were made in conjunction with the naval forces who were anxious to prevent any German vessels escaping from the port. Eight of the attacks were made by Bomber Command, beginning with a bombardment on the gun emplacements on August 5 and terminating on September 2 with an attack against ships in the dry docks.

At Le Havre after a week of bombardment (September 5-11), when 949 tons of bombs were dropped in seven attacks, Col Eberard Wildemuth surrendered the garrison of 11,300 men, in spite of an order from Hitler to fight to the last man. The cost to Allied ground forces was a mere 50 soldiers. Six of the seven attacks were marked by 8 Group and on each occasion more than one strong point was attacked.

On September 8 the five aiming points were 7-8/10ths cloud-covered wtih base varying from 1,000 feet to 4,000 feet, tops 8,000 feet. W/Cdr H.A. Morrison on the third A/P caught a glimpse of the *Oboe* TIs as he approached the target and ordered the crews to orbit until he found the cloud base. He made three runs going lower each time and on the fourth broke cloud at 1,000 feet to be greeted by three bursts of flak which ripped off the starboard aileron, damaged the starboard wing and set the mainplane ablaze. The Lancaster was uncontrollable so he jettisoned his HE and ordered 'abandon aircraft'. The aircraft crashed on the shore, the TIs exploded and everyone was killed except W/O W. Hubiak, the rear gunner, the only crew member who had time to bale out.

On September 10, when eight separate coastal batteries were marked, the areas were given names of motor cars for reasons best known to the raid planners; Buick I and II, Alvis I to IV and Bentley I and II. Because of the nearness of Allied troops, in addition to the Master Bombers and Deputy Master Bombers, a Long Stop[16] was added to control the whole attack. His duty was to cancel any wild marking or bombing by dropping yellow TIs. When Buick II was covered with smoke he advised the Master Bomber to abandon the mission because the Main Force was tending to overshoot. On Alvis IV, the Main Force got too enthusiastic when a bomb dump exploded and he stepped in to help the Master Bomber, S/Ldr M.S. Mingard. On Bentley II, although the Master Bomber, W/Cdr. B.H.D. Foster, ordered crews to bomb the accurate *Oboe* greens, many crews continued to bomb the less accurate reds, so G/Capt P.H. Cribb put down a 'not beyond this point' line of yellows to help him. The remaining two

---

16. In the first instance, Master Bombers carried yellow TIs which were called Long Stops, but later, to distinguish the role from that of the Master Bomber, the term became personalized.

strong points, Cadillac I and II, were attacked on September 11. The Long Stop had no worries: the Main Force were well behaved and did some excellent bombing on accurate TIs. The next day the Germans surrendered.

The single demonstration of the might of Bomber Command on September 17, when 762 bombers dropped 3,347 tons of HE, was sufficient for the Commander at Boulogne and more than 9,500 prisoners were taken. In August and September, 6,017 bombers dropped 28,346 tons of bombs on the fortresses for a loss of 21 aircraft; the highest casualties occurred on September 24 when 127 bombers attacked Calais. Five aiming points were marked by 21 out of 25 *Oboe* Mosquitoes with a Master Bomber, Deputy, Backer-up and 30 bombers on each. The ground defences, helped by low cloud, had a successful day. Seven crews were shot down, including the Long Stop, F/Lt K.P.C. Doyle, and many other bombers were damaged. F/O D.G. Murray, a Master Bomber, was making a run to assess the markers, when the Lancaster's starboard outer was hit and, as it would not feather, he handed over to the Deputy, F/O R.P. Roberts, and retreated to Manston. In turn, the Deputy's Lancaster was hit and the control column was affected so he handed over to the Backer-up, 2nd Lt S.J. Hausvik. As the 2nd Lt made his run to assess the TIs, his Lancaster was hit and the starboard inner had to be feathered; on the second run to drop his markers the port inner was damaged but he continued to control the attack until all the aircraft had bombed.

Two Master Bombers were in the firing line on September 26. W/Cdr C.W. Palmer was shot down three miles south of the target, the TIs exploded and, although the Long Stop put down a line of yellows, some crews still bombed in that area. W/Cdr R.W. Cox's Lancaster was hit by flak, the elevator controls were cut and the control column jammed. The Wing Commander climbed to 4,000 feet and made directly for Woodbridge.

After six attacks between September 20 and 28, Calais capitulated. Nearby at Cap Gris Nez, after two air attacks on September 26 and 28, when 3,700 tons of bombs were dropped, the army had only to mop up the dazed and bemused defenders. In less than a month, Bomber Command had cleared the Germans from the Channel ports: 8 Group spearheaded the vast majority of the attacks and *Oboe* Mosquitoes dropped the initial markers.

Antwerp was taken by the army on September 4 with the port facilities almost intact, but the Germans held on grimly to the mouth of the Scheldt preventing the Allies from using it. The fortress of Walcheren, and to a lesser degree, Fort Fredrich Hendrich and Breskens controlled the approaches to the port so once again a call to High Wycombe brought the army's 'long-range artillery' into action.

Between September 16 and 23, six attacks were made on four gun emplacements on the Island of Walcheren, but there seemed to be no rhyme or reason behind the attacks. The weight was insufficient to blast the gunners into submission and there was no follow-up by the army or navy. It was obvious more drastic measures would be necessary to capture the Island so, on October 3, in daylight, eight successive waves of bombers, 30 in each wave, attacked the sea wall near West Kapelle. *Oboe* Mosquitoes put down the initial markers for each wave and 4 PFF Lancasters backed them up. Accurate marking, combined with controlled bombing, breached the dykes without the aid of 617 Squadron's 12,000-pounders. It was thought that it might require one or two Tallboys to loosen the 200-feet-thick foundations but the concentrated pounding from the Main Force was sufficient. The breach was made during the fifth wave's attack and the sea water began to cover the fields and encroach on the borders of the town. All the efforts of the sixth wave were concentrated on widening the gap. Cloud had been thickening throughout the attack and the seventh and eighth waves merged into one as G/Capt Cribb, the Master Bomber, exhorted the crews to come below the 2,500 feet cloud base to bomb. The breach was widened and by the end of the attack the sea was rushing through a break of more than 100 yards.

The ground forces made no immediate attempt to follow up, in fact they sat back and watched the bombers drive the Germans out of Fort Fredrich Hendrich and Breskens, pound the gun sites on Walcheren and make a second breach at Flushing. The Marines did not go in until November 1, four weeks after the initial flooding, and after eight days of mopping up the last Germans had surrendered.

OIL Eisenhower had plumped for the Transportation Plan because it might help the invasion whereas the Oil Plan was a long-term policy. After the Allies were established on the Continent, he asked Harris to co-operate in attacking oil targets chiefly in the Ruhr area. General Spaatz had continued his attacks on oil, but the Americans were naturally reluctant to send their formations deep into Happy Valley through the most concentrated ground defences in the world.

The Germans too realized how much their mobility depended on oil and shortly after the invasion Edmund Gielenburg was put in charge of restoring damaged plant. Special safety precautions for plant and workers were introduced, ground defences were increased, and smoke screens and decoys were intensified. The first attack by the Main Force was on the Nordstern plant near Gelsenkirchen on June 12-13. The raid was a *Musical Parramatta*, and the six Backers-up did some precise bomb-aiming so the reds and greens were closely grouped around the aiming point. In the initial stages, the bombing was very concentrated, the whole plant being heavily damaged. Bomber Command estimated that it would be out of production at least until the end of July. A stray red TI which probably fell when a Mosquito opened its bomb-doors, was at least 10 miles from the target, yet more than thirty crews bombed it. On June 16-17 at the Holten plant, Sterkrade, crews had to bomb the glow of TIs just visible through 10/10ths cloud. Bombing was more scattered than at Nordstern but useful damage was done, nine separate units being affected.

Two attacks led by 5 Group over 10/10ths cloud on June 20-21 were disastrous; neither of the plants received any notable damage and over 17% of the force was shot down. Four weeks later, Pathfinders marked the same targets; at Scholven two explosions followed by fires and thick black smoke told their own story. Nearby at Wesseling, the report was almost identical. From the two raids only five bombers were missing. Two nights later (July 20-21) at Homburg the Main Force kept up its previous standard, but at Bottrop, where the thick ground haze reduced the TIs to a dull red glow, bombing was scattered. The presence of nightfighters in the target area may have been a contributory factor: 28 bombers were shot down.

Two attacks on Donges on the nights of July 23 and 24 began a four-week assault on the storage depots and refineries in occupied territory. The spectacular results from attacks on oil targets afforded crews great satisfaction. Risk was measured against achievement; explosions, raging fires and thick clouds of smoke made it all worthwhile.

Although buildings at Donges could be seen in the fires, the daylight attacks on Pauillac near Bordeaux, on August 4 and 5, afforded the Master Bombers better opportunity to direct the Main Force: in good visibility they could pick out individual buildings and bomb-aimers were able to drop their loads with greater accuracy. After the success of August 4, when flames and smoke could be seen from 100 miles, 96 crews attacked the adjacent depot the next day. The Master Bomber, W/Cdr J.B. Voyce, chose a large building near the aiming point as easily identifiable and directed the attack on to it. Crews trying to emulate their friends of the previous day soon destroyed it. Then, towards the end of the raid, Voyce noticed that a line of oil tanks had miraculously escaped damage, so he directed the bombers on to them. Determined to leave nothing standing, the Main Force did some excellent bombing and almost immediately the area was ablaze. When Voyce left the target, fires were raging and a pall of thick black smoke, rising to 6,000 feet, covered the area. Close by, at Bassens, drifting cloud made bombing difficult but crews waited patiently for a gap in order to make a good bombing run. On the east bank of the Gironde at Blaye a third force set fire to the storage tanks and the target area was soon enveloped in smoke.

Targets hidden in woods were *Oboe's métier* and on 8 and 9 August,

105 and 109 Squadrons marked four oil dumps.[17] Aided by their markers, the Master Bombers had no difficulty in identifying the aiming points and at de-briefing it was the same story from all the attacks; fires, explosions and smoke obliterated the target.

For the last attacks in this pleasant diversion, the attention switched to Belgium: Ertvelde-Reime, on the canal between Ghent and Terneuzen, was attacked on August 18-19. The daylight attack was a Controlled *Oboe* and the Master Bomber, W/Cdr D.M. Walbourn, exhorted the small force to come below cloud. Those who did started some good fires whereas the less adventurous tended to bomb short of the TIs. The Controlled *Newhaven* attack in the evening, by 113 bombers, rekindled the fires and started new ones. The Master Bomber, S/Ldr R.B. Roache, found the Main Force more amenable to advice and the bombing was consequently concentrated. He reported that the whole area was ablaze, the heat causing many explosions and, when he left the target, smoke was rising to 4,000 feet.

Towards the end of the Battle of Berlin when Harris was asking the Chiefs of Staff for a large force of protective nightfighters the possiblity of daylight bombing was discussed. Harris was totally against the idea, but in June when the *Luftwaffe* had made only a few forays over the invasion beaches, Portal and Churchill thought the idea worth trying. The attack of June 14, on Le Havre docks was made in the evening and subsequently daylight attacks over France were increased. At night, the *Luftwaffe* was far from a spent force and when the nightfighters intercepted the bombers the toll was always heavy. The 5 Group attacks at Scholven and Wesseling and the Main Force attack on Bottrop proved the point, even when the penetration was only as far as the Ruhr. Unlike the Americans, British crews could not fly in tight formation to protect themselves but the *Luftwaffe* had made no attempts to intercept the bombers in daylight, unless they were making deep penetrations into Germany. Consequently, the only unknown factor was how much more effectively the ground defences could operate in daylight. Bomber Command's 'gaggle' might be advantageous in these circumstances because the AA gunners would have to shoot at individual aircraft. Only a trial by battle could answer the question so, on August 27, Harris sent 216 Halifaxes to Homburg plumb in the middle of Happy Valley, for this first daylight attack in strength on the Ruhr. *Oboe* Mosquitoes, flying in pairs [18] were detailed to open the attack and mark the target at intervals. All but one of the seven pairs made successful runs and Pathfinder Lancasters backed-up their reds. The 5-8/10ths cloud made bombing difficult but most crews saw the TIs.

---

17. Foret de Chantilly, Foret de Lucheux, Foret de Mormal and Foret d'Englos.

18. A primary and a reserve flying in formation so that, if the primary failed, the reserve aircraft would be ideally placed to take over the run.

The cloud also hindered the anti-aircraft guns; the Spitfires drove off a lone German fighter, so there were no losses.

Between the last attack on Le Havre (September 11) and the one on Boulogne (September 17) Bomber Command made a three-day assault on six Ruhr oil refineries. A total of 945 aircraft were involved in these attacks and 18 were shot down, none of them by fighters; seven were from PFF, a loss rate of 5.6%, and, in addition, their damage rate was very high.

From 13 Lancasters of 156 Squadron detailed to attack Gelsenkirchen on September 11, one was shot down and ten were badly damaged by flak. S/Ldr P.A. Williams's Lancaster was one of five from 582 Squadron damaged in the Castrop Rauxel raid. The starboard inner received a direct hit and the starboard outer was hit twice; the DR compass was rendered unserviceable and the tailplane was damaged. There were eight flak holes in the bomb-bay, five in the fuselage and two in the mainplane.

The following day, at Wanne-Eickel, 6 out of 12 Lancasters from 405 Squadron were damaged and one was shot down. F/Lt V.T. Woods, whose Lancaster had been badly damaged the previous day at Castrop Rauxel, saw the Lancaster in front of him hit by flak and explode, but as he was on his bombing run he had to press on and his Lancaster received two direct hits which tore gaping holes in the petrol tanks. Knowing he was running short of fuel, Woods had fortunately kept some height in hand for, on approaching the Suffolk coast, all four engines stopped and he had to glide the last 5 miles into Woodbridge.

These attacks shew the mettle of Pathfinder crews: to mark targets accurately against such fierce opposition required courage of the highest order. The PFF Lancasters, who marked Kamen on September 11, merit special mention; their attack was a Controlled Visual. The Master Bomber S/Ldr A.J.L. Craig, his Deputy S/Ldr R.P. Stroud and the Primary Visual Markers put down a compact group of markers and 'smoke to 15,000 feet from a flaming base' was the graphic description of the attack. Four sorties to Bottrop and Sterkrade on September 27 and 30 only served to prove that they were equally well defended.

GERMAN TOWNS After three weeks of self-denial, Harris switched part of his force to German targets and between April 20 and 27, Cologne, Brunswick, Dusseldorf, Munich, Karlsruhe, Essen and Friedrichshafen were bombarded. The heaviest raid was on April 22, when 567 out of 596 bombers severely retarded the Dusseldorf *Gauleiter's* rehousing competition. Although only 5 out of 12 Mosquitoes coped, the backing-up was of a high order and the *Oboe* reds had a recentering effect. The two Rheinmetal Borsig factories were extensively damaged and, as almost half of the Berlin branch had been destroyed on November 26, 1943, this new damage was a serious blow to their production figures.

Harris, in his 'Despatch', described the Friedrichshafen raid on April 27-28, as one of the most outstanding raids of the war: all six factories of importance were completely devastated. The aiming point, identified and successfully marked by PFF, was so placed that any creepback would be over the town. In the event it was only the incendiaries that dropped short, most of the HE falling in the marked area. The zero hour was changed in flight and S/Ldr Cresswell, the Master Bomber, whose wireless receiver was unserviceable, arrived late on target, but he directed the attack after the TIs had burnt out thus ensuring that no bombs were wasted.

Nineteen aircraft failed to return but news of one of them, captained by W/O R.G. Peters, came from the British Embassy in Switzerland. Peters saw a twin-engined fighter attacking from ahead and immediately put the Lancaster into a corkscrew. The enemy made only one attack hitting the starboard outer engine which had to be feathered. As this seemed to be the only damage to the Lancaster Peters continued the sortie, completing the last 50 miles without further incident. Shortly after leaving the target the wireless operator, F/Sgt M.T. Bartle, on duty in the astrodome, saw tracer coming up from astern and Peters dived away. Fire which broke out in the fuselage filled the cockpit with smoke and set both turrets ablaze. The Lancaster went into a spin and Peters, being unable to see the instruments for the smoke, ordered the crew to bale out. After the navigator and flight engineer had baled out through the front hatch the wind cleared the cockpit. The Lancaster, now in a flat spin, was only losing height gradually and Peters by throttling back on the port engines regained control at 3,000 feet. F/Sgt N.C.W. Davis, the bomb-aimer, came forward and told him that F/Sgt D.A. Balmer and Sgt I. Graham, the gunners, were injured and their parachutes burnt, and that his own had opened prematurely. To crash-land in the Alps was too risky so Peters decided to ditch on Lake Constance. It was a courageous choice for it was a dark night with no moon; the Lancaster was on fire and was flying on three engines; the front hatch had been jettisoned so the aircraft would undoubtedly sink quickly. The crew took up ditching stations and Peters made a perfect landing on the lake. The Lancaster sank three minutes later but everyone was safely in the dinghy. They pulled for the Swiss shore and 1½ hours later landed on neutral territory.

Peters was not the only Pathfinder to be intercepted during the Friedrichshafen sortie; S/Ldr Cresswell and F/Lt T.E. Ison had brushes with nightfighters after leaving the target, and W/O J.M. Bourassa was intercepted twice, once near the target and again over the English Channel, but excellent crew co-operation prevented the nightfighters damaging the Lancaster. Sgt R.A. Edie, the rear gunner, shot down a Ju88 attacking from astern: as it dived away with the starboard engine ablaze Sgt R.H. Chapman, the mid-upper, saw another Ju88, silhouetted by the burning fighter, coming in to attack, but as soon as he opened up the German broke away without firing. Continued vigilance was rewarded when, just after leaving the enemy coast, Edie saw an Fw190 climbing to attack: a corkscrew to port gave both gunners a chance to fire and the fighter broke away. Bourassa had just resumed course when Chapman called, 'Corkscrew port! Go! Go! Go!' and opened fire on the Focke-Wulf making a second attack from the same quarter. As Edie swung his turret he saw the mid-upper's tracer hit the fighter which dived away towards the sea.

In May, because Bomber Command was primarily concerned with the *Overlord* campaign, there were only three attacks on Germany. The lull in activities had given the ground defences in Holland few opportunities to show their skill, so when the Main Force attacked Duisburg on May 21, they were keen to go into action. Flying over Holland without encountering a flak battery was not as easy as the intelligence officers made it out to be, particularly in the Rotterdam area. There was no margin for error between Rotterdam and The Hague and, having bisected the road connecting them, there was always a reception committee waiting at the Hook. North of the Hague, Valkenburg airfield was suspicious of any aircraft and downright unfriendly if it had four engines: fly south of Rotterdam and into the waiting guns on the island of Over-Flakkee, which could have been a Chinese description of a flight across it. In order to miss Soesterberg airfield and Utrecht, F/Sgt P.S.M. Robinson had gone too far south of track and, although there was plenty of flak activity to the starboard everything seemed peaceful ahead. It was typical of Rotterdam. Experience had taught ground crews that it was more rewarding to wait patiently for the bombers to find them rather than reach out with their tentacles of light trying to catch the wayward. Suddenly the whole sky lit up and hell broke loose; Robinson and the flight engineer, F/Sgt F.C.V. Tuck, were injured and the aircraft went out of control with the starboard outer on fire. Robinson's immediate reaction was to order 'abandon aircraft' and W/O K.C. Taylor and Sgt D.R. Scopes jumped, but after recovering from the initial shock of being wounded he regained control of the Lancaster and rescinded the order. The starboard outer Graviner[19] was pressed and the fire went out. A direct course was set for Manston where he made an excellent landing. Apparently, 'the man with the chopper' considered he had not scared the crew enough for Robinson found himself taxiing toward a petrol bowser with insufficient brake pressure to avoid a collision – but the axe didn't fall; there was neither fire nor explosion.

F/Lt R. Temple also finished the sortie landing on a strange aerodrome. With no brake pressure the Lancaster careered off the end of the runway,

19. Fire extinguisher fixed in engine cowling.

crashed through a gun position and came to a halt on some tree roots bulldozed out of the ground preparatory to lengthening the runway. The crew were pulled out of the burning Lancaster by Dutch airmen manning the station. About 20 minutes after leaving the target the Lancaster had been attacked by a Ju88 from astern. The Junkers opened up from beyond the Brownings' effective range and severely damaged the Lancaster. Accurate defence by Sgt W.V. Cooper, the rear gunner, and F/Sgt L Reynolds, the mid-upper, forced it to break off the engagement. Almost immediately an Me110 came diving down with guns blazing hoping to complete the kill. Reynolds, although wounded in the head and neck during the initial burst of fire from the Junkers, continued to man his guns and the Messerschmitt too was driven off. Neither of the Huns had stomach for a second attack even though, by now, the Lancaster was defenceless. Although the engines appeared to have escaped damage the rest of the aircraft was in a sorry plight. The hydraulics were shattered, the compasses damaged, and all the wireless operator's and navigator's equipment was unserviceable. Both turrets were out of action and the aircraft responded only sluggishly. Temple pointed the aircraft away from the flak, his only indication of the general direction of England and, as he was flying between two layers of cloud, the flak remained his only pointer, so unwittingly Robinson may have helped Temple in his plight. After about an hour one engine burst into flames, but the fire did not spread. After what seemed an eternity a break in the clouds revealed some lights below and they tempted the skipper to explore. Making regular orbits was a recognized way of telling the British ground defences an aircraft was in trouble and, as Temple circled the lights (it was in fact Guildford railway station) the searchlights came on. The drill was to sweep towards the nearest aerodrome and then form a cone over it to indicate its precise location.

After the war when Temple was attending a conference in Amsterdam, two Dutchmen came up to him and asked if he had ever been to Dunsfold. Temple said he crash-landed there once and the Dutchmen said that it was they who had pulled him out of the burning Lancaster. That was worth the price of a drink in any coinage.

The following night at Dortmund skies were clear and an excellent *Musical Parramatta* was carried out. Bombing was well concentrated around the markers, fire and bomb damage were extensive. The ORS said: 'It is estimated that 70,000 man-months were lost through this attack.' S/Ldr H.W.B. Heney was the victim of the inevitable consequence of concentrating a large number of bombers over the target in the shortest possible time. He was hit by incendiaries dropped from another aircraft. One exploded on the port outer engine and another in the port rudder, and with flames shooting out 50 yards to the rear he became the centre of attraction for the searchlights. Having completed the bombing run, he ordered the crew to stand by to bale out. Diving from 18,000 to 13,000 feet, he succeded in putting out the fires, but the searchlights still held him. Being coned at 13,000 feet in Happy Valley was to be in no-man's-land but, because the damaged Lancaster was gradually losing height, he dare not go down to escape the attention of the heavy guns for fear of crashing later. The gunners at Munchen Gladbach and Cologne took full advantage of the rare opportunity of engaging a single aircraft at a suicidal height and scored several hits. Heney contested every inch of height with the Lancaster but it was down to 2,400 feet when it crossed the English coast yet the crew were now prepared to give odds on getting back to Little Staughton. At Mepal, 30 miles from base, they were intercepted by an intruder which raked the Lancaster with cannon fire: miraculously no one was injured. With both turrets unserviceable it became a contest between Heney's skilful evasive action and the German pilot's ability. The enemy came a poor second. Later, Heney made a good landing at base: GT-R had flown its last sortie; it was certified Category 'E': damaged beyond repair.

The four Main Force attacks on Germany in June and the early part of July were directed against oil targets but, towards the end of the month Harris, finding his *Overlord* commitments less demanding, switched his force to what he still considered its vital role: attacking industrial towns.

There was an air of nostalgia at Wyton on July 23 when 14 Lancasters of 83 Squadron landed. Eight marker crews and six supporters were back in the group to help their hard-pressed friends. The squadron marked Kiel for more than 600 bombers and showed they had lost none of their skill. The attack was a resounding success, most of the bombs falling in the port area and the torpedo boat harbour was severely damaged.

The night's activities provide an excellent example of the sophistication in Bomber Command's routeing and spoofing for the tactics were well planned and thoroughly carried out. In addition to the raid on Kiel, 100 Lancasters bombed the oil storage depot at Donges, near St Nazaire; Les Catelliers and Les Hauts Buissons V-1 sites were attacked by 102 Halifaxes; 27 LNSF Mosquitoes made the long trip to Berlin and 4 out of 5 *Oboe* Mosquitoes dropped HE on Duren; 2 Stirlings and 6 Lancasters were 'gardening' in the Brest and Kiel areas. In addition, 180 crews made a diversionary sweep and other aircraft from OTUs dropped leaflets over France. Fortresses, Halifaxes, Stirlings and Wellingtons of 100 Group were supporting the operations; 13 aircraft were operating the *Mandrel*[20] screen; over Kiel 8 more were dropping a new type of *Window*; 13 were operating *Jostle*[21] and 2 Fortresses were operating ABC.

---

20. Jammed GCI.

21. Device for jamming German radar used in connection with barrage A.A.

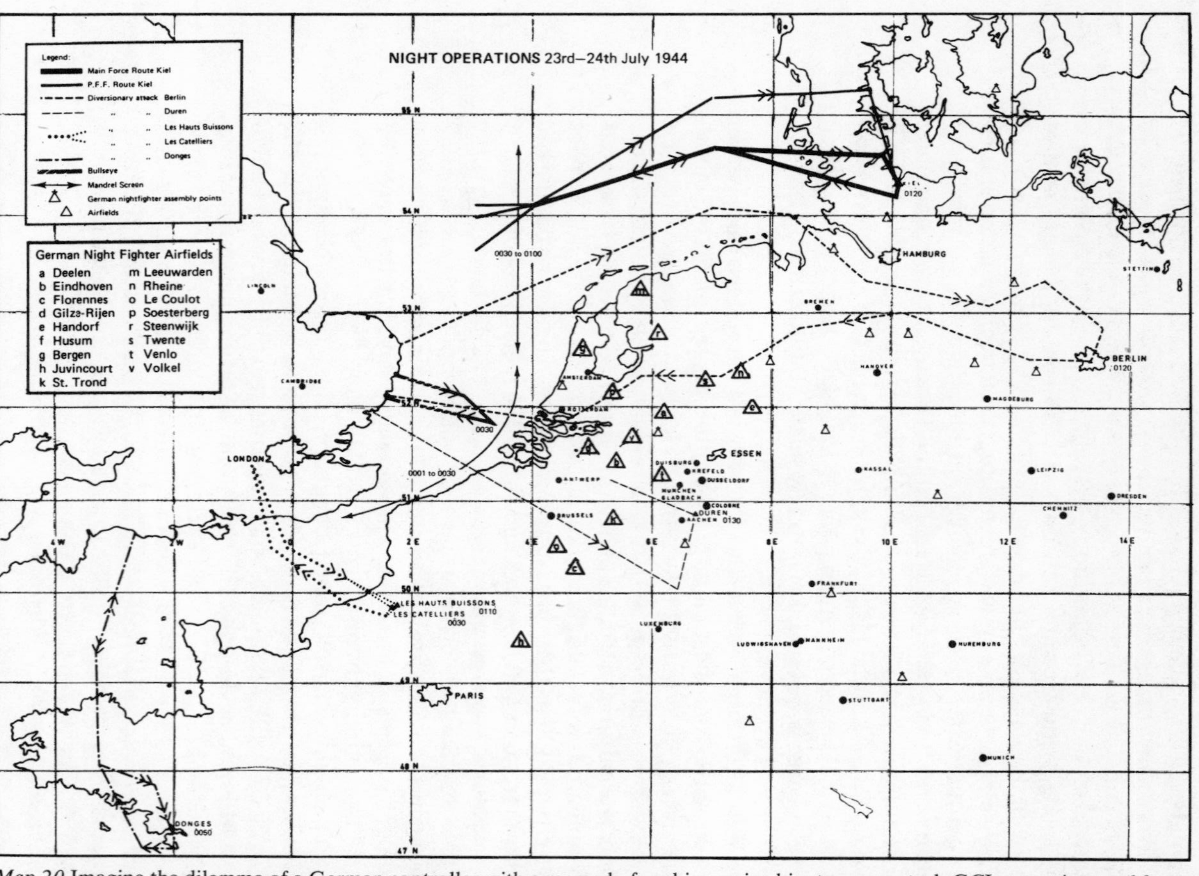

Map 20 Imagine the dilemma of a German controller with a memo before him urging him to save petrol; GCI screen jammed from the air and from the ground; knowing something was afoot. As the screens clear reports come through of five separate forces hundreds of miles apart. Knowledge is as bewildering as uncertainty. Kiel, the main target, already having had a visit from a group of 'gardeners', probably didn't go into the hat. Only 4 bombers were lost to fighters on this target.

The elaborate plans were designed to protect the Kiel force from nightfighters based in Holland, Belgium and France by outflanking them over the North Sea. At midnight, as the Donges force crossed into Brittany, the Halifaxes were approaching Dieppe and the *Mandrel* screen was operating over the North Sea. It was extended northward to conceal the Kiel force which was flying at 2,000 feet to keep below the German GCI and assembling 30 miles north of Texel. From this point the bombers climbed to operational height with the Berlin Mosquitoes flying a parallel route nearer the enemy coast. At the same time the *Mandrel* screen was allowed to break down gradually in the south revealing the diversionary force approaching Flushing. The Controllers thinking, as they were intended to, that this force was bound for the Ruhr, deployed 5 *Gruppen* to meet the threat, the remainder being sent to oppose the Halifaxes.

Isolated interceptions were made as the Kiel force crossed the enemy coast and single-engined fighters were seen over the target, but there were no casualties until the force was homeward bound and then only four bombers were shot down.

Between July 24 and 28, three attacks were made on Stuttgart. Weather took a hand in all the attacks: on July 24 and 28 the target was cloud-covered, and on the 25th, electrical storms and severe icing were encountered *en route*. After helping with the marking on July 24, 83 Squadron returned to Coningsby and 97 Squadron flew in to assist on the following day. It was the best of the three raids and was notable because many of the Blind Marker crews used GPI to make their bombing run. Full reconnaissance was not obtained until after July 28, so it was impossible to attribute specific damage to any raid. Damage was extensive throughout the town; an area from the main railway station to the south-west was devastated. Fourteen factories, including one making ball-bearings, were damaged. Many buildings were hit including the railway station and the post and telegraph office.

On the night of July 28-29, when Hamburg and Stuttgart were raided, it was estimated that 300 nightfighters were active, 200 of them against the Stuttgart force. In all, 62 aircraft were lost and 28 of them are known to have fallen to fighters, but Bomber Command had an unprecedented success; 27 fighters were destroyed, 6 probably destroyed and 12 damaged. There was scarcely a crew who did not see some fighter activity even if they were lucky enough not to experience a combat; 7 Squadron completed a successful week by shooting down three. On the Sunday, at Kiel, F/O J.F.S. Wainwright had claimed a 'probable' when an Fw190 which attacked his Lancaster appeared to be out of control as it entered cloud. The following night, at Stuttgart, F/O N.F. Brundle, F/Lt R.G. Williams's rear gunner, had shot down an Fw190. On July 28, S/Ldr A.J.L. Craig and P/O P.G. McCarthy each claimed their gunners shot down a Ju88. News of the third success came from Bradwell Bay where

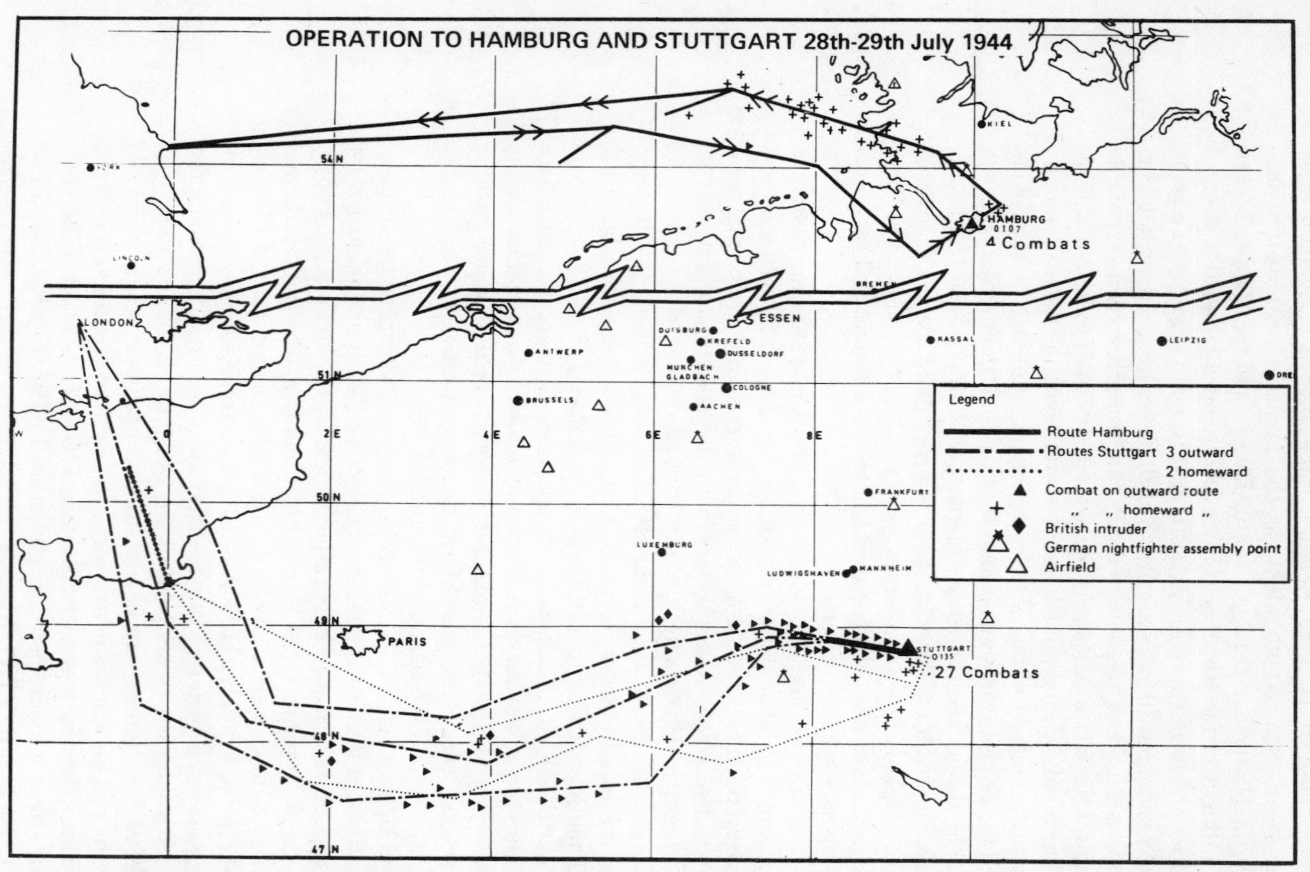

Map 21 Crews, who came to the squadrons after the Battle of Berlin, smiled condescendingly as senior crews described their ordeals of flak and fighters. Weaned on French and Belgian marshalling yards they had little conception of what was in store for them at Stuttgart. With an estimated 200 fighters opposing them they grew up overnight and thereafter treated with greater respect those who had faced such ordeals every sortie. The Hamburg force was pursued over the North Sea as far as 06°00E.

S/Ldr R.P. Todd had made a forced landing. The Squadron Leader withstood a simultaneous assault by two nightfighters and, although his gunners, P/O W.R. Drinkwater and P/O T.L. Tracy, drove off one and shot down the other, the Lancaster was so severely damaged that Todd was forced to jettison his bombs over France and had to abandon the sortie.

F/O R.G. Herbert was only 50 miles form Stuttgart when his Lancaster was hit by a projectile believed to be a rocket, the port wing and the bomb-bay being severely damaged. The nightfighter made only one assault and fired from well beyond the range of the Lancaster's armament. The same night, at Hamburg, three Pathfinders had combats and the 8 Group gunners got the best of the exchanges. F/Lt R.W. Beveridge and S/Ldr L.D. Leicester both claimed their gunners had shot down a Ju88 and F/O R.P. Robert's gunners drove off two Fw190s, which made a simultaneous attack from both quarters. The fighter pilots had spotted the Lancaster when the port outer engine had been set on fire by flak.

Three experienced crews of 156 Squadron were finishing their tour of operations on the Hamburg raid: F/Lt R.C. Wiseman was on his 70th sortie, S/Ldr T.W.G. Godfrey on his 61st and S/Ldr J.F. Slade on his 58th. Slade's bomb-aimer was ready to drop his markers when the Lancaster received a direct hit; the port wing broke upward from the tip to the outer engine, causing the aircraft to go into a slow spiral, completely out of control. Slade orderd everyone to find their parachutes and stand by to bale out, telling them not to panic as there was plenty of height. He throttled back and by using the rudder and varying the throttle speed he regained control and levelled out. He then ordered the flight engineer, F/Sgt J.A. Brookes, to check the engine temperatures, oil pressures and petrol. As everything seemed in order, he asked the navigator for a course telling him that turns to port would be dangerous. He told the crew to relax but warned them that they were not yet out of the wood; there was still the flak belt on the coast to negotiate and evasive action was out of the question. The bomb-aimer reminded him they still had four TIs and two 1,000-pound HEs on board, but as the bomb-doors began to open the Lancaster became unstable and lost height rapidly, so they were unable to jettison them. Brookes suggested that if they used the petrol from the port side first it might improve the balance and make the aircraft easier to handle. Having cleared the enemy coast without further mishap, Slade asked the navigator for a course which would allow him to fly parallel to the enemy coast 25 miles offshore until they could make the shortest sea crossing to Woodbridge. The Lancaster had been slowly losing height all the time but, when the English coast appeared with Woodbridge dead ahead, Slade still had sufficient height (1,500 feet) not to cause any problems. The aerial had been shot away so. although the wireless operator kept broadcasting, he had no means of knowing whether he was being received. Slade got a green from the ever-alert Woodbridge flying control, the undercarriage was lowered and the 'locked in position' lights came on. Everyone except Brookes was ordered to crash positions as Slade made a long fast approach.[22] When the Lancaster touched down, the port undercarriage collapsed and the broken wing dug into the ground. The aircraft cartwheeled, the fuselage broke in two and the Lancaster skidded off the runway on to the grass. However the plane did not catch fire and the crew scrambled clear. Slade went back to check everybody was out. He had nothing but praise for the flight engineer and navigator – but what of the man himself? Any momentary loss of concentration from the time the aircraft left Hamburg could have resulted in disaster; the idea of flying parallel to the enemy coast to give the crew a chance of being saved if anything went wrong and his calmness over the target with the aircraft out of control mark him as an outstanding captain.

A new form of *Newhaven* was given its first trial at Russelsheim on August 12-13. Visual identification of the aiming point at night was always difficult and anything burning on the ground, even TIs, tended to dazzle bomb-aimers so the Blind Marker Illuminator force was split. Blind Illuminators went in first and dropped flares, closely followed by the Visual Markers; the Blind Markers were next on target but only dropped their TIs if the Visual Markers had failed to mark. This method helped Backers-up too, and indeed the Main Force, because it was easier to bomb small compact groups of TIs. If the attack became a *Parramatta*, the greens of the Backers-up would tend to form a concentration within the Blind Markers' yellows. On the night, haze prevented the Visual Markers identifying the target and, because of the 5-10/10ths cloud, there was some wild bombing.

The first real test came on August 18-19 when the marker force found clear skies and good visibility at Bremen. Timing by the Blind Illuminators was excellent and their hooded flares enabled the Visual Markers to identify the aiming point and mark it accurately. Backing-up and recentering were of a high order and the Main Force, untroubled by nightfighters, because of successful spoofs on Hanover and Hamburg, turned in a fine piece of concentrated bombing. The LNSF crews on Berlin said they could see the fires from the capital and a reconnaissance Mosquito from 1409 Flight reported 'intense unbroken fires with black smoke to 23,000 feet'.

A week later, when the target was the Opel works at Russelsheim, conditions were similar and all the Visual Markers dropped their TIs within the factory area. The attack was scheduled to last 10 minutes so that the 400-strong Main Force would be bombing the initial markers and most crews bombed within the time limit. Thirteen crews of 5 Group, realizing their attack on Darmstadt was a complete failure, wisely

22. Earlier he had discovered the aircraft stalled at 140 knots.

41. (*Top*) G/Capt K.R. Rampling, CO of 7 Squadron during the Battle of Berlin, and his crew. Their tally of 2 DSOs, 7 DFCs and 2 DFMs proclaim them as experienced Pathfinders

42. (*Bottom*) Lancaster III NK 709. Her crew proudly pose for a picture following the painting-on of the 100th bomb symbol. She was one of only two known Pathfinder 'centenarians'. She began life with 35 Squadron but was handed over to the newly formed 635 Squadron in April 1944. She also served with 592 and 405 Squadrons and completed at least 110 sorties

Pathfinder VCs

43. S/Ldr I.W. Bazalgette crashed after a raid on Trossy St. Maximin on August 4, 1944

44. S/Ldr R.A.M. Palmer shot down over the target on December 23, 1944

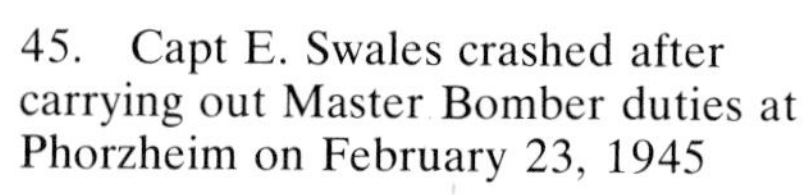

45. Capt E. Swales crashed after carrying out Master Bomber duties at Phorzheim on February 23, 1945

46. (*Top*) G/Capt H.E. Bufton was associated with *Oboe* from its inception and flew the first *Oboe* sortie. After six months as CO of 109 Squadron he became Station Commander at Bourn

47. (*Bottom*) Capt E. Swales and his crew

48. (*Top*) 'One of our aircraft is missing'. The cold, bland radio announcement was all the public learned about the deaths of a gallant crew whose Lancaster exploded after a direct hit by flak over Wesel

49. (*Bottom*) The burnt out wreck of S/Ldr I.W. Bazalgette's Lancaster which crashed at Servantes in France

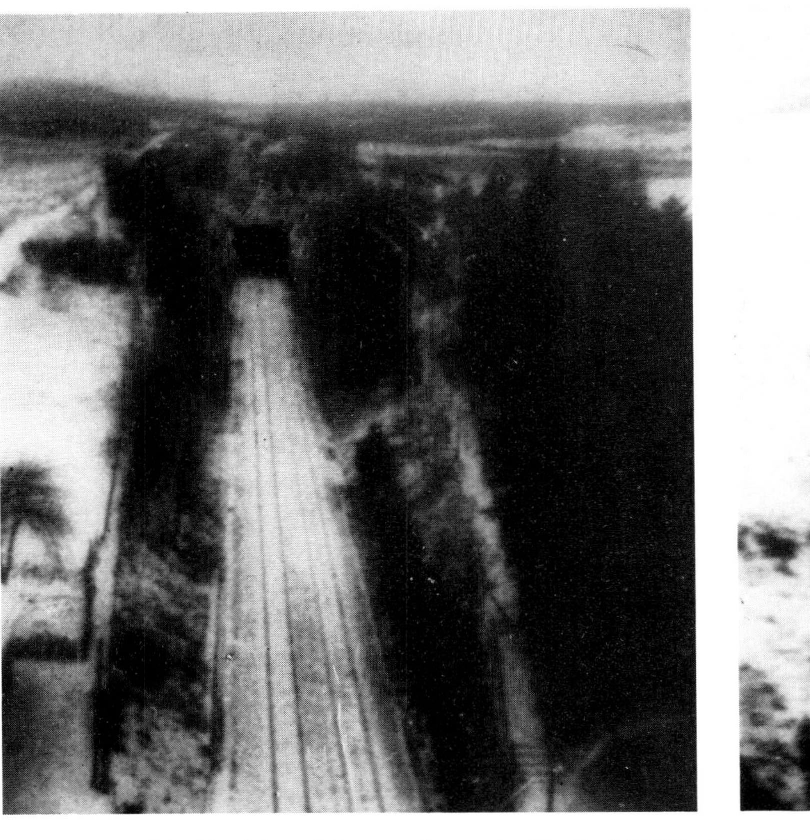

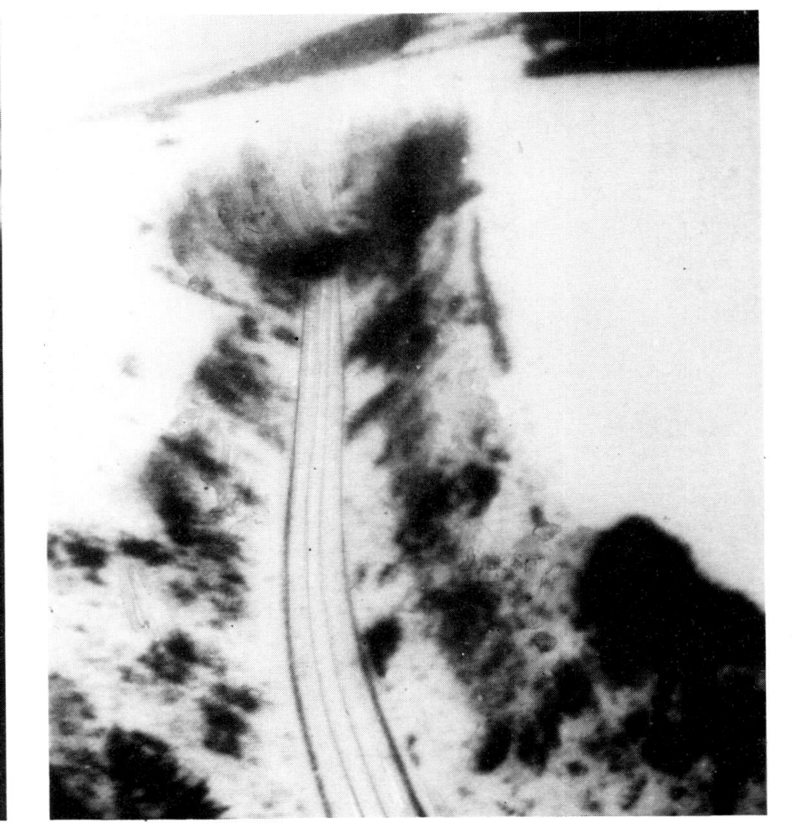

50 & 51. Two of the tunnels attacked by the LNSF in daylight on January 1, 1945. *Left* (50) F/Lt G.C. Crow had a straight run to the target. *Right* (51) the dust and smoke spewing from the tunnel's mouth proved that S/Ldr R.G.S. St. C. Wadsworth's Cookie had found its mark

52. (*Top*) The awesome sight at Cleve which paid the penalty of harbouring German armour and troops; attacked on February 7-8, 1945

53. (*Bottom*) Dulmen was pulverised by Bomber Command on March 22, 1945, seven days before the town fell into Allied hands

54. (*Top*) After repeated Bomber Command attacks Gielenburg found it impossible to repair many of the Ruhr oil plants. His problems are manifest in this ground shot of Sterkrade

55. (*Bottom*) This ground shot of a tramway depot at Dusseldorf reveals the chaos below the twisted metal

56. (*Top*) Cologne cathedral survived despite the severity of the bombing and being in the vicinity of the railway station

57. (*Bottom*) Devastation in the city. Most of the buildings still standing are mere shells. Almost 2,000 acres or 61%, of the built-up area was destroyed

bombed Russelsheim where they knew their bombs would do worthwhile damage. All the key units in that part of the factory which had been converted to manufacture aircraft components were damaged. The whole factory was at a complete standstill the following day and extensive damage to machine tools held up production for some time. Although only 15 aircraft were missing, 66 were intercepted by the strong force of nightfighters operating over the target and *en route*. The enemy engaged 10 PFF Lancasters but only F/Lt W.J.L. Weicker's was seriously damaged. Homeward-bound, he was near Saarbrucken when tracer enveloped the Lancaster. He dived steeply to starboard but, when he tried to level out after losing 1,000 feet, he found the controls had been damaged and the Lancaster would not respond. When he apprised the crew, the engineer, wireless operator and mid-upper gunner took this to be an order to bale out. The rear gunner, W/O M.J. Martin, called out on the intercom: 'I'm hit, and the rear of the fuselage is on fire.' The navigator made his way to Martin and found the blaze had died down but the fire was still smouldering. The Lancaster had lost another 7,000 feet before Weicker regained control. In addition to the damaged starboard elevator which had caused the alarm, the rear turret and the bomb-doors had been hit and the H2S was rendered unserviceable. The fighter made only one attack, and Weicker was left in peace to solve the problems of flying the Lancaster back to base.[23]

At Kiel, on August 26, an effective smoke screen ruined the Visual Markers' chances of identifying the aiming point and saved the town from the destruction meted out to Russelsheim on the previous evening. As in the July raid crews were briefed to fly out at 2,000 feet, but some of them climbed to operational height early. The Germans, forewarned, had nightfighters waiting over the North Sea and two Pathfinders, F/Lt I.B. Hayes and F/Sgt D. Owen, were intercepted before reaching the enemy coast.

F/Sgts R. Smith and D.W. Aspinall, F/O J. Cuthill's gunners, were always on the alert and had on more than one occasion driven off the enemy.[24] Over Kiel Smith saw an Me110 some 600 yards away and, although he was not certain GT-S was its intended victim, he ordered a dive to starboard. Aspinall too was taking no chances and opened fire on the Messerschmitt, which dived away steeply out of control and crashed.

S/Ldr S.J. Long was making his bombing run when his Lancaster was attacked by a Ju88. His gunners, P/O S. Freedom and F/Sgt J.F. Stearn,

---

23. The incidence of fighters making only one attack increased in the final stages of the war and it must be assumed that new nightfighter crews were advised to employ this tactic until they had gained more experience.

24. At Russelsheim, the previous night, Smith had damaged an Fw190 although at the time of the combat his turret was being shot to pieces by a 'friendly' aircraft.

opened up as Long made a corkscrew to port but the German pilot followed the manoeuvre and pressed home the attack. Both starboard engines were put out of action; the port elevator was shot off; the hydraulics were hit and there was a gaping hole in the fuselage 2 feet square. The enemy was shot down for his temerity: following an explosion between the port engine and the fuselage the Junkers turned over on its back before going down in an uncontrollable spin. G/Capt L. Cheshire wrote: 'It (the Lancaster) had the strength to survive damage that would have toppled other aircraft out of the sky . . .'[25] GT-B proved him correct on the morning of August 27. After dragging its battered frame from the target on two engines the port inner seized when it was over the North Sea yet it still struggled back to England. Some of the the credit had to be shared with Long for it was not the easiest of pastimes to fly an undamaged aircraft on an outer engine and GT-B had half the controls damaged or shot away.

At first, six aircraft were posted missing from the group but later news came through to Upwood that F/Lt R.M. Etchells's crew had ditched in the North Sea. The outward journey had passed without incident and when Kiel came up on ETA half their worries were over, or so the crew thought.[26] The bomb-doors had scarcely closed after releasing their HE when the tail gunner yelled, 'Enemy fighter astern, corkscrew port,' and opened fire on a Ju88 only 300 yards away. The Junkers fell away with the port engine and fuselage on fire and was probably destroyed. Its cannon fire had ripped across the Lancaster diagonally, shot away the tail assembly on the port side, tore a large hole in the fuselage and put both starboard engines out of action.

Back over the North Sea the TIs were jettisoned but then the bomb-doors would not shut and the port wheel, which had come down when they were opened, would not retract. About an hour after leaving the target the port inner caught fire, and the Lancaster began to lose height rapidly. Etchells made an excellent ditching and everyone clambered on to the wing near the dinghy which by then had inflated.

At 0200 hours (Sunday) an aircraft flew low over them and they fired off two reds. the aircraft circled, dropped a flare and then flew off. Three hours later, a Lancaster flew over them, they fired more reds and received an OK from the downward identification lamp. Now their biggest fear was that the Germans might rescue them first. Shortly after 11 o'clock, three air-sea rescue Hudsons making a square search spotted them. One

---

25. D.B.Tubbs, *Lancaster Bomber*.

26. F/Lt J. Goldsmith was not the crew's regular navigator. There was always some tension when there was an 'odd bod' in the crew because they worked as a team. The navigator was a key member of the crew so when they arrived on track on time, much of the apprehension died down.

dropped an inflatable boat, but the sea anchor did not release and it drifted out of reach. One of the other two dropped a Lindholme dinghy which was secured after ten minutes. Three of the crew transferred to it and they tied the two dinghies together.

There was always one Hudson chaperoning throughout the day. At dusk another returned and dropped an airborne lifeboat but it took them most of the night to reach it. Safely aboard, they decided to wait for daylight before starting the motors knowing the Hudsons would be back.

At 0800 on Monday, as the first Hudson appeared on the horizon they started the engines and set course for England, but the boat, damaged by the fall, began to break up in the rough seas and all seemed lost. The Hudsons, realizing their plight, searched the area and, sighting a small Danish sailing boat nearby, directed it to the lifeboat and the Danes soon hauled them aboard. At first the four fishermen were reluctant to take them to England but later, after a Hudson had dropped a message cannister instructing them to set 250° on the compass, they agreed to do so. On Tuesday, at 1700 hours, an air-sea rescue launch intercepted them and seven hours later they disembarked at Grimsby.

Although no 8 Group aircraft took part in Operation *Hackle* the outcome was eagerly awaited by Bennett. On August 12-13, 373 Main Force heavies all equipped with H2S took off to bomb Brunswick without the aid of markers. The results were appalling. At most, 23 bombed the target; Hallendorf – where 50 crews dropped their bombs on Goering's steel city – was the most popular error. Shades of 1941. ORS partially excused the force by saying the target was cloud-covered but, if the object of the exercise was to find out what percentage of the Main Force was capable of finding the target navigating by H2S, then the cloud made the results authentic.

Because to date no one has written a comprehensive history of Bomber Command in Europe, space which should have been devoted to Pathfinder deeds has had to be used describing the devastation caused by the bombing. In its turn it has tended to detract from PFF's significant role in the bomber offensive. This raid illustrates how much Bomber Command owed to Pathfinders.

VII The Long Finale

During the period October 1944 to VE Day, Bomber Command had almost complete freedom of the skies. Crews had learnt how to bomb with precision and, as the loss rate was low, there was always a high percentage of experienced crews available. These advantages, however, were not fully exploited. Many armchair strategists condemn Harris for persisting with area bombing in the last stage of the bomber offensive and certainly he was at loggerheads with the Air Staff to the extent that he offered to resign, but if there has to be blame on this score then Portal must take his share, for he could at any time have replaced the AOC-in-C.

Harris was held in high esteem by his crews but that did not mean they would not have followed a new commander, nor would there necessarily have been a lowering of morale. Like other great leaders he was not infallible; in fact he had misjudged the Germans' resilience as well as the capabilities of his own force. In 1942 his single-minded determination had been an all-important factor but now, to bring the war to a speedy close, Bomber Command needed an enlightened leader capable of exploiting its versatility and other recently developed operational capacities. The arguments of 1942-3, sound though they were then, no longer obtained. Area bombing was not the only manner in which the force could be employed effectively, nor were oil and communications still to be rated as 'panacea-targets'; in fact they proved to be the vital factors in breaking German resistance. Yet the word panacea appeared in most of the AOC-in-C's letters to Portal.

If the sole aim at this stage had been to break the German economy then undoubtedly area bombing would have been the correct strategy and Speer agreed that German industry would have crumbled eventually under the weight of Bomber Command's attacks. However, the need of the times, which was to win the war quickly, called for all-out attacks on oil and transport to bring the German war machine grinding to a halt for lack of oil and, by striking at transport, to cause chaos in the assembly plants of those essential war industries which had been forced to disperse in 1943-4 to escape the attention of British bombers. Much of this was done in 1945, but the chance to win the war before the Russians had overrun half Germany was missed. That the Germans would have capitulated before Berlin was besieged is sheer conjecture but the Russians' occupation of the capital produced a stark fact in post-war politics which perhaps had been made possible through a lost opportunity.

From October to December 53% of Bomber Command attacks were on German cities, a mere 14% on oil and 15% on transport. It is only fair to say that area bombing did damage oil plants and more frequently railway installations and marshalling yards, but they were by way of a bonus rather than the intention of the AOC-in-C. The German cities were accorded less prominence in 1945 and oil and transport received a much higher percentage of the bomb load, but this was because of governmental pressure. If Germany could not support herself economically after the war then the task of the Allies would be almost insuperable. Not only Germany herself but the economy of the Low Countries depended on German industry.

THE SECOND BATTLE OF THE RUHR Harris celebrated his freedom from Eisenhower's control by opening a new offensive against targets in the Ruhr. While the second Battle of the Ruhr was no more homogeneous than the attacks of 1943 yet, of the 86,669 tons of bombs dropped on German cities during the last three months of 1944, more than 60,000 were dropped on towns in the Ruhr area. Duisburg, Dortmund, Essen, Cologne and Dusseldorf were the main targets but, in addition, ten other Ruhr towns were bombed between October and December.[1]

The significant difference between these attacks and those of March 1943 was the preponderance of HE in the bomb loads. Harris explained that there was little left to burn, which was certainly true, but the colossal damage done in this period poses the question of whether the proportion of IBs might not have been too high previously. However, the AOC-in-C did not believe this because, when the target was one not previously attacked by Bomber Command, he reverted to the 1943 load.

The battle opened on October 6-7 when 483 out of 525 bombers attacked Dortmund. Although 105 Squadron had a disastrous night – only one of the twelve crews coped – 109 Squadron with ten copes maintained a steady supply of TIs backed-up throughout by the Lancaster marker crews and, despite the ground haze, the outlines of buildings could be seen in the glow. The bombing on the whole was concentrated within the marked area of 800 square yards and an oval of fires, aided by four large explosions, was extending outwards. Finally, an enormous

1. Bochum, Gelsenkirchen, Hagen, Hamm, Leverkusen, Munster, Neuss, Oberhausen, Solingen and Witten.

explosion, starting its own fire, lit up the surrounding area. The entire railway communication system was so gravely disrupted that less than half of the through lines had been cleared after a week's intensive effort. The Werk Dortmund steel plant was at a standstill for more than two weeks.

Although cloud came to the town's aid for the daylight attack on November 29 when 291 crews dropped their cargoes, according to post-war reports, damage was extensive. Werk Hoerde steel plant, damaged in this raid, had only recovered to 50% output after fourteen weeks.

Two attacks in 1945 completed the town's destruction. On February 20-21 the target was cloud-covered again but, as it was night, the glow of the TIs could be seen and they were quickly replaced by the glow of healthy fires. Further extensive damage was done but CIU had not completed their assessment before the final attack in strength on March 12. More than 1,000 bombers took part in the raid made in daylight above 10/10ths cloud. *Oboe* Mosquitoes were dropping blue Smoke Puffs and the PFF heavies greens: crews were briefed to give priority to the blues. Production at Werk Hoerde and Werk Dortmund came to a complete standstill. The damage to the essential services of Dortmund was so severe that it would have been months before work could have been resumed. The gas supply was cut off and had not been reconnected when the Allies took the town in the middle of April; 90% of the fresh water supply was affected and there was no electricity for three weeks.

In the first battle of the Ruhr Harris had given Duisburg far more attention than its importance demanded and, although, with its wide open spaces between the built-up areas, it was a difficult target to devastate, the town appeared to be singled out for destruction on an unparalleled scale. At 0700 hours on October 14, crews from the first of five waves took off to attack the town. In all 1,063 bombers took part in the sortie and, although *Oboe* Mosquitoes marked five different aiming points, layer cloud between 8,000 and 10,000 feet made identification of individual A/Ps almost impossible and only a few Backers-up were able to mark. Crews dropped their loads on the glow of TIs and, later in the attack, on the glow of fires.

When 1,005 bombers, attacking in two waves, arrived over the town in the early hours of October 15 the cloud had dispersed. The huge force, encouraged by excellent marking in both phases, started new fires and extended those still burning from the day attack and, by the end of the raid, the whole town was well ablaze. Damage was widespread, large areas being completely devastated.[2] In 24 hours, Bomber Command flew 2,647 sorties and dropped over 10,300 tons of bombs, more than 9,000 tons on Duisburg. This was a far greater weight of bombs than was

2. On this night, 1,575 Bomber Command aircraft took off on a variety of missions, 5 Group's attack on Brunswick by 240 bombers being the second in importance.

dropped in the ten-day Hamburg ordeal, but the Ruhr was so inured to such bombardment that hardly a squeal was heard beyond the city boundaries. It was Bomber Command's peak effort for any 24 hours.

Two further attacks on November 30 and December 17 spread and intensified the damage and PRU photographs, taken two months later, showed that craters in the railway yards had not been touched. For a final attack by 323 bombers on February 20-21, 1945, the aiming point was the railway yards. Lord Teddar had long been advocating the isolation of the Ruhr from the rest of Germany and although this raid anticipated operation *Bugle* by fourteen days, transport was second in Bomber Command's priorities at this time. The first TIs fell on the northern end of the yards and although cloud to 15,000 feet made backing-up and bombing difficult some Visual Recenterers did go below cloud but the Main Force bombed initially on the glow of the TIs. Later, as the cloud began to break up, bomb-aimers could see the markers and dropped their loads with greater precision.

The destruction of Essen, and in particular Krupps, which had begun on March 5, 1943, was finally completed in October 1944. Two *Wanganui* attacks, the first on the night of October 23-24, the second by daylight on the 25th, were made over cloud and more than 200 separate buildings came toppling down under the weight of 7,326 tons of HE. A single bomb which cut the main water pipe from the Ruhr stopped all steel production and the works ground to a halt. Further attacks in November and December demolished any lingering hopes of repairing the damage. Elsewhere in Essen, 13 other factories, four railway stations, two gasworks and two power stations were hit.

One final assault on March 11, 1945, by 1,105 bombers paralysed the essential services of gas, electricity and water and caused a complete breakdown in road and rail transportation, which almost isolated the town until it was captured by the Americans. *Oboe* Mosquitoes, flying in the now familiar pattern of primary and reserve in formation, kept the target marked with blue Smoke Puffs throughout the attack. The Main Force was so keen to dot the last 'i' and cross the last 't' in the town's destruction that the Long Stop had no problems and the American troops close by had no palpitations.

Except for a sharp reminder on April 20-21, 1944, that the town was still on Harris's books, Cologne had not been heavily bombed since July 8, 1943. Three attacks during the last four days of October destroyed the few important buildings left standing in the centre of the city – miraculously the cathedral escaped – and spread the damage to the outlying districts. Mulheim was almost wiped out in the daylight raid on October 28. This attack was in two waves, both controlled *Musical Parramattas*; the planners must have had a hunch that the *Oboe* copes would be low because the reserves, flying in formation, were instructed to drop their markers on their primaries' release signal. Backing-up was of a high order and most of the Lancasters dropped their markers. W/Cdr. B.W. McMillan controlled the first phase as a *Parramatta* until the TIs were completely obscured by smoke and later crews were ordered to bomb the centre of the smoke.

The second aiming point was on the west side of the Rhine and here, although the bombing was generally more scattered, dust and smoke enveloped the target, so F/Lt D.B. Everett, the Master Bomber, ordered crews to select and bomb worthwhile targets. The Knapsack power station, south of the city, was bombed in the first instance by a handful of crews; others, seeing the activity in the area, joined the attack and soon it became the main target. More than 60 bombers dropped their loads on the power station; its destruction necessitated enforced power-cuts over a wide area and few people enjoyed a hot Sunday dinner.

Flak was intense over the city and many aircraft were hit. F/Lt G.C.J. Vann made his escape to the south, searching for a quiet piece of sky, but four mounted railway guns in a siding at Sieburg shattered all his hopes. Their marksmanship was excellent; all four engines were hit and the port inner and starboard outer had to be feathered. The Lancaster was badly damaged and Vann decided to take a private land route home to avoid the long sea crossing.

Cologne's heaviest raid took place on October 30-31[3] when 870 bombers dropped 4,040 tons of bombs on the town. The attack was a *Musical Wanganui* and, although no results could be observed, the red glow from fires augered a busy night for the fire brigades. The following night, 3 out of 5 *Oboe* Mosquitoes dropped TIs on the city and 10 LNSF Mosquitoes bombed on the glow of them. The weary townsfolk were just thanking God it was only a small raid when the sirens sounded again and, minutes later, the drone of heavy bombers foreboded another night of misery. Many senior crews among the 491 who bombed said the skymarking was the best they had experienced. The *Kölnische Zeitung* said: 'It has been a hard blow full of chaos and bitterness . . . Cologne has acquired new areas of silence and death.'

After the two heavy raids in 1943, the *Gauleiter* of the Dusseldorf region ordered all citizens to co-operate in building emergency housing. All their efforts had been nullified by the raid of April 22, 1944. Many Ruhr firms had offices in the town and they alone would have made it an important target, but its value to the Germans lay in its steel plants still working at more than 50% capacity.

On the night of November 2-3, conditions were ideal for bombing and *Oboe* reds, accurately placed, were backed-up by Pathfinder heavies so

---

3. Not the largest number to attack: 898 out of 1,047 attacked the town on May 31, 1942, but dropped only 1,455 tons of bombs.

that, when the 946 bombers arrived over the town, the target was enveloped in a pool of coloured illumination. The raid was aimed at the northern districts which had fortuitously escaped in previous attacks. Here Rheinmetal Borsig had two of its most important factories and they were severely damaged. There was not a single building left in either factory with its roof and walls intact. Mannesmann steel-tube works, close by the Rath branch of the combine, was devastated. Rail and road facilities were seriously affected as also were the essential services.

The route took the bombers over Krefeld and the ground defences there were very active claiming F/O H.A. Hannah as one of their victims. At 1935 hours, his Lancaster was coned and hit several times by heavy flak; he was wounded in the neck and twice in the back, one piece of shrapnel piercing his lung – he became unconscious in less than a minute. The bombs were jettisoned immediately and for the next 15 minutes the Lancaster performed its own version of evasive action as the crew struggled to get the captain out of his seat. Over Remscheid the aircraft's gyrations became too much for the rear gunner who, having received no reply to his oft-repeated question, 'What's happening?' baled out. F/Lt G.A. Martin, the navigator/set operator, took over the controls and flew the aircraft back to Gransden Lodge. When base did not reply on the RT, he switched to the 'Darkie'[4] frequency and Debden answered his call giving him a course to the aerodrome. Martin warned flying control that he would have to crash-land and they gave him every assistance, guiding him down safely. 'It's a good landing if you can walk away from it' was a common RAF phrase and Martin's came into this category: there were no further casualties. He was awarded an immediate DSO for an outstanding piece of airmanship. Hannah, sad to relate, died under the anaesthetic when the doctors tried to remove the schrapnel from his lung.

Few people in the West have any conception of the retribution wrought on the German people for supporting Hitler's ambitions and trying to prove themselves to be a super race. The *Luftwaffe* at the height of its power, destroyed 5% of Coventry; Britain trembled and the World was shocked. By the end of 1944 Bochum was 83% destroyed. Two raids on October 9-10 and November 4-5, 1944 caused most of the damage. PFF Lancaster crews were given a stand-down on October 9 so the two *Oboe* squadrons were responsible for the marking and, to cater for the uncertain weather conditions, TIs and *Wanganui* flares were dropped. Between 8-10/10ths thin stratus covered the target so the 404 Main Force crews had the option of bombing skymarkers or on the glow of the TIs.

The second attack on November 4-5 was an outstanding success. *Oboe* Mosqutioes dropped a steady supply of red TIs for a *Musical Parramatta*

4. SOS Frequency.

and the backing-up of the Visual Centerers[5] was of a standard in keeping with their more imposing title. More than 700 Main Force crews provided the final requirement, concentrated bombing within the marked area. An interesting ploy was used in this attack. The German tactics of putting up a flak barrage around skymarkers was exploited; Pathfinder Lancaster crews dropped a *Wanganui* flare after releasing their bombs to draw the weight of the ground defences away from the bombing force.

The importance of Bochum to Ruhr industry was far greater than its size would seem to indicate; it was the centre of one-third of the total output of coal in the valley and, among many other important industries, its four Vereinigte Stahlwerk factories were particularly important, two of them making high-grade alloy steel. All four plants were extensively damaged in the two raids. One of them at its peak produced 1,000,000 shells a month; bombing had gradually reduced this figure to 150,000 and after the November raid production ceased entirely.

Beyond the Ruhr five towns in north and central Germany were attacked and in south and south-west Germany thirteen attacks were made on eleven towns; 5 Group were responsible for more than 50% of these raids and their results varied from poor, at Wilhelmshaven on October 5, to brilliant at Brunswick on October 14-15 and at Heilbronn on December 4-5. Their techniques were always at the mercy of the weather and, after abandoning off-set marking because it was too costly, their initial consistency was not maintained. By contrast, the improved standard of 8 Group's skymarking resulted in few bombs being wasted irrespective of weather conditions over the target.

Pathfinders involvement ranged from a daylight jaunt to a highly efficient night attack in southern Germany. At 0420 hours on Wednesday, October 4, the villagers at Downham Market were awakened when 8 Lancasters took off for Bergen – a Master Bomber, S/Ldr P.H. Swann, a Deputy, two Primary Visual Markers and four Backers-up. It was just light enough to pinpoint the Norwegian coast when the first crews made landfall and Pathfinders had no difficulty in identifying the target visually. The Germans were building submarine shelters in the port and 100 bombers were determined to postpone their completion by some months. The attack opened at 0930 hours and within 2 minutes they had started a large fire giving off volumes of smoke which quickly obscured the aiming point, and later crews were ordered to bomb the centre of the smoke.

If the U-boat commanders were relieved to see the 'gaggle' fly directly to the TIs their relief was short-lived, for 20 Lancasters broke away from the main stream and attacked the port. Four submarines in the harbour received direct hits and one bomb-aimer is probably still boring his

---

5. A more grandiose title for the erstwhile Backers-up.

children with a graphic account of how he hit a ship attempting to leave the harbour.

The night of November 27 saw two forces in action, one against Neuss in the Ruhr and the other against Freiburg in southern Germany. At Neuss, the 200 bombers had to contend with 10/10ths thin stratus but *Oboe* Mosquitoes where dropping both ground and skymarkers and so crews had the choice of bombing on the green flares or on the glow of the red TIs. The initial fires were in the central districts spreading westwards but later crews started fires in the eastern half of the town. Here the explosions were described as 'fierce and frequent' and a reconnaissance crew from 1409 Flight, reported that there were numerous fires throughout the city and to the east the explosions were still occurring.

Oboe ground crews, operating from mobile caravans on the Continent, brought towns like Freiburg, near the Swiss border within *Oboe* range and five Marker crews from 105 and 109 Squadrons laid the foundation for what the Germans described as one of the most outstanding attacks of the year. The Illuminators, often a maligned force, made the Visual Markers' task easy by lighting the aiming point. W/Cdr T.E. Ison controlled the attack admirably and, although the 5/10ths broken cloud made accurate bombing difficult, the Wing Commander persuaded most crews to exercise a little patience and wait until they had a clear bombing run. According to reports from neutral sources large areas of the town were completely devastated and the main railway station, the marshalling yards, the railway repair shops and the post office were demolished. News had filtered through that German troops were massed in the town and their presence made the raid an excellent example of how the strategic and the tactical merged. The Germans reported that the death toll ran into four figures and, as the Karl Barracks was completely destroyed, it was hoped that the casualties were soldiers not civilians.

TROOP SUPPORT From October 1 to the end of the war 153,000 tons of bombs were dropped in support of the ground forces. The first call for help came from General Montgomery early in the month. The British Second Army had pushed on beyond Antwerp and this advance left its right flank exposed to German forces assembled in Cleve and Emmerich. By the night of October 7, Montgomery had one less worry because earlier, in daylight, two Bomber Command forces had wiped out the opposition.

The enemy forces at Cleve, even if they had not experienced the terror of a Bomber Command support attack, had undoubtedly heard lurid accounts of their devastating effects. A lone Lancaster, inquisitively circling the town, could mean only one thing – they were about to be attacked. On cue the first Mosquito dropped its markers and the guns opened up. W/Cdr T.L. Bingham-Hall, whose Lancaster had created the hollow emptiness of fear, was in the direct path of the first shells to explode, his Lancaster was hit and the starboard inner burst into flames. The fire died out when the engine was feathered but valuable time had been lost checking the damage. Meanwhile other TIs had been dropped and the Main Force, reverting to type, had started to bomb the first markers they saw. Some crews, having apparently made the trip merely to add 5 points towards the required 150 for a tour, in fact cheated because they did not cross the German border; their bombs fell nearer Nijmegen than Cleve and W/Cdr T.E. Ison, the Long Stop, stepped in lest their frailty became infectious. When a salvo of TIs fell near the aiming point Bingham-Hall was able to convince the Main Force of the error of their ways and from then onwards the bombing was concentrated around the aiming point. The late-comers were instructed to bomb the centre of the smoke which had quickly enveloped the town.

At Emmerich the raid went like clockwork. W/Cdr. B.D.H. Foster, the Master Bomber, having visually identified the target, sat back and watched the TIs cascade into the railway centre. The Main Force obeyed his instructions to the letter. Soon smoke obscurred the target but two oil fires served as TIs and by the end of the attack the whole town was ablaze. A reconnaissance crew confirmed that both attacks were successful and reported that a cloud of thick brown smoke, rising to 15,000 feet, covered the whole area around Emmerich.

On November 16 Bomber Command was called in to support the American ground forces for the first time; 8 Group marked Duren and Julich for more than 800 bombers and the towns were obliterated. The 8 Group report covering these attacks said: ' . . . everyone did his job magnificently, hardly a building remained unscathed.' The 1st and 9th US Armies were more than pleased with the result.

The Von Rundstedt offensive opened on December 16 with a thrust through the Ardennes and, by December 23, the Germans had pushed the Allied forces back more than 60 miles on a 20-mile front. Widespread fog over England and low cloud over the Continent kept the Allied air forces grounded and the offensive prospered until they were able to create chaos behind the enemy lines.

The enormous success of the Transportation Plan in France prompted Eisenhower to call on Bomber Command to attack marshalling yards in the Ruhr and Coblenz areas and also to help in the attacks on the Ruhr airfields. Bonn and Cologne Nippes marshalling yards were marked by PFF on December 21 but, because of 10/10ths cloud, crews had to bomb either on the skymarkers or the glow of the TIs.

The next night, at Bingen, *Oboe* groundmarkers which fell across the aiming point were immediately backed up and some useful bombing by 90 Halifaxes of 4 Group, reduced in strength because of bad weather at bases, caused three explosions in quick succession. The same night the marshalling yards at Coblenz were groundmarked by PFF, but because of cloud most crews had to bomb on the Emergency *Wanganui* flares.

On the morning of December 23, a small force of Pathfinders, 27 Lancasters and 3 Mosquitoes, took off from Little Staughton, Graveley and Bourn to attack the Gremburg marshalling yards at Cologne in three formations, each led by an *Oboe* Lancaster with an *Oboe* Mosquito acting as reserve. This ill-fated sortie got off to an inauspicious start when two Lancasters collided over the Thames estuary. Some crew members escaped by parachute but, although rescue vessels were on the scene within 20 minutes, they died from exposure. Cloud over Cologne was forecast as 10/10ths with tops at 10,000 feet but the cloud ended 20 miles short of the target and the formations, flying at 17,000 feet, were exposed to murderous heavy and light flak visually predicted. The leading Lancaster, with S/Ldr R.A.M. Palmer of 109 Squadron at the controls, was hit; two engines were set on fire; flames and smoke were pouring out of the nose and the bomb-bay was ablaze. In this type of formation crews released their loads when they saw the leading aircraft bomb, so Palmer knew that if he jettisoned or released too soon all the other bombs would miss the target. Facing almost certain death he maintained his course until the release signal was sent from the ground station and his bombs were seen to hit the target. Seconds later the Lancaster spiralled to earth and crashed in flames; there was only one survivor. Palmer was awarded the VC for this act of conspicuous bravery, the culmination of an operational career which spanned three years and ended on this his 110th sortie against the enemy. Equally courageous was F/Lt E.C. Carpenter immediately behind in a Mosquito. The Mosquito had one engine feathered, the other on fire and four enemy aircraft on its tail, but he too knew he must not bomb before the leader because the rest of the formation might bomb when they saw his bombs falling. The Mosquito also crashed in flames, both members of the crew being killed.

Part of a force of 250 German fighters, which had been sent to oppose USAAF activity in the vicinity, attacked the formation and, in addition to the Mosquito, shot down 3 Lancasters. F/O R.P. Terpenning's Lancaster was hit by flak over the target; the starboard inner was damaged, the port inner put out of action and the hydraulics rendered unserviceable. As the bomber turned away from the target it was engaged by 5 fighters, a mixed pack of Fw190s and Me109s. They attacked in turn, the first opening up from 900 yards; the range lessened after the second one had damaged the Lancaster. Cannon shells ripped into the rear turret and navigator's compartment; the instruments on the control panel were shattered, the starboard aileron control severed save for a single strand and the port petrol tanks were holed. Although the Lancaster had withstood the combat it was obviously doomed and as he was over Belgium, behind

Allied lines, the captain ordered the crew to bale out. Miraculously none of them had been injured and they landed safely if somewhat unconventionally. The Lancaster crashed a few miles away and was burnt out.

W/Cdr J.H. Clough had an inconclusive combat with an Me109 and Capt E. Swales survived a running battle with 8 Me109s and an Fw190. The Focke-Wulf was shot down and two of the Messerschmitts were damaged. Swale's gunners did not panic in spite of the odds and made every shot count. Although lead seemed to be flying everywhere no one was injured.

By comparison the other two formations appear to have had an easy ride but none of the participants would agree. They were fortunate only in the fact that the fighters concentrated on the leading formation. The ground defences knew the target, the height and the track of the bombers. The flak was so intense and accurate that both formations broke and dive-bombed the target visually, leaving the two *Oboe* Lancasters, with their Mosquitoes in tow, to brave it alone. S/Ldr G.W. Harding, whose Lancaster was extensively damaged by flak, three engines being hit, saw his bombs straddle the target. S/Ldr H. Almond's Mosquito was also hit by flak, rendering the hydraulics unserviceable and, as the bomb-doors would not open, he had to bring his bombs back. The third *Oboe* Lancaster, piloted by F/Lt R.E. Jordan, was hit seven times by flak and fire broke out in the fuselage so he jettisoned his load as soon as he saw the marshalling yards. S/Ldr G.W.A. Parker, in the reserve Mosquito, waited for the release signal and saw his Cookie burst in the yards. Although he could offer only moral support Parker stayed in formation with Jordan until he reached the safety of cloud. Both *Oboe* Lancasters force-landed at Manston where, earlier, three other severely damaged Lancasters from the sortie had found refuge. One Mosquito was shot down and the other two damaged: 5 Lancasters were shot down, 2 collided, 20 were damaged by flak and 2 were also damaged in combat. After the raid it was worse than treason to mention *Oboe* Lancaster formations in 8 Group.

In the afternoon, four *Oboe*-led Mosquito formations attacked the Sieburg marshalling yards at Cologne and because of bad weather at bases all of them were diverted.[6]

Two controlled *Musical Parramatta* daylight attacks on airfields on the Rhine on December 24 were both successful. At Mulheim (Essen) it was obvious the force was expected but, in spite of the fierce opposition, the runways were left well cratered and several buildings were hit. The attack at Lohausen (Dusseldorf) appeared to be more successful for, in addition to bomb damage to the runways, several Fw190s were destroyed on the ground and a large hangar was almost completely gutted.

In the evening, 6 *Oboe* Mosquitoes and 14 PFF heavies marked the

---

6. For more detailed account see LNSF.

Nippes marshalling yard at Cologne for a small force of 81 Lancasters of 1 Group. Fortunately, High Wycombe was shrouded in fog and the clear skies were over the target, for 700 airmen, whose original plans for Christmas Eve had been to extend goodwill to all men in as lavish a manner as they could afford, were turned into vengeful monsters. Accurate bombing around a well concentrated cluster of TIs reflected the mood of the crews. The yards could be seen clearly in the bomb flashes; damage to rolling stock was extensive and almost all of the tracks were hit. The yards were completely unserviceable for 24 hours. All PFF heavies were diverted.

A highly successful Controlled *Musical Parramatta* at St Vith on Boxing Day by 282 heavies probably did more to aid the Allied counter-offensive than any other single factor. The vital crossroad there was blocked by piles of rubble that minutes earlier had been a village, and the cratered area was so extensive that it was impossible to detour. It was a week before the roads were usable.

Troop concentrations at Houffalize were attacked on December 30-31 and again on January 5-6, 1945, causing utter confusion by demolishing the town and cratering the surrounding area. The attacks bore a close resemblance to those on Villers Bocage in June and south of Caen in July 1944 but with more devastating effect. The main roads in the salient converged on the town and its destruction forced the Germans to disperse as they retreated, at a time when they were trying to regroup to slow the Allied advance.

OIL Harris has been criticised because he did not concentrate on the Wehrmacht's oil supply in the last quarter of 1944; in mitigation it must be said that more than 23,000 tons of bombs were dropped on oil targets and this represents more than half the weight dropped on all targets in the corresponding period of 1943. Allied air attacks on these targets through the summer months had reduced the March monthly output figure of 480,000 tons by 75%. During October and November, production figures rose but, by the end of the year, when Speer had hoped supply would exceed demand, the output had been reduced to little more than 10% of the March figure.

With the exception of the Chemischewerke at Kamen, which was already out of production, the ten main plants in the Ruhr were attacked.[7] The Leuna synthetic oil plant at Merseburg and the Politz plant near Stettin were also bombed. There were 27 attacks on 15 plants but Pathfinders were concerned in only ten of them, three being carried out

7. The other nine where Nordstern, Scholven, Wesseling, Homburg, Wanne Eickel, Sterkrade, Castrop Rauxel, Bottrop and Dortmund.

on skymarkers and one mainly on DR because of the weather conditions.

In daylight on October 6, small forces attacked Scholven Buer and Sterkrade Holten. Marking on both targets was accurate and concentrated and many Main Force crews, aided by the TIs, were able to identify the targets visually. The reports of fires, explosions and smoke were almost identical but PRU cover showed the Sterkrade damage to be the more severe. Equally identical was the intensity of the flak and 9 out of 292 crews were shot down: marker crews on both targets seemed to be the focus of attention. All 6 aircraft of 635 Squadron on Scholven were hit by flak and F/Lt G. A. Thorne's Lancaster was so badly damaged that he had to make a crash landing at Woodbridge. A direct hit killed Sgt J.D. Crabtree and wounded the gunners. At Sterkrade where 35 and 156 Squadrons were on duty several aircraft were hit and one seriously damaged. Just before reaching the target, F/O L.N.B. Cann was wounded when his Lancaster received a direct hit by heavy predicted flak. He collapsed over the controls and the flight engineer and navigator/set operator, perhaps thinking he was dead, baled out. Cann recovered quickly and pressed on to the target. After piloting the Lancaster away from the defences he was in a state of complete exhaustion; the navigator and wireless operator had to drag him out of his seat and carry him to the rest bed. Sgt R.V. Fisher, the navigator, then took over the controls and brought the Lancaster back to base. Cann was helped back into the pilot's seat and landed the aircraft. He was given an immediate award of the DFC and Fisher the DFM. For his outstanding display of leadership Fisher was granted an immediate field commission.

Although, unknown to Bomber Command, production at the Holten plant Sterkrade was at a standstill, a second raid was made on the night of November 21. Skies were clear and the 247 crews had a compact group of reds and greens to aim at. Their bombs stifled all hopes of repairing the plant. Earlier in the evening 260 bombers had attacked Castrop Rauxel. Here too the marking was excellent and the bombing was a credit to 1 and 6 Groups. The damage was extremely severe throughout the plant and almost every individual building was damaged. The September raid had halted production for five weeks and earlier in November, just when the plant was getting back into its stride, a 3 Group daylight attack had stopped it again. After the night attack, Edmund Geilenberg, who had been especially commissioned by Hitler to keep the plants active, threw in his hand: the plant was beyond repair.

Pathfinders led two attacks to Wanne Eickel on October 12 and November 18-19. For the daylight attack on the 12th, the marking was excellent with reds and greens forming a circle around the aiming point, but they were quickly obliterated by smoke. A direct hit on an oil storage tank early in the attack started a fire and the thick black smoke blew across the target. Main Force crews bombed the smoke and as it spread to the north-east the bombing spread in that direction too.

For the November attack, 6 Non-*Musical* Mosquitoes flew in with the first *Oboe* crews and after *Windowing* the target made an orbit to bomb their reds. Cloud was 6-9/10ths but the diligent 'heavy' Pathfinders maintained the marking and achieved an excellent concentration. The Main Force too was patient and waited for gaps in the cloud. The raid was notable for the large number of explosions, and one in particular, seen from 40 miles away, shot out an enormous jet of flame lighting up the sourrounding area for three or four seconds.

On December 6 at Leuna, PFF's only oil target outside the Ruhr, the 10/10ths cloud made the planned *Newhaven* attack hopeless. Blind Markers dropped TIs and skymarkers but the flares drifted in the strong wind and there could be little hope of a good attack. For the last oil attack of the year, at Scholven on December 29, crews bombed on the glow of the TIs seen through the 10/10ths stratus. The *Oboe* Markers must have been accurate because thick black smoke forced its way through the cloud and rose to 12,000 feet.

After the shock of the von Rundstedt offensive[8] more than a quarter of Bomber Command's effort was devoted to oil targets and 69 attacks were made on 44 plants and refineries involving, 11,418 aircraft. The number of attacks, rather than the weight of bombs dropped, gives a clearer indication of Bomber Command's effort in the oil offensive; large forces were required to demolish a city whereas comparatively smaller ones could cause devastation in the plants and refineries.

The ten large synthetic oil plants in the Ruhr were capable of producing one-third of Germany's output. One by one they had been put out of action by Bomber Command and at the end of November production was at a standstill. Moreover, at least four of them were damaged beyond repair. The three main plants outside the Ruhr were at Leuna (Merseburg), Politz and Brux and, in the New Year, Bomber Command turned its attention to them. On January 14-15, Pathfinders spearheaded the second of a two-phase attack on Germany's largest synthetic oil plant, Leuna. When S/Ldr C.P.C. de Wesselow, the Master Bomber, arrived over Merseburg the target was covered by 10/10ths low stratus at 2,000 feet. There was little evidence that a raid by more than 200 aircraft had taken place four hours earlier, although one or two crews reported small fires to the north of the target. De Wesselow called for *Wanganui* flares and as the winds were light at 15,000 feet[9] they drifted only slowly which helped to keep the bombing concentrated. Two large explosions started

8. High Command had been confident that German oil stocks were too low to permit an offensive.

9. *Wanganui* flares were usually fused to burst at heights to between 15,000 and 16,000 feet.

fires which gave off black smoke billowing well above the cloud tops and they provided additional target markers for later crews.

PRU reported severe damage throughout the plant, the northern half being heavily hit, and the ORS gave a list of the vital parts affected, their significance being intelligible only to someone in the industry. When PRU visited the plant a month later it was totally inactive and there were no signs that any repair work had been attempted.

Most 8 Group aircraft were diverted to Ford and Exeter so news of crews who had met with misfortune came secondhand. Over the target, bombs from a 'friendly' aircraft had severed the rear turret from S/Ldr D.B. Everett's Lancaster and the rear gunner, F/O R.T. Salvoni, fell with the turret and was presumed to have been killed. Everett, as Johnson had before him, found that the Lancaster could be controlled provided it was only required to respond slowly. A sudden clampdown in the weather at 8 Group bases meant he had an extra 200 miles to fly before he landed safely at Exeter.

F/O F. Lloyd's Lancaster was also hit by falling bombs. The mid-upper gunner had a narrow escape when two of them went straight through the fuselage just in front of his turret and out through the bomb-bay. The main damage was to the starboard mainplane and the starboard engines seized, causing the Lancaster to make a diving turn to starboard. Lloyd ordered the crew to bale out. As the aircraft dived from 18,000 to 10,000 feet most of the crew found the 'g'[10] too great for them to obey the order, but the bomb-aimer managed to jump. At 10,000 feet, Lloyd regained control and rescinded the order. The North Sea crossing was a nightmare: the struggle to keep the aircraft level and on course with the power all on one side; the graph of loss of height over distance covered foreboded a watery climax to the sortie, and the damaged starboard wing, shuddering under the strain, looked for all the world as if it were waving goodbye. The Kent coast made a timely appearance with the Lancaster at 2,000 feet and Lloyd made a masterly landing at Manston.

Having unsuccessfully tried to destroy the important plant at Politz near Stettin, on January 13-14, 5 group were given first bite of the cherry on February 8-9. Crews in the second phase had to contend with cloud along the whole of the route but 20 miles from the target the skies cleared and conditions were ideal for a Controlled *Newhaven*. The six fires burning in the target area from the 5 Group attack were not bright enough to prevent the Deputy Master Bomber, F/Lt G. Lewis, and the Primary Visual Marker, F/Lt R.H. Phillips, from making a visual identification: the Deputy's TIs fell right on the A/P and those of the Primary Visual Marker close by, and they provided the nucleus of a good group of markers all within the factory boundaries. Backing-up was consistently

10. Due to aircraft falling at a greater rate than the body.

good and maintained throughout the sortie. Most crews were on time and bombing was well concentrated. Within minutes the whole target was a mass of flames and numerous explosions were reported, one lighting up the whole area. No one doubted the raid was a resounding success; PRU cover was a mere formality.

The Fates were unkind to Everett; having successfully piloted his damaged Lancaster back from Leuna in January against the odds, he was shot down on March 7 over Hemmingstedt Heide when he was on duty as a Master Bomber. In consequence the attack lacked the concentration required for this type of target, but it was given only 13 days remission for, between 0330 and 0400 hours on the 20th, a force of more than 400 bombers destroyed the plant. Two hours earlier at Upwood, F/Lt T. Grant had started his engines and, on the run-up, found one of them faulty. He and his crew made a quick switch to the reserve aircraft, taking off 10 minutes late. As Master Bomber, Grant was expected to be over the target 6 minutes before zero hour, so he opened the throttles to make up lost time. The starboard inner found the strain too much and seized, but the other three shouldered the extra load and got him there on time. The attack was a Controlled *Newhaven* and Grant found two groups of reds and greens awaiting his assessment. One group was near the aiming point and he called in a Visual Centerer to reinforce it. He warned the Main Force of the stray markers and told them to watch for cascading TIs if they were uncertain which was the correct group. Explosions, fires and thick black smoke, the basic ingredients of a successful oil attack, were the just rewards of his endeavour and the fruits of a bombing force which took the trouble to bomb accurately.

GERMAN TOWNS On February 23-24, almost the entire built-up area of Pforzheim was completely devastated by 368 heavies. The raid, a Controlled *Musical Parramatta*, was carried out from a low level. Bomber Command tried out a new ruse: the *Mandrel* screen was used to cover a *Window* feint and the Main Force was sent in unprotected but with instructions to fly below 5,000 feet until it reached 07 °00E and then climb on track to 8,000 feet, the operational height. The experiment was unsuccessful – the German nightfighters were assembled in the Stuttgart area only minutes away from the actual target.

The Master Bomber, Captain E. Swales, the Deputy and two Primary Visual Markers readily identified the A/P aided by the Blind Illuminators' flares released around accurately placed *Oboe* TIs and within minutes the marker force had established a good concentration of reds and greens. Obeying the Master Bomber's instruction almost to the letter, the Main Force turned in a fine piece of bombing, one of the best ever achieved. The Visual Centerers' TIs were superfluous for creepback was negligible and the fires, which began early in the attack, spread rapidly until the whole of the target area was covered by smoke. Hardly a building remained intact throughout the town, in which almost every house was a small workshop, making precision parts for instruments and munitions.

Swales was one of 10 crews shot down by the enemy. Eight minutes after dropping his TIs and while still controlling the attack, Swales's Lancaster was attacked by an Me410. First sighted on the starboard quarter level by the rear gunner, P/O A.A. Bourne, the fighter was lost to view when it dived. Seconds later Bourne spotted it climbing up to attack and he ordered a dive to starboard. Swales, broadcasting instructions on the VHF, did not hear the order so no evasive action was taken. Bourne pressed the starboard indicator as the fighter pilot opened up from 800 yards, and returned the enemy's fire. Although he could see tracer hitting the Messerschmitt it came in relentlessly and when his four guns jammed in quick succession, the German raked the Lancaster with another long burst. The mid-upper, F/Sgt B. Leach, picked up the fighter at 400 yards, but was unable to get a bead on it until it broke away to port. He too scored hits and suddenly the Messerscmitt rolled off the top and dived away vertically.

During the enemy's first burst, the tailplane and rudder were damaged and the port inner burst into flames, but the fire subsided when the engine was feathered. Cannon shells from the second burst hit the starboard inner and it too had to be feathered. A fuel tank on the starboard side was also holed. The crew were told to don parachutes but the order was rescinded when the aircraft seemed to be performing satisfactorily and even responded when the captain asked it to climb. The chief anxiety at this stage was how long the electrics would last as the generator was driven off the inner engines, and lack of current later caused the DR compass to fail. Even then the situation did not become critical until the Lancaster had to fly in cloud associated with a cold front. Loss of all blind-flying equipment, particularly the artificial horizon, caused endless problems in cloud, and turbulence associated with cold front conditions added to the difficulties of maintaining level flight. Swales, realising that the odds on survival had changed dramatically, ordered the crew to bale out. With the last crew member safely away he tried to make a crash landing but the Lancaster spun in and the petrol tanks exploded, turning the aircraft into a blazing inferno. The citation for the captain's VC concluded '. . . Intrepid in the attack, courageous in the face of danger, he did his duty to the last, giving his life that his comrades might live'.[11]

Harris was 'requested'[12] to bomb Dresden, Chemnitz, Leipzig and

---

11. Capt E. Swales was the only member of the South African Air Force to operate with PFF.

12. Letter, Bottomley to Harris, dated January 27, 1945.

Berlin as part of the combined offensive in support of the Russian advance. Dresden and Chemnitz were on Harris's original list of German area towns and now their importance was enhanced because they were vital centres of communication for men and materials in transit to the Eastern Front. The Americans had already attacked the Dresden marshalling yards on January 16 before the proposals had been put forward, and almost three weeks before the idea was discussed with the Russians.

Bomber Command in general and Harris in particular have been cast as inhuman monsters for their part in the destruction of the city, and in some quarters it was said that because of this attack Mr Attlee did not honour the AOC-in-C in a manner similar to the commanders of the other forces. It was curious, too, how after the war the Germans, who needed America's financial aid, played down the USAAF's part in the attacks; they flew more than 500 missions to the town in the two days following the Bomber Command attack. As Webster and Frankland put it: 'The operations against Dresden were, therefore, only a part of a concerted action and the Bomber Command attack was only an element in a combined Anglo-American assault.'[13]

The attack, which took place on February 13-14, was in two phases. The bank of cloud, which had prevented 250 crews of 5 Group from making a concentrated attack, had moved 10 miles south of the target by 0130 hours when S/Ldr C.P.C. de Wesselow and W/Cdr H.J.F. Legood, the Master and Deputy from 8 Group, arrived over the town. Fires, smoke and haze prevented Visual Marker crews from identifying the aiming point and, working on Bennett's edict – a longhand circular, 'Markers – better not drop at all than not reliably' – they withheld their TIs. De Wesselow called up the Blind Markers and Legood went down to spot some well placed ones. At 0129 a group of reds fell just short of the river and de Wesselow ordered crews to bomb them with a 2-second overshoot. The water mains were hit in the early stages of the attack and fires were able to spread unchecked. Soon they had gained an uncontrollable hold and later crews were told to bomb the centre of the smoke.

In this one night the havoc created was equal to, and many say exceeded, that caused at Hamburg. In the narrow streets, flanked by tall buildings, similar firestorms were started and, as at Hamburg, the river proved to be the sole protection against the intense heat. The following day, and again on February 15, the USAAF poured more bombs into the holocaust. More than 16,000 acres lay devastated. British PoWs brought in to clear the shambles said that the scenes of death and destruction were indescribable. As the news spread across Germany the people's morale finally broke. Realizing that Bomber Command could, in favourable conditions, mete out similar devastation anywhere in Germany their fear

13. 'The Strategic Air Offensive Against Germany', Vol III, page 190.

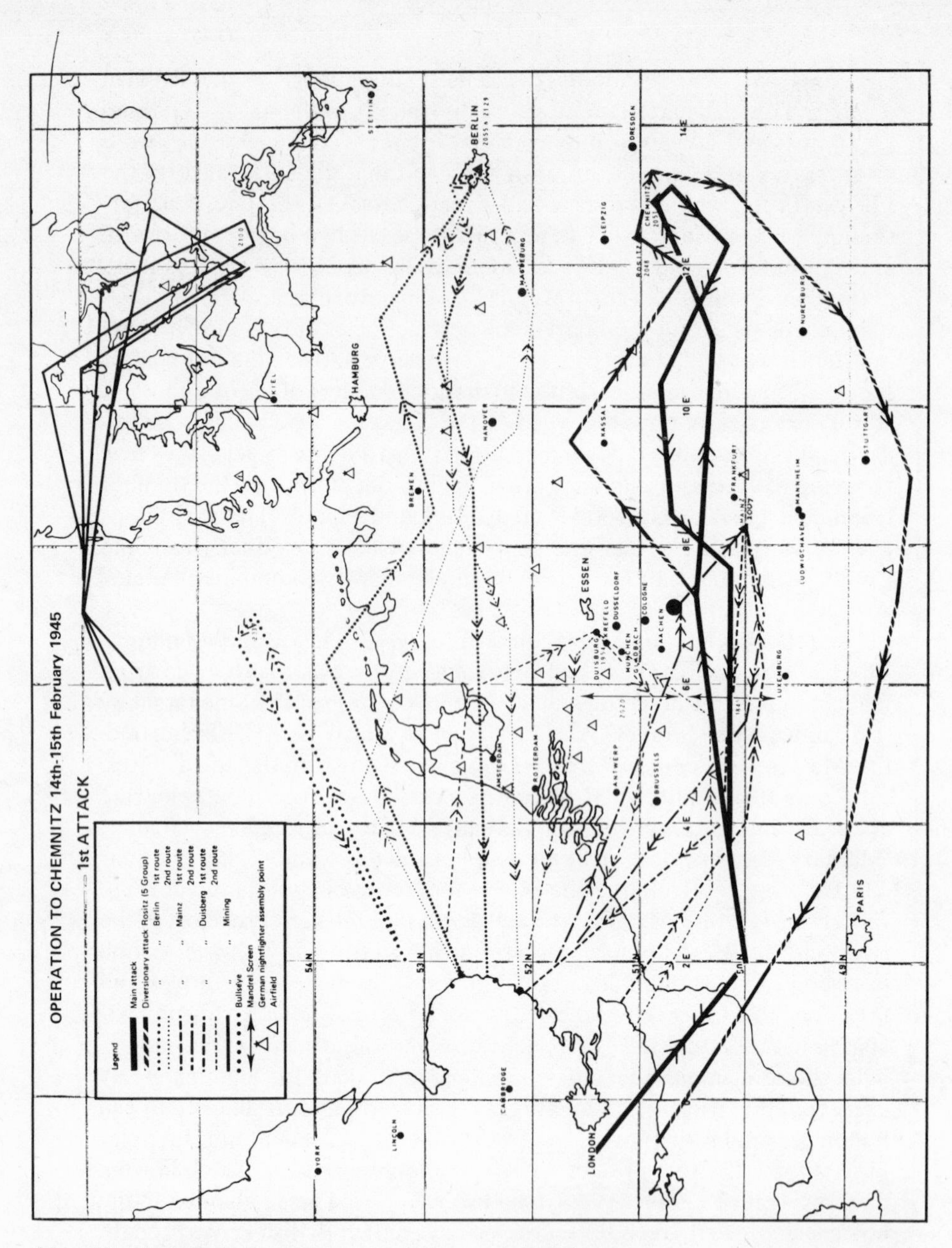

Maps 22 and 23 show the elaborate plans made to protect the Main Force in 1945. The Germans, having lost the advantage of their early warning systems combined with the acute shortage of petrol, were forced to keep the nightfighters on the ground until they were certain of the target. Then it was usually too late to make a telling interception. Had not the weather taken a hand Chemnitz might well have become a second Dresden.

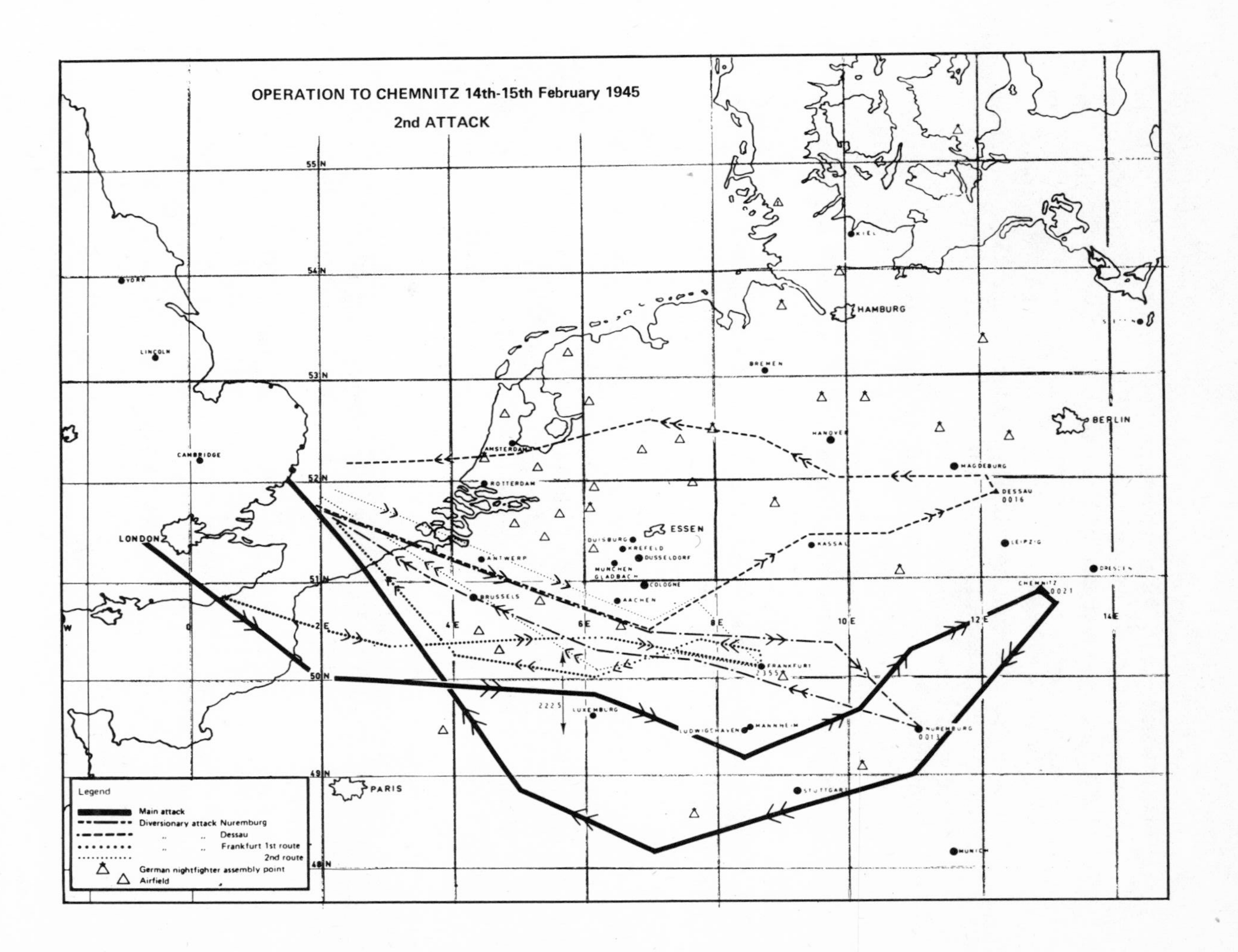
OPERATION TO CHEMNITZ 14th-15th February 1945
2nd ATTACK
55N
54N
53N
52N
51N
50N
49N
48N
W
0
2E
4E
6E
8E
10E
12E
14E
YORK
LINCOLN
CAMBRIDGE
LONDON
PARIS
KIEL
HAMBURG
BREMEN
HANOVER
BERLIN
MAGDEBURG
DESSAU
0016
LEIPZIG
DRESDEN
CHEMNITZ
0021
AMSTERDAM
ROTTERDAM
ANTWERP
BRUSSELS
ESSEN
DUISBURG
KREFELD
DUSSELDORF
MUNCHEN GLADBACH
COLOGNE
AACHEN
KASSAL
FRANKFURT
2355
2225
LUXEMBURG
LUDWIGSHAVEN
MANNHEIM
NUREMBURG
0013
STUTTGART
MUNICH
Legend
Main attack
Diversionary attack Nuremburg
Dessau
Frankfurt 1st route
2nd route
German nightfighter assembly point
Airfield

of the Gestapo was no longer paramount. It might seem banal to point out that the military objective was achieved. The railway station was completely destroyed and four bridges across the Elbe were damaged or destroyed.

The following night, February 14-15, Bomber Command laid on one of its most elaborate night operations (see Maps 22 and 23), a two-phase Main Force attack on Chemnitz with a 5 Group diversion on Rositz. There were a bewildering number of feints even from a British point of view: mining, *Bullseyes* and numerous LNSF spoofs, a protective *Mandrel* screen, and 100 Group put up intruders and aircraft to jam German radar. As so often happened the weather had the last word: cloud prevented visual identification and the Master Bombers on both phases had to call for Emergency *Wanganui* flares.

A second attack on March 5-6 was also made from above cloud but as it was forecast Pathfinders, reverting to the Berlin Method, provided a continuous supply of *Wanganui* flares sufficient to the needs of the 686 bombers. When 6 LNSF Mosquitoes attacked later they reported that the fires were concentrated and burning fiercely. The town centre was almost entirely burnt out and to the south another blaze had completely gutted most of the built-up area. Bomber Command showed no favouritism; every factory had received a calling card.

F/O J.C. Gould, one of the Blind Markers, had dropped his bombs but because of the cloud condition had retained his TIs. Back over England the Lancaster crashed near Chesham in Buckinghamshire. After a sudden explosion believed to have been a TI bursting, the aircraft plummeted to earth and all the crew were killed except Sgt G. Hart, the rear gunner, who was blown clear.

Two nights later at Dessau the attack started as a *Wanganui* but, when the cloud began to clear, crews were able to bomb groundmarkers. Almost immediately fires spread throughout the town and Siren Tour Mosquitoes said they covered an area of 2 x 1 miles.[14] The whole of the city was laid waste; all four Junkers factories were hit, the railway station and marshalling yards severely damaged.

The losses, 20 from Chemnitz and 18 from Dessau, although low in comparison with those of the previous March, showed that the nightfighters, when given an opportunity, could still make their presence felt. P/O L.E. Larson was still in the target area, having dropped his bombs, when the rear gunner, W/O R.W. Hainsworth, shouted, 'Dive port, Skipper,' and then calmly shot down a fighter coming in from the port. Before he could swing his turret a second fighter had come in close

---

14. Fire damage was high on these targets because of the percentage of IBs dropped: 60% on Chemnitz; 56% on Dessau and, although only 44% on Dresden, it was nevertheless more than 1,000 tons.

and cannon shells ripped into the rear turret setting it on fire. W/O G. Hobbs, the mid-upper, got a bead on it as it broke away and when last seen it was falling in flames. P/O R.B. Van Metre, the wireless operator, heedless of his own danger, forced his way into the blazing rear turret. He found Hainsworth slumped over the guns oblivious of his burning parachute. Although he believed Hainsworth to be dead, Van Metre still tried to pull him clear but without success. As the fire was getting out of control, he took the only other possible course, which was to bale him out. Meanwhile, a third fighter had strafed the bomber causing further damage and putting one engine out of action. When pulses had slowed, after the feverish battle with the fire had been won, the journey seemed interminable as the three Merlin engines dragged the severely damaged Lancaster back to Gransden Lodge.

Perhaps the most remarkable feature of the bomber offensive at this stage was the concentration achieved in *Wanganui* attacks, particularly in daylight. 'Widespread damage' of 1943 was superseded by 'devastation' in the final phase. This was, of course, due to all-round teamwork in the marker squadrons helped by a new weapon, the coloured Smoke Puff: it was readily identifiable, one of the main essentials of a good marker, and remained visible longer than a flare. But an even more important factor was that Pathfinder navigators had become adept in the use of the GPI and so were able to augment *Oboe* skymarkers with an accuracy which often vied with their high-flying team-mates.

Wuppertal Barmen was the most devastated town in the Reich, 94% destroyed: its first major attack on May 29-30, 1943, when the town was almost demolished, has been recorded.[15] By March 13, 1945, it had recovered to 50% of its former output. On that day 354 bombers dropped 897 tons of HE and 256 tons of IBs on accurately positioned Smoke Puffs dropped by Pathfinders, and life in the town ceased.

The Town Clerk kept precise accounts of the damage and his records show that in the combined towns of Barmen and Elberfeld 1,186 factory buildings were totally destroyed and 776 heavily damaged. During the final raid, the destruction of the gas and power stations added to the misery of the willing dupes who, in the space of two years, had twice seen their livelihoods disappear and their homes turned into a heap of rubble.

COMMUNICATIONS, TROOP SUPPORT AND CLIMAX In the cross-section of the 30 towns attacked by Bomber Command in 1945 the two-fold nature of the attacks, the strategic and the tactical, became more closely allied, not because of any change in the method but chiefly in the timing. There was always an element of the tactical in Bomber Command strategic attacks

15. Battle of the Ruhr, page 44

even in 1943. U-boat batteries at Hagen, shipping at Hamburg, rail centres and oil targets were damaged in the Battle of the Ruhr, the raids on Kassel delayed the V-1 launchings; the incidents were grouped under the heading 'bonus' because they were the result and not the intention. At Dresden and Chemnitz the devastation tended to overshadow the tactical importance, but the raids coincided with the new Russian offensive and the chaos behind the German Eastern Front was an important factor in the Russian's success.

The attacks on marshalling yards and rail centres were of a more direct tactical nature and as, in general, the timing coincided with an Allied advance they can be combined with the direct troop support – which accounted for 29.8% of Bomber Command's effort in 1945.

Although the ground lost in the von Rundstedt offensive had been regained by the middle of January, the confidence of the Allied ground forces had been severely shaken and Eisenhower cosseted them by calling on the air forces to soften up the opposition. In January, Saarbrucken was attacked four times in two days and Kornwestheim and Zuffenhausen, two of Stuttgart's outlying marshalling yards, were destroyed ahead of the 3rd and 7th US Armies' advance into the Saar Basin. Mainz, in the same theatre, was the target for 261 heavies on February 1.

In the north, Cleve and Goch were wiped out on February 7-8 as a prologue to the Canadian Army's advance into the territory between the Meuse and the Rhine. Cloud base was at 5,000 feet over both targets and the Master Bombers ordered crews to come below the cloud. The attacks were *Musical Newhavens* and accurate *Oboe* Mosquito proximity TIs combined with brilliant illumination made the Primary Visual Markers' task a formality. At Goch at Z+10 the whole target area was covered with smoke. Bombing then tended to become erratic, mainly as a result of crews not coming below cloud. Although less than a third of the force of 464 had bombed, S/Ldr A.W.G. Cochrane cancelled the attack because Canadian troops were close to the town.

Ten miles away, W/Cdr Baker had no problems: 286 out of 305 in his force completely demolished Cleve; 1 Group's bombing was of the same high standard as 8 Group's marking, and the Long Stop had no worries. In his message to Harris, the GOC-in-C 1st Canadian Army described the bombing as being of the '. . . usual super quality . . .'

The American 1st and 3rd Armies were camped on the banks of the Rhine by the end of February. In daylight on March 2, 858 British bombers were sent to attack German troops and armour which were concentrated in Cologne to oppose the American 1st Army seeking to make a bridgehead at Remagen, south of Bonn. *Oboe* Mosquitoes dropped *Wanganui* Smoke Puffs, but there was no cloud and the target could be seen clearly; S/Ldr P.F. Clayton called in the Lancaster crews to drop groundmarkers. As 0900 hours approached, he could see the gaggle of more than 800 bombers stretching back for miles and realized that they were not going to arrive on time, so he held up the marking for two minutes. The first waves pounded the area around the TIs and soon the whole area was covered in smoke and dust. Clayton then gave the order '*Pickwick*', which was the code word for 'bomb with upwind edge of the smoke'; 686 crews attacked and turned the target area and southward for 3½ miles into a mass of rubble. It was so heavily cratered that the armoured vehicles were marooned in Bomber Command's version of tank traps, and the Tactical Air Forces had a busy day mopping up. By mid-March the American 1st Army had established the bridgehead at Remagen and the 3rd and 7th were pushing out of the Saar Basin.

Eisenhower planned to make a second bridgehead to the north of the Ruhr and then, with a pincer movement, isolate it from the rest of Germany. Paratroops were to be used to establish the bridgehead and, to avoid a second Arnhem, the Allied air forces had to ensure that no German troops could get into the area and Bomber Command made 17 attacks to help the plan.

D-Day for the drop was March 24 and 8 Group's first task was to mark the marshalling yards at the important rail and road centre Rheine, some 60 miles behind the German lines. A happy omen – the first day of spring was bright and sunny and W/Cdr D.A. Cracknell map-read his way to the target and obtained an excellent pinpoint on the yards. The 6 *Oboe* Mosquitoes coped and, when the Deputy, F/Lt D.J. Butters, and the Primary Visual Marker, F/Lt N. Alexander marked the A/P visually, TIs were more than adequate for Cracknell's needs. Some 140 Halifaxes were detailed to do the damage and, although from time to time volumes of smoke masked the TIs, under Cracknell's excellent directions the yards were left in complete chaos. The many explosions and healthy fires were also a good augury: urgently needed supplies would never reach their intended destination.

The following day, the targets were much nearer the front. Once more the marking was of a very high standard. At Dorsten, the *Oboe* TIs fell on the aiming point and the Master Bomber, F/Lt G.A. Thorne, dropped his yellows on top of them. The bombing force of 110 Halifaxes were over the target on time and showed their appreciation of this superb marking by starting fires which spread so quickly that within five minutes the whole area was covered with smoke which was forming a cloud at 10,000 feet by the end of the attack.

Dulmen, on the main route from Munster to Wesel, was an important road centre and harboured a GAF fuel storage depot. Here the Master Bomber, F/Lt R.M.B. Cairns, and his Deputy, F/Lt J.E. Brown, dropped their TIs on the A/P, but only the six 8 Group Supporters and a handful of Halifax crews were on time to take advantage of the excellent marking. Cairns ordered his Visual Centerers to hold their TIs until the main gaggle got nearer. Drifting smoke from the fires started by the first bombers gradually obscured the markers and Cairns, by ordering the last wave to bomb the upwind edge of the smoke, kept the bombing near the aiming point. Two huge explosions, patently in the fuel depot, were followed by fires thus reducing the *Luftwaffe's* rapidly dwindling stocks of fuel. On the night of March 23-24, *Oboe* Mosquitoes marked the north-western edge of Wesel for 218 Lancasters of 5 Group, who made a devastating attack. The first troops crossed the Rhine as the bombing ceased and the town was taken for the loss of only 36 Commandoes. Ironically, the only hazards facing the parachutists were made by the Allies: dust and smoke from the Wesel bombing and from dawn attacks by TAF were drifting across the dropping zones.

Throughout March 24, Allied air forces continued their role of interdiction with Bomber Command crews on Munchen Gladbach and Sterkrade. At Munchen Gladbach, when F/Lt L.B. Lawson arrived over the target, *Oboe* reds were burning on the A/P. The Deputy, F/Lt W.N. Cook, made an excellent run and his TIs also fell by the reds. Not to be outdone Lawson dropped his TIs right in the middle of both groups. Within a minute, the Main Force had the central area of the town shrouded in dust and smoke. As the northern districts had escaped so far Lawson ordered crews to bomb the northern edge of the smoke. There was devastation throughout the town and, judging by previous attacks, those of the troops who survived the bombing would be in no condition to fight for some time.

The 150 Halifax crews sent to Sterkrade were in a truculent mood and, at the beginning of the attack, bombed short of the excellent group of markers. With *Oboe* reds near the aiming point (the marshalling yards) and a group of red-greens on the A/P there was no excuse for this slackness and W/Cdr S.P. Coulson told them so in no uncertain manner Later crews, stung into proving their mettle, started fires, giving off dense smoke, and the many explosions pointed to the complete destruction of the military freight known to have been in the yards.

Two small forces attacked the Mathias Stinnes oil refinery at Bottrop and the Harpenerweg plant near Dortmund. W/Cdr J.W. Fordham, the Long Stop at Bottrop, had to cancel one group of TIs, but they were so far from the A/P they had no effect on the results. Explosions and smoke to several thousand feet summarized an excellent attack. At Harpenerweg, accurately placed *Oboe* TIs enabled F/Lt T.S. Harris, the Master Bomber, to identify this remotely sited target visually. Later *Musical* markers maintained the accuracy and the Backers-up too were right on the button. Fires, explosions and black smoke at both targets proved that small forces could cause extensive damage by concentrated bombing.

'An episode of valour and courage which might never have been recorded had it not been for superb airmanship on the part of the captain and the selfless devotion to duty of the survivors' was the dramatic prologue in the 156 Squadron ORB to F/O G.B. Hampson's ordeal at Harpenerweg. The Flying Officer was on his bombing run when his Lancaster received a direct hit near the bomb-bay and the flight engineer, Sgt D.R. Bowers, was wounded in the thigh. The aircraft, which was on fire and full of smoke, had assumed a nose-down attitude so Hampson ordered 'abandon aircraft' and the navigator and the wireless operator jumped from the front exit. F/Sgt J.R. Mann, the rear gunner, scrambled his way forward past the gaping holes in the fuselage, reporting that the mid-upper gunner was missing but his parachute was still in his turret. It was presumed that because of the smoke, he had not seen the large shell hole beneath his turret and had fallen through it. The flak was too close for comfort and as Hampson struggled with the controls in an effort to take evasive action, the Lancaster suddenly responded so he reversed the order to abandon aircraft. F/Sgt F.G. Reynolds, the navigator/set operator who had been helping the Bowers to bale out, called Mann to come and help him get the wounded flight engineer back on to the flight deck. As he was being dragged into the aircraft another direct hit shattered his left leg at the knee severing it save for a few tags of flesh. Bowers, an ex-medical orderly, supervised the dressing of his wound and injected himself with morphia. He continued giving advice on the state of the fuel and superintended all his normal duties. Mann stayed and helped his captain and Reynolds navigated the Lancaster back to Manston. The aircraft was graded 'Cat E', beyond repair. Excellent teamwork by the depleted crew and the outstanding courage of Bowers enabled them to survive.

If Essen and Dortmund were considered to be excellent examples of Pathfinders' devastatingly accurate skymarking on a large scale, then Paderborn must rank as one of the finest on a small scale. The daylight attack on March 27 was scheduled to be a *Musical Parramatta*, but a Mosquito from 1409 flight, sent ahead to report on the weather at the target, warned the Master Bomber, W/Cdr Coulson, of the 10/10ths cloud. He, in his turn, instructed his Lancaster marker crews to be prepared to drop their Emergency *Wanganui* Smoke Puffs. The marking was so accurate that a mere 270 bombers destroyed the town. As at Hamburg and Dresden, its narrow streets helped the fires to spread and a pall of smoke, one mile in diameter, formed above the cloud. Weeks later a ground observer said that there was little trace of separate buildings and streets and, even where roads had been cleared, it was done at the expense of the pavements, which were piled high with debris.

From a force of 482 bombers 11 aircraft, 3 of them Pathfinders, were shot down over Hamburg on March 31, a sharp reminder that the Hun must still be treated with respect. This attack brought Bomber Command's busiest month to a close; 21,341 sorties had been flown and of these 8 Group conrtributed 4,258. During the month, PFF had marked 39 major targets.

On April 1 the 1st and 9th US Armies met in the region of Soest and the Rhur armies were completely surrounded. The 1st and 9th then made a parallel push across Germany towards Magdeburg and Leipzig, and the 2nd British Army pushed towards Bremen and Hamburg. Ahead of the 1st Army, Bomber Command totally destroyed the military barracks at Nordhausen in two daylight attacks on April 3 and 4. On the night of April 4-5 more than 1,000 bombers were out, attacking oil targets at Lutzkendorf, Leuna and Harburg. 'Explosions, starting several fires, emitting large quantities of black smoke', was the report from Lutzkendorf, and the overspill destroyed two large buildings near the railway yards, where tracks were cut and rolling stock destroyed. At Leuna the attack was made above cloud and the bombing tended to be scattered, but the Rhenia plant at Harburg was left ablaze, following good bombing around a tight cluster of TIs: ten of the 19 storage tanks were gutted.

On April 10 the Englesdorf and Mockau railway centres at Leipzig were severely damaged, ahead of US troops, and the following day *Oboe* Mosquitoes continued their marksmanship by dropping TIs in the marshalling yards at Bayreuth, where smoke to 10,000 feet was reported. Further south, 14 Pathfinder Lancasters marked the marshalling yards at Nuremberg visually; in clear weather, the Primary Visual Markers had no difficulty in identifying the aiming point. The weight of the attack fell in the western half of the yards; explosions, fires and smoke, which later obscured the TIs and brought problems, nevertheless indicated a successful attack.

Four large explosions and smoke to 8,000 feet were the more modest claims from Schwandorf on April 16-17. Accurate *Oboe* reds were backed by very concentrated greens on and around the A/P, and the bombing rivalled the marking. It was the last attack on communications, but the German Navy remained a threat and the enemy was given a stern warning that the 'Wolf's Lair' was not impenetrable from above.

On April 6, Harris received his last directive: area bombing was to be discontinued and built-up areas attacked only at the request of the ground forces. Attacks on oil and communications were of the highest priority and the shipyards at Bremen, Hamburg and Kiel might profitably be attacked. The last of three attacks on the Blohm und Voss shipyards at Hamburg was made above cloud on April 8-9. More than 4,500 tons of bombs were dropped on the yards: damage was severe and widespread, many buildings being wholly or partly destroyed. The power-house was completely gutted and the gas-works were damaged in the last raid bringing the yards almost to a standstill. PRU photographs showed wrecked prefabricated submarines lying amongst the devastation.

A simultaneous attack on two A/Ps in Kiel harbour was a novelty and was carried out successfully. The 1409 Flight Met Mosquitoes reported the target clear of cloud and 8 non-*Musical* Mosquitoes *Windowed* ahead of the marking force. Blind Illuminator flares were accurately placed enabling the Primary Visual Markers on both A/Ps to mark accurately. The high quality of marking was maintained and the Main Force added three important scalps to its belt: the pocket battleship, the *Admiral Scheer*, capsized; the *Emden* burnt out; and the *Admiral Hipper* was wrecked. Almost every building in the Deutsche Werke suffered some damage many being gutted.

The island fortress of Heligoland and the Dune airfield were attacked by more than 900 bombers on April 18. There were three A/Ps, the main island, the naval base and the airfield. Whole areas were laid waste – only photographs could convey the utter devastation[16]. Marking, from the initial *Oboe* TIs to the last Backer-up, was of a high standard and the Master Bombers kept a tight rein on an enthusiastic Main Force. The next day, 33 Lancasters of 5 Group, 6 carrying Grand Slams and the remainder Tallboys, sent to flatten anything left standing, reported that the centre of the island was still ablaze.

A week later the coastal guns on Wangerooge were silenced, but most crews on the sortie were envious of the force sent to attack Hitler's country seat in the redoubt at Berchtesgaden. When W/Cdr J.W. Fordham and F/Lt C.G. Hitchcock, the Master and Deputy, arrived over the target the A/P was readily identifiable in the clear mountain air. As the first Mosquito, high above at 39,000 feet, circled round without marking Hitchcock went in and dropped his TIs. Marking and bombing befitted the occasion, everyone wanting to make each bomb count and hoping all the while that Hitler was at home. The SS barracks were largely destroyed; direct hits were scored on both wings of the chalet and the private residence of the SS chief was severely damaged. Bomber Command, twice chastened by the *Luftwaffe*, first by day and then by night, finally emerged triumphant and 'the almost contemptuous ease and success of the attack (Berchtesgaden) was a demonstration both of complete victory in the air and of the final defeat of Hitler's Germany'[17] This was the Pathfinder heavies' final blow against the Reich and, although the Mosquitoes continued bombing sorties until May 3, they too were running out of targets.

Before the end of April the Dutch airfields were back in the heavies' sights but the cargoes were food supplies for the starving population, and even the burning of the stand on The Hague racecourse by an *Oboe* TI did not dampen the cheers nor lessen the flag-waving from the grateful populace below. On April 24-25 medical supplies for prisoners of war

---

16. Plate number 59-62.
17. *Bomber Command Review*, 1945.

were dropped at Neubrandenburg and leaflets (Fig 2) were scattered over PoW camps warning the Germans of the dire consequences which would befall them if they harmed the prisoners.

The next pleasant task was to bring back PoWs. Everything, except bare essentials, was stripped out of the Lancasters and, between May 7 and 9, Pathfinders ferried 2,858 PoWs home to England, the first aircraft

Alliierte Kriegsgefangene

WARNUNG AN JEDEN, DER FÜR IHRE BEHANDLUNG VERANTWORTLICH IST

DIE Regierung von Grossbritannien, die Regierung der Vereinigten Staaten und die Regierung der Sowjet-Union richten hiermit zugleich im Namen aller Vereinten Nationen, die sich im Kriege mit Deutschland befinden, eine feierliche Warnung an alle Kommandanten und Bewachungsmannschaften, die Befehlsgewalt über alliierte Kriegsgefangene in Deutschland oder im deutsch-besetzten Gebiet haben, sowie an alle Angehörigen der Geheimen Staatspolizei und an alle anderen Personen, gleichgültig welchen Dienstzweiges und welchen Ranges, die alliierte Kriegsgefangene in Händen haben, sei es im Kampfgebiet, auf den Verbindungswegen oder im rückwärtigen Gebiet. Sie erklären hiermit, dass sie alle diese Personen ebenso wie das deutsche Oberkommando und die zuständigen deutschen Heeres-, Kriegsmarine- und Luftwaffe- Behörden für die Sicherheit und Wohlfahrt der ihnen anvertrauten alliierten Kriegsgefangenen persönlich verantwortlich machen.

Jedermann, der alliierte Kriegsgefangene misshandelt oder solche Misshandlung zulässt, gleichgültig ob im Kampfgebiet, auf den Verbindungswegen, im Lager, Lazarett, Gefängnis oder wo auch immer, wird rücksichtslos verfolgt und seiner Bestrafung zugeführt werden.

Sie weisen darauf hin, dass sie diese Verantwortung unter allen Umständen als bindend betrachten: auch kann diese Verantwortung nicht auf irgendwelche anderen Behörden oder Einzelpersonen abgeschoben werden.

Winston Churchill *Harry S. Truman* *Josef Stalin*

UNG 1

Fig. 2 A warning to camp Commandants and guards that they would personally be held responsible for the safety of PoWs Rumours had percolated through to the Allies that the German High Command had issued orders that PoWs, who could not be moved deeper into Germany, had to be shot rather than let them be released by the advancing armies.

58. Ground photographs showing damage to the Krupp works at Essen. A & C, medium and heavy guns; B, foundry; D, loco work shop; E, armoured trains

59 & 60. The fortress island of Heligoland, an important naval base, was saturated with 4,971 tons of bombs on April 18, 1945. Inset in this PRU photograph taken before the attack is an aerial shot of the naval base subsequently

61 & 62. Two oblique photographs showing the utter devastation in the northern half of the island

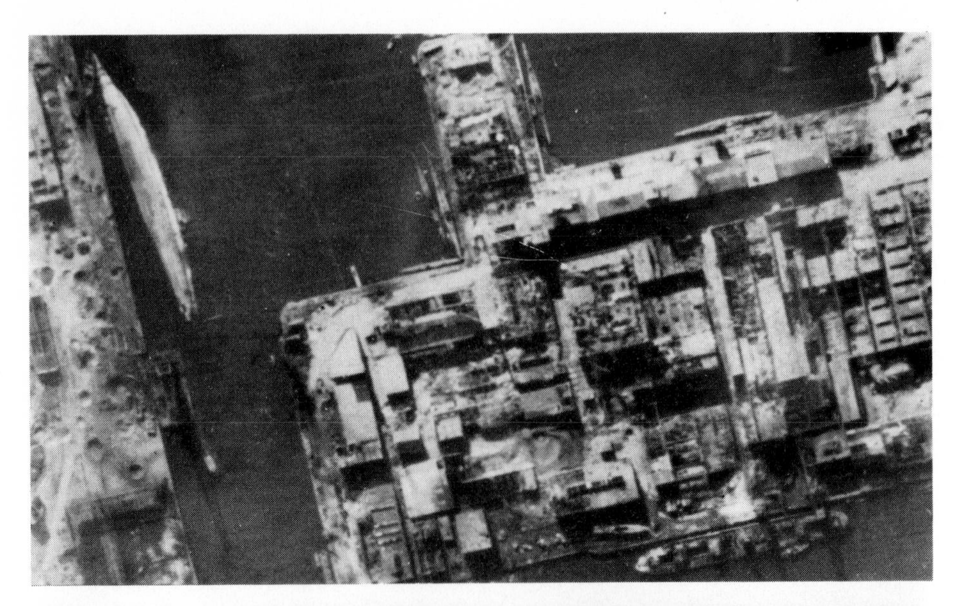

63. (*Top*) Photograph of Kiel Harbour showing part of the damaged shipyards after the raid of April 10, 1945. The attacks were primarily against U-Boats but the *Admiral Hipper* and the *Emden* were destroyed and the *Admiral Scheer* can be seen capsized at her moorings to the left

64. (*Bottom*) To demonstrate to the Nazi hierarchy that Bomber Command could search out and bomb any hide-out, however small and remote, a daylight raid was carried on the *Redoute* at Berchtesgaden on April 25, 1945. Unfortunately the owner was not in residence

being flown by Bennett. On May 10, 51 Lancasters took off for Lubeck-Blankensee and 39 of them returned with 894 happy airmen. The other 12 crews stayed overnight to ferry the stragglers but there were more aircraft than PoWs; the last three came home in grand style, being able to pick and choose their willing hosts.

VIII Mosquitoes

OBOE MOSQUITOES *Oboe*'s contribution to the success of the bomber offensive was second to none and, although from time to time other marking methods stole the limelight, its consistent accuracy in all weather conditions made it the king of all marking devices. The limitation of range with height curtailed its usefulness to Bomber Command during the second half of 1943 but, with the advent of *Overlord*, its unique ability to pinpoint targets, however small or well concealed, made its value inestimable. Later, when mobile stations were set up on the Continent, all targets in Germany within 250 miles of the western border could be marked. Finally, in 1945, the constant wish of 105 and 109 Squadrons' crews was granted, Berlin itself came within range.

Although 109 Squadron was a founder member of the Pathfinder Force and the crews had logged a lot of flying hours between August 18 and December 20, 1942, none of them had been against the enemy. The gremlins, having settled their differences with the Wellington Mk VI, took umbrage when the *Oboe* equipment was transferred into the Mosquito Mk IV: the transmitter in the aircraft started giving trouble and there was also intermittent interference which proved difficult to locate. Modifications were suggested, wrangled over, and some were eventually approved. The problems were not resolved until June 21, 1943, but Bennett's impatience and the crews' keenness to become operational resulted in the squadron going into the front line using unmodified equipment.

At 1755 hours on December 20, 1942, S/Ldr H.E. Bufton took off from Wyton to bomb the coking plant at Lutterade in Holland and at 1927 hours his navigator, F/Lt E.L. Ifould, released three 500-lb MC which fell a mere 200 yards from the aiming point – an excellent start to a brilliant future. Other bombing sorties followed and, on New Year's Eve, Bufton dropped skymarker flares over Dusseldorf for eight crews of 83 Squadron who dropped their bombs through 10/10ths cloud on to the unsuspecting town below. The bomber crews, briefed to fly on a predetermined heading, released their cargoes when they had a flare in their bombsights – the first *Wanganui* of the war. Eight similar attacks were made during January, the number of bombers increasing from 20 on the 3rd to 70 on the 13th. Essen was the target for seven of the attacks, the exception being on January 8 when Duisburg had its first experience of *Wanganui*. Dusseldorf, having been the stage for the first *Musical Wanganui*, was also the target for the first *Musical Parramatta* when, on January 27, 3 out of 5 Mosquitoes dropped red TIs for a force of 162 heavies. This was the first time the squadron had dropped groundmarkers for the Main Force and the 10/10ths stratus would have saved the town from attack had it not been for *Oboe*.

On February 2 both *Oboe* and H2S were used to mark Cologne, but the experiment left much to be desired.[1] There was no good concentration of TIs and the bombing was scattered. From February 2 to 26, the squadron carried out *Overture*[2] raids on six Ruhr targets apparently selected haphazardly and a new type of target, a nightfighter aerodrome, was bombed on February 16. The *Oboe* equipment failed in the first Mosquito sent to mark Cologne on February 26, so many of the 354 Main Force crews had bombed either visually or on ETA before the reds went down at Z+9. PFF heavies, having put in 10 minutes' unscheduled practice at taking evasive action, quickly surrounded the salvo of reds with a compact group of greens and the bombing, which a minute earlier had seemed doomed to be labelled 'scattered', became concentrated round the TIs.

The next marking attack was on February 28 when 2 out of 4 *Oboe* Mosquitoes dropped green TIs on St Nazaire. The Backers-up were also dropping greens and there were TIs burning throughout the duration of the attack. The last crews reported that the target area was a mass of fires with smoke enveloping the port.

Harris was a shrewd commander for, although he had been opposed to forming a pathfinder force[3], after he had been overruled he was determined to make it a success.[4] He could easily have made Pathfinders take all the blame for the unsuccessful attacks in the early stage, but he wisely did not relieve the Main Force crews of the responsibility of identifying the aiming point for themselves until PFF had its two main requirements, an accurate means of locating the target (H2S and *Oboe*) and a distinct method of marking it (TIs).

Pathfinders had been operating for six months before he put them to the supreme test. Essen, probably one of the most important targets in

---

1. C.M. Sharp and M.J.F. Bowyer in *Mosquito* say that the 11 Lancaster Backers-up were equipped with H2S. 83 Squadron were the Backers-up but, although they were the first Lancaster squadron to be equipped with H2S, they did not receive them until May 1943.

2. Code name for *Oboe* HE sorties.

3. He considered 'pathfinding' essential but he was opposed to an '*élite*' force.

4. He reacted in precisely the same manner when ordered to implement the Transportation Plan.

Germany, had to date escaped serious damage; its smoke haze hid it from the keenest bomb-aimer's eye. Gee, even before it was jammed, had proved too inaccurate for either the *Sampson* or *Shaker* techniques to be successful and the '1,000-bomber' raid of June 1, 1942, had missed the mark. Having no distinct shape and no outstanding features it was just a mass of echoes on the H2S screen, so all Bomber Command's hopes were centred on *Oboe*. The new blind bombing aid was equal to the challenge. On March 5, when 5 out of 8 Mosquitoes dropped their TIs in the Krupp works while their comrades in the Group some 10,000 feet below backed them up and kept the target marked throughout the duration of the attack. PRU photographs showed over 300 acres of devastation in the town, of which 66 acres were in Krupps, and the fires had raged for two days. So began the series of attacks which left the Ruhr towns charred ruins and their industries staggering under the weight and accuracy of British bombs.

Because of bad weather the high key of March was not maintained during April, but under such conditions it is doubtful if there would have been any success at all before the formation of PFF. The raid on Dortmund on May 23-24 caused frightful havoc and six days later, at Wuppertal-Barmen, the Main Force turned in a fine piece of concentrated bombing around closely grouped markers. Although the Backers-up earned the plaudits, the *Oboe* TIs ensured the accuracy. The planners must take some credit too: the elongated town was scarcely 2 miles wide and the aiming point was so placed that the inevitable creep-back was along the longer axis.

On June 11-12 the heart was torn out of Dusseldorf and three days later the colossal damage at Oberhausen, by 203 heavies which bombed 109 Squadron's skymarkers, was a complete vindication for this type of attack. 'K' Oboe was used for the first time at Krefeld on June 21-22 and, although Bomber Command was apprehensive about the serviceability before the raid, the clear signals allowed the pilots to make accurate runs and the marking was spot on. Cologne did not come into the firing line until late in June but three quick raids left the Rhineland capital at the top of the 'Severely Damaged Towns' league.

The Mosquito's remarkably low loss rate was also a feature of the attacks: only two aircraft were missing due to enemy action, one which came down in the North Sea on March 26 and a second shot down during the Essen *Wanganui* of May 26. It was all the more remarkable because crews could not take any evasive action during the 10-minute run-up to the target.

Both 105 and 139 Squadrons were transferred from 2 Group to 8 Group on June 1 and 105 Squadron became the second *Oboe* unit; 109 Squadron moved from Wyton to Marham on July 4 and the two *Oboe* squadrons operated from the same station until March 1944.

On July 9, 1943, S/Ldr W.W. Blessing and F/O W.E.G. Humphreys flew 105 Squadron's first *Oboe* sorties, dropping HE on Gelsenkirchen. The first marking sortie came on June 25 when five crews helped nine from 109 Squadron to put down a steady stream of accurately placed TIs which enabled more than 600 Main Force crews to do more damage to Essen in 50 minutes than the total in all previous attacks. Again, on June 30-31, the two squadrons were primarily responsible for the virtual destruction of Rhemschied. The next attack was not until August 22 when only 4 out of 13 marked Leverkusen for the Main Force – charitably the 10/10ths cloud received most of the blame because the Backers-up could only see the glow of the *Oboe* markers and so did not drop their TIs.

The next night found the two squadrons dropping route-markers for the Main Force, which was attacking Berlin. *Oboe* Mosquitoes were used from time to time in this role until early 1944 when it was considered that the markers were probably helping the nightfighters as much as the Main Force. On August 30-31, when 20 Marker crews were on duty, 14 of them marked at Munchen Gladbach, where more than 600 bombers started fires which could be seen from 120 miles away, and 3 out of 6 marked an ammunition dump near Valenciennes for 34 Wellingtons from the three training groups. The next night, on the same target, 5 Halifaxes of 35 Squadron were sent to back up the reds. Two more French targets, the Foret de Mormal and the Foret de Raisaines, were attacked on September 2 and 3 respectively. These sorties gave the senior crews in the training groups operational experience of bombing on TIs in relatively mild surroundings.

One such sortie, however, code-named operation *Starkey*, was used to compare the accuracy of full *Oboe* with that of a Bailie Beam and an *Oboe* release.[5] On September 8-9 the training groups were strengthened by aircraft from 1, 3 and 6 Groups and by 5 Fortresses from the USAAF making a total 270 bombers, and two targets near Boulogne were successfully attacked. The Bailie Beam gave, by comparison, a poor result, which was no surprise to *Oboe* pilots. The raids, because they were closely scrutinized by CIU (Central Interpretation Unit), brought to light the fact that, although TIs were released 'salvo', they actually fell in stick form because the distributor gear on the bomb-release mechanism moved too slowly. It was relatively unimportant in area bombing but it could be vital in precision attacks. After marking Bochum on September 29 and Hagen on October 1, the *Oboe* crews reverted to route-marking or dropping HE on selected targets in Happy Valley.

From the *Oboe* point of view the most exciting raids in October were the five on Emden. The Repeater System,[6] which would have enabled

5. See Trinity in Appendix I.

6. See Appendix I

Oboe to mark targets deep in Germany, was used for the 'Cat' signals and, although the copes were above average, Bomber Command was not interested.[7]

At Emden, on October 18, one Mosquito dropped a TI which had a photoflash encased among the candles. The flash, fused to burst near the TIs when they were cascading, produced night photographs showing ground detail even when taken from 29,000 feet.[8]

The chapter on the LNSF reports that the Germans developed flak to burst at heights up to 30,000 feet and, although it was produced to appease the moaning Berliners, the Ruhr received a high percentage of the output. The gunners were usually accurate for height and speed, but fortunately a small error on the ground became large enough at 30,000 feet to make direct hits rare.

For their run-up to Dusseldorf on November 15, the Mosquitoes were routed over Krefeld. It was a clear night and, once the Germans had established the track, 30-40 searchlights swept the area until they spotted a Mosquito then they formed a cone and the gunners shot into the centre of it. *Oboe* crews just had to sit and take it because variations of speed or height and deviations from track affected the accuracy of the bombing. In all, 4 out of 10 Mosquitoes were damaged by flak: F/O W.E.G. Humphreys was hit in the foot and had to land at Hardwick; F/Sgt D.T. Burke was wounded in the hand by a piece of shrapnel piercing his navigation board, which fortunately cut down the momentum; and one crew, F/Lt J.R. Hampson and F/O H.W.E. Hammond, were shot down.

The Germans, unwittingly, must have had some radiating device on the track to Leverkusen which interfered with *Oboe* signals. On August 22 only 4 out of 13 crews had copes and on November 19, of 10 Mosquito crews sent to mark the target, none was able to make a good enough run to drop markers: 10/10ths clouds forced Main Force crews to drop on ETA. Yet again, on November 22 when crews were sent to bomb the town, only 4 out of 12 made successful runs. Many of the failures in the last quarter of 1943 were due to the Germans jamming Mk I, but equally disappointing was the constant failure of Mk II. It was not until the *Aspen* Mk II reached the squadrons in January 1944 that the number of copes showed any significant improvement.

Bennett had realized that the Mosquito could play an important part in the bomber offensive, so he resolved to build up a Mosquito bombing force within the Group. Until it was large enough to warrant its own

---

7. Reports elsewhere that it was used in 1944 are wrong. It was never used operationally after October 31, 1943. In fact bomber command had told TRE to stop development on August 9. These raids were made to try to make them reverse that decision.

8. The highest night photograph of the war, taken by F/Lt J.W. Jordan over Osnabruck, April 18-19, 1944.

Pathfinder Force the *Musical* Mosquitoes carried a mixed load of TIs and HE to help them locate the aiming point. When, in early 1944, the LNSF started carrying 4,000-pounders, *Oboe* TIs provided them with a pin-point so they could drop their worthwhile load where it would do most good, or harm depending whether one was at 26,000 or zero feet.

The tie-up with the V-1s between the strange structures being built in the Cherbourg Peninsula and the Pas de Calais area was finally established in December 1943. Bomber Command's assault opened on December 16 when 105 Squadron dropped TIs on two sites near Abbeville for 20 bombers from each of 3 and 5 Groups. It was this series of attacks which made the Germans realize the sites were vulnerable to air attack and so they abandoned them, later replacing them with smaller constructions.

There was a gradual drift away from route-marking to spoof route-marking as on the night of January 27-28 1944, the *Musical* Mosquitoes dropping markers near Aachen when the Main Force route took the bombers miles to the north and out over the Dutch coast. However, this was not the only diversion carried out by Mosquitoes; in the New Year they bombed nightfighter bases in Holland, sometimes catching the fighters before take-off and often making the airfields unserviceable so that they had to be diverted, causing many to crash because they ran out of fuel.

On March 2 S/Ldr P.A. Kleboe with F/Lt J.E. Jefferson took off from Graveley for Krefeld with a 4,000-pounder. Unfortunately, the special equipment failed so Jefferson had to drop his cargo on DR. S/Ldr H.B. Stephens tried his luck the following night, but with the same result. On March 4 the target was changed to Aachen, but for S/Ldr R.C.F. Law the equipment failed for the third time. It was left to F/Lt R.Hartley to score the first success when at 2205.30 hours on March 5 his navigator, F/O A. Burnett, released his Cookie over Aachen on a signal from the ground station. It was 105 Squadron's turn on March 7 but F/Lt A Caesar-Gordon made an unsuccessful run to Duisburg. The squadron had to wait for its first success until five days later when S/Ldr J.S.W. Bignal and F/Lt G.F. Caldwell attacked Hamborn.

The first marking sorties of the month was on March 2 when 2 out of 6 crews dropped their red TIs on the SNCA du Nord assembly plant at Meulan-les-Mureaux 15 miles north-west of Paris. The Germans had taken over the plant and were turning out an average of 15 Messerschmitt Me108s a month and in addition were making components for Me109s and Dornier Do24s. W/Cdr H.J. Cundall was first on target but his special equipment failed just before release so he did not drop his markers.[9] The

9. Sharp and Bowyer in *Mosquito* claim that W/Cdr Cundall dropped his TIs. Oboe crews never dropped TIs unless they received the release signal from the ground station. If Cundall's equipment failed he would disappear from the ground station screens so (a) the

106 Halifax crews waited patiently for the first TIs which were dropped at 0310 hours. They could be seen clearly through the gaps in the 3-10/10ths stratus at 8,000 feet. Marker crews reported the bombing as being concentrated, with several sticks bursting across the reds. There were scattered fires throughout the factory and an enormous one, in the southern section, was obviously out of control.

Paris had its second air-raid warning of the month on the 6th when 4 out of 6 Mosquitoes marked Trappes marshalling yards for 235 heavies, the opening gambit in the attacks on the railway systems in France and the Low Countries. In the three months before D-Day Bomber Command flew 13,349 sorties in this campaign, which paralysed the whole railway system from the Rhine to the Normandy area. *Oboe* Mosquitoes opened almost all of Bomber Command's attacks, and Master Bombers from the Group controlled the majority of them. After D-Day the chaos caused by these attacks delayed reinforcements of men and munitions from reaching the invasion area, and in no small way contributed to the success of the Second Front.

Earlier on March 6 S/Ldr Law led a formation of 6 Mosquitoes of TAF, the first of eight similar daylight sorties to bomb V-1 sites through 10/10ths cloud. These attacks were continued from time to time throughout April and May and, when both Groups became more adept, 2 Group sent 12 Mosquitoes for each formation.

On March 7 W/O J.W.G. Eaton, on a bombing sortie to Aachen, was comfortably settled on the beam with the 'dits' just sounding through the equi-signal note, intently watching his instruments, keeping his height and airspeed correct, dreaming of a zero error, when cannon shells came tearing into the nose of the Mosquito. As the fighter made only a single attack he pressed on and bombed the target. The reception committee below were equally determined that he should regret his temerity: the Mosquito was further damaged by flak and after releasing his load Eaton dived away to safety. There were holes in the fuselage, the hydraulics were shot away and the pitot head damaged. He set a direct course for Manston and his navigator, W/O J.E. Fox, began the long and arduous task of pumping down the undercarriage by hand. Eaton made an excellent landing without flaps but, having no brake pressure, he was unable to prevent the Mosquito careering off the end of the runway and crashing. However, the crew escaped unhurt.

On March 11, *Album Leaf* Mk II flew its first successful sortie, a bombing raid on Munchen Gladbach. Mk I still had many sorties to fly before the squadrons were fully equipped with either Mk II or Mk III and played an important part in the D-Day preparations.

---

release signal would not have been sent, (b) even if it had been sent he would not have heard it so would have retained his TIs.

Bomber Command, knowing the two *Oboe* squadrons were to play a vital role in the pre-invasion plans and, fearing the Germans might make an attack on Marham to wipe them out, played for safety by splitting them, transferring 105 Squadron to Bourn and 109 Squadron to Little Staughton. Marshalling yards, gun sites on the coast, radio and radar stations, airfields and ammunition dumps: there was scarcely a target attacked during the spring and summer which did not call for *Oboe*'s accuracy.

During the *Overlord* preparations the constantly expanding LNSF became Bomber Command's main instrument in attacks on German industry. With the ever-increasing proportion of Cookies in the bomb-load they became a menace to the Germans rather than a mere nuisance and *Oboe* Mosquitoes continued to mark targets for them in the Ruhr.[10] In addition to their role of marking for the Main Force and the LNSF they did *Overture* sorties to the Ruhr, airfields in France and to ammunition dumps, sometimes with spectacular results. On May 3-4, when 8 out of 14 crews attacked the ammunition dump at Chateaudun, as F/Lt D.C. Dixon turned away from the target after dropping four 500-pound MC bombs, a large orange fire started followed, seconds later, by a violent explosion with sheets of flame shooting up to a great height, triggering off sympathetic explosions. The fires could be seen from 100 miles away and every now and then the sky would light up as more ammunition exploded.

When 5 Group demolished the important radar site at Ferme d'Urville two nights before the invasion, the Master Bomber gave credit to *Oboe*'s initial marking – high praise from an unexpected quarter. On the eve of D-Day 25 Mosquitoes from the two squadrons marked ten gun sites in the Normandy area and more than 1,000 bombers silenced all but one of the guns. The call on the two squadrons had increased drastically; from 255 sorties flown in February the number had risen to 725 in June.

The continued absence of the *Luftwaffe* in strength over the Normandy battle area persuaded Bomber Command to try daylight attacks. Enemy shipping, sheltering in Le Havre and Boulogne, was attacked on June 14 and 15 with devastating results. Spitfires, sent to protect the bombers, did not have to fire a shot in anger. Being able to operate by day or night gave Bomber Command more freedom from the weather.

At times, when Bomber Command was called upon to bomb enemy troop concentrations, Allied troops were only 1,000 yards away and, because the Mosquito crews opened the attacks, the initial responsibility for the safety of our troops was in their hands. The first troop-support raid took place on June 30 and F/Lt K. Wolstenholme's Mosquito was challenged by two Spitfires. The pilots, who obviously had not paid sufficient

10. The heavies made only three attacks on Germany in May. In June four were made but they were against oil targets.

attention at briefing, were apparently surprised to see a Mosquito in the target area. Fortunately, they did not open fire but, having closed in to 50 yards, contented themselves with shepherding Wolstenholme away from the target.

At Caen on July 7, S/Ldr Blessing was on his marking run when he was intercepted by a fighter. P/O D.T. Burke, his navigator, was reaching forward to pick up a chart when cannon shells ripped into the Mosquito. Blessing, an old hand at evasive action,[11] put the aircraft into a dive and lost the fighter. After levelling out, he noticed the starboard engine was over-heating and, looking across at Burke to tell him to feather it, saw him pointing to the starboard wing, 3 feet of which had been shot away. Blessing, seeing one of our Normandy landing strips, decided to land there and called up Biggin Hill to tell them his plans. Suddenly the aircraft went into a spin and Burke was ordered to bale out. After that, he remembers nothing until he came round on a stretcher behind our lines. Eyewitnesses on the ground saw one man leave the Mosquito and then, seconds later, the aircraft broke into pieces. Blessing, 'A' Flight Commander at the time, was one of the squadron's most experienced pilots.

All the close-support attacks were opened by *Oboe* markers as were those on the coastal fortresses. The climax in this series came on October 3 when 261 aircraft were dispatched to breach the sea wall at West Kapelle on the island of Walcheren. Command had thought some Tallboys would be needed to destroy the foundations, but accurate *Oboe* marking combined with the Master Bomber's skilful directions, not discounting concentrated bombing by the Main Force, made 5 Group's participation unnecessary and W/Cdr J.B. Tait, as soon as he saw the breach effected, ordered his crews back to base as the 12,000-pounders were in short supply.

The pressure on the railway systems was maintained after D-Day until August 18-19 when Eisenhower considered further damage would hinder rather than aid the Allies. Airfields were also attacked during the summer but often without the aid of *Oboe*, particularly when the attacks were made in daylight.

Shortly after D-Day the V-1s were launched against London and Southampton, but the modified sites, being smaller and situated in or near woods, were difficult to pinpoint. It was left to *Oboe* to mark them precisely for the Main Force. To maintain the pressure in conditions of 10/10ths cloud, which was no protection against *Oboe*, daylight formations were flown again, but in conjunction with the heavy squadrons. Because of the difference in cruising speeds the formations were often ragged, so 3 Lancasters were fitted with *Oboe* and pilots from 105 and 109 Squadrons flew them down the *Oboe* run.

---

11. He was awarded a DSO for his part in the low-level Mosquito daylight raid on Jena.

On July 20, 109 Squadron led two formations of Lancasters to the Foret du Croc where, instead of the forecast 10/10ths cloud, the skies were clear. The second formation, led by an *Oboe* Lancaster, was engaged by light flak shortly before reaching the target. The *Oboe* Lancaster was hit and, although it was on fire, S/Ldr F. Foulsham pressed on to the target to bomb but then crashed in flames. Foulsham knew he was too near the target to allow the reserve aircraft, a Mosquito, to take over in time and also knew that if he jettisoned his bombs the other Lancasters would bomb too soon. Unfortunately, this outstanding feat of courage was wasted because the Lancaster immediately behind the leader was set on fire too; the pilot jettisoned his bombs and broke formation but the other crews did not realise he was in trouble, and they released when they saw his bombs go down.

Altogether, 44,334 tons of bombs were dropped in this campaign and 25 sites were completely knocked out, but only the attacks on the storage depots had any real effect. *Oboe* Mosquitoes opened almost all of Bomber Command's attacks on flying-bomb sites. The ground forces were indebted to Bomber Command for many favours but they reduced the debit when they overran the Pas de Calais in August and so released crews for tasks which were more in keeping with their role of defeating the enemy. Harris for one was delighted. Having been relieved of two irksome diversions, bombing marshalling yards and flying-bomb sites, he was able to reopen his offensive against German industry.

Before returning to *Oboe*'s involvement in this sphere, Bomber Command's attacks on oil during the summer months have to be recorded. Harris, who had consistently opposed the directives which ordered him to attack oil, diverted his force to oil targets in the Ruhr on Eisenhower's request: he must have 'asked him nicely'.[12] Because the Ruhr plants were (a) within *Oboe* range and (b) difficult to pinpoint, being small and often in remote parts of small towns, the two squadrons spearheaded most of the attacks. The first in the series was on June 12-13 when 276 out of 294 heavies put the Nordstern plant near Gelsenkirchen out of production for six weeks. Solid Cloud saved Sterkrade Holten from a similar fate on June 16-17 but 300 out of 321 crews bombed the glow of *Oboe* TIs and nine separate units in the plant were affected.

When 10 *Musical* Mosquitoes attacked the Scholven Buer plant on June 28-29 accurate bombing started fires in the plant, but the Ruhr gunners were also on target and several aircraft were hit. F/Lt D.M. Russell was intercepted by a fighter in the target area and the Mosquito was set on fire. At full throttle, and with 29,000 feet to lose, he probably still holds the record for a flight between Scholven and the English coast.

---

12. 'Ask me nicely' was a common phrase of the period, if someone was reluctant to grant a request.

At 0210 hours the watch tower at Manston saw an aircraft in flames approaching from the direction of Ramsgate; ground crews, trained to deal with such an emergency, were alerted and Russell was given a green. Forced to make a belly landing, he eased the Mosquito down gently but, as it skidded along the runway, the fires spread until the whole aircraft was a mass of flames. Miraculously, the crew scrambled clear, Russell escaping with a burn on the forehead and his navigator, F/O J.G. Barker, with second and third-degree burns on the face and hands. But who was complaining? The word 'future' a minute before had had no meaning.

The Top Brass, preening themselves because of the success of the tactical switch to daylight bombing on targets in Occupied Territory, decided to press their luck and lay on a daylight attack to the Ruhr. Bacon and eggs at 1000 hours on August 27 – an early lunch for the insomniacs, an unexpected breakfast for the lie-a-beds – presaged a noon take-off for 230 Halifaxes and 13 PFF Lancasters; 6 Mosquitoes from Bourn and 8 from Little Staughton took off some 30 minutes later and, shortly afterwards, could be seen flying in pairs. For this operation, the *Oboe* reserves were flying in formation with their primaries so that they could take over immediately and be on the beam within seconds if the primary had PD (Precision Device) failure. Of the 7 pairs, 6 coped and the Backers-up dropped their greens among the *Oboe* reds.

Broken clouds made bombing difficult and the Master Bomber exhorted the Main Force to wait until they could see the TIs. Following an explosion a large column of thick black smoke spread across the target area and, as if to emphasize the accuracy of the bombing, a salvo of red TIs cascaded into the middle of it. An excellent raid with a satisfactory ending – no bombers were lost.

When the ground forces overran France the mobile ground stations moved forward enabling the two *Oboe* squadrons to penetrate deeper into the Reich. During September, Aschaffenburg, Heilbron, Karlsruhe and Lubeck were attacked and in October 243 sorties were made using continental stations. Pforzheim, Frankfurt, Wiesbaden, Coblenz and Schweinfurt were added to the list, and Mannheim-Ludwigshafen was marked for the Main Force and the non-*Musical* Mosquitoes.

October saw the opening of the second Battle of the Ruhr and marker crews from the two squadrons spearheaded these attacks. *Oboe* markers opened a dawn attack by the LNSF on Cologne on October 14 as a prelude to Bomber Command's busiest day. At 0700 hours, the first of 20 *Musical* Mosquitoes took off to mark four aiming points at Duisburg for 998 out of 1,065 heavies. In the evening 32 crews (16 primaries and 16 reserves) were detailed to mark the same target for a two-wave attack, again by more than 1,000 bombers. Two crews of 105 Squadron marked Mannheim for a spoof attack, their markers being backed by greens dropped by 4 non-*Musical* Mosquitoes who had *Windowed* Duisburg *en route.*

Earlier, on October 4-5, F/Lt Russell was in trouble again. His Mosquito was severely damaged by flak over Heilbronn and later the crew had to bale out. Russell was wounded in the right foot and sprained his ankle when landing, his navigator, F/Lt Barker, being uninjured. On October 25 at Essen, three crews of 109 Squadron were hit by flak and HS-P had to make a forced landing at Manston.

November saw the same round of experimental and U/T targets but the monthly report warned that some crews were taking evasive action on the bombing run. Perhaps the incidents were not widespread and the evasive action not violent for records were kept of each pilot's run and it was an unusually lenient way for Bennett to issue a warning.

However, marker crews were not in his black book; Dulmen and Julich were accurately marked ahead of the ground forces; the Battle of the Ruhr continued unabated with notable successes at Bochum and Dusseldorf and the oil war was stepped up with very good attacks on Sterkrade and Castrop Rauxel. In the same sphere, on the 29th, *Oboe* crews led a formation of non-*Musical* Mosquitoes to Duisburg. This was the first in a series of similar attacks which continued throughout December.[13]

The weather deteriorated as the month progressed, but any hopes that fog-bound aerodromes would be allies to a Merry Christmas were shattered when von Rundstedt made his counter-offensive. The danger from hitting low-flying birds principally on take-off was very real, particularly in summer, but this winter they were not a hazard – they were walking; 1,000 yards visibility was considered excellent. One crew was briefed four times in one day, made abortive trips to two stations and eventually took off at 0300 hours with the aid of Fido. It was almost unheard of to take off and land at the same aerodrome. For the WAAF drivers, ferrying crews to and from aerodromes, December was a nightmare. True the main roads had 'cat's-eyes' to help, but vehicles travelling in the opposite direction were using them too, and the American lorries had steel bumpers, which made them more terrifying to meet at night than any German fighter.

Eisenhower had called on the Air Force to bomb marshalling yards and aerodromes to help the ground forces stop the Ardennes counter-offensive, and when on the morning of December 23 the weather forecast for the Rhine and Ruhr towns was 10/10ths cloud below 15,000 feet, blind formation bombing was the only recourse.

Shortly after 1000 hours 27 Lancasters and 3 Mosquitoes took off from 8 Group stations to attack the Gremburg marshalling yards at Cologne. Having broken cloud, the Lancasters settled down in three formations each led by an *Oboe* Lancaster, with a Mosquito acting as reserve. The account in 'The Long Finale' (Chapter VII) left the *Oboe* Lancasters in

---

13. See p. 210 for more detailed account.

sad disarray: one shot down, the other two having force-landed at Manston. The two surviving Mosquitoes arrived over Bourn at 1400 hours. S/Ldr Parker put his Mosquito down safely and was wiping the perspiration off his brow when he saw GB-D skidding towards him along the grass. S/Ldr Almond, with a full bomb load and without flaps or undercarriage, had made a masterly single-engined belly-landing on the grass along the side of the runway to lessen the risk of fire and explosion. Parker almost became airborne in his effort to get out of the way.

In the afternoon four all-Mosquito formations attacked Sieburg marshalling yards at Cologne. Even at Mosquito height, visually predicted flak could be uncomfortably accurate and the formations tended to be a gaggle. The weather in the meantime had clamped down at bases and all crews were diverted. The next day, when four crews took off from Bourn to mark the airfields at Essen and Dusseldorf, they could not be seen from the control tower and, needless to say, were all diverted.

For the daylight attack of December 29 on the Mosel marshalling yards at Coblenz, because ground haze was expected in the target area, 8 Mosquitoes (4 primaries and 4 reserves flying in formation) dropped Cookies instead of TIs to help the Master Bomber identify the A/P – a reversion to the early 1943 technique, when the Pink Pansy's flash was used as a target marker. There can be few crews in 8 Group, and perhaps in the whole of Bomber Command, who do not have a grim memory scar of the last ten days of 1944.

Due almost entirely to the pounding given to the supply lines by the combined effort of the Allied air forces the von Rundstedt offensive ground to a halt and when Allied forces pushed the Hun back, first St Vith (December 26) then Houffalize (December 29 and January 5) were attacked adding confusion to the German troops who were vainly trying to regroup. *Oboe* markers were the focal point of these raids which were highly successful.

The fact that the Hun was able to mount an offensive came as a shock to Eisenhower and his advisors and the offensive against oil was stepped up. In this sphere, 8 Group led attacks to Ludwigshafen, Bochum, Zeitz, Leuna and Duisburg and the LNSF attacked Sterkrade in strength, with *Oboe* Mosquitoes in the van on all targets except Zeitz and Leuna.

Weather conditions at bases, although better than in December, caused cancellations of all operations on ten nights in January. A period of snow brought its problems and at Bourn on the 7th, F/O J.L. De Beer swung on take-off and crashed into the snow piled on the side of the runway. The crew were unhurt, but the engineering officer acquired several grey hairs as he watched the armourers digging the snow and mud off the Cookie to get at the arming pistol; they did not treat it with the respect he thought it deserved.

A call from the Army to destroy Cleve and Goch ahead of the Allied troops on February 7 had been answered with a completeness which continued to amaze the ground forces. As the Germans were driven back Wesel became the most important target north of the Ruhr but, like Berlin in the winter of 1943-4, the town was perpetually cloud-covered. Four attacks in February, all made above cloud, had effectively destroyed the town but by the beginning of March it was estimated that 3,000 vehicles were sheltering among the ruins.

On March 6, following a 3 Group sortie above cloud in the morning 8 Group took over the attack. Six formations of Mosquitoes, comprising an *Oboe* leader and reserve backed up by 6 non-*Musical* Mosquitoes, bombed the town; in the last two formations, all aircraft were carrying 4,000-pounders. Five out of six made successful attacks – four primaries and one reserve coping – but the sixth formation found itself leaderless and had to abandon the sortie, S/Ldr G.M. Smith and F/Lt J.F.Carnegie of 109 Squadron having collided 10 miles south-east of Southwold. Carnegie's Mosquito went into a spiral dive with the port aileron jammed. By manipulating all the controls violently he managed to free it, pulled out at 13,000 feet, and made for Woodbridge where he landed safely. Smith was seen by crews of 571 Squadron to crash into the sea. Of the 51 *Oboe* Mosquitoes which attacked at intervals throughout the night, 45 dropped either four 500-pound bombs or Cookies. S/Ldr R. Burrell had an eventful evening. Having lost the port engine because of icing, he made a single-engined landing at base. He took off later, attacked his objective, and was returning to base without navigational aids when, shortly after crossing the English coast, he was intercepted by one of our own nightfighters. At the time of the attack he was actually in touch with Bourn, and giving them his approximate position. The nightfighter pilot demonstrated that his aim was as good as his aircraft recognition was bad. The crew was compelled to abandon aircraft, the port engine being of fire. Burrell sustained shrapnel injuries in the leg, but F/O J. McCulloch had only superficial injuries as a result of his jump.

On February 22-23, S/Ldr I.L.T. Ackroyd, having bombed Erfurt from 32,000 feet, realized his petrol consumption was high, so he reduced boost and revs and gradually lost height. On reaching the Belgian coast he had petrol left for only 20 minutes, so, knowing cloud was down to 1,500 feet over England, he decided to land on the Continent. None of our airfields answered his call so the crew baled out near Bruges. His navigator, F/Lt E.F. Casey, landed 4 miles from the town and made a fantastic sight as he marched down the centre of the road clutching his parachute which refused to be subdued by his embrace. Meanwhile, Ackroyd had landed on the roof of the Grand Hotel in Bruges and spent an alarming 5 minutes performing feats of daring more in keeping with Douglas Fairbanks.

F/Lt J.T. McGreal had just cleared the target area after successfully dropping his HE and Smoke Puff over Cologne on March 2 when P/O T. Lynn saw two Fw190s coming in to attack. By diving and pushing the throttles through the gate McGreal got sufficient speed out of his Mk XVI to persuade them that it was pointless to continue the chase, and when Lynn last saw them they were mixed up with a pack of fighters, which he fervently hoped were ours.

On March 11, for a daylight attack on Essen by more than 1,000 bombers, 36 Mosquitoes (18 primaries and 18 reserves, flying in formation) were on duty. The target was expected to be cloud-covered so, with the exception of two primaries and their reserves who were carrying TIs against the chance of clear skies, all crews were armed with two Smoke Puffs and two 500-pound MCs.

Again, the following day, the call was for 36 aircraft. The bomb-loads were the same; in fact many of the Main Force crews were the same. For this raid on Dortmund, 1,079 out of 1,107 crews attacked, the highest number ever to attack one target, dropping the heaviest bomb-load, 4,851 tons.

The mobile caravans moved forward almost on the heels of the Allied armies and by April 8 Berlin was within range. To F/Lt I.B. McPhearson went the honour of making the first *Oboe* run on the Big City. The following night three crews dropped markers for 41 out of 44 crews of the LNSF. By April 20 the Russians were on the outskirts of Berlin and, although the LNSF were there in strength, ironically it was not one of the season-ticket holders who dropped the last bombs on Berlin: that distinction went to F/O A.E. Austin.

On April 22, 16 Mosquitoes marked four A/Ps at Bremen for a daylight attack, but 10/10ths cloud forced the Master Bombers to abandon the sorties. *Wanganui* was out of the question because of the nearness of the British troops. The port was full of troops opposing our forces so, at regular intervals throughout the night, 40 Mosquitoes dropped HE on the town, the aiming point being the concentrations of German armour.

Amidst all the success there was one big disappointment. On April 25, eight crews coaxed their Mosquitoes up to 39,000 feet in order to mark Hitler's hideaway at Berchtesgaden. The 'Cat' purred contentedly for the whole of the 10-minute run, but not a squeak from the 'Mouse': someone forgot to look out of the window – there was a mountain between the caravan and the aircraft.

The previous night *Oboe*'s accuracy had been put to a pleasant use; crews dropped Monroe bombs on PoW camps, and marked for 3 Lancasters dropping medical supplies on the one at Neubrandenburg. On Sunday, April 29, the targets were in Holland, the mission a peaceful one, marking for Lancasters dropping food for the starving people, and these sorties were flown daily until May 8 with the exception of the 6th when low cloud made the mission impossible.

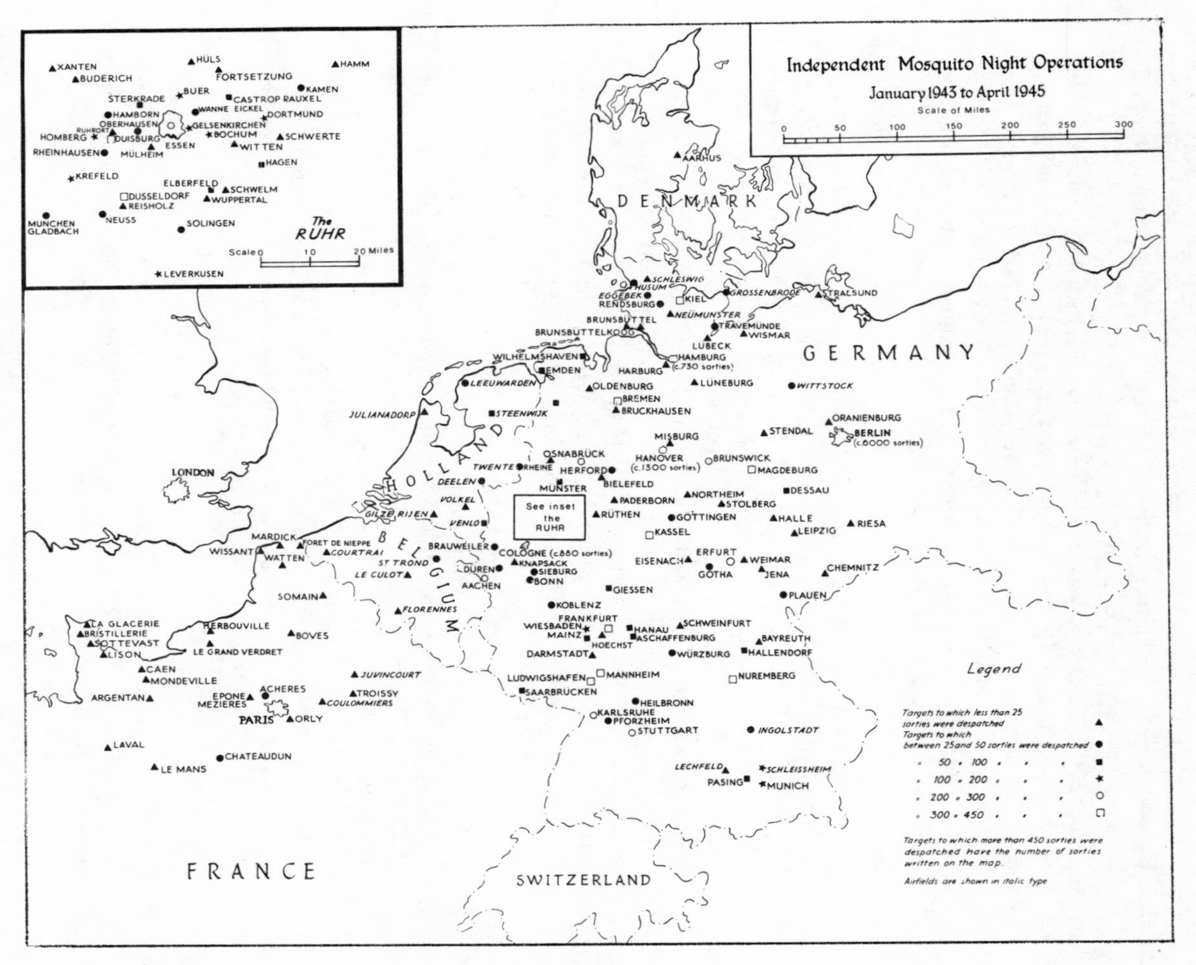

Independent Mosquito Night Operations
January 1943 to April 1945
Scale of Miles
0 50 100 150 200 250 300
The RUHR
XANTEN
BUDERICH
HÜLS
FORTSETZUNG
HAMM
KAMEN
STERKRADE
BUER
CASTROP RAUXEL
WANNE EICKEL
DORTMUND
HAMBORN
OBERHAUSEN
GELSENKIRCHEN
RUHRORT
HOMBERG
DUISBURG
BOCHUM
SCHWERTE
ESSEN
WITTEN
RHEINHAUSEN
MÜLHEIM
HAGEN
KREFELD
ELBERFELD
SCHWELM
DUSSELDORF
WUPPERTAL
REISHOLZ
MÜNCHEN GLADBACH
NEUSS
SOLINGEN
Scale 0 10 20 Miles
LEVERKUSEN
DENMARK
GERMANY
HOLLAND
BELGIUM
FRANCE
SWITZERLAND
LONDON
AARHUS
SCHLESWIG
HUSUM
EGGEBEK
RENDSBURG
KIEL
GROSSENBRODE
STRALSUND
BRUNSBÜTTEL
NEUMÜNSTER
TRAVEMÜNDE
WISMAR
BRUNSBÜTTELKOOG
LÜBECK
HAMBURG (c.730 sorties)
WILHELMSHAVEN
HARBURG
EMDEN
LEEUWARDEN
OLDENBURG
LÜNEBURG
WITTSTOCK
BREMEN
BRUCKHAUSEN
JULIANADORP
STEENWIJK
ORANIENBURG
STENDAL
BERLIN (c.8000 sorties)
MISBURG
OSNABRÜCK
HANOVER (c.1300 sorties)
BRUNSWICK
TWENTE
RHEINE
HERFORD
MAGDEBURG
DEELEN
MÜNSTER
BIELEFELD
DESSAU
See inset the RUHR
NORTHEIM
PADERBORN
STOLBERG
VOLKEL
GILZE RIJEN
RÜTHEN
GÖTTINGEN
HALLE
RIESA
VENLO
KASSEL
LEIPZIG
MARDICK
FORET DE NIEPPE
BRAUWEILER
COLOGNE (c.880 sorties)
ERFURT
WISSANT
COURTRAI
WATTEN
ST TROND
KNAPSACK
EISENACH
WEIMAR
CHEMNITZ
DÜREN
SIEBURG
GOTHA
JENA
LE CULOT
AACHEN
BONN
GIESSEN
SOMAIN
PLAUEN
KOBLENZ
FLORENNES
FRANKFURT
WIESBADEN
HANAU
SCHWEINFURT
LA GLACERIE
HERBOUVILLE
MAINZ
ASCHAFFENBURG
BAYREUTH
BRISTILLERIE
BOVES
HOECHST
SOTTEVAST
LE GRAND VERDRET
DARMSTADT
WÜRZBURG
HALLENDORF
LISON
CAEN
JUVINCOURT
LUDWIGSHAFEN
MANNHEIM
NUREMBERG
MONDEVILLE
ACHERES
TROISSY
SAARBRÜCKEN
ARGENTAN
EPONE
MEZIERES
COULOMMIERS
HEILBRONN
KARLSRUHE
PARIS
ORLY
PFORZHEIM
STUTTGART
INGOLSTADT
LAVAL
CHATEAUDUN
LE MANS
LECHFELD
SCHLEISSHEIM
PASING
MUNICH
Legend
Targets to which less than 25 sorties were despatched
Targets to which between 25 and 50 sorties were despatched
50 - 100
100 - 200
200 - 300
300 - 450
Targets to which more than 450 sorties were despatched have the number of sorties written on the map.
Airfields are shown in italic type

Map 24.

Rumours were rife that the Hun was trying to gather a force at Kiel to flee to Norway and continue the hopeless struggle there. On May 2-3, *Oboe*, H2S and Main Force Mosquitoes turned out in strength to mark and bomb Kiel, and 16 *Oboe* crews were detailed to bomb Husen and Eggebeck airfields. That night, F/Lt D.P. Dalcom dropped the last bomb in anger on the European front.

A grand total of 9,624 sorties had been flown against the enemy, 2,266 of them in June, July and August 1944, the majority of them marking duties pinpointing small targets for the Main Force. But perhaps the best remembered feat was the marking of Krupps on the night of March 5, 1943, Bomber Command's first real success against this temple of German autocracy.

THE LIGHT NIGHT STRIKING FORCE The introduction of Mosquito bombers to the Group proved to be one of the significant events of 1943, not only for PFF, but also for Bomber Command. At the end of May when 2 Group left Bomber Command, 105 and 139 Mosquito Squadrons were transferred to 8 Group.[14] Bennett's foresight and 139 Squadron's brilliant achievements added a new dimension to the bomber offensive.

From nuisance raids in June, 139 Squadron turned to *Windowing* targets ahead of the Pathfinder Force. At Essen on July 25, they went in with the leading marker crews, dropping *Window* on their first run and then going round again to bomb. On July 29 they *Windowed* Hamburg ahead of the marker crews.

In August, when spoofing became fashionable, the squadron added another role to is expanding repertoire. When the Main Force were attacking Nuremberg on August 10 they carried out a spoof raid on Mannheim. This was the first time the squadron dropped TIs: they *Windowed* and marked the target on the first run and then made two runs dropping HE. On August 17 they carried out a spoof on Berlin to draw the nightfighters to the capital and so reduce losses at Peenemunde. As a result, fighters did not arrive over the main target until the last wave was attacking. Altogether 139 Squadron operated on 21 nights in August, flying 152 sorties.

On August 31 Main Force crews on Berlin reported seeing white flares along the route in and out of the target; it was presumed their purpose was to help the *Wild Boars* locate the bomber stream. So, as a countermeasure on the next Berlin raid of September 4. the mosquitos after *Windowing* the target, proceeded to drop White Drip flares at intervals marking a false route some distance away from that of the Main Force. Such tactics inevitably drew the fighters to the Mosquitoes, but aircraft

14. 105 Squadron changed its role becoming the second *Oboe* marker squadron.

and crews proved equal to the challenge.

September showed the Germans were not going to treat the new menace lightly: they had developed flak which burst at heights up to 30,000 feet and with this the ground defences achieved some success. At Dusseldorf on September 5, F/Lt A.A. Mellor was coned for several minutes. His Mosquito was hit, the port engine being put out of action and the starboard one damaged; but, by gradually losing height, Mellor nursed the aircraft back to base. W/O B.C.N. Wright too was coned and hit and many of his instruments were damaged: the starboard engine had to be feathered and he was forced to make an emergency landing at Coltishall.

At Brandenburg on September 14 S/Ldr D.A. Braithwaite was coned for ten minutes and received ten direct hits. The spirit of the squadron can be measured by this incident for lesser men would have jettisoned their load, whereas the Squadron Leader pressed on to the target, Berlin. Two days later, F/O J. Patient was hit by flak over Berlin and the starboard engine had to be feathered. On the homeward route he was coned twice and reduced height to escape searchlights and flak. Manoeuvring was not easy on one engine so it was not surprising that his Mosquito received further damage when two Fw190s jumped it over Holland. The Focke-Wulfs scored hits on the wings and the fuselage and the navigator, Sgt N. Gilroy, was wounded. To escape, Patient dived to 2,000 feet. The crippled Mosquito staggered into Manston where it crash-landed 5 minutes after the petrol gauges had been reading zero. Before Patient had time to breathe a sigh of relief 'a Typhoon nipped up behind him and removed the whole of the tailplane'.[15]

S/Ldr D.C. Skeene flew the squadron's first Mk IX Mosquito operationally on October 3 to Hanover; by carrying two 500-pound MC bombs under the wings the bomb load was increased to 3,000 pounds. The squadron wished they had flown all their new Mk IXs because one was destroyed on the ground when an intruder dropped a stick of bombs on Wyton.

ARI 5525, the service number for GH, flew its first operational sortie on October 4 but had to wait three days for its first success, on Aachen. The squadron pioneered this '*Oboe* in reverse' precision device but it was only an interim measure, its limitations being the same as *Oboe*'s.

Once Pathfinders had found their feet the full moon, which had once been Bomber Command's main target-finder, helped the enemy more than the bombers and so the heavies enjoyed a stand-down over this period. From November 4 to 18 they did not attack any German targets, and it was left to the three Mosquito squadrons to carry the war to the Reich. On November 5, six crews were sent to Hamburg where, except

---

15. From 139 Squadron ORB.

for a single hole, cloud covered the target. Three of them, obviously types who could not resist testing 'Wet Paint' notices, felt themselves irresistably drawn towards it. F/Lt P.W.W. Nock was the first to explore and, seeing the docks below, he dropped his bombs. Silhouetted against the cloud background by the searchlights he was an easy mark for the AA gunners, who peppered the Mosquito with flak; he made for the safety of the cloud with all speed. Having caught one victim the Germans realized that it was the one place they could see the enemy so they concentrated their searchlights there, turned them off and waited for their next victim. They did not have long to wait. F/O A.B. Stovel, who had noticed that Heligoland was clear, said to his navigator: 'Let's just look through that hole to see if we can recognize anything. If not, we'll go back to Heligoland.' He did not see anything because he was blinded by the searchlights. Flak burst all around and the reason the Mosquito was not badly damaged was probably because Stovel's evasive action was so violent. It was 5 minutes before he escaped into cloud and set course for Heligoland. Then the Germans got set for their third victim, F/O J.R. Goodman. Immediately coned and with the AA guns primed for height and direction, he got a warm reception. He needed no convincing he was in the correct place: he dropped his bombs, opened the throttles and was away as fast as possible. 'Remind me not to do that again.'

Bennett, finding he had a surplus of crews and Mosquitoes sufficient to form another flight, was given the choice of making 139 Squadron into three flights or forming a new squadron. He decided on the latter and on November 12 eight crews from 139 Squadron were transferred to Oakington as the nucleus of 627 Squadron.

On November 22, when 10 Mosquitoes of 139 Squadron went to Berlin, six attacked with the Main Force and dropped spoof fighter flares; three arrived just after the Main Force had left the target, to keep the Berliners in the shelters; 1½ hours later a lone warrior arrived to the sound of sirens and wake them all up again.

The following night P/O M.J. Izatt and F/Sgt A.W. Bains had just crossed the Dutch coast at 26,000 feet when Izatt noticed lights on the port side: almost immediately a burst of tracer came towards the Mosquito, just missing the tail. Izatt made a diving turn to port while Bains searched for the fighter. At 20,000 feet he turned back on track and started to climb again. Three minutes later tracer came from the starboard quarter and again missed the bomber. As Izatt dived to starboard the fighter streaked past and was not seen again. The crew had lost 8 minutes and, knowing they would be too late for the Berlin attack, they bombed Emden.

Ten days after 'The Ruhr Express'[16] had made her unsuccessful maiden

16. The first Canadian Lancaster flew on November 22, 1943.

voyage to Berlin, the first Canadian-built Mosquito XD-H (KB 161) made its maiden sortie. F/Lt G. Salter, knowing the disappointment over the Lancaster's failure, pressed on to Berlin in spite of engine trouble and frozen controls.

It was 139 Squadron which was scheduled to lead the New Year's Eve celebrations by marking Cologne for the LNSF, using GH, but the set was unreliable and no TIs were dropped. Lack of success did not prevent the celebrations going ahead.

The New Year saw the formation of 692 Squadron at Graveley under the command of W/Cdr W.G. Lockhart. For many reasons the new squadron did not operate in January, but 139 and 627 Squadrons were by no means chair-borne, flying 184 successful sorties. On January 5, 1944, when the Main Force was attacking Stettin, they simulated an attack on the capital by dropping TIs and *Window*. The ruse was successful; the nightfighters assembled over Berlin. No Main Force aircraft were intercepted on the outward route and only five combats were reported on the way home.

The intention was to groom 139 Squadron to be the marker squadron for the LNSF. When GH proved unsuitable Bennett turned to H2S and Mosquito XD-U was modified to take a set. F/Lt D.G.W. Tayler and F/Lt C.F. Bedell flew it operationally for the first time on January 27 and five days later marked Berlin for a small number of Mosquitoes, including one from 692 Squadron piloted by the commanding officer: it was the squadron's first sortie.

When the Main Force made its heaviest attack on the Big City on February 15-16, the Mosquitoes were there *Windowing* and dropping spoof fighter flares. S/Ldr S.D. Watts, having laid a false route out of the target, was checking to see if his flares were being backed up when, to his surprise and amusement, he saw a German aircraft following behind reinforcing them.

There was always something new going on in the Mosquito world, it seemed as if the 'powers that be' were trying to find the limit of its capabilities. As early as April 1943 it was proposed to modify the bomb-bay to accomodate a Cookie. The conversion was the easiest part. The movement of the centre of gravity, due to the extra weight, altered the attitude of the aircraft and introduced instability; the problem was never completely solved on MkIVs and MkIXs. Two modified MkIVs arrived at Oakington for 627 Squadron but were immediately handed over to 692 Squadron.

At 1903 hours[17] on February 23, S/Ldr Watts with F/O C. Hassell

17. F/Lt G. McKeand, also carrying a Cookie took off at 1901 hours and dropped at 2048 hours so obviously it was a two-horse race. There was also an element of luck. The bomb had to be dropped on a TI to win the bet: the gamble was on 105 Squadron's timing.

roared down the runway at Graveley in P3-B and right on their tail followed F/Lt V.S. Moore with P/O P.F. Dillon in P3-H: the race was on to drop the first Cookie on Germany from a Mosquito – 105 Squadron was doing the honours and the TIs went down accurately and promptly. Dusseldorf was given the privilege of staging this historic occasion. Hassell released his bomb at 2045.30 hours and logged the half-minute because it might have made all the difference. P3-M was coned for 4 minutes and was hit by flak so Moore lost precious time taking evasive action. As he did not reach the aiming point until 2046.30 hours the drinks were on him.

There was so much change and movement going on in the Group during March it is astonishing that time was found to operate, yet the three LNSF squadrons successfully completed 489 sorties out of 509 flown. A successful spoof attack on Munich was made by 627 Squadron on March 1; only four heavies were missing from the Stuttgart raid. There were no interceptions reported by the 557 Main Force crews before the target and only 17 on the return journey, a remarkably low figure at that stage of the bomber offensive.

As the force increased in strength and accuracy so the Germans treated them with more respect and, as well as the flak already mentioned they used decoy TIs to lure the Mosquitoes away from the centre of the town, but the one at Hamburg on March 11 was too far south for any of the bombers to be deceived. That night 139 Squadron had put up four 'Y' aircraft to mark the target for 16 Mosquito bombers, and they also fired green Very cartridges over Amrum Island as route-markers, so the bombers were approaching the target along the same track as the 'Y' aircraft towards the correct TIs.

There was a marked increase in the size of the Mosquito attacks during April: 41 sorties were flown to Cologne on Apr 3 for a *Musical Parramatta* and one *Oboe* crew dropped a TI Floater as a safeguard against the target being cloud-covered. On April 8-9 at Essen, 40 non-*Musical* Mosquitoes and 7 *Oboe* crews attacked Krupps. Many crews saw a tremendous explosion, near an *Oboe* TI, with a fire growing by the minute. Altogether 308 sorties were flown to eight German towns.

A fourth LNSF squadron was formed at Downham Market on April 7; 571 Squadron was originally intended to be a two-flight squadron but instead some of the aircraft were transferred to Bourn to make 'C' Flight of 105 Squadron. With the emphasis on smaller targets within *Oboe* range the call on 105 and 109 Squadrons was very heavy and Bennett, although keen to expand the LNSF, chose to deploy his force where it would best serve to bomb the Hun into submission, irrespective of his personal ambitions.

Two crews from 571 Squadron were among the 39 Mosquitoes which attacked Osnabruck on April 12-13. The marking was done by one *Oboe*

Mosquito and two 'Y' aircraft from 139 Squadron. The next night was notable because eight of the 29 Mosquitoes were carrying Cookies to Berlin for the first time. The extra fuel needed to transport the 4,000-pounders was supplied by a 50-gallon drop tank attached to each wing. The weather over the Dutch coast was appalling and storm clouds, rising to 28,000 feet, caused several crews to turn back, but the eight crews with Cookies succeeded in reaching the capital. Five of them were coned, two suffering flak damage as they orbited, waiting for the arrival of the 'Y' aircraft, which were late on target. Six of the crews carrying 4,000-pounders were from 627 Squadron. It was the squadron's last operation in the Group: later in the month it was transferred to 5 Group for low-level marking duties. The LNSF flew 553 sorties during the month for the loss of only one aircraft.

Ludwigshafen was attacked seven times by the LNSF during May and 139 Squadron marked the target on each occasion. On the 1st May it put up five markers for an attack by Mosquito bombers. Two nights later, the Commanding Officer W/Cdr, G.H. Womersley acted as Master Bomber. First he ordered the 27 Mosquitoes to bomb TIs dropped by 'Y' aircraft but then, having made a visual identification of the A/P, he ordered all bombing to stop until he had marked. The night of the 22nd was clear and the markers were well grouped: timing was good and all crews bombed the TIs. One huge explosion and three fires were reported. The attack on the 26-27th was almost a replica, with one huge explosion, characterized by a flash lasting ten seconds and this started fires which soon got a hold. Unfortunately the constant practice was improving the AA gunners aim and two aircraft were missing from the attack on the 26th-27th.

Just before dawn on May 13 the AA guns at Heligoland were alerted by green Very cartridges being fired to the north of the island. 'Y' aircraft from 139 Squadron were marking the turning point for 13 Mosquitoes of 692 Squadron, each carrying a mine. Turning south-east from this point and gradually losing height to 8,000 feet they flew towards the datum point 54°08N 08°59E, 14 nautical miles from the Kiel Canal. At briefing the crews had been told that the 3½-mile stretch chosen was undefended. That brought a laugh for most of them were old hands and they had heard that story before. The next piece of information also produced a laugh; Mosquitoes of 100 Group were to go in before them and shoot up the (non-existent) AA guns.

The attack was in two waves, the first six to identify by the moon and dawn: zero hour was 0340. Red Spot Fires were dropped on the datum point and with 250 knots IAS (Indicated Airspeed) on the clock and losing height from 8,000 feet to 300 feet, the 14 nautical miles took 3 minutes. Some 6 minutes later the second wave started their run from the same point but with the additional aid of flares to help them pick out the dropping zone for it was thought it might not be healthy to dawdle in the area once the enemy had been aroused. Altogether, 11 out of 13 dropped their mines from between 50 and 250 feet and did not run into flak trouble until after bombing. Not unnaturally the ships in the canal resented the intrusion and they proved to be the main hazard, although F/O H. Goodwin narrowly missed the barrage balloons on the Albersdorf railway bridge. One crew brought their mine back having failed to make a visual identification and P/O D.M.T. Burnett was missing. The enemy was taken by surprise and started a smoke screen after the attack was over. The results were most satisfactory. The canal was closed for a week until a channel was cleared for limited traffic, but after 3 days it was closed again for a further 3 days.

Port installations at Brunsbuttel, where the 11-mile canal joins the North Sea, were attacked by 12 Mosquitoes as a diversion for the 'gardeners'. They did their own share of damage to the canal mouth and the lock gates were set on fire.

On 1-2 June 692 Squadron sent five 'gardeners' into the Baltic to drop 'vegetables' just south of Aarhus. Again the enemy were caught by surprise, the lights of Aarhus could be seen in the distance. Unfortunately the mines had to be dropped by Gee/DR because 139 Squadron had H2S unserviceability and no TIs were dropped.

Returning from an attack on Dusseldorf on May 27-28 F/O T. Dickinson was cruising peacefully over the North Sea with 210 knots on the clock, gradually losing height, when at 22,000 feet and only 50 miles from Woodbridge, tracer came flashing past the cockpit. Dickinson made a steep diving turn to port and quickly lost 6,000 feet. Kneeling on his seat – not praying, for this was the only way the navigator could look to the rear easily – F/O D.W. Griffiths saw the fighter coming in for a second attack. Forwarned, Dickinson took violent evasive action, which included a steep dive and a half roll, levelling out at 6,000 feet. During the first attack the starboard engine nacelle and the bomb-doors were hit and the tailplane badly damaged. Dickinson made a crash landing at Wittering.

In June, when Bomber Command was too busy with *Overlord* commitments to attack the Reich, the LNSF still carried the war to the heart of Germany. Eleven different targets were bombed; Berlin was attacked seven times and claimed four victims. On the 10th-11th, 139 Squadron dropped green TIs and the Germans, who were caught unprepared, fired red decoys which naturally attracted no attention. This was the best of the seven attacks and explosions followed by fires were reported.

However, the best attack of the month took place on June 23-24 when 31 out of 32 crews attacked Bremen. The Germans were again caught off their guard: the route had bypassed the town and then the Mosquitoes came in from the north. Marker crews were on time and the bombers carried out a concentrated attack, starting many fires. The Mosquitoes were clear of the target before the Germans had manned the ground defences. During June, 692 Squadron put up 232 aircraft and altogether the three squadrons flew 661 sorties. Eight aircraft were missing, a higher than average loss rate.

July followed the same pattern with nine sorties to Berlin and a continuance of the attacks, begun in June, on oil targets in the Ruhr. *Oboe* Mosquitoes usually marked for these attacks and, although the results were unspectacular, useful damage was done. Hamburg, Hanover, Bremen, Mannheim and Stuttgart also felt the Mosquito's sting.

On August 1, 608 Squadron was formed at Downham Market and S/Ldr J.D. Bolton flew its first operation to Wanne-Eickel four days later. The following night *Oboe* and LNSF crews combined to start fires in the oil plant at Castrop Rauxel and the thick black smoke was proof that they were in the right place. Two sorties to Cologne, on August 8 and 23, were very successful. During the second attack an enormous explosion lasting for 45 seconds lit up streets and buildings; fires could be seen from 100 miles away. On the 9th, 16 Mosquitoes were briefed to drop mines in the Dortmund Ems canal making a DR run from *Oboe* TIs dropped on Osnabruck. Eleven saw the TIs and duly 'planted their vegetables'. Mosquito crews had to take a fair amount of ribbing from the heavy crews and, reporting on this low-level attack, Oakington ORB remarked wryly that it 'disproves the rumour that Mosquito crews "black out" under 20,000 feet.'

Two Mk III H2S sets were allocated to 139 Squadron in August and one was operating before the end of the month; 571 Squadron were being fitted with Loran,[18] which was developed to help navigation beyond Gee range. Although it was not as accurate as Gee, crews were able to bomb larger towns blindly when no TIs were visible. Because both aids were designed to operate from the same set, navigators did not lose the accuracy of Gee during the earlier and later stages of the sortie.

The keeness of LNSF crews to improve their standard of bombing was shown in their eagerness to overcome the problems which beset the installation of the Mk XIV bombsight. Early in 1944 RAE (Royal Aircraft Establishment) had approved the trial of a Mk XIV in a Mosquito; within a week 8 Group had installed and tested the bombsight and sent their findings and recommendations back to RAE. In June, Bennett, despairing of ever hearing from them, ordered his own technicians to work on the problem; within a month the difficulties[19] had been overcome and by the end of August modified bombsights had been fitted in 28 Mosquitoes.

---

18. See Appendix VII.

19. The Mk XIV was far more accurate than the Mk IX under operational conditions: without getting too technical, much of the Mk XIV's automation relied on suction and, at Mosquito height, the rarer atmosphere impaired the smooth running of the parts.

September began with an excellent attack on Bremen, 34 out of 35 crews bombing TIs dropped by 5 out of 6 'Y' aircraft of 139 Squadron. The groundmarkers were grouped in the dock area, several explosions were reported and fires were spreading as the last crews left the target. Karlsruhe on September 4 was another success: the six 'Y' aircraft marked and 41 out of 43 crews dropped thier bombs on the well-grouped TIs.

On September 5, No. 128 Squadron was formed at Wyton and operated for the first time on the 10th when the whole complement, two, set out for Berlin; one, however, had to make an early return. For 139 Squadron the following night was one of those occasions when little went according to plan. They put up two bombers and nine marker crews, but only two dropped their TIs; one crew was shot down and two were damaged. P/O H.A. Fawcett's Mosquito was hit by flak during the bombing run, the hydraulics were damaged and an engine was put out of action. As the bomb-doors would not open the crew had to return with the HE on board and, because the hydraulics were unserviceable, the undercarriage would not work. Fawcett made a single-engined crash landing at Woodbridge. The Mosquito was a wonderful aircraft and its single-engined performance was remarkable but, being made of wood, it broke up easily when it crashed. Fawcett's Mosquito was completely wrecked, but the crew escaped with minor injuries.

During August and September the calls on the Main Force to help in the *Overlord* campaign decreased and Harris immediately stepped up his attacks on Germany. The LNSF resumed its roles of spoofing and *Windowing* the target for Pathfinder crews. Some 9 Mosquitoes *Windowed* ahead of the heavy squadrons on each of the two attacks on Kiel, on August 16 and 26, and again at Frankfurt on September 12. Sometimes the force was divided into smaller groups to carry out spoof attacks as at Kiel and Frankfurt on August 12-13, when the Main Force was attacking Russelsheim. On September 15-16, when the Main Force attacked Kiel, the LNSF was divided into three groups: 9 went to Lubeck laying on a successful spoof attack by *Windowing*, marking and bombing the port; 7 *Windowed* Kiel before the main attack and 30 went to Berlin.

The heavy squadrons did not attack the Fatherland until October 5 but the LNSF kept the sirens sounding with the help of the two *Oboe* squadrons. Five targets were attacked on October 1 and four the next night. On both occasions Brunswick was the main target and, in spite of cloud, useful damage was done. The Germans sent fighters, including jets, to intercept the force the next night when 41 crews attacked Kassel.

Brunsbuttelkoog is at the western end of the Kiel canal and the port was attacked on October 5 by 4 out of 5 crews from 139 Squadron and then three of them went on to drop datum-point markers for four crews of 571 Squadron and five of 692 Squadron 'gardening' in the canal. All of them successfully released their mines from between 150 and 250 feet and the Mosquito's speed took most crews clear of the light flak. S/Ldr E.J. Greenleaf of 571 Squadron had just dropped his mine when an AA shell burst near the cockpit and pieces of shrapnel tore into the aircraft. P/O K.L. Rendell, the navigator, was killed instantly and Greenleaf was wounded in the left shoulder. The Squadron Leader was temporarily blinded by perspex splinters but experience made him carry out the correct manoeuvres instinctively. Once clear of the target area he set course westward on the long 400-mile return journey. He had to fight fatigue caused through loss of blood and his radio was destroyed when the plane was hit, so it was a fight agains the odds. As he crossed the English coast he recognised the long wide runway at Woodbridge. With only one arm he had to set the flaps and the engine speed for the landing, knowing he would be unable to make any adjustment on the approach. Flying control, ever alert, gave him a 'green' and he landed safely. In October the total sorties exceeded the thousand mark, 1,105 being flown and, in addition to the mining raid, 25 attacks were made on nine German town for the loss of seven aircraft.

No. 142 Squadron was formed at Gransden Lodge on Oct 25 and sent two aircraft to Cologne on the 29th and the following night two to Berlin. This attack was in two phases 2½ hours apart, and more than 60 Mosquitoes took part in the raid.

In November bad weather caused cancellation on nine nights but the LNSF still exceeded its October total by 109 sorties. The force switched its attention from Berlin to Hanover, which was bombed nine times during the month. Mobile *Oboe* ground stations on the Continent moved forward with the advancing ground forces and by November towns in central Germany as far as 11° East were within range. Stuttgart, well within these limits, was marked by *Oboe* Mosquitoes on November 5-6 for 65 non-*Musical* Mosquitoes, 139 Squadron acting as Backers-up. The attack was in two phases, 3½ hours apart, and crews on both phases reported many explosions with substantial fires taking hold. Two crews saw jet fighters but there were no interceptions and no losses.

On the night of November 6-7, following a successful daylight raid by 600 heavies, 58 Mosquitoes were detailed to attack Gelsenkirchen. It was impossible to mistake the target; fires were raging over an area 5 miles square and plumb in the middle of them were the TIs dropped for their attack.

F/O J.N. Cambell and F/Lt A.A.B. Cleaver made an abortive sortie to Stuttgart on November 21; their Cookie hung up and their efforts to shake it free were unsuccessful. Cambell decided to land at Manston and just after landing the 4,000-pounder jolted off and exploded. The Mosquito was a bare 100 yards away and the blast caused the undercarriage to collapse. The aircraft caught fire but the crew scrambled clear uninjured.

They were treated for shock at sick quarters and returned to Oakington the next day. When H2S marker crews arrived over Nuremberg on November 25 the street lights were still burning. The Germans could not make up their minds whether the aircraft were friend or foe: as the marker crews were getting their bearings the lights were switched off and on twice and finally doused only after the markers had been dropped.

In March 1944 *Oboe* Mosquitoes had led small formations of 2 Group Mosquitoes in attacks on flying-bomb sites. It seems astonishing that all-Mosquito formations were not used again until November 29 when three formations set out to bomb the tar benzol plant at Meiderich, a suburb of Duisburg. The pattern was the same as the earlier formations, an *Oboe* leader and reserve with eight bombers flying in pairs in line. Only one of the three formations made a successful attack; 571 Squadron failed to make contact with their *Oboe* Mosquitoes at either of the rendezvous points but wisely joined on to the rear of 692 Squadron's formation, with 105 Squadron in the lead. Dame Fortune had the last laugh – owing to PD failure, they all had to bomb on DR.

The next day four formations were sent to attack the same plant and all were successful. A reconnaissance report on the attack said that a huge column of brown smoke turning black was rising through the cloud to a height of 10,000 feet. The bomb-load for each aircraft in two of the formations was a 4,000-pounder. As the whole formation released on a signal from the leader there is no reason to suppose that the ten Cookies did not explode almost simultaneously: they would have fallen within an area the size of Wembley Stadium, so the damage from the blast must have been enormous, and they must have made a very impressive bang.

December followed the familiar pattern with the Mosquitoes operating when weather permitted: on eight nights all operations were cancelled and when the LNSF was 'scrubbed', the conditions were invariably what was aptly described as 'bird walking weather'.

The average number of Mosquitoes operating on main targets was now more than 60 and when, on December 4-5, Bennett sent 54 Mosquitoes to make a spoof attack on Hagen, it was the weight of the attack that helped in the deception. An example of the strength of the force was when, on December 11, *Oboe* Mosquitoes led ten LNSF formations to oil targets in the Ruhr and, although 80 non-*Musical* Mosquitoes had taken part in these attacks, Bennett was able to muster 56 crews for night attacks on Hanover and Hamburg.

New crews from 139 Squadron, and later from 162 Squadron, were sent on 'Siren Tours' to gain H2S experience. They ranged far and wide over the Reich dropping a 500-pound bomb on each of three or four different targets. Invariably, when they appeared over a town the sirens were sounded, hence the appellation. Although the bomb did little damage man-hours were lost in factories, the townspeople lost sleep and the ground defences were kept on the alert. The first sorties were flown on December 23 when seven crews attacked Bremen, Hanover, Osnabruck and Munster.

To help stem the flow of supplies to the Ardennes counter-offensive four Mosquito formations took off to bomb the marshalling yards at Sieburg on December 23. The weather forecast was for 10/10ths cloud but the target was clear which may have been the reason why there were no clear-cut formations. The *Oboe* leaders and their reserves flew their tracks while non-*Musical* Mosquitoes followed in a gaggle. Due to bad weather at bases all the aircraft on this raid were diverted to aerodromes outside the Group.

By Boxing Day von Rundstedt's offensive had been halted but it was still important to prevent German reinforcements getting through to the front. On New Year's Day, 1945 17 crews of the LNSF were detailed to make daylight attacks with 4,000-pounders on 15 selected railway tunnels in the hilly districts to the west of Coblenz and Mainz and north of Trier. The aim was to dive down to 200 feet and drop the Cookie in the tunnel entrance. The bombs were fitted with short delay pistols to allow the aircraft to get far enough away from the blast.

Four crews of 128 Squadron including the CO, W/Cdr R.J. Burroughs, made accurate attacks, and F/Lt J.D. Armstrong with F/O W.E. Whyte saw 'a mushroom of smoke covering both ends of the tunnel' after their Cookie exploded. F/O A.W. Heitman and F/Lt I.J. Fawcett were the only crew from 128 Squadron to experience any opposition. As they made their approach light flak batteries opened up and they were forced to turn away. They found another tunnel in the vicinity and bombed it. The CO of 571 Squadron, W/Cdr R.J. Gosnall, took this rare opportunity to do some authorized low flying. The five crews from the squadron made successful attacks, two of them with spectacular results. S/Ldr H.D. Dawlish and Sgt P.E.C.L. Richard saw a column of brown smoke billow from the tunnel's mouth. P/O D.R. Tucker and Sgt F.A.J. David found three tunnels in their area and did a dummy run on each. The villagers came out to watch. The middle tunnel seemed to offer the best prospects and David dropped the 4,000-pounder right into the entrance. Tucker went round again to assess the damage and found the whole tunnel had erupted causing the hillside to collapse in the path of an approaching train. S/Ldr R.G.S. St C. Wadsworth and F/O R.E. Scholes of 692 Squadron pinpointed Mayen and flew down a valley to the tunnel. There was little room for error, the gap between the hills being only 150 to 175 feet, roughly three times the Mosquito's wing span. Wadsworth was flying at 100 feet when Scholes released the Cookie, which fell into the tunnel; after the explosion smoke and dust poured out of the other end. Two very important tunnels were on the 692 Squadron list, one south-east of Urft Dam and the other north of the Nurburgring, so they sent two aircraft to each of them. F/Lt G.C. Crow with F/O C.E. Earl and F/Lt F. Hill with F/O J. Simkin, having identified the checkpoint, a quarry near Scheven, destroyed the northerly tunnel.

It was not entirely a success story: F/Lt C.H. Burbridge with F/Sgt I.L.H. Ramage and F/Lt G.H.T. Nairn with Sgt D. Lunn made their run from Dumpelfeld. Burbridge made a shallow dive and Ramage's aim was true. Unfortunately they alerted the light flak batteries near the tunnel and on the high ground to the west, so that, when Nairn and Lunn made their run, they ran into a withering cross fire. Both engines were set on fire and the blazing Mosquito crashed into a hill. F/Lt T.H. Galloway made two dummy runs over the target near Kochem before dropping his bomb. The village nestled between two hills with the tunnel only a short distance away. Galloway had to dive down one hill and then immediately pull back the stick in order to avoid crashing into the other. After two close calls he told Sgt J.S. Morrell to drop the bomb on the next run because, even if the Mosquito could take the strain a fourth time, his nerves could not. The bomb overshot and crashed into the village. Earlier at Wyton F/Lt L.C.R. Wellstead crashed on take-off and both he and F/Lt G.P. Mullam were killed.

With two new squadrons helping to swell the numbers the LNSF could muster more than 150 aircraft without putting up a maximum effort. No. 162 Squadron, formed at Bourn on December 18, 1944, flew operationally for the first time on the 23rd, their target being Limburg; 163 Squadron reformed at Wyton on January 25 and sent four aircraft to *Window* Mainz on the 28th.

After the daylight on January 1 it was back to routine for the rest of the month, Berlin being the main target. When F/O F. Henry and F/Sgt T.A. Stinson were over the capital on January 5 their Mosquito was hit by a burst of flak. The starboard engine was put out of action and the feathering mechanism would not work; the instruments were damaged and the starboard undercarriage set came down. Because of the extra drag, caused by the milling engine and the undercarriage, the Mosquito would not maintain height so Henry decided to take a land route home. This proved to be a wise choice because the aircraft began to behave erratically and finally, after it had gone into an unscheduled dive, Henry decided to abandon aircraft. The escape hatch was jammed so the crew had to jettison the roof panel in order to bale out. Stinson jumped when the aircraft was at 4,000 feet and Henry struggled free seconds later. They landed safely near Marchiennes in northern France and the Caterpillar Club gained two new members.

On January 14 F/O J.H.B. Richards became a victim of the German gunners. Over Berlin his Mosquito was hit by flak, the starboard engine had to be feathered and the generator became unserviceable. He crossed the east coast just north of Orford Ness and made an emergency landing at Friston. It was probably lucky he landed at the nearest aerodrome because the weather at 8 Group bases was deteriorating rapidly and all crews arriving back after 0200 hours on January 15 had difficulty in landing. The 14 crews of 608 Squadron were diverted and S/Ldr R.J.G Greene and his navigator, F/Lt J.H. Robson, had a fatal crash while attempting to land at Little Staughton. After this crash, by a very experienced pilot, other crews were diverted to stations outside the Group, and two crews of 128 Squadron, short of petrol, were compelled to bale out.

Although this chapter is only a *précis* of the LNSF's achievements, reference to one of their failures may bring into sharper focus the fact that it was almost entirely a success story. On January 28-29, when 79 Mosquitoes set out to bomb Frankfurt the marker crews, usually so reliable, for once were not agreed on the aiming point; there were two groups of markers 15 miles apart. Most of the bombing force selected the wrong markers and started fires at Weisbaden where the smoke was rising to 5,000 feet when the last crews left. It is difficult to imagine these old campaigners being attracted by fires but the fact remains that, although markers were burning at Frankfurt throughout the scheduled duration of the attack, few bombs were dropped there.

It was 'bird walking weather' again on January 29 when 59 Mosquitoes took off to attack Berlin: only one managed to land at base, the other 58 all being diverted.

The ever-growing strength of the Mosquito force was shown when, on February 1-2, eight separate targets were attacked and 176 sorties flown. Although Bomber Command could find nothing novel for the LNSF to do in February, the month is notable because the Mosquitoes started a campaign against Berlin which it alone could achieve. Beginning on February 20, they bombed the Big City on 36 successive nights with an average of 60 Mosquitoes on each raid. The smallest number was 19 on February 25-26 and the largest on March 21-22 when 118 out of 139 Mosquitoes attacked the capital for the loss of one aircraft. The attack was in two phases with a gap of 6½ hours. Two sorties were made by 20 aircraft and there can be nothing but praise for the ground crews who, within the space of 2 hours, had these aricraft serviced and bombed up.

In February and March 2,538 sorties were flown to Berlin and 2,409 were successful; 855 Cookies were dropped on the capital during these two months, more than half the total weight. A further 572 were dropped on other German targets, 1,020 tons from the total weight of 1,600. This large proportion of the tonnage, comprising 4,000-pounders, combined with the greater concentration being achieved, resulted in the attacks causing severe local damage and, when fires started, local devastation.

Four GH raids by 3 Group on Wesel between February 16-19 had caused severe damage to the town, but now the German armour, which had retreated across the Rhine when the Allies advanced into Cleve and

Goch, was assembled among the ruins. Cloud had persisted over the town so Harris called on 3 Group to make a further attack during the morning of March 6. Then in the afternoon 12 *Oboe* Mosquitoes (6 primaries and 6 reserves) led formations of non-*Musical* Mosquitoes: 5 out of 6 were successful, 4 primaries and one reserve coping. Crews could see the glow of fires, which were still burning throughout the night when 105 and 109 Squadrons, using their PD, continued the assault by dropping HE. In the evening 38 out of 42 non-*Musical* Mosquitoes made a concentrated attack on Berlin in clear weather. Crews reported a terrific explosion in the Rheine area and a large fire-glow was still visible 2 hours later when they were homeward bound.

On April 11-12, when 109 out of 113 Mosquitoes attacked Berlin, the raid was divided into three phases and marking was done by *Oboe* Mosquitoes for the first time. LBTI reds (long-burning) were dropped and the bombing was concentrated around them. When the 37 bombers in the second phase arrived there were six fires burning from the previous attack with fresh TIs falling into the area of the fires. The 16 non-*Musical* Mosquitoes of the third phase were sent to keep the fires burning and they had a choice of four large or several small ones at which to aim their bombs.

There were seven sorties to the Big City between April 11 and 20 and *Oboe* markers were dropped during some phase of the attacks. By April 20 the Russians were on the outskirts of the town and Bennett, realizing this was the finale, laid on an extended programme. At 2250 hours 4 *Oboe* Mosquitoes marked for 24 crews of 128, 142 and 608 Squadrons, and the TIs could be seen through 10/10ths cloud. Twenty minutes later 8 *Oboe* crews dropped red TIs for a further 22 out of 24 bombers[20] and most crews saw the 'very large explosion' reported in the ORBs. Green and yellow TI Floaters were dropped during both phases. Next came four of 109 Squadron dropping HE and then three waves of H2S Mosquito bombers[21] who reported seeing numerous fires burning. At 0200 hours the first of 4 *Oboe* Mosquitoes of 105 Squadron attacked with HE and finally, at 0215 hours, F/O A.E. Austin's navigator, F/O P. Moorhead, released four 500-pounders. So ironically it was not one of the 'commuters' who dropped the last bomb on the capital.

As the ground forces advanced, worthwhile targets were at a premium. A very successful attack on Munich over 10/10ths cloud on April 25-26 caused a large explosion and fires giving off clouds of smoke. The glow of a concentrated group of *Oboe* TIs could be seen through the overcast and 80 out of 82 LNSF Mosquitoes made full use of the excellent marking.

---

20. Four each from 128, 142, 162, 163, 571 and 608 Squadrons.

21. 6 of 139 Squadron at 0030 hours; 5 of 162 Squadron at 0100 hours and 6 of 139 Squadron at 0130 hours.

After Berlin had been overrun by the Russians the Mosquitoes turned their attention to Kiel and five attacks were made on the port during the last ten days of April. No operations were flown to Germany between April 27 and May 2; the ground forces were making steady progress and the Tactical Air Forces were well able to take care of any pockets of resistance.

By May 2 Montgomery's troops were close to Lubeck and Kiel but the Germans had assembled a fleet of boats in the two harbours ready to make a dash across to Norway. On the night of May 2-3, all the 8 Group Mosquito squadrons were on detail to make Bomber Command's last sorties to Germany in anger: 16 Mosquitoes attacked Husen and Eggebeck airfields and 124 out of 126 bombed Kiel. The raid on Kiel was in two phases an hour apart. H2S Mosquitoes opened the attacks at 2315 and 0015 hours, 10 bombing in the first phase and 11 in the second. Then 5 minutes later *Oboe* Mosquitoes dropped ground and skymarkers. Most crews bombed the green TI Floaters because the target was 9-10/10ths cloud-covered.

In the words of *Bomber Command Review* 1945: 'The value of the Mosquito attacks as a supplement to the attacks by heavy aricraft is unquestioned and their contribution to the success of the combined bomber offensive was both significant and praiseworthy.'

1409 FLIGHT Perhaps, outside 8 Group, the least known of the Mosquito fraternity was 1409 Flight. Formed at Oakington in 8 Group on Apr 1 it performed the same tasks as the recently disbanded 521 Squadron of Coastal Command so that Bomber Command could obtain its own Met information. The pilots were usually tour-expired and most of them had Mosquito experience; the navigators too were usually on their second tour. Knowledge of cloud formation and conditions of icing were essential, and photography also played a large part in their operations. Deep penetration of enemy territory in daylight was common, for Bomber Command relied on their observations to determine weather conditions at the target. Only by having a complete knowledge of the Mosquito's capabilities and the skill to use it could they hope to survive, for evasive action and strategic use of cloud were their only defence against flak and fighters.

One important piece of information they had to obtain was the height at which condensation trails formed. This was important for their own safety as it was for all high-flying aircraft, because fighters flew along them to make an interception. Most pilots avoided cloud for fear of icing but the *Pampa*[22] crews had to fly through it to find the depth of the icing layer

22. Code name for a Met Flight sortie.

and estimate its severity. *Pampas* were often flown at night to obtain weather information for the USAAF; then flares were used to calculate the height and base of cloud. They also photographed the American missions so that their Top Brass could estimate the tightness of the formations. They performed the same service for 3 Group when they were using GH in daylight.

Stand-by crews were ready to take off at a moment's notice and, although the call on the Flight increased as Bomber Command attacked several targets in one evening, it still put up crews to operate in many roles. They dropped flares along the Kiel Canal when the LNSF made its dawn 'gardening' raid; they made reconnaissance sorties to obtain an immediate report on Bomber Command attacks; they flew ahead of the Main Force to get up-to-the-minute information of weather conditions at the target and broadcast their findings to the Master Bombers; they flew ahead of Churchill on all his overseas missions, and when King George VI flew to Italy a Met Mosquito flew ahead relaying weather conditions.

This brief account does less than justice to the important part they played in the bomber offensive and to the bravery of the crews whose survival rested chiefly on their skill.

Epilogue

'Genesis' gave a brief summary of Bomber Command's disappointing record before the introduction of Pathfinders, and traced the underlying factors which made such a force essential. The period from August 1942 to the end of the year was one of experimentation yet, using only the same equipment as the Main Force, PFF brought about an improvement in concentration. During this period Pathfinders' role had been chiefly to identify the target and the Main Force had been briefed to locate the aiming point for themselves. In the New Year, when TIs were introduced, the policy was gradually changed and crews were ordered to bomb the markers. There were occasions when the Main Force were given the option but these were the exception rather than the rule. By the end of February, even discounting the previous gross errors and the proportion dropped on decoys, the percentage of bombs plotted within the MPI of the bomb pattern had increased from 35% to 50%.

This was a remarkable improvement but, unfortunately, a new problem was introduced. Whereas previously the MPI had been near the aiming point, now the resulting bomb-pattern was determined largely by the TIs. The displacement between the MPI and the A/P was called the Systematic Error, and this reduced the overall improvement to 5%. Bomber Command, at this stage, was working to a limit of within 3 miles of the centre of concentration.

As would be expected with Bennett at the helm, much was done to improve the standard of marking, but little to improve the standard of bombing. Creepback was the main offence: the MPI changed alarmingly as the raid progressed and the undershooting became more pronounced. Moreover, crews enjoyed bombing fires, and once there was a good fire blazing TIs were neglected. On an average only 30% of the Main Force bombed within 3 miles of the aiming point yet there were few markers outside those limits. Another Main Force habit, which persisted until the end of the war, was to bomb the first TIs they encountered although they were briefed to bomb the centre of all the markers. Concentration was the keynote of success but clever planning could capitalize on the frailties of the Main Force, as at Wuppertal when creepback spread the damage into Barmen.

When Bomber Command was required to destroy marshalling yards in occupied territory as a prelude to *Overlord*, speaking from experience, Harris proclaimed that his force was incapable of the precision required, but fortunately his crews proved him wrong. *Oboe* attacks had always been more concentrated than H2S *Parramatta* and *Newhaven*, but their markers proved to be insufficiently accurate to allow the Main Force to bomb them without guidance.

Master Bombers had been used to encourage the Main Force to brave defences, and generally to direct the attacks, but now the relationship became more intimate. Crews were guided to the aiming point and instructed how to overcome the TI error. It was this expert advice which enabled small targets to be demolished and, after the invasion, enabled Bomber Command to give close support to the ground forces. First on target and last to leave, Master Bombers and their Deputies were exposed to the defences for longer periods and, when the target was cloud-covered, they risked their own lives to find out if it was safe before ordering the Main Force to come below cloud.

Being part of a group where keenness was a way of life, they found it difficult to understand why many Main Force crews seemed reluctant to press home the attack and, serving under an AOC whose minimum standard was perfection, they could not comprehend the mentality of those who, having risked their lives, did not take the trouble to aim their bombs accurately. Fortunately this *malaise* was not widespread for it is doubtful if the Second Front could have been opened without air supremacy, and even more improbable that the beachheads could have been held without the chaos behind the German lines created by Allied bombing before and after D-Day. As a prelude to each important advance by Allied ground forces bombers softened up the enemy.

In the final phase the full weight and potential of Bomber Command was realized – that it was effective was entirely due to PFF. As Bennett put it in his victory message to all personnel: 'Bomber Command's share in this great effort has been a major one. You, each one of you, have made that possible. The Pathfinder Force has shouldered a grave responsibility. It has led Bomber Command, the greatest striking force ever known. That we have been successful can be seen in the far-reaching results which the bomber offensive has achieved. That is the greatest reward the Pathfinder Force ever hopes to receive, for those results have benefited all law-abiding peoples.'

Outside the Air Force it was unusual for someone of lower rank to be in charge, but when flying on operations the pilot was invariably the captain and the rest of the crew took orders from him. This egalitarian principle was more marked in 8 Group than anywhere else in the Air Force. It was of course chiefly because marking was a team effort and each man was selected for his fitness to perform a specialized task. Two examples will illustrate the point. S/Ldr Cranswick and S/Ldr Cresswell were equally capable of performing Master Bomber duties but on the raid when Cranswick was shot down his role was Primary Visual Marker; Cresswell had been made Master Bomber because he knew the target. Again, at Dresden, W/Cdr de Wesselow was in charge of the attack and W/Cdr Le Good, who outranked him on the ground, was acting as his Deputy. In the air rank did not count and everyone accepted this anomaly. The quality of Pathfinder crews was again shown when, at Dortmund on March 11, 1945, a Squadron Leader – his equivalent rank in the Army a mere Major – was in command of more than 7,000 men, many of them his seniors on the ground.

Other groups quote their heroes and crack squadrons but for Pathfinders anonymity was the key word, Bennett refusing to have a public relations officer in the group. There were, of course, outstanding personalities in Pathfinders, but giants appear as tall men when all men are tall. Tempting though it is, it would be invidious to single out individuals without making unfair omissions when team work was so essential. G/Capt J.E. Fauquier has been described as 'King of the Pathfinders' not for any outstanding act of bravery, nor indeed for any brilliant feats of marking, but because he embodied the qualities so necessary in a force whose job was to lead: courage, reliability, tenacity, the ability to blend into a team and, above all, to press on resolutely with continued enthusiasm, in spite of adversity, with his allotted task to help to win the war.

Appendix I
Oboe

Oboe was the name given to a ground-controlled blind bombing device of unique accuracy. From 30,000 feet at speeds of over 300 m.p.h. the average operational error was only 300 yards: for lower heights it was even less. A flight of 109 Squadron, which was one of the original five transferred to the Pathfinder Force, was at that time in the process of being equipped with *Oboe*.

In summer 1940, when the Germans switched to night bombing, they used three types of beams to direct their bombers to the target, *Knickebein, X Gerat* and *Y Gerat.* No. 80 Wing was given the task of identifying the type, measuring the width, finding the exact wavelength and locating the source.[1] The crews suggested it would be no more hazardous to try to bomb the source at the same time, and permission was granted to do this. Blind bombing at night was something new and several methods were tried, one of which was a ground-controlled release. An IFF set in the aircraft was used as a signal repeater and a CHL (Chain Home Low)[2] set as a monitor. It was, in fact, the early-warning system in reverse and was known as a 'howler chaser'. One navigator thought the note of the CHL set sounded like an oboe and gradually the name became associated with blind bombing.

The failure more than the success started TRE thinking about blind bombing techniques and many ideas were discussed, but it was not until June 1941 when Dr F.E. Jones joined A.H. Reeves that a satisfactory system was devised. By this time they had seen the varied fortunes of *Knickebein* and the *X* and *Y Gerat* techniques and were able to capitalise on this knowledge. They worked out a system using two stations each with a different role: one, the tracking station – code name 'Cat' – sent

1. The crews assigned to this task formed the nucleus of 109 Squadron attached to 80 Wing. The squadron was therefore associated with *Oboe* from the start, was the first to use it operationally and continued to use it throughout its wartime career, and it was a crew from 109 Squadron who dropped the last bomb in anger in the European theatre.

2. CHL receivers were used in RDF stations sited around the coast to forewarn the country of approaching hostile aircraft.

dot-dash signals to the pilot; the other, the releasing station – code name 'Mouse' – measured the groundspeed of the aircraft, warned the navigator of the approximate time before bomb release and gave the release signal. Both stations operated on the same wavelength but used different pulse radio frequencies (PRFs). A pulse repeater in the aircraft responded to both PRFs so each station could measure the aircraft's range independently. The purpose of the repeater was to boost the signals to increase the range. The track to the target was along an arc of the Circle of Constant Path Range passing through the point of bomb release (R/P) with the 'Cat' at the centre. To overcome jamming it was proposed to operate in the centimetre (S) band and, to avoid German interference with the information sent to the crews, it was to be incorporated in the pulse frequencies. As the beam[3] was an arc it was estimated that the average time for a pilot to settle on it and fly it accurately would be 10 minutes. A position on the track, called point A, equal to 10 minutes' flying time, was measured back from the R/P, and given to the crews at briefing, together with the height and airspeed at which the run must be made. Height and airspeed were vitally important because they were part of the complicated formula to calculate the R/P and were used to determine point A. The navigator's job was to get the aircraft to point A 10 minutes before time on target. This was invariably done with the aid of Gee, but for marking operations, as a safety precaution, a Bailie beam was laid on to a position near point A called the Waiting Point. The *Oboe* equipment was switched on, with the exception of the repeater, prior to reaching the Waiting Point to make sure it was working. Most crews listened to the progress of the aircraft on target before them; it was useful to know if they were early or late, and also the pilot could assess the quality of the signals. Each crew had its own call sign and this was transmitted from both stations. When they heard their call sign, then and only then, the navigator switched on the repeater. Almost immediately the pilot would receive dots or dashes depending which side of the track he was on. If he was on the side nearer to the station he received dots, if on the far side dashes. When he settled on the beam he got an equi-signal tone, in other words a steady note.[4]

If the aircraft was some distance from the beam both stations sent an X, Y or Z in morse indicating it was 5, 10 or 15 miles adrift. If it was further from the target than point A an S was sent. The 'Mouse' sent A, B, C and D to the navigator indicating 10, 8, 6 and 3 minutes from the R/P; finally the release signal, 5 dits and 2.5 second dah, was given. When the

---

3. While technically *Oboe* was not a beam in the accepted sense of the word, because of its aural similarity it is referred to as a beam.

4. Saward in *The Bomber's Eye* says the dashes were on the near side, but I can assure him and the reader this was not so.

navigator pressed the bomb release it automatically cut out the aircraft transmitter and so the ground stations knew the exact time of release. He switched off the transmitter as soon as possible after dropping the bombs so that the next aircraft could be called.

When the idea was put to the Air Staff they were not very enthusiastic. Ten minutes on the run meant only six aircraft an hour. The plane could not take evasive action during that time without affecting the groundspeed calculations, and subsequent planes all flew the same track. This would make them an easy prey for both ack-ack and the nightfighters. Finally, because the signals travelled at a tangent to the earth's surface, distance and height were irrevocably linked; so the range was limited by the aircraft's ceiling.

Dr Jones was put in charge of development, but scarcely had he got his team together before Bomber Command was knocking at the door: 'Could anyone remember bombing German radio beacons?' They wanted to try the idea on the *Scharnhorst* and *Gneisenau*, so the majority of the team high-tailed it down to West Prawle to take part in what was known as the Trinity project.

Reeves had argued that, when the target was heavily defended, if a diversionary raid took place in the same area simultaneously then it might be some time before the Germans realized special equipment was being used, its accuracy being attributed to luck. Here was an opportunity to prove the point.

Although some sources quote these raids as the first *Oboe* sorties they were, in fact, more like *X Gerat*, which used two beams, a Lorenz beam for the pilot, the other to control a reversible clock for the release. A Bailie beam was set up at Helston in Cornwall to provide the track, the *Oboe* station at West Prawle sending the release signal. Stirlings from 7 Squadron were fitted with the special equipment; crews from No. 109 joined the Stirling crews to operate it during the final straight and level run. About 100 Wellingtons, attacking in waves, bombed the harbour at Brest as a diversion. Several attacks were made in November and December 1941 and, much to everyone's surprise, no Stirlings were lost.

At this stage of development the release station was using the reversible clock principle. An *X Gerat* clock had been captured in working order from a crashed Heinkel He111; its mechanical ticking reminded one of the salvage party of a 'Mickey Mouse' clock, so it was christened 'Mickey Mouse'. Although the clock at West Prawle was electrical it too was called Mickey Mouse. This was later shortened to Mouse and the station became known as the Mouse station. By association of ideas the tracking station was eventually called the Cat.

Because *Oboe* had a low priority only limited S-band equipment was available. In addition to its other objections the Air Staff was sceptical about the paper claims of blind bombing. With these two points in mind it was decided to develop *Oboe* in the 150-cm band and the S-band simultaneously. The 150-cm could develop unrestricted; the Boffins could prove their point with regard to accuracy; crews could be trained; ground experience too would be gained. Eventually, when priorities were given, many teething troubles would be avoided and an S-band prototype would be ready.

Despite the Trinity diversion everything was ready for the first full trials by April 24, 1942. Bomber Command sent down F/O B.W. Finn as their observer. His reports were glowing – he had seen amazingly accurate bombing through 10/10ths cloud at least as good as visual daylight bombing. Bomber Command realized here was the aid needed to drop the TIs which were being developed at this time.

Although it was never intended to use Mk I operationally, because it would be easy to jam, Command insisted, so everything else was dropped to get it into service. At Malvern (TREHQ) it was sheer bedlam; anything useful was commandeered or 'borrowed', and those not on the project had virtually to chain everything to their benches. Sir Robert Renwick conjured 90 airmen from somewhere overnight and they were immediately put to work stripping CHL sets for the ground stations. ASV Mk II receivers and transmitters, with slight modification, were used for the aircraft sets but the modulators had to be built from scratch. RAF Kidbrooke obliged with the first transmitters and 60 Group were called in to install the equipment in the newly built ground stations. By August two ground stations were ready and sets for the aircraft were coming through at a steady pace.

Meanwhile things had been happening outside Malvern. TIs had not yet been used operationally and it was thought that ten would be the minimum required to light a target. The pressurized Wellington VI had a ceiling of 30,000 feet and could carry this load, so two were assigned to 109 Squadron for *Oboe* trials. A marking exercise by heavies was laid on at Larkhill bombing range for the Top Brass to see a demonstration of TIs. In case there was cloud on the night it was suggested one of the Wellingtons should stand by: there was 10/10ths cloud, so the Wellington was called in. It did a successful run and the TIs fell within 70 yards of the target. By one of those curious quirks of fate, which often alter the course of war, only three of the TIs fell; some electrical fault caused the other seven to 'hang up'. In the post mortem on the exercise it was unanimously agreed that three TIs provided adequate illumination. New vistas were opened, the Mosquito could carry this load, its ceiling was well above 30,000 feet, its speed much faster than any German nightfighter: these were significant factors when flying straight and level for 10 minutes. The Air Staff sanctioned the use of the Mosquito for *Oboe* on July 18, 1942.

The Wellington had one advantage over the Mosquito; it was pressurized. The aircraft equipment, which had been designed for the Wellington and had previously given no trouble, started burning out in the Mosquito and the fault took weeks to locate. Because of the lower pressure the high-frequency circuits in the transmitter were arcing and they had to be redesigned to obviate this: once rectified it gave no further trouble even at heights of 35,000 feet. Intermittent interference was also causing trouble. One school of thought considered the source to be local and the squadron wanted to do an operation to prove the point. The others argued that, by fitting a double frequency modulator into the aircraft transmitter now, not only would this trouble be cured but also, when the enemy eventually began jamming, it would prevent spurious pulses being transmitted to the ground stations. It was decided to make the modification first and K *Oboe* (K for coincidence) was the name given to this form of Mk I. Two receivers were fitted into the aircraft and tuned to different frequencies; the pulses were transmitted coincidentally from the stations on the two frequencies and, unless the aircraft received both pulses, the transmitter did not operate.

The squadron had the last laugh. Because the modifications were taking longer than anticipated Bennett was champing at the bit and Command was getting impatient, so the first *Oboe* sorties took place in unmodified Mk Is. On December 20, 1942, six aircraft attacked Lutterade, each carrying three 500-pound MC; 3 out of 6 made successful runs, and the beer flowed in the Wyton mess that night. Other bombing sorties were made before the squadron was called upon to mark. The honour went to S/Ldr H.E. Bufton. On December 31 he dropped a skymarker over Dortmund for 8 Lancasters from 83 Squadron to bomb. Then followed several successful sky and groundmarkings until, on March 5-6, 1943, Command took its courage in both hands and sent *Oboe* to mark its *bête noir*, Essen: 5 out of 8 crews marked successfully for a force of 442 heavies. In 40 minutes they did more damage to Essen and dropped more bombs on the town than in all the previous raids put together.

K *Oboe* was having its problems as breakthrough was occurring when more than one pair of stations were operating at the same time; this was cured by Latching (see (ii) below). This further modification to the aircraft meant more delay; so it was not until mid-June 1943 that all the aircraft were fitted with the double frequency sets.

To maintain the marking satisfactorily at least two aircraft must bomb within a period of 10 minutes. There were three ways of overcoming the problem:

(i) More pairs of stations operating on different wavelengths. This method was used for Mk I, its limitation being the number of radio frequencies available on the waveband. Three were allotted for Mk I, so the limit was three pairs of stations. The fact that K *Oboe* used two radio frequencies made no difference as three still provided three pairs – AB, AC and BC.

(ii) Latching was sending out two signals a definite number of micro seconds apart. The receiver in the aircraft had a built-in delay of an equal number of micro-seconds for the second signal to catch up and the transmitter responded only when it received both signals simultaneously. Latching was never used to create more channels but was used with K *Oboe* to prevent breakthrough.
(iii) Different pairs of pulse frequencies on the same radio frequency. This method was used on Mk IIM and Mk III.

Getting Mk I operational and converting to K *Oboe* retarded progress on Mk II, so it was necessary to institute a crash programme to provide 40 sets in the S-band in case Mk 1 was jammed. For S-band *Oboe* it was intended to extract the information sent to pilot and navigator from the ground signals before they were retransmitted. To do this a tunable valve was essential. Also, to accommodate several pairs of PRFs, a width modulator had to be designed instead of the space modulator used on Mk I.

There were four different types of Mk II developed: *Penwiper, Pepperbox, Fountain Pen* and *Album Leaf.*

Penwiper was the name given to the first Mk II sets. It used the Klystron (CV70) tunable valve and incorporated a new IF amplifier. Fortunately Mk I was not jammed until late 1943; because *Penwiper* was a failure as was its successor.

Pepperbox was a modification of *Penwiper* using a higher-powered Klystron (CV150). The valve had the power lacking in the CV70, but at height it had a disappointingly short life, and proved too unreliable for operational use. The scheme was abandoned in November 1943.

The Magnetron, so vital to H2S, was a more powerful and more durable valve than the Klystron: a non-tunable one was being used in Mk II ground-station equipment. The Americans, who were carrying out parallel development, had a tunable Magnetron (2J54), which worked in conjunction with a special transmitter (ASG3). Besides being light and compact[5] the transmitter was pressurized and sealed, which meant it operated equally well at all heights. The Americans, being very interested in *Oboe*, readily agreed to barter ASG3 transmitters and the 2J54 valves for British receivers.[6]

Fountain Pen[7] (Mk IIF) also used the *Penwiper* receivers as these were the only ones available in numbers. By combining these with the ASG3 and the Magnetron, S-band *Oboe* was tranformed overnight from a nightmare into an operational fact. The advent of *Fountain Pen* was

---

5. Two important considerations: space and weight were always problems when fitting equipment into a Mosquito.

6. The Americans used *Oboe*; flying 627 missions, involving 1,663 sorties.

7. Or *Aspen* as it was called in 8 Group.

timely because the Germans were jamming Mk I ground stations from the Pas de Calais area, and the airborne sets from the Ruhr. The copes fell off alarmingly in December 1943 but, by the end of January, things were looking up; pilots and navigators were speaking to each other again, and ground crews managed an occasional smile.

Album Leaf was the code-name for Mk IIM; it incorporated all that was good in the other Mk IIs; the Magnetron, the ASG3 and a new IF amplifier. It also had far more sophisticated filters (Type 166) for the width modulator. Mk IIM did not come into service immediately, because the filters were in short supply. The heavy call on the *Oboe* squadrons to mark *Overlord* targets brought about an urgent need for aircraft sets, so a further modification had to be made, using space modulators; and six mobile ground stations had to be converted to operate them.

Reeves considered *Oboe* the ideal bombing medium and so he devised a system which overcame Bomber Command's criticism that six planes per hour provided no concentration and that the danger was increased because they all used the same track. Twenty different pairs of PRFs and two radio frequencies would enable 40 planes to be in the target area at the same time. By using the Delta technique of control, aircraft within ±45° of the CPR could be controlled directly on to the target (Fig. 3). This technique gave a dot-dash modulation based, not on which side of

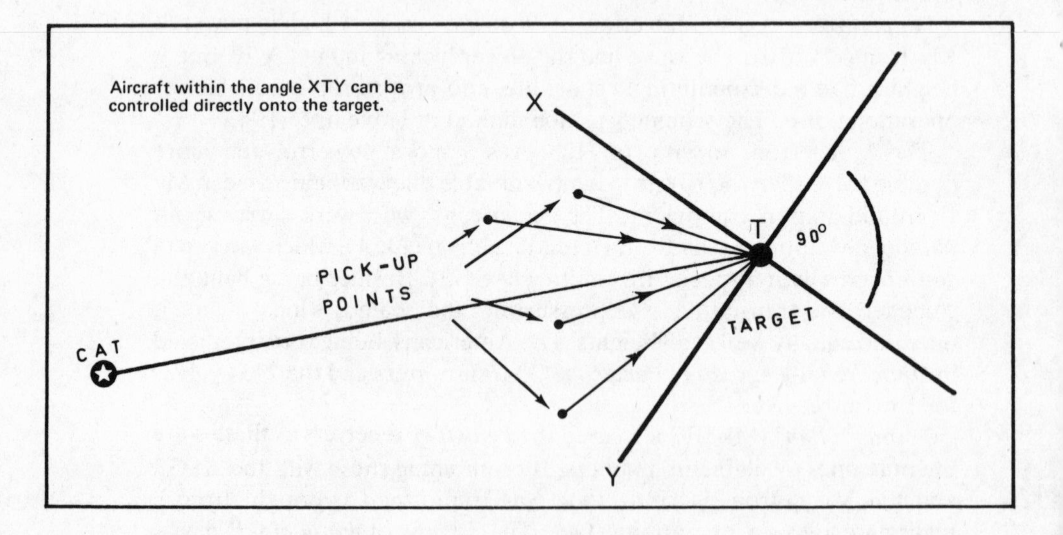

Fig. 3 The Air Staff's main objections to *Oboe* (it was designed to be an accurate bombing device) were too few aircraft per hour, and they all flew the same track. Multi-approach was designed to cover the second criticism. By using the Delta Approach (Fig. 5) all aircraft within the limits of XTY could be controlled directly onto the target. The order of bombing would be made by a controller at the Cat station who could see the relative position of the aircraft on his screen.

the track the aircraft were, but on their rate of approach to it (Figs 4 and 5). By controlling the rate of approach so that the point of intersection with the track was in all cases the A/P then no two succeeding planes would attack from the same angle. Two radio frequencies enabled two planes to be controlled at the same time and a 3-minute run would be ample as the pilot did not have to settle on the beam. A master controller would call the aircraft, selecting the one in the best position to attack.[8] The idea was never developed beyond the experimental stage (although ground stations were built) because *Oboe* was being used primarily for target-marking, and also Bomber Command wanted to attack more than one target simultaneously, which necessitated using a different radio frequency for each of them.

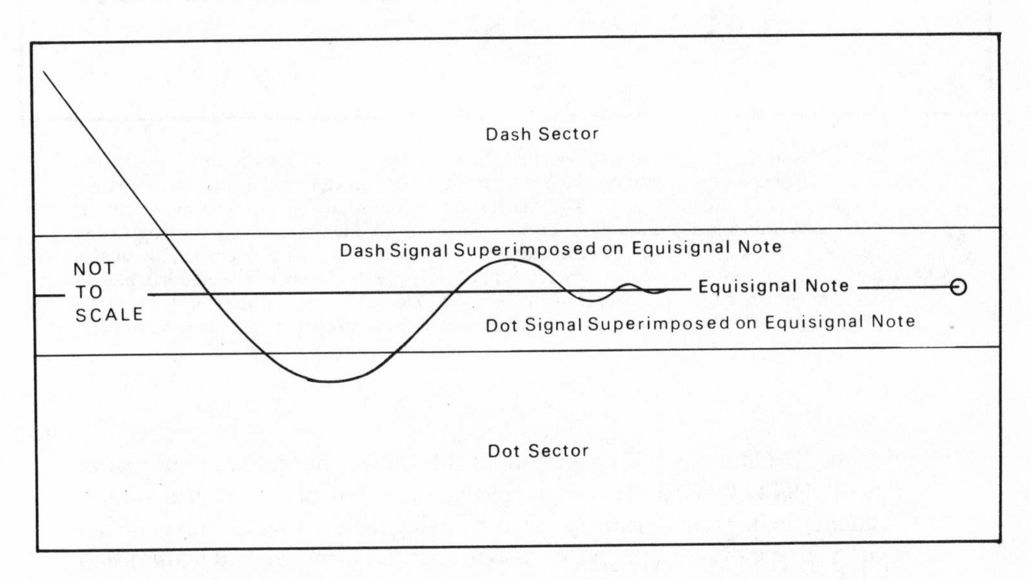

Fig. 4 Although the navigator gave the pilot his course for the run-up to the target calculated on his latest wind even if it were accurate the pilot still had to ease himself onto the beam gradually. He would try to settle down with the dots just sounding on the equisignal note because the curvature of the beam would bring him onto the correct track with little or no alteration of course. The aircraft's heading at the time of bomb release was the most important factor when bomb-aiming. Height was important; too low resulted in an undershoot; too high an overshoot.

8. The description has been simplified because it never became operational. It is obvious that if any degree of accuracy were to be maintained a series of R/Ps would have to be calculated to cover all angles of approach. This contingency was covered by using an Instant Velocity 'Mouse' coupled to an automatic bomb release.

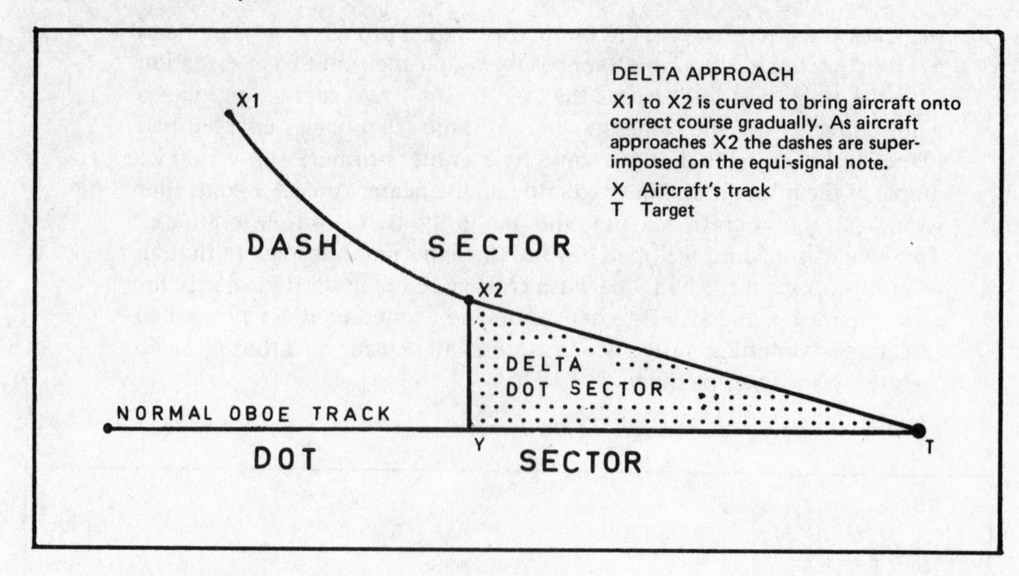

Fig. 5 The Delta Technique was designed to direct pilots without beam experience to the target. The crew were required to be within the limits laid down in Fig. 3, and not more than 5 minutes away from the target. The Cat station then plotted their track to the target, (it bore no relation to the radius track). Dot-Dash information was sent according to the aircraft's position in relation to the Delta track. It was never used operationally in this manner. However, unknown to most *Oboe* pilots, because their experience enabled them to beat the system, it was used operationally between D and the target. When coupled with the Instant Velocity Mouse the electronically controlled release signal was more accurate.

Mk III *Oboe*, as this development was called, became operational in April 1944. It used Mk III ground stations but operated in a similar manner to its predecessors because, by flying the CPR the planes could be controlled more accurately and also the danger from flak and fighters had proved negligible. The airborne equipment was almost identical to Mk IIM and so it too was held up because of the shortage of Type 166 filters, and also for modifications at the ground stations. It was not until July 1944 that it was used extensively when it replaced the Mk I sets on the squadrons, and by the autumn Mk I had ceased to function operationally.

THE REPEATER SYSTEM The boffins were alive to the tangential problem of *Oboe* and they worked out a method of increasing range without increasing operational height. Two repeater aircraft, one for Cat and the other for Mouse, would fly the station beams acting as go-betweens for other planes attacking targets as far afield as Berlin (Fig 6). They would re-radiate the signals from the ground stations to the operational aircraft and re-transmit the return signals back to the ground. Several trial raids were made on Emden during September and October 1943, using a repeater for the Cat, the Mouse being controlled normally. Although these raids were successful, further development was abandoned because the Air Staff over-optimistically thought H2S sufficient to their needs for targets beyond normal *Oboe* range.

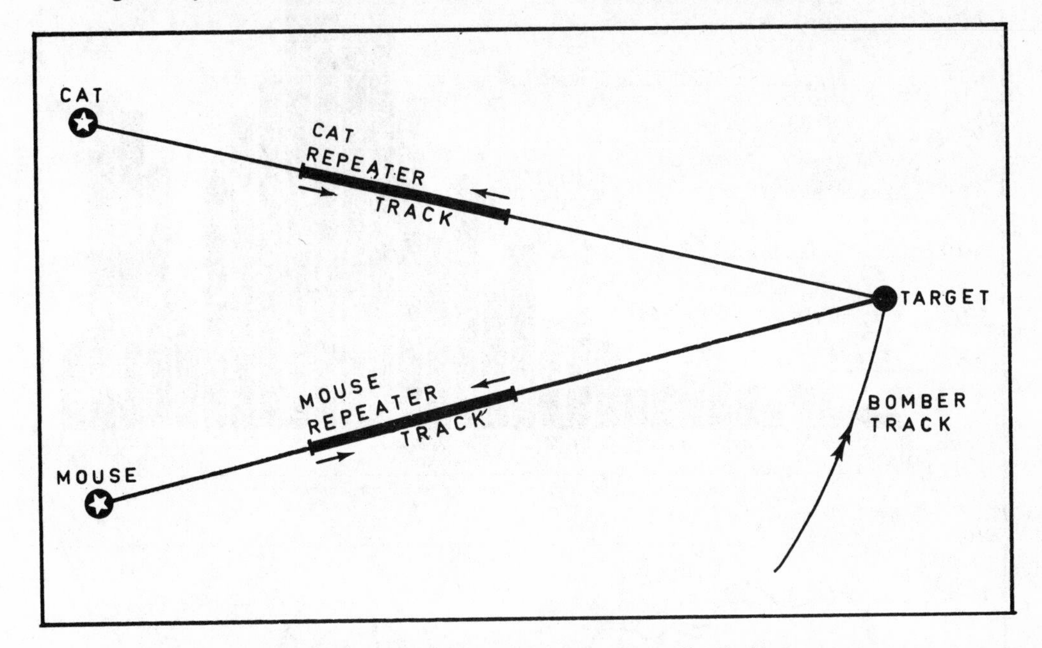

Fig. 6 Height and distance were irrevocably linked in *Oboe* due to the earth's curvature, so the aircraft's ceiling determined the device's range. The Repeater System overcame this limitation by employing intermediaries in the sky. Signals to and from the bomber sent by the Cat station were relayed by the Cat repeater aircraft, and similarly its distance from the target was relayed by the Mouse repeater aircraft. Berlin could have been marked by *Oboe* in late 1943 had the ploy been used. In fact the Mosquito's range, which was no problem, would have been the limiting factor.

Ground stations were an integral part of *Oboe* and, when the call came to 'get operational' in May 1942, they rated the same priority as aircraft sets. The two existing stations were on the south coast and so were of no use for German targets. New stations were sited at Trimingham, near Cromer and Hawkeshill Down, between Dover and Deal. More were built to satisfy the increasing demand and mobile caravans were equipped against the day when they could be set up on the Continent. By D-Day there were 13 home stations and six mobiles with another four almost completed. These gave a continental coverage from Nantes to Emden in an arc including Paris, Cologne and the Ruhr.

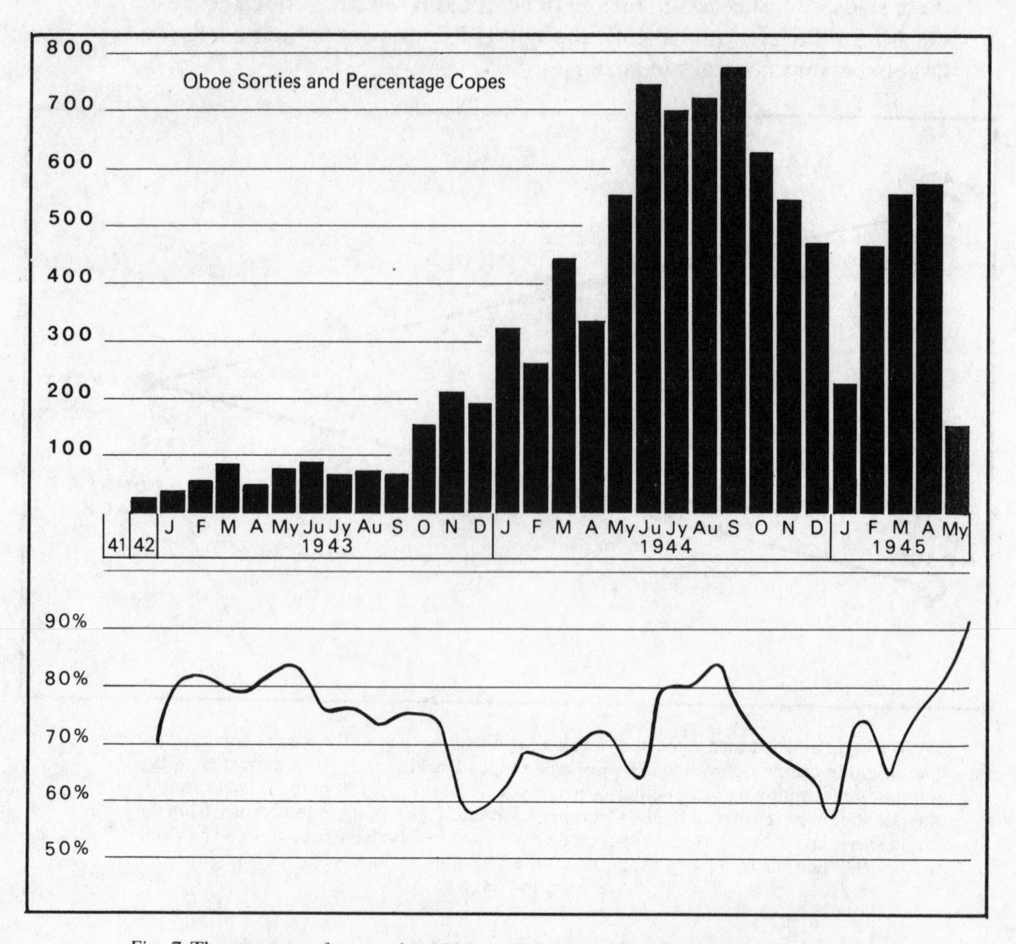

Fig. 7 The average of more than 700 sorties during the summer months of 1944 bears witness to the high regard in which *Oboe* marking was held. Few Bomber Command attacks were launched without its help. The copes maintained a good average. The first low was caused by the Germans jamming MkII. The low in May was the result of unscheduled modifications on the ground equipment: a fault at one ground station meant no copes. Teething troubles with mobile ground stations was the cause of the downward trend in the autumn of 1944. However, PFFHQ thought that bad navigation played its part, crews being too far away from the waiting point for the ground station to pick them up on their screens. Senior crews sent an *Overture* sorties had a much higher percentage of copes which tended to prove the point.

Ground staff to man the stations was also an urgent need and two training schools were formed, one for maintenance staff, the other for ground controllers. Shortly after the Trinity project five officers were transferred to *Oboe* to learn ground control and they were the nucleus of a team which expanded to more than 50 by D-Day. A total of 50 officers and 150 other ranks, including WAAF, were assigned to *Oboe* for the maintenance of ground and airborne equipment.

Appendix II H2S

H2S was the second of Bennett's blind bombing aids and flew operationally for the first time on January 30, 1943, when 7 Stirlings of 7 Squadron and 6 Halifaxes of 35 Squadron marked Hamburg. Its obscure title is credited to Lord Cherwell who, having seen a demonstration of the equipment, realized it was the type of aid that Command needed. When told how long it had been waiting for priorities he said: 'This whole affair stinks.' Laughingly he added: 'Call it H2S.' The equipment had two significant advantages over Gee and *Oboe*. Because it did not depend on ground stations, it could not be jammed, and even more important it had no range limitations.

In July 1939 Dr E.G. Bowen had navigated blindly using an AI, and in February 1940 Prof P.M.S. Blackett had drawn attention to the possibilities of ASV as a navigational aid for picking up coastlines and rivers, and suggested using a radio altimeter to measure the aircraft's height above the ground accurately. However, at that time, defence was the operative word and no one had time to listen, so it was not until the autumn of 1941 that any action was taken. At a Sunday Soviet[1] in October, when the topics were the Butt Report and the urgent need for new navigational aids, the merits of AI were put forward, and this time everyone listened. If AI were feasible then development in the centimetre band would improve its definition enormously.

A 9cm AI in a Blenheim, with the aerial angled downward, was tested on November 1 and the possibilities were manifest. Six flights were made and it was established that rivers, coasts and towns gave responses of different intensity. Radiated VHF pulses travel in straight lines and are reflected back (echoes) from suitable surfaces in varying degrees. When the echoes are displayed on a cathode-ray tube they fall into three distinct categories:

---

1. A Sunday Soviet was an informal, though serious, gathering at the Superintendent of TRE's house for tea every Sunday afternoon. Boffins and Service officers dropped in to discuss their problems. All views were argued on their merits, rank or position bearing no weight, hence the appendage 'Soviet'.

(i) Water looks dark, because it is a poor reflector.
(ii) Land appears lighter so the coastlines stand out, also estuaries and banks of rivers.
(iii) Built-up areas contain a number of 'corner reflectors'[2]; these give a powerful return without scatter. This characteristic response is readily distinguishable from ordinary ground returns because as well as being brighter it also produces a recognizable shape.

It was quickly realized that the rotating beam (scanner) and Plan Position (PPI) display used by the GCI units would give a vastly superior weapon to that which might be obtained by making refinements to AI or ASV. The scanner, sending out narrow horizontal beams of radiation with a wide vertical sweep below the aircraft, when coupled to a rotating synchronized time base display on a cathode-ray tube, would give a radar map of the ground beneath the aircraft. Pulses would appear on the screen whenever the scanner pointed at them and, with the help of an afterglow, remain for one revolution of the scanner. With the aircraft at the centre of the screen objects appeared in their true relative position and their bearing and distance could be calculated.

Two Halifaxes[3] were allocated to TRE and the first trials, carried out at 8,000 feet, enabled them to inform the Air Staff that the system offered 'the likelihood of successful target identification and accurate location with the possibility of selective bombing within the area.'[4]

To date the Klystron valve had been used to power the pulses, but TRE wanted to use the Magnetron so that definition could be maintained at operational heights of over 20,000 feet. This put the cat among the pigeons. Britain was well ahead of Germany in centimetre radar and the Chiefs of Staff wanted to keep it that way: the two valves alone put us streets ahead of the enemy in this field. The Magentron was more powerful than the Klystron and was virtually indestructable. The last virtue was a vice as far as H2S was concerned, for the first set lost on the other side would give away its secrets to the Germans. Even when detonated it still retained sufficient form for a Dr Pleydl[5] to reconstruct it. The Navy was vitally concerned because it was being used, highly successfully, by Coastal Command in the latest ASV for U-boat spotting. and the senior naval officers among the Chiefs of Staff fought remorselessly to retain its exclusive use. They sought to strengthen their case by pointing out that the valve would destroy Bomber Command if it came to be used in the enemy nightfighters. The Americans supported this view: they had no

---

2. It is a scientific fact that, when three reflecting surfaces are at right angles, then rays return along their own path. This principle is known as a 'corner reflector'.

3. The Halifax was selected because it offered a greater choice of position for the scanner.

4. TRE report, April 1942.

5. Responsible for *X and Y Gerat*

faith in H2S and said it was presenting the Magnetron to the Germans on a crazy enterprise. The other side protested that there was no point in having a lead if it could not be exploited and, even if the Germans realized its significance, it would take time for them to develop a counter-offensive. Meanwhile we would have enjoyed the benefits.[6]

At this point tragedy struck the project. On June 7 the Halifax equipped with the Magentron set crashed in Wales with six of the H2S Boffins on board: there were no survivors. It was certainly a time for men with stout hearts, and had it not been for the faith and inexhaustible energy of Prof P.I. Dee and Dr (now Sir Bernard) Lovell H2S might never have become operational. The tragedy in Wales brought one aspect to the notice of all concerned; H2S did not recognize mountains. To overcome this a radio altimeter was incorporated to give the height of the aircraft above the ground irrespective of air pressure.

A month later Bennett went to Defford for a demonstration in the Klystron Halifax and was impressed. He immediately saw its potential and asked Command for the first sets to equip his newly formed Pathfinders. Bennett stood by at Defford for most of July and, realizing that many of the flights were being postponed because of aircraft unserviceability and not because of faults in the H2S sets, he imported a 'gen' ground crew to service the Halifax. He caused considerable turmoil by trying to organize everyone and raise them to his immaculate standards, and eventually his keenness to get going and reluctance to stop broke Lovell's equanimity, 'The man's only happy when flying at 5.30 a.m. or midnight.' On July 15 the Chiefs of Staff gave the Magnetron their blessing, but with a proviso, that its operational use depended on the Russians holding the line of the Volga. This was the needed boost: Dee and Lovell were overjoyed.

By December 5, 35 Squadron had taken delivery of six sets and 7 Squadron had nine by December 21. By mid-January, another three sets had been delivered to each squadron. Only 25 of the first 42 sorties were successful;[7] imperfections in the polar diagram were the chief cause of failure, while inexperience both on the ground and in the air were contributory factors. Despite this on February 9 Command announced: 'The problem of accurate navigation under almost any weather conditions is solved by H2S when operated by a trained navigator.'[8] Twenty towns and five different groups of islands had been pinpointed and coastlines stood out clearly: the rivers Rhine and Elbe had been iden-

6. *Naxos*, German radar equipment, was fitted to the U-boat snorkels and warned them of the approach of planes carrying ASV. The German nightfighters also used it with marked success to 'home' on to bombers operating H2S but it did take time.

7. This figure includes seven early returns not due to H2S, and one aircraft missing.

8. ORS, February 9, 1943.

tified, Hamburg docks, the Zuider Zee and the lakes near Lyons too.

Priority was given to improving serviceability, and once this was achieved, there was some time to consider the quality of the picture. Gaps in the PPI display were an inconvenience but, from the general navigational point of view, the results were satisfactory. Inside the larger towns it was a different story; 'clutter'[9] made it impossible to identify the aiming point. Another problem needing urgent attention was that the picture became a complete blur when the aircraft banked or took evasive action. It was hoped to overcome clutter by using the 3cm band instead of the 10 cm,[10] and to secure the picture in spite of aircraft manoeuvres by fitting a roll stabilizer.[11] In the meantime an improved aerial and mounting were fitted (Mk IIA), which filled in the gaps in the PPI and work was put in hand on a new type of scan-corrected indicator (Type 184) to improve the centre of the picture (Mk IIB).

About this time, in June 1943, the Americans, who less than a year before had condemned the device, came forward with a scheme to equip PFF with 3cm sets. The introduction of an American element was strongly opposed by Command, 8 Group and TRE because they realized it might disrupt the close co-operation between the Boffins and the squadrons. The Americans had to be content with making 3cm ASVs and designing their own H2S, which they called H2X.

Bennett knew that Harris was on the point of opening the Battle of Berlin. It was over the Big City that Pathfinders found clutter such a problem and if the previous raids on Berlin were any criterion, most of the attacks would be made over 10/10ths cloud, so no visual identification of the aiming point would be possible. For these attacks skymarkers would be used and this meant that success of the attacks would depend entirely on H2S Blind Marker crews. Bennett, Lovell and S/Ldr D. Saward[12] planned to equip six Lancasters with 3cm 'lash-ups'.[13] These sets, made at TRE, were ready by the time official permission was obtained. Lancasters JB352, JB355 and JB356 were delivered on November 13, the other three on the 17th. Harris opened his campaign on November 18. But for the foresight of Bennett, Lovell and Saward, the Battle of Berlin would have made a stark comparison with the Battle of Essen in pre-PFF days.

Bennett tried to keep H2S exclusively for Pathfinders but had wisely

---

9. Too many corner reflectors resulted in no recognizable shape, this was called 'clutter'.

10. The shorter the wavelength in the horizontal plane the better the definition.

11. A gyro.

12. RDF Liaison officer at Bomber Command, author of *The Bomber's Eye*.

13. Equipment fitted into an aircraft not designed to take it. In many cases it had to be tied (lashed) in position, as there was no other means of fixing it, and no time to carry out a modification.

been overruled. His argument, that H2S needed highly skilled navigators to get the best out of the equipment, was undoubtedly true but no fair-minded person could claim all the capable navigators were in 8 Group. Again it was pointless marking a target if the Main Force never reached it or if it arrived too late to see the TIs. Although 150 sets had been lost before the Battle of Berlin began there were still some 330 front-line aircraft fitted with H2S when the battle opened and, by the end of the year, 90% of the Main Force had been equipped with it. PFF still got innovations and modifications first.

H2S was blamed for the inconclusive result of the Battle of Berlin and TRE came to its defence by criticizing both Harris and Bennett. They claimed Bennett was not using Mk III to the best advantage[14] and that the AOC-in-C was a great antagonist of TRE. They further claimed that it had been developed for blind bombing and that Harris refused to employ it in this fashion. Their conclusions were sent to Air Ministry (March 1944) and then the fur began to fly. Harris resented criticism and when it was made by people who did not know all the facts he did not pull his punches.[15] He called the Boffins 'a bunch of pimply prima donnas, struggling to get into the limelight', and told Air Ministry to tell them to 'mind their own bloody business'. TRE was not amused – no one had made any friends.

By May 1944, the improvements were coming into service, although very slowly. The Type 184 indicators (Mk IIB and Mk IIIB) had been fitted to 300 sets and the roll-stabilizer conversion, begun in March, was progressing satisfactorily, the modifications being carried out by Bomber Command. Fitting another variant, a barrel-type scanner (Mk IIC), was not started until 1945 and many aircraft were still unmodified at the end of the war.

Meanwhile, at Malvern, experiments with a 6-foot scanner, nicknamed *Whirligig,* were being tried and Dr S. Devons was working on the latest version, coded *Lion-Tamer,* in the K-band (1¼ cm). At successive meetings priorities were changed and no one at TRE knew what Command really wanted. The truth was that Command didn't know either. Another proposal to combine all that was good in H2S (proved operationally) into one set received little support; even Bennett was against the idea unless it included *Whirligig.* The pervading apathy was not confined to the Services. The progress of the armies made everyone think victory was just around the corner and manufacturers were chary of tooling-up for an order which would undoubtedly be cancelled if hostilities ceased. In fact

---

14. Bennett was using Mk IIs and IIIs indiscriminately for blind marking and using the same colour markers for both. Mk III was not reserved for experienced crews.

15. Harris was right. The Main Force were not competent enough to use H2S without PFF markers, viz Operation *Hackle*.

Mk IIIF *(Whirligig)*, Mk IV and M VI *(Lion-Tamer)* were never used on operations although work was continued against the possibility that they might be used in the Far East. The need did not arise because the atom bomb brought hostilities to an early end.

Because H2S was used by PFF primarily as an aid to marking, and TRE's insistence that it should be developed for blind bombing, it is necessary to stress that it was an excellent aid to navigation and a great deal of time and trouble was expended on this side in the early stages. As has been stated earlier, the Boffins worked closely with Bomber Command and were always ready and willing to make modifications. Lovell and Dee were no exceptions and their liaison work with F/Lt E.J. Dickie, a tour-expired navigator, was a credit to all concerned.

Dickie pointed out that navigators plotted on a chart with True North at the top; it was therefore common sense to project the PPI picture with

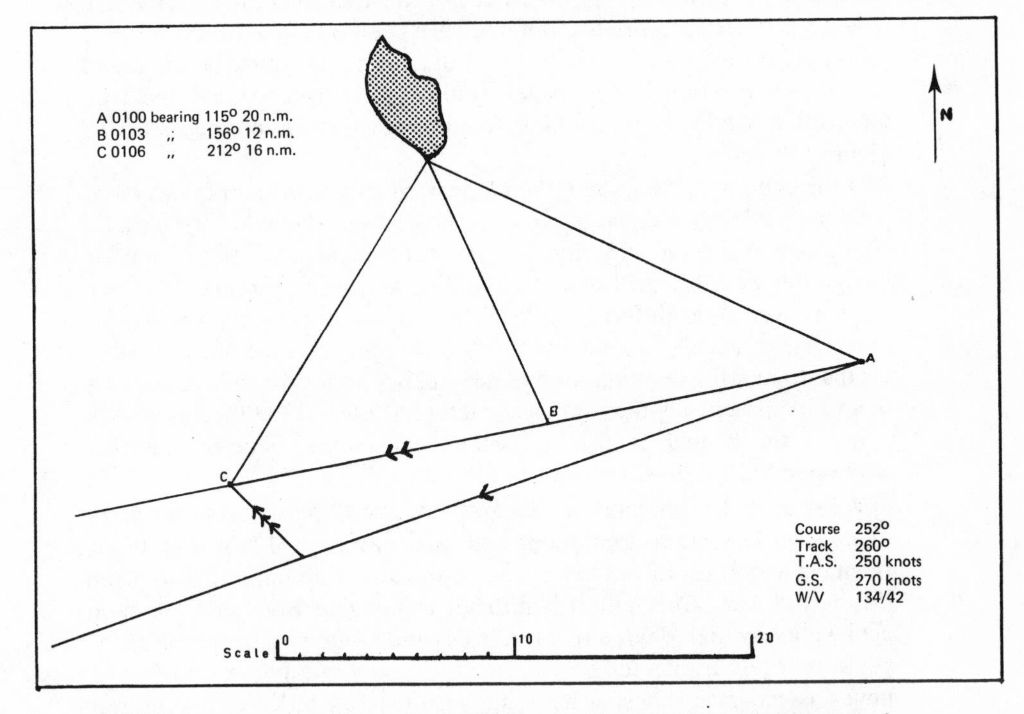

Fig 8 describes the method of obtaining a wind from an unknown position. This was one of the standard methods used in conjunction with H2S. In this instance the distance from the object could be measured on the P.P.I. so a track, ground speed and wind velocity could be calculated. Had the position been known a fix could have been obtained. Then it was not essential to know the distance. Three bearings similar to the example above are taken, and by transferring bearing A and bearing B along an assumed track the point where they cross bearing C is the aircraft's position. The lines rarely crossed precisely a small triangle (cocked hat) was usually formed and the fix was assumed to be at the centre of the triangle. Accepting *Oboe* precision, navigators were able to obtain a fix from Mosquito land markers.

True North at the top; displacing the natural image the aircraft's heading (true course). This was achieved by connecting the picture to the DR compass, the aircraft's heading being indicated by projecting a radial line on to the tube.

A perspex screen was fitted on the front of the PPI with parallel pairs of lines at equal intervals. The centre pair had two arrows on them, the navigator's symbol for track. Four pairs of lines, two on each side of the track lines, were inscribed at angles of 10° and 20°: these were known as drift lines. By reading the number of degrees between the track lines and the radial line (true course) the navigator had a constant check on drift.

By rotating the perspex screen until the track line passed over an echo on the PPI, its bearing could be read opposite the azimuth marker at the bottom of the tube and its distance calculated from the centre of the tube (i.e. the centre of the aircraft). If two or more bearings were taken of the same echo, the track and groundspeed of the aircraft could be obtained. The aircraft's true course was obtained in a similar manner to the bearing on the echo – track line along course radial line; true course bearing read at azimuth position. With track, ground speed, true course and true airspeed, a wind velocity could be found (Fig 8). It was not necessary to identify the echo.

If the echo were identified, then a bearing and distance measurement gave the navigator a fix, and, provided he had maintained an air plot, he could obtain a wind velocity. So the three main uses of the set for navigation were for drift and wind finding and fixing position.

There were four different scales (100, 50, 30 and 10-mile radius) for the navigator to choose from, but the 30-mile range was the one invariably used until nearing the target, when he switched to the 10-mile scale. This scale gave practically the same-size picture as the 1/250,000 continental maps or the ¼-inch British equivalent, and so the shape on the map corresponded to the shape on the tube. [16]

Webster and Frankland in *The Strategic Air Offensive Against Germany* say: 'Despite its limitations and disadvantages, H2S was certainly the most widely useful aid to navigation and bomb-aiming ever produced during the war.' Certainly it is difficult to imagine Bomber Command achieving any high degree of success beyond *Oboe* range without H2S; yet the quotation gives too rosy a picture. Blind bomb-aiming on H2S was never as accurate as visual bombing with the Mk XIV bombsight, nor could it compare with blind bombing using *Oboe*. As an expedient, for instance in conditions of 10/10ths cloud, it was invaluable – PFF usually

16. The different methods of releasing bombs using H2S are dealt with in the section on the Mk XIV bombsight (page 243) because an understanding of the bombsight and its computer are necessary.

carried *Wanganui* flares for such emergencies – but the Main Force crews bombed on H2S only as a last resort.

H2S did have advantages over Gee and *Oboe*, yet its limitations and disadvantages were also very real and cannot be set aside. The chief limitation was clutter. TRE's protestations apart, the picture on the H2S screen, even on the 3cm sets, was never free from clutter nor easy to interpret. Only on rare occasions was it possible to pick out the aiming point on the PPI, so blind bombing on H2S was only as good as the navigator's pinpoint and target wind.

H2S needed highly skilled operators to get the best out of the equipment. It was an exercise in recognizing shapes, and the old-type observer, who had been trained to map-read rather than to excel at DR proved more able to interpret what he saw on the screen. This led to the practice of using two navigators, one to plot the information and navigate, the other to operate the set and drop the bombs. Even the specialists needed particular features to be certain of a pinpoint. Most navigators would accept a Gee fix without question whereas they only trusted H2S when it was confirmed. So H2S excelled when everything was going right and when Met winds were correct, but it was viewed with scepticism at other times.

On the other hand H2S did enable Bomber Command to operate over the Reich in periods of no moon and in conditions of 10/10ths cloud, and also the attacks could be pressed home even if the weather was not as forecast. It meant that the German people were not able to sleep peacefully, wherever they were, and whatever the weather conditions over the Reich: respite came only when the weather at bases made it too hazardous to get the Main Force down.

Appendix III The Mk XIV Bombsight

The Mk XIV bombsight was an integral part of Bomber Command's increasing potential, in particular when the demand was for more accurate bombing on smaller targets in 1944. Its predecessor, the CSBS (Course-setting Bombsight) was designed for daylight bombing and required a straight and level run to the target with little or no evasive action for small errors in the air meant large errors on the ground. Apart from PFF and a few special squadrons it was the standard bombsight in Bomber Command until the summer of 1943 when it was gradually superseded by the Mk XIV or T-1, the American version. The need was for a sight which would indicate the point on the ground where the bombs would fall if released at that moment, irrespective of the manoeuvres the aircraft might be carrying out.

The Mk XIV was a stabilized vector sight and worked on the same principle as the CSBS but was more automatic, which made it easier to operate. As it was designed during the war it had a more realistic approach to the requirements of war conditions. It was fitted with a gyro which could cope with a 60° bank and a 40° dive without spinning. Evasive action on the run-up to the target did not affect its accuracy provided the last 8-10 seconds were steady flight (not necessarily level or straight) and, provided it was correctly banked[1] – preferably in not more than a rate-one turn – the aircraft could be banking at the moment of bomb release without affecting the accuracy. Yet it was a precision instrument only within its own type. It was called the Area Sight and had an acceptable aiming error of 150 yards. It was considered too inaccurate for 617 Squadron dropping Tallboys and Grand Slams.

The bombsight consisted of two major units, the sighting head and the computer. The sighting head was in fact the actual bombsight. It had four main components: the collimater, the reflector, the drift scale and the gyro. The collimator was a tube which projected a graticule (Fig. 9) on to the reflector. When the bomb-aimer looked through the reflector he got

1. Without sideslip.

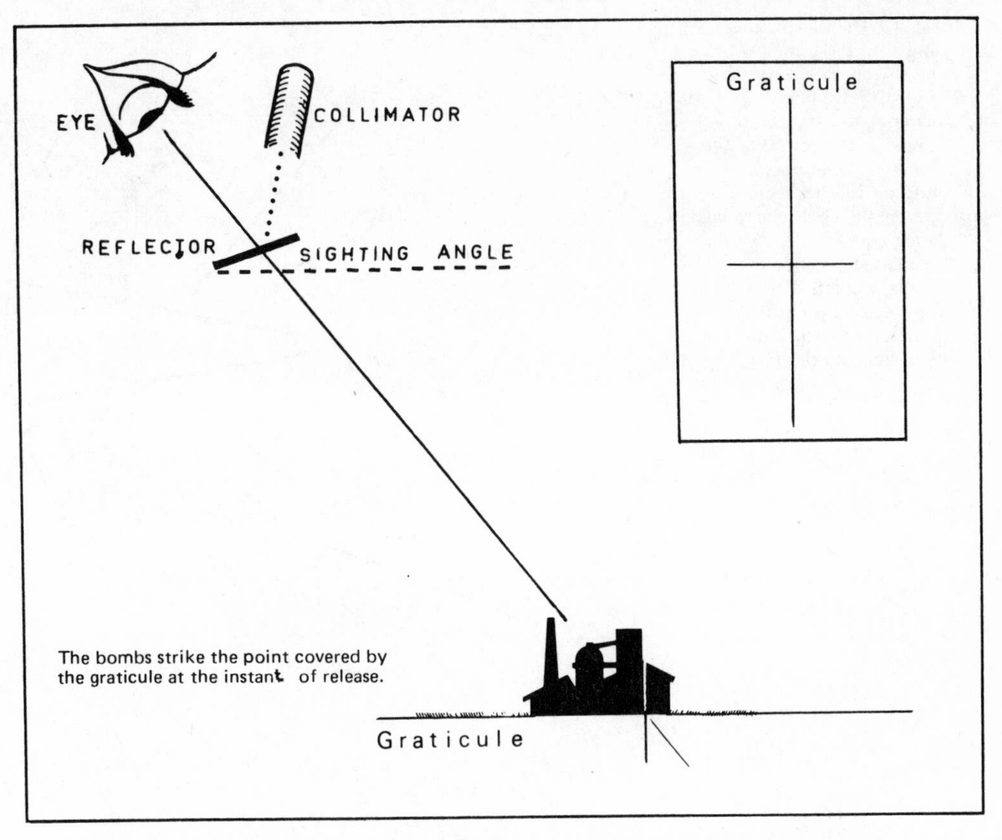

Fig. 9 The graticule, projected onto the reflector from the collimator, appeared to be on the ground and the target, if the course was correct, came frustratingly slowly down the longer axis. The bomb-aimer, fighting all his instincts of self preservation, waited until the shorter axis bisected the target before releasing the bombs.

the impression the graticule was on the ground. Provided the bomb-aimer had the correct wind velocity, objects on the ground appeared to travel parallel to the longer line and the bombs were released when the target reached the shorter line. The reflector was connected to the gyro and was geared 2:1, so if the aircraft banked 40° the reflector moved through 20°. The collimator moved with the aircraft and consequently the sighting plane remained vertical through the bank. The reflector was adjustable through the fore and aft plane (the sighting angle) to allow for the terminal velocity (TV) of the bombs and the different attitude of the plane according to the all-up weight. It was usually preset but could be altered in flight if necessary – for example, change of bombing height or where the load was not dropped in one salvo – and cards were attached to the computer showing corrections for different permutations. The sight-

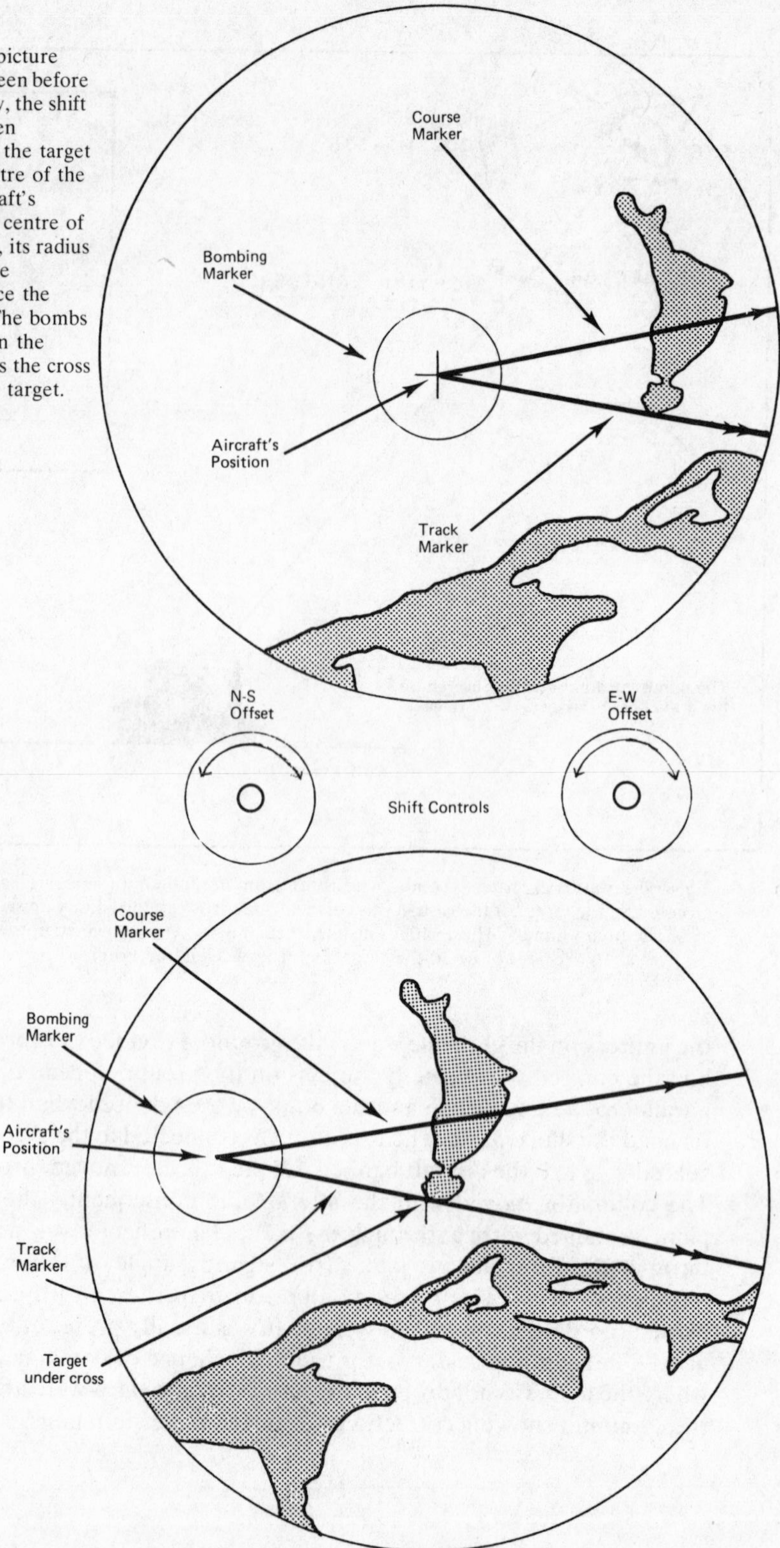

Fig. 10 The top picture shows the PPI screen before it is frozen. Below, the shift controls have been manipulated and the target is now in the centre of the screen. The aircraft's position is at the centre of the smaller circle, its radius being equal to the calculated distance the bombs will fall. The bombs are released when the perimeter touches the cross lines beneath the target.

ing angle adjusted automatically for up to 5° climb and 20° glide. Even without the computer, it was a far superior weapon to the CSBS.

The computer put it in a class apart.[2] Aircrew were amateurs doing a highly skilled job under very exacting conditions, and anything automatic was welcomed.[3] Six manual settings had to be made to get the sighting and drift angles. Four of these, sea-level pressure at target, target height above sea level, the terminal velocity of the bombs and the setting of the all-up weight, could be made before take-off. The wind speed and direction were fed into the computer just before the run-up to the target. The computer measured the airspeed and height automatically and calculated the indicated airspeed (IAS). The height combined with the present sea-level pressure and target height, gave the desired height above the target. The course was fed in by the DR compass. Changes in speed or direction altered the drift angles and these adjustments were automatically conveyed to the bombsight. Provided the navigator's wind was a good one the target came slowly and inexorably down the long graticule.

The computer was also designed to work with H2S for blind bombing runs. The same information was fed into the computer as for a bombsight attack, but instead the computations were relayed to the PPI (Fig. 10). During this operation the picture, instead of moving normally across the screen, was frozen and the aircraft's movement recorded. The target was brought under two cross-lines at the centre of the tube by juggling two shift control knobs, one giving a north-south movement, the other an east-west. In addition the PPI was provided with a bombing marker and this projected on to the screen as a circle with radius equal to the forward throw of the bombs calculated by the computer from the TV of the bombs.[4] A track marker was also projected on to the screen as a radial line, duly calculated by the computer from the wind velocity, airspeed and course. The bomb-aimer then gave instructions to the pilot as on a normal bombing run, and released the bombs when the bombing marker and track marker intersected the target under the cross-lines.

A second method was used when the aiming point was not easily identifiable. Some salient point not more than 10 miles from the target was pre-selected and its bearing and distance logged. The aircraft was flown over the salient point when its echo would be in the centre of the tube. The set was then switched to the static state and the point moved by the shift controls to its true relative position in relation to the target; this automatically brought the target to the centre of the tube under the

---

2. See plate No 27.

3. In the strict sense of the word the sight was not automatic because some information had to be fed into it manually.

4. The aircraft's position on the screen was, of course, at the centre of the bombing marker circle.

cross-lines. The run and bomb release then followed the same pattern as in the first instance.

The Mk XIV sight had a height limit of 20,000 feet so, when the Lancaster IIIs, Halifax IIIs and, of course the Mosquitoes were regularly bombing above this height a modified sight was fitted, the Mk XIVA, or the American version, the T-1A. As Saundby[5] put it, 'This type of bomb-sight could never be as accurate, under ideal conditions, as a tachomatic sight . . . But, owing to the tactical freedom allowed to the aircraft during the approach, it proved in practice to be the most accurate sight under operational conditions.'

5. Sir Robert Saunby in *Air Bombardment*.

Appendix IV
API and GPI

The API (Air Position Indicator) gave the exact position of the aircraft in conditions of no wind. It was connected by a multiplicity of pipes and wires to the ASI (Airspeed Indicator), the altimeter and the DR compass. This meant that evasive action, variations in airspeed when climbing and also any accidental errors in speed, height or direction were all accounted for.

The original sets displayed four windows marked north, south, east and west, and the figures in the windows changed as the aircraft progressed along its course. The navigator read the recorded latitude and longitude when he took a fix. Later a modified set was introduced, which was sighted over the navigator's table, so that when he aligned his plotting chart correctly a pinpoint of light indicated the air position. At the moment of taking a fix the navigator marked this spot on his chart; then, by connecting this position with the fix, an average wind from the moment of take-off was obtained. It was possible to reset the API in the air by using the last fix as the new starting point, but this was seldom done in practice.

The GPI (Group Position Indicator) was an attachement to the API: It was used for making DR runs to the aiming point from a known position. The navigator fed his latest wind into the GPI and aligned the pinpoint of light on to the known position on the map. The light, being controlled in precisely the same way as the API, behaved in a similar manner but, because it had additional information, a wind velocity, it traced the track of the aircraft. This obviated errors on the DR run to the target caused by pilots having to take evasive action, and they could be redirected on to the aiming point if a change of course was necessary. The bomb-aimer dropped his bombs when the light was over the A/P. Patently, the aircraft's actual track would be wrong if the applied wind was inaccurate so a good fix and an accurate target wind were essential to its success. Towards the end of the war Pathfinders used this method for blind bombing and marking with good results, particularly over well defended targets. It proved more accurate and easier to operate than a corresponding run directed from the H2S screen. The highly concentrated *Wanganui* attacks in the final phase were almost entirely due to the fact that Pathfinder Lancasters were able to supplement *Oboe* skymarkers using GPI and, equally important, lay down an accurate and concentrated group for targets beyond *Oboe* range.

Appendix V
Target Indicators

Target indicators were just as essential to the effectiveness of a Pathfinder Force as were accurate navigational aids and an efficient bombsight. PFF was required to locate the target and then to indicate the aiming point. To make the most of *Oboe* and H2S as target-finders, the aiming point had to be marked in some definite continuous manner.

Employing a TI is analogous to aiming a rifle bullet as opposed to using grapeshot: with the latter the chances of hitting the target are enhanced, but with the rifle bullet the probability of killing or seriously injuring is much higher. If bomb-aimers dropped their load in the centre of a group of TIs then the attack would be concentrated.

During the German blitz on England, it was discovered that incendiary fires were easy to imitate so decoy fires were lit outside the area and they attracted the bulk of the bombs if the original fires could be put out quickly. It was obvious the Germans would employ similar tactics and there was no reason to suppose that Bomber Command crews would be more discerning than the enemy's had been. They weren't. Fires had a magnetic attraction for bomber crews, whether British or German. Air Marshal Sir Robert Saundby says: 'It is unbelievable the amount of attention they (decoy fires) received.'[1] The Chiefs of Staff had realized this and progress had been made with rudimentary target markers, Red Blob Fires and Pink Pansies. Red Blob Fires were 250-pound incendiaries filled with a mixture of benzol, rubber and phosphorus which burnt with a red glow. Pink Pansies were 4,000-pound bomb casings filled with the same ingredients and coloured so that the initial flash was of a distinctively brilliant pink.

From August to December 1942, PFF had to use these makeshift markers while specially designed TIs were being developed and put into production. The only other available pyrotechnics were reconnaissance flares and their usefulness was very limited as the Raid Leaders had discovered in early 1942. Although under ideal conditions they helped

1. *Air Bombardment.*

crews to identify the target visually and were used to indicate the boundaries of the target area they were of no use for marking the aiming point. To get concentration in the right place and to nullify the effects of decoy fires, a target indicator had to have:

(i) Good ballistic properties, to ensure accuracy.
(ii) A clear pyrotechnic display, unlike any bombing phenomena yet easy to recognize and difficult to imitate.
(iii) Colours which caught the eye; the Main Force did not want to hang around, particularly in heavily defended areas.

Bennett was given special permission to discuss his ideas with the Ministry of Aircraft Production directly and a liaison officer was installed permanently at MAP to assist in the decision and development, and to co-ordinate PFF requirements. This was a necessary step as TIs were of the highest priority and normal channels were slow and cumbersome. Working very closely with Bennett, Dr W.F. Coxon was the brains behind the TI's development.

The first problem was to find a suitable groundmarker which could be carried by Mosquitoes as well as the heavies. In fact, 250-pound bomb cases were available in quantity and it was decided to fill them with 12-inch pyrotechnic candles; 60 candles fitted snugly into the case and a barometric fuse in the nose was used to eject them. The candles then ignited and cascaded to the ground where they burnt for 3 minutes (Fig. 11). Fused to function at 3,000 feet the TI made a ground pattern of

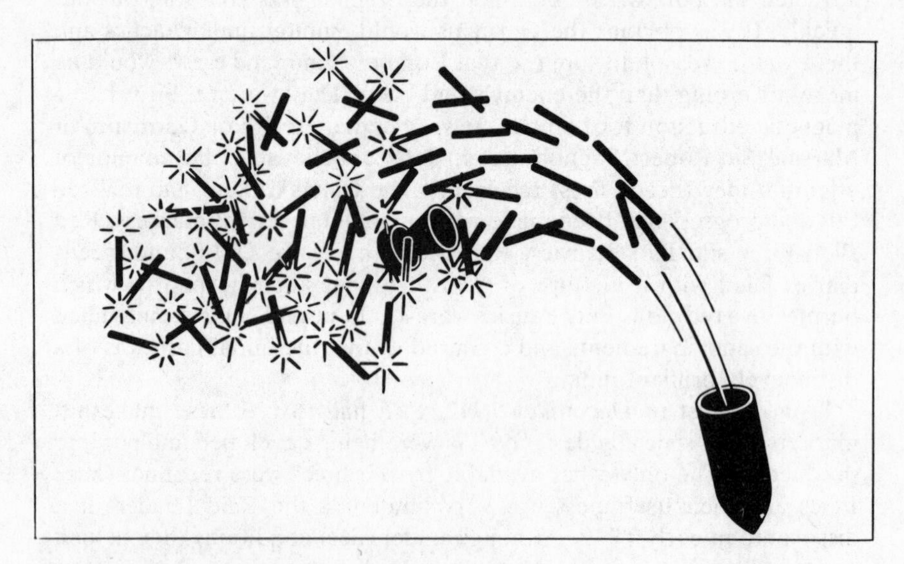

Fig. 11 For the first official TI, 60 candles, each with its own ignitor, were ejected from a 250-lb. casing; the bursting height being controlled by a barometric fuse.

approximately 100 yards in diameter, but fused for 1,500 feet it was reduced to 60 yards in diameter. The lower height was more accurate because the parent case was more stable ballistically than the 'children' – the candles. Red, green and yellow candles were used and the gross weight of the bomb was 220 pounds. These were first used on Berlin on January 16-17, 1943.

Because, in the early days of *Oboe*, the shortest interval between Mosquito attacks was 5 minutes, it was necessary to develop a long burning TI (LBTI) to avoid gaps in the marking. This was achieved by igniting 20 of the candles at the initial burst, 20 after a 2½ minute delay and the remaining 20 after a 5 minute delay. In this way, the overall burning time was extended to approximately 7 minutes but, because fewer candles were burning, the display was smaller and less intense. By varying the delay times and the number of candles burning at one time the life of the TI could be extended to 12 minutes – a very long burning TI (VLBTI). From time to time a number of explosive candles was included in the TI to discourage the enemy from dousing them, or at least make the job more precarious. As many as 30 explosive candles were used, some of them armed with delay fuses.

Groundmarkers were usually dropped in salvoes and this increased the marked area threefold. A salvo invariably included one or more Long Burning TI. Bomb-aimers were briefed to bomb the centre of the salvo and not single TIs which would probably be decoys or strays. For greater accuracy on small targets two types[2] of TI were made with no cascade. One, the candle type, used an impact fuse with a 2½ or 5-minute delay to ignite the candles. The second type contained 56 incendiaries which burst on impact: they burnt with a bright white light for 4 minutes and subsequently for 10 minutes with a yellow light from the molten slag.

As early as April 1943 it was thought that the Germans had developed a decoy TI, but the first positive evidence came on the Bochum raid of May 13-14. The enemy fired the TIs from the ground and although they burst and cascaded at a lower height the simulation was quite good. Burning time on the ground varied from 30 seconds to 2½ minutes. The enemy cunningly varied his method of employing decoys: on occasions he used them on their own, and sometimes in conjunction with decoy fires or smoke screens.

To prevent crews bombing decoys a Red Spot Fire TI was developed and it was first used on the Peenemunde raid of August 17-18. The 250-pound casing was filled with cotton wool soaked in a solution of metallic perchlorate dissolved in alcohol. It burnt on the ground as a single spot of deep red for 15 to 20 minutes. A Green Spot Fire was introduced later. Spot Fire TIs, because of the small diameter of fire, were

2. Later a third, the Red Spot Fire, was added.

soon obliterated by fire and smoke and so were used mainly on small precision targets or as route-markers.

Bombing decoy TIs was a very real problem and, although in theory it could never happen if briefing instructions were adhered to, the fact remains that on five occasions between May and October 1943 more than 25% of the force reported having had red TIs in their bombsights when none were burning. At Kassel on October 22-23, the figure was as high as 33%. Even worse, taking October 1943 as an example, on four occasions crews reported bombing red TIs when none were dropped: this ranged from 12% on Stuttgart on October 7-8 to 26% on Kassel on October 3-4.

With the aim of reducing these figures, three types of TIs were introduced: candles which emitted two Morse letters successively for a period of 22 minutes, another had candles strapped in bundles of three which burnt with clearly defined pinpoints of light, and a third which changed colour every 15 seconds, but they did not provide the answer.

In April 1944, a further effort was made to overcome the problem. A 1,000-pound casing was filled with 200 candles: this marker gave a much larger area of colour and the intensity was maintained throughout the burning time. Four burning times were available: 3, 7, 12 and 20 minutes, the duration being controlled by delaying the ignition of some of the candles. Because of the intensity of the enemy was never able to match the colour precisely. In PFF the 1,000-pound TIs were carried only by the heavies.[3] Unfortunately, they were ballistically unstable when dropped from a height and accounted for many of the stray TIs which the Main Force enjoyed reporting.

In the second half of 1944 when Bomber Command started attacking in daylight it was found that smoke and dust soon obscured the TIs and that in any case the colours did not stand out clearly, so the 250-pound casings were filled with candles which emitted coloured smoke. Smoke Puffs were made in red, blue, green and yellow and they burnt for 8 minutes, but the smoke actually hung around until dispersed by the wind.

Radar navigational and bombing aids did not depend on seeing the ground so Pathfinders could mark the target area irrespective of weather conditions. When the target was 10/10ths cloud-covered, skymarkers were used which burst at a predetermined height and the Main Force, flying on a heading (course) given to them at briefing, dropped their bombs when they had a skymarker in their bombsights using a zero wind.

Skymarkers were usually flares although candle TIs fitted with parachutes were developed. Flares could be dropped either singly or in clusters and in both instances an air-burst fuse was used to draw the pyrotechnic from the container. With the exception of the White Drip,

---

3. Mosquitoes of 627 Squadron when they joined 5 Group were modified to carry the 1,000-pound TI.

employed mainly by the LNSF the 4.5-inch flare was the standard type used. When the flare was free from the container the parachute opened and the flare burnt for 3 minutes, the rate of fall being between 500 and 700 feet per minute. Originally the flares were either red or green but a variant of this type, which ejected seven stars of contrasting colour at intervals of 20 seconds with each star burning for 8 seconds,[4] was soon brought into use. The effect was similar to a roman candle used on Guy Fawkes night – indeed the firework manufacturers were involved in the production of all RAF pyrotechnics.

The 30-pound White Drip skymarker was in the same category but behaved differently. The composition was solid magnesium with a thermite core, and the white molten magnesium dripped from the core producing a 'tail' of up to 1,000 feet in length. It was used chiefly by the LNSF because of its short life, the Mk I and Mk II lasting only 100 seconds and the Mk III only a little over 2 minutes.

In January 1944, cluster flares came into operational use. A suitable parent for stowing the flares was essential and seven 4.5-inch target flares were packed into a 1,000-pound case or four 4.5-inch flares into a 500-pound case. By fitting delay capsules it was possible to obtain a vertical chain with a maximum of 600 feet between each flare.

There were two types of TI skymarkers used by PFF, the TI Floater and the Smoke Puff. For the former 25 non-delay candles, each attached to a separate 3-inch parachute, were ejected from a parent and floated in a bunch giving a candelabra effect, the burning time being 3 minutes. This was the first used over Berlin on January 20-21, 1944 and again on the Nuremberg raid on March 30-31, 1944. When Bomber Command began large-scale daylight attacks in the autumn of 1944, the difficulty of seeing the various types of skymarkers led to the development of a sky Smoke Puff. A 250-pound case was filled with coloured pigment which when ejected, burned as a large ball of colour suspended in the air. The smoke was the same colour as the ball of fire with the same colour range as the ground Smoke Puffs. It was also packed into a 1,000-pound casing but although this gave a larger ball of colour the burning time was the same as that of its smaller brother, 3 minutes. As with the ground Smoke Puff, the smoke remained visible until dispersed by the wind.

As the LNSF grew in strength selected crews of 139 Squadron dropped markers for them. The Germans had so much respect for this force that they used both decoy TIs and decoy fires to try to lead them astray. To help the non-markers distinguish the true from the false, marker crews, at the same time as they dropped their TIs, fired a TI cartridge from a Very pistol and this burnt for 25 seconds in bright red, green or yellow. They

---

4. The colours were red/green stars, red/orange stars, green/red stars and green/orange stars.

were also fired by the marker aircraft at turning points. The Very pistol TI was a very useful addition to PFF pyrotechnics because it saved a station on the bomb rack: it was an important factor as there were only four stations on the Mosquito.

Another TI which also saved a station was the Photoflash TI. This incorporated a 4.5-inch photoflash with 40 TI candles in a 250-pound bomb case. It enabled crews to photograph the ground detail as their TIs burst. The highest night photograph of the war was taken by F/Lt J.W. Jordan of 105 Squadron from 36,000 feet using the TI photoflash on April 18-19, 1944, over Osnabruck. (see plate 29).

For some time before PFF was formed reconnaissance flares had been used by bomber crews to help them identify the target. It was a cordite bomb which ignited when drawn from a canister by a parachute. The glare from the flares tended to blind the bomb-aimers and so early in 1943 development began on a hooded flare. The experiment included altering the size and shape of the parachute and giving the material maximum opacity, but the project met with all kinds of problems and it was not until January 1944 that they were solved and the flares came into regular operational use.

Flares were originally dropped through a flare chute by hand and they could only be dropped singly and at a rate which depended on the ability of the operator. *Window* was also dropped through the flare chute until the spring of 1944 when the long-awaited dispenser became operational, so meanwhile life was getting hectic in this part of the aircraft. By packing the flares into suitable parents, 500-pound, or 1,000-pound casings, they could be dropped from the bomb-bay in clusters, which disintegrated by the action of a fuse set at a predetermined height, each flare normally having a 2-second delay igniter. By employing flares with delay candles and appropriate delay igniters, continuity of burning could be achieved.

Fuses were an integral part of TI accuracy and of the correct functioning of flares. Practically all PFF pyrotechnics were armed with air-burst fuses. Three types were used, Barometric, combustion and clockwork. Barometric fuses functioned at a predetermined height above the ground independent of the height of release. Delays could be incorporated to retard ignition. They were also used if the aircraft should be below the bursting height when the TI was released to ensure the safety of the aircraft.

Initially TIs were fitted with nose fuses, (860 and 869 delay) but they were liable to be activated as the bombs approached their terminal velocity and so they burst higher than intended causing the worst type of fault, an undershoot. Tail fuses (867 and 885) were developed to overcome the problem but, although solving the one they introduced another: when the bombs jostled one another as they fell from the bomb-bay the oscillations caused the fuses to operate unpredictably as to height. As

1,000-pound TI'S were more ballistically unstable than 250-pounders, they were usually nose-fused. With the 250-pound TI the advantages of the lower bursting height (terminal velocity had no effect on the tail fuse) more than outweighed the disadvantages of the occasional stray.

Combustion fuses (848 and 949) were delay fuses which functioned at a pre-determined time after release; their bursting height therefore depended on the height of the aircraft. These were used in flares, and the delay capsules associated with this type of fuse were also combustion fuses.

Clockwise fuses were American and sometimes used by PFF: they provided a pre-set variable delay from 5-92 seconds. As with combustion fuses, the functioning height depended on the height of the aircraft.

On rare occasions, for pinpoint marking on special tarkets, the airburst fuse was considered too inaccurate, then PFF used a Bomb 874 fuse, a sensitive piece of equipment which functioned on impact.

Appendix VI Pathfinder Marking Techniques

Although basically there were only two methods of marking a target – groundmarking and skymarking – marking was technically divided into three main categories: blind groundmarking (*Parramatta*) visual groundmarking (*Newhaven*) and skymarking (*Wanganui*). The explanation of the strange code names is simple: Parramatta was Bennett's home town; Corporal Ralph, Bennett's personal WAAF, came from Newhaven; and S/Ldr Ashworth was a New Zealander from Wanganui.

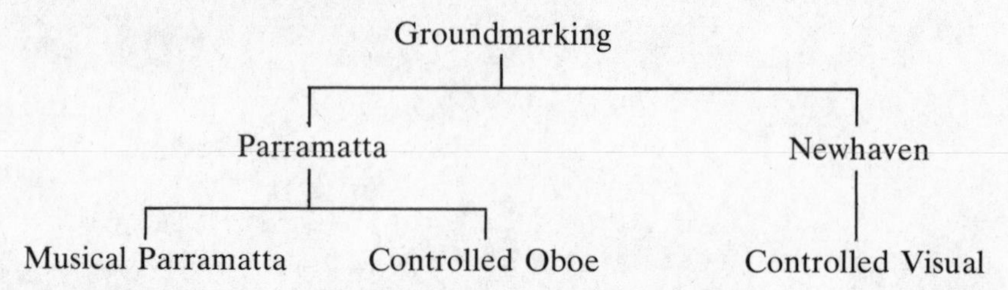

PARRAMATTA (Fig.12) 'Y' aircraft, provided their H2S equipment was working satisfactorily, dropped their TIs blindly on the target, usually before zero hour. Backers-up followed closely behind the Blind Marker aircraft and dropped TIs of a contrasting colour on the MPI of all the original markers.[1] The Main Force was briefed to bomb the MPI of the secondary markers and to bomb the primaries only when no secondary markers were burning.

MUSICAL PARRAMATTA When *Oboe* Mosquitoes dropped the primaries the marking followed a different pattern. Whereas all the 'Y' aircraft dropped their TIs at the beginning of the raid *Musical* markers were dropped at intervals throughout the attack. Bomber crews were briefed to give preference to the primaries. The duty of the Backers-up on this type of attack was to keep the target marked at all times. Unserviceability in the *Oboe* equipment could cause gaps in the marking with the result that the

1. As the colour patterns were changed from time to time for tactical as well as technical reasons the usual colour patterns have been omitted.

primaries would burn out. Backers-up were detailed to fill in the gaps.
CONTROLLED OBOE Although *Oboe* was a very accurate blind bombing device, technical and human errors often resulted in two groups of TIs being 500-800 yards apart. Such errors were relatively unimportant on towns but when extra precision was required for targets in France, and later when supporting Allied Ground Forces, these errors could have been disastrous.

For these targets a Master Bomber was sent to assess the *Oboe* TIs and, having selected the best placed ones. inform the Main Force of their position in relation to the A/P. The Master Bomber and his lieutenants carried TIs but they were dropped only on a direct order from the Master Bomber.
NEWHAVEN (Fig.13) In this type of attack markers were withheld unless the aiming point was positively identified visually. From time to time the aids to identification were changed as also was the colour scheme. The chief aid was blind illumination and hooded flares were specially designed for this purpose. 'Y' aircraft dropped flares at intervals across the target area and the Visual Markers, following closely behind, attempted to identify the A/P in the light of the flares. Originally the Illuminators were also Blind Markers and in addition to flares dropped TIs. Anything burning on the ground, even markers, made visual identification more difficult so when sufficient crews were available the role was divided and Blind Markers dropped TIs only if the Visual Markers were unable to mark the target.
CONTROLLED VISUAL or MUSICAL NEWHAVEN In April 1944 an offshoot of visual groundmarking was introduced. The need for precision marking on railway marshalling yards in France and Belgium necessitated modifications to the area techniques and Controlled Visuals were introduced. *Oboe* Mosquitoes dropped proximity markers and Illuminators dropped their flares around them. Primary Visual Markers following closely behind dropped their markers if they positively identified the aiming point. A Master Bomber and Deputy were in attendance and were part of the marking force. The Master Bomber selected the best placed TIs and then broadcast precise bombing instructions to the Main Force.
WANGANUI (Skymarking) (Fig. 14) When the target was obscured by cloud selected crews dropped marker flares and the Main Force, flying on a pre-determined heading with zero wind on their bombsights, released their cargoes when they had a flare in their bombsight. In the final phase Bomber Command carried out daylight *Wanganui* attacks but the flares proved difficult to see so coloured Smoke Puffs attached to parachutes were developed and, because they were readily identifiable above cloud, many devastating daylight raids were carried out. Originally *Musical Wanganui* was the only successful method but, after the development of GPI, the heavies were able to mark with an accuracy which rivalled even that of *Oboe*.

EMERGENCY WANGANUI was in essence the same as *Wanganui*. In the early stages of the war lack of precise information on weather conditions over the target resulted in many sorties being abortive because the town was cloud-covered. To obviate this, Pathfinder crews carried *Wanganui* flares which were dropped when the groundmarkers could not be seen. During the Battle of Berlin, when deep penetration was the order of the day, both ground and skymarkers were dropped irrespective of cloud conditions (Berlin Method) and Main Force crews were briefed to attack the groundmarkers and only bomb on the *Wanganui* flares as a last resort.

General remark

Almost all Pathfinder pyrotechnics were fitted with air-burst fuses. Only rarely were more than four TIs dropped in one salvo. It was, in fact, the Mosquito's maximum load.

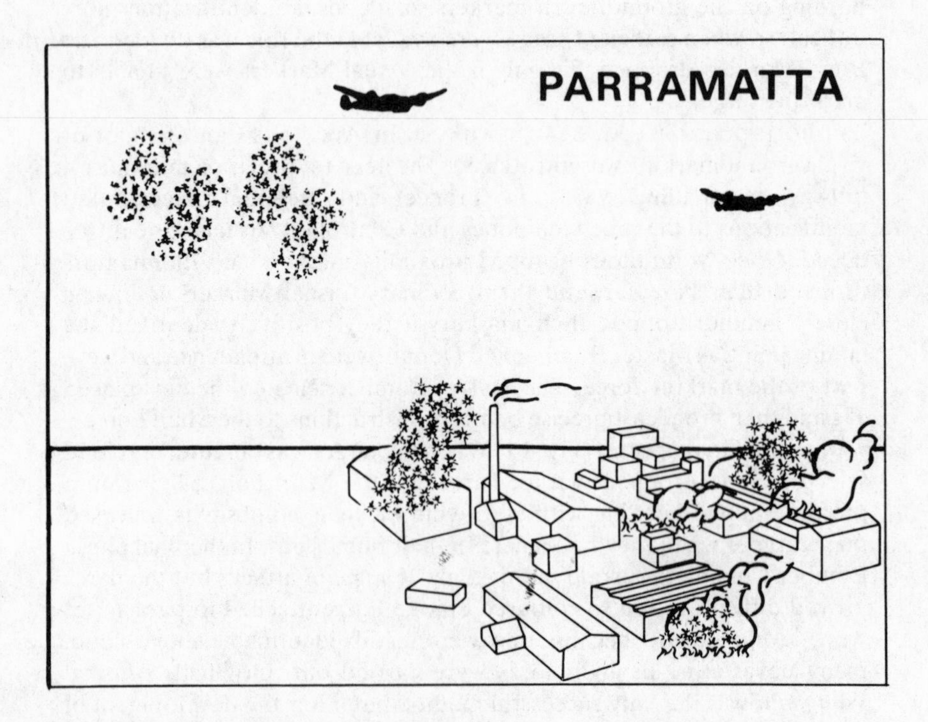

Fig. 12 Blind groundmarking by H2S or *Oboe* aircraft. The prefix *Musical* was added when *Oboe* aircraft were responsible for the marking.

Fig. 13 Visual marking using Mk. XIV bombsight, aided at night by a flare force (Illuminators). For *Parramatta* and *Newhaven*, to keep the target marked continuously, a secondary force, (Backers-up) dropped TIs of a contrasting colour.

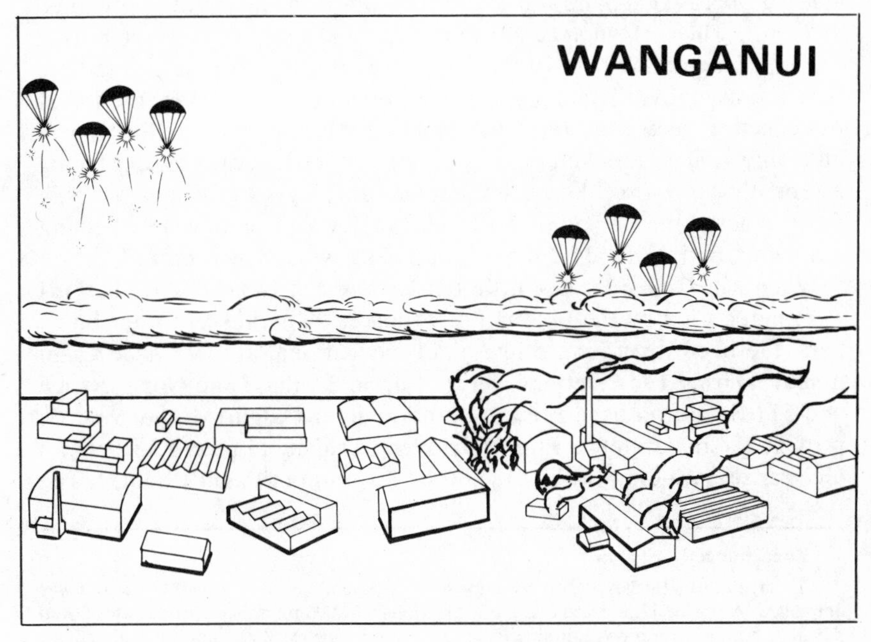

Fig. 14 Blind skymarking, using flares, TI Floater or, in daylight, Smoke Puffs, dropped by H2S or *Oboe* aircraft. Crews were brief to attack the flares on a given magnetic heading with zero wind on their bombsights.

Appendix VII
Loran

While Gee was being developed in this country, work on the Loran[1] system was proceeding independently in the United States. Gee was more advanced than Loran and the close co-operation between the teams enabled the Americans to benefit from British experience. Both systems used the same hyperbolic principle and were designed to be interchangeable in Allied aircraft. Loran was intended for use over the sea whereas Gee, and indeed all British navigational aids, were designed to operate chiefly over land. One of the main differences between the two was that Gee used three stations to obtain a simultaneous fix whereas Loran stations operated in pairs and so only one position line could be obtained at a time.[2] The performance of Loran over land was very poor but during the experimental work it was discovered that if an extremely long time base was used (over 1,000 miles) it was possible to synchronise the waves by reflecting them from the ionosphere. As this method could be operated only at night the Americans were not interested, the USAAF being essentially a day force. Some of the teams did play with the idea but only from an academic viewpoint. Sufficient work was done to warrant giving it a name, and they called it SS Loran (Sky-wave Synchronized).

When Mk II Gee proved little better than Mk I and H2S radiations were being used by the German nightfighters to home on to our bombers, the need for a long-range night navigational aid was once again urgent. During 1944 stations were set up in Scotland and North Africa and 571 Squadron used Loran operationally in August of that year. It provided a moderately accurate fix over Germany in places far beyond Gee range, including Berlin, one of the Mosquitoes' nightly haunts. The

1. Long-Range Navigation.

2. To save plotting a running fix a compromise, originally used in astro-navigation, was employed. A position line from one pair of stations was taken and the co-ordinates noted down. A minute later a position line from the second pair was taken and the time noted. Another minute later a further reading from the first pair was taken and the two readings averaged. This average was plotted with the line from the second pair, so obtaining a fix. The time of the fix was the time noted when taking the second pair.

Gee sets in all 8 Group Mosquitoes, and also in some of the heavy squadrons, were modified so that either system could be used. After some aerial improvements, the tests all being carried out by 571 Squadron, the accuracy was considered good enough to drop bombs blindly on the Big City.

Appendix VIII
Monica and Fishpond

MONICA was the name given to a warning device for the tail gunner. Radiated signals to the rear of the bomber were reflected back (echoes) when another aircraft was behind it. These echoes were translated into 'pips' and fed into the intercom – the nearer the aircraft the closer the pips. While keeping everyone on their toes, the main disadvantages were that it did not distinguish friend from foe, nor did it give any indication of the angle of approach of the other aircraft. When, for better protection against nightfighters and with the aim of saturating flak and searchlight defences, the Main Force began flying in streams, much of *Monica*'s value was lost because it was perpetually on the 'bleep'. SN2, the German version of our AI, used the radiations from *Monica* to home on to British bombers, and many crews considered it to be of more use to the enemy than themselves. *Monica* was first used operationally on June 16-17, 1943. A later version, the Mk IIIA, substituted a visual for the aural warning but, apart from providing relief from the incessant nerve-racking 'bleep', the disadvantages were the same as in the earlier versions.

FISHPOND When H2S came into more general use in Bomber Command *Fishpond* became an economical proposition and it gradually superseded *Monica*. Originally called *Mousetrap* the code name had to be changed because it was alread in use. *Fishpond* worked in a similar manner to *Monica*, but the echoes were received on a cathode-ray tube. The normal H2S tube displayed signals only at the aircraft's height (ground signals); for *Fishpond*, Lovell, whose brainchild it was, used that part of the time base not normally used, the radiations between the ground and the aircraft. Using the H2S scanner, echoes were projected on to a separate tube with the ground return at the outer edge looking like a halo, the centre dark as some unfathomable pool, the light round the edge giving it an eerie look. Anything between the ground and the level of the aircraft would be recorded on the tube in its relative position. The advantages were:

(i) The *Monica* bleep was replaced by a silent signal – a blip on the screen.
(ii) The bearing and distance of the approaching aircraft could be measured.
(iii) If several blips appeared on the screen and one was approaching much faster than the others it was odds on that a nightfighter was closing in.
(iv) The danger of collisions in the dark was lessened.
(v) If there were no blips then the indications were that the aircraft was not where it should be – in the bomber stream. The eerie dark of the tube had a sinister appositeness.

Its two disadvantages were:

(i) The signals were recieved only when the aircraft were below the bomber. This was not such a big disadvantage as it at first seems because the German nightfighters using *Schrage Musik* attacked from below the aircraft.
(ii) When the German nightfighters were fitted with *Naxos* they used H2S and *Fishpond* signals to home on to the bombers.

Appendix IX
Aircraft

When the five original squadrons came to PFF, they were equipped with different types of aircraft; 156 Squadron with Wellingtons; 7 Squadron Stirlings; 35 Squadron Halifaxes; 83 Squadron Lancasters; and 109 Squadron had two pressurised Mk VI Wellingtons. This had a profound effect on the efficiency of the force during its first nine months. One of the main arguments in favour of forming a separate force was to ensure uniformity of equipment, but this was impossible when all the replacements had to come from the parent group. It could be argued that they were no worse off than the majority of the Main Force but less notice was taken if Main Force crews performed indifferently. Pathfinder crews, on the other hand, were sniped at from all angles if their marking was not on the top line. The Lancaster was really the only plane suitable for the role. This can be said without slandering the other three types, for they had neither the ceiling nor the reserves of speed essential to pathfinding. It was almost impossible to mark the target accurately when ploughing through a flak barrage; yet this was the constant lot of the Stirling. The Wellingtons and Halifaxes fared little better. Timing was as important as accuracy, so that if Met winds were wrong or if there were adverse weather conditions, lack of performance inevitably made them late on target.

H2S attacks suffered enormously in the early stages because the first two squadrons to be fitted with it were flying Stirlings and Halifaxes. The Halifax had been chosen as the experimental plane because it offered a greater choice of positions for the scanner. To make matters worse, Churchill, when approving the operational use of H2S, had said in pique[1] that they could equip two squadrons of Stirlings. The result was that during the first half of 1943, Nos. 7 and 35 Squadrons had to bear the brunt of pathfinding beyond the Ruhr and outside *Oboe* range.

---

1. Churchill was fed up with the wrangling over H2S and after giving his approval to equip two squadrons, paused, scowled , and then added 'of Stirlings'. No one dared argue in case he changed his mind and withdrew his approval.

The Vickers Wellington, The Wimpey as it was affectionately known to Servicemen and public alike, was the backbone of Bomber Command during the formative years, 1941-2. In the '1,000-bomber' raid on Cologne, 599 were Wimpeys. Because of its geodetic design it was immensely strong and could take tremendous punishment, particularly from flak. As raids increased in strength the Germans concentrated their defences and the Wellington's ability to absorb punishment was tested to the full. Its inadequate defence of four .303 guns and its lack of speed made it an easy prey for the German nightfighters unless it escaped by skilful evasive action. In the race to be first Pathfinders to cross the enemy coast it was a Wellington of 156 Squadron which took the honour. When in January 1943, PFF became a group, Bennett immediately made plans to convert his heavy squadrons to Lancasters and 156 Squadron was the first to re-equip. It was a more protracted operation to convert 156 than the other heavy squadrons, which were already using four-engined aircraft, because the pilots had to be instructed in the art of flying with four engines, and crew strength had to be increased from five to seven because Wellingtons did not carry a mid-upper gunner or a flight engineer.

The Short Stirling was the first four-engined monoplane to enter service with Bomber Command and 7 Squadron received its first Stirling in August 1940. It had the distinction of being the only four-engined monoplane to be originally designed as such, but its performance was limited because the 1936 specifications laid down a maximum wingspan of 100 feet[2] and this seriously reduced its ceiling. Only the robust construction of the Stirling and the quality of its crews enabled it to withstand the mauling from German flak and perform in its new role.

Some Mk IIIs were allocated to 7 Squadron but it found that the more powerful Hercules XVI engines improved performance only marginally. The service ceiling was given as 17,000 feet, but most pilots would have been pleased to get within 1,000 feet of that. Bennett had PFF Stirlings stripped of all non-essentials to improve performance, and for Bennett the protective armour came into this category. But 7 Squadron continued their Blind-Marking and Blind Illuminating duties in Stirlings until 83 and 156 squadrons were equipped with H2S in May 1943. Bennett was then able to give them a brief stand-down in order to re-equip with Lancasters.

The Handley Page Halifax was the second four-engined monoplane to come into service and 35 Squadron was the first to get them. Although the Stirling was its senior by three months[3] it had the honour of being the first four-engined bomber to attack the Fatherland (Mar 12-13, 1941). The H.P.56, from which it was developed, was designed to the same specifications as the Manchester but Air Ministry persuaded Handley

---

2. So that the bombers could be housed in the existing hangars.
3. Operationally by one month.

Page to glue four Rolls-Royce Merlins on the wings in place of the two Rolls-Royce Vultures. Halifaxes had nasty habits particularly on take-off and landing.[4] Yawing, which was not conducive to accurate bombing, was cured only when rectangular fins were adopted (Mk II Series 1A). That all was not well could be clearly seen from the fact that there were three series of Mk I and also three of Mk II. The modifications were chiefly to overcome problems of aerodynamics and performance and both the front and dorsal turrets were sacrificed in the process.

When the Stirling became obsolescent in 1943 the demand for the Hercules XVI engines eased and so it was possible to power the Mk III Halifax with these 1,615 H.P. units, giving it an all-round increase in performance. No. 35 Squadron received its first Mk III production aircraft in July 1943 and gradually exchanged its Mk IIs for them. It was the last heavy squadron in PFF to convert to Lancasters and this was not until March 1944, after the Battle of Berlin. When 405 Squadron was transferred from the newly formed 6 Group on April 19, 1943, it was equipped with Halifaxes and operated in them until August 1943. It was then re-equipped with Lancasters.

The Avro Lancaster was the outstanding heavy bomber of World War II. Its performance – 260-270 m.p.h. at 22,000 feet with an all-up-weight of 60,000 pounds – put it in a class apart and only in defensive armament could the Fortress and Liberator claim to be superior. Its flying characteristics were superb; it was easier to service and its enormous bomb-bay accommodated the Tallboy and, when modified, the Grand Slam. It was the only aircraft capable of carrying these bombs. It inherited its bomb-bay from the Manchester from which it was developed.

By contrast, the Manchester was an abject failure and its service with Bomber Command was short lived. Its failure put A.V. Roe out of favour with Air Ministry and when they asked for materials to develop a four-engined bomber they were told to 'dig for it'. Fortunately Avro did not take the rebuff too seriously and proceeded to make a four-engined prototype which was called the Manchester III. It used the Manchester I airframe with the three-fin tail, and was powered by four Rolls-Royce Merlin X eingines. It was virtually what Air Ministry had suggested Handley Page should do in 1937, yet Avro had now to sell the idea back to them.

Between January 9, 1941, when the first prototype flew, and Ocotober 31, when the first production Lancaster took to the air, several modifications had been made; the central fin had disappeared and the twin fins and rudders of the Manchester IA had been fitted instead; dorsal

---

4. At Pocklington, the flying control tower was near the intersection of the runways, and after many near misses from swinging aircraft a trench was dug around it to trap the offenders. It was probably the most unpopular Flying Control posting in the RAF and when posted out the officers talked of having 'done a tour'.

and ventral turrets had been added and the aircraft now boasted four Merlin XXs in place of the Merlin Xs. No. 44 (Rhodesian) Squadron of 5 Group received the first operational Lancasters and the whole Group was equipped with them by the time 83 Squadron was tranferred to PFF in August 1942.

156 Squadron was re-equipped with Lancasters in January 1943 and when, in April 1943, 97 and 405 Squadrons were transferred to Pathfinders, No. 97 came from 5 Group and so was already flying Lancasters. By the end of August Nos. 7 and 405 Squadrons were operating Lancasters; which left 35 Squadron the odd one out. Bennett wanted to equip the whole Group with Lancasters but Harris insisted that he kept one Halifax squadron for crews volunteering from 4 Group who would have been operating in them and there were also Halifax squadrons in 1 and 6 Groups. This was an unnecessary precaution because the pilots could have done their conversion while the navigators and bomb-aimers were undergoing their intensive course in Pathfinder techniques.

The ventral turret of the Mark III gradually gave way to the H2S cupola and this eventually became standard on all Bomber Command Lancasters. The Mk III came to Pathfinders via 156 Squadron in March 1943: it differed from the Mk I only in engines, being powered by Packard Merlins made in America under licence; 8 Group seemed to get more than its fair share of them, for no apparent reason, but it did help towards standardisation.

When Avro were developing the Lincoln, using the two-stage Merlin 87 engines with four-blade propellers, they realized the new engines, which developed 1,625 h.p., would increase the performance of existing Lancasters, so they earmarked ten to be fitted with them. Of these, six did service trials with Bomber Command and all were allocated to 8 Group: five were sent to 635 Squadron and 405 Squadron had the sixth. In fact, 635 Squadron was not greedy with its special charges and lent them to 7, 83 and 582 Squadrons. S/Ldr Craig did fourteen Master Bomber sorties in one of them (JB 675). One was lost to the enemy and the other five were withdrawn from active service towards the end of November 1944. The operational experience greatly reduced teething troubles in the Lincoln development.

In March 1944, Bennett was allowed to convert 35 Squadron to Lancasters and this was completed by the end of the month. So PFF had been in existence for over eighteen months before it was fully equipped with the two finest bombers to be built anywhere in the world during the Second World War, the Lancaster and the Mosquito.

There were in all 43 Marks of Mosquito but it was so versatile that only five of them come within the scope of this book. The Mosquito was a twin-engined[5] monoplane with an all-wooden airframe and it was origi-

---

5. Rolls-Royce Merlins on all bomber versions except the Mk XXV.

nally developed as a private enterprise by de Havilland. In 1938 the idea of an unarmed bomber, relying on its speed and manoeuvrability to evade fighters, was too way-out for the Air Council. The exception was Sir Wilfred Freeman who had sufficient faith in the project to fight for it whenever it came on the agenda. In spite of the fact that it was designed as a bomber all the British bomber versions had a corresponding PR version, and in fact its first role with Bomber Command was photographic reconnaissance.

No. 105 Squadron was the first to operate it as a bomber, carrying out daring daylight raids on its own and with 139 Squadron, usually from a low level. The destruction of the Quisling Headquarters at Oslo on September 25, 1942, the spectacular attack on the Philips works at Eindhoven in December 1942 and the attack on Jena on May 27, 1943 (one of the deepest daylight penetrations of the war), were just three out of more than 100 forays.

The Mk IV had a cruising speed of over 300 m.p.h. and a ceiling of just under 29,000 feet. It was originally designed to carry a bomb-load of 2,000 pounds, but later Mk IVs were modified to carry Cookies. Its ceiling and speed made it the most suitable aircraft to carry *Oboe* and 109 Squadron received its first Mk IV on July 21, 1942.

The Mk IX had more powerful two-stage Merlin engines which increased the ceiling and the cruising speed, and in addition to its normal bomb-load it could carry either two 500-pounders under the wings or two drop tanks when extra fuel was needed. Like the Mk IVs some were modified to carry Cookies. No. 109 Squadron received its first Mk IX on April 21, 1943, but they were not used operationally until June 11-12 in a raid on Dusseldorf.

The Mk XVI was the pressurised version of the Mk IX and performance varied more from aircraft to aircraft than between the different Marks; the flat-out speed was 400 m.p.h. The slightly pregnant appearance of the bomber when standing next to the PR and fighter versions proclaimed her ability to carry the Cookie. Some XVIs were fitted with paddle blades to increase performance at height and this enabled them to reach 40,000 feet, but the price was loss of performance at lower heights.

In November 1943, the first Mk XXs, the Canadian-built Mosquito Mk IX, were delivered to 139 Squadron and its maiden sortie was to Berlin on December 2. The last bomber version to enter service during the war was also built in Canada, the Mk XXV. It differed from the Mk XX only in engines, being powered by the American Packard Merlin 225. The only disadvantage with Canadian-built Mosquitoes was that none of them was modified to carry the 4,000-pounder.

The Mosquito was the only British plane to attack Berlin after March 1944. *Oboe* Mosquitoes took part in daylight marking and daylight formations which included many to the Ruhr: the formations to Happy

Valley were done in conjunction with the LNSF. Yet, in spite of having no defensive armament, the loss rate in 8 Group was only 0.4%. From a modest 133 sorties in June 1943, the number increased to a peak in April 1945 when 2,405 were flown including 1,000 to Berlin.

Appendix X
Personnel

PFF eventually became the best equipped Group in Bomber Command but the Second World War was not a war of robots or guided missiles, although the German V-1s and V-2s did make a brief appearance. The fighting forces still depended on the human element and the best were drawn to the RAF. The irresistible magnets were the glamour, the opportunity of displaying individual skills, the chance to use powers of leadership, the thrill of flying, the opportunity to show courage. In addition, the force was the youngest and, in spite of the achievements of the Great War, its tradition was clearly in the making. The Battle of Britain, Bomber Command's part in the ultimate victory, Coastal Command's destruction of the U-Boat, all bear witness that they were correct in their judgment of where the vital challenge lay. The sky was a symbol of freedom and that was what the war was about.

No. 8 Group was composed of heavies and the LNSF, *Oboe* and Met flight Mosquitoes, each requiring different types of courage and skills. Getting crews for the heavies was the chief problem; the 'chop rate' on Mosquitoes was so low that there were always plenty of volunteers. All crews were volunteers (even the founder members) and in the early days Bennett had little choice in who came, but much say in who stayed. He was a hard taskmaster and only crews who reached his standards were allowed to remain. The best crews from the groups were supposed to be transferred to his force. Inevitably, it was not the case; with equal inevitability the inferior ones were weeded out and posted back. This did not help recruitment because if they did not make the grade they were blacklegged when they returned to their Groups.

At first, because they knew the odds, only experienced crews had any chance of being accepted. PFF had to open the attacks and this meant it had to brave the flak before the Main Force swamped the defences. Crews had to be 'press-on' types but they had to be more; they had to keep calm and assured because a TI in the wrong place was worse than no TI at all. Reliability was another essential characteristic as not only the Main Force but others in PFF depended on each aircraft being at a certain place at a definite time. Timing was the navigator's responsibility but even the best navigator was only as good as his pilot's course and airspeed; the accuracy of his navigation depended on the pilot maintaining a good course at a steady airspeed. Navigation was a skilled trade carried out under trying conditions: plotting on a chart; measuring angles and distances precisely, although cramped for space and with poor lighting; working to a regular time schedule taking fixes, then calculating new courses and ETAs were a full-time occupation. Maintaining a good air plot and keeping an accurate log were essential to good navigation, but the best navigators had that something extra – confidence in themselves. To use a wind which was entirely different from the forecast wind needed moral courage. If you were wrong and the nightfighters didn't have you for breakfast then you were meat and gravy for the Squadron Navigation Officer. On the other hand, if you used the Met wind you knew you would not be alone.

Dropping TIs in the right place required both precision and courage in the bomb-aimer. He alone of the crew was looking directly down on the flak. It was an awesome sight to see it coming straight towards you and bursting all around; or to watch a searchlight drifting ever closer knowing what was in store if you were coned. Throughout, he had to give directions to the pilot and keep his nerve until the target was in his bombsight. A good concentration of TIs was essential to a good attack so he had to guard against an 'itchy' finger. The chief crime was to undershoot because the tendancy of most attacks was creepback. He had to be a good map reader from height. When H2S was introduced the bomb-aimer worked in conjunction with the navigator and operated the set. If *Window* had to be dropped it was his job.

The flight engineer was constantly watching the instruments, checking and logging the fuel supply, working out the petrol consumption. By generally lending a helping hand, checking the course, height and airspeed, a good engineer could be a boon to his captain. He was required to have an extensive knowledge of the workings of flaps and undercarriage and when the bomb-aimer was otherwise gainfully employed he took over the task of dropping *Window*. He had to be proficient in the use of a sextant and in star recognition. He had to have a knowledge of bomb-aiming procedures and be able to use the Mk XIV bombsight.

The wireless operator (known as the 'Wop') had a longer list of duties than the flight engineer. Originally he was trained to double with the air gunner but as the war progressed his compartment became so filled with gadgets there was little room left for him. He was responsible for the various airborne jamming devices designed to make life difficult for the German nightfighters. He had to be proficient in Gee manipulation and be able to supply necessary W/T aid. When *Fishpond* was introduced he worked the set and warned the gunners of approaching nightfighters, giving them a bearing and distance.

Then the two lonely jobs – the gunners. There was no relaxation for them. From the moment of take-off until landing the lives of the crew rested on their vigilance. No admiring the 'wizard prang' or counting the searchlights to relieve the monotony, that was the moment the fighter struck. Instant recognition immediately a plane came into view; fire first to discourage him from attacking and to show him you were awake. These were the rules, for they were outgunned both in power and in range and few fighters gave a second chance. The tail gunner never saw another crew member throughout the sortie. Although certainly in the hot seat, it was nevertheless a cold and lonely job. Both gunners had to be familiar with the theory and practice of deflection aiming and the tail gunner had to be able to take a drift with his gun-sight.

Each crew member had to be an expert in his own field and yet weld himself into the team whose strength depended on their confidence in each other. This team spirit was invariably the final responsibility of the pilot. He had to impose his personality on the crew and gain their respect so that his decisions were accepted without question and obeyed instantly. In order to make correct decisions he had to have some knowledge of everyone's job and, for Pathfinders, be above average at his own. In particular, it was necessary for him to have a comprehensive knowledge of navigation and also be able to map-read from height. In PFF, bombs (TIs) and flares were dropped only on a direct order from the captain, who had to be certain the correct target was being approached and the bombing run an accurate one; then he would order the bomb-aimer to carry on and attack. Those were the requirements: the reader can judge whether they were met.

Pathfinders had to work as a team and each crew had a specific task. In a cricket team the side is chosen to suit the ground and the expected weather conditons, and also the type of match being played. The selectors have to consider which form of attack is best suited to the conditions – the number of seam bowlers and whether to include one or more slow bowlers. All rounders and specialist fielders are essential – wicket-keeper, slip, leg-slip and cover point – yet it must be a balanced side.

Similarly, Bennet had to decide which type of attack was most suited to the target and the expected weather conditions. Each method of marking called for different skills and the squadron commanders had to choose the crews most suited to meet the requirements. All crews did not mark but this did not mean that the other jobs were less important, although experienced crews did do the actual marking. Originally crews did not specialize in one role[1] and were sometimes called upon to perform more

1. With the exception of *Oboe* crews.

than one task on a raid. It was up to the squadron commander to judge what was a crew's *métier* and, when possible, select them for that job. In 1944 there was a move towards specialisation but the boundaries were not rigid.

Here the analogy ends because the size of the team and the duties varied with each raid and Bennett had to decide how many crews would be needed to keep the target marked throughout the attack. Extra crews were allotted to each category to guard against mechanical and special equipment failure. This was always a difficult decision: too few and the attack suffered; too many and the crews were exposed to danger to no good purpose. As an added precaution, because the weather at the target was often not as predicted, Bennett often laid on an alternative method of marking to cater for all contingencies.[2]

For a full-scale attack here is the batting order with a brief description of the duties:

(1) Route-markers[3] dropped flares or TIs at important turning points to help the Main Force crews keep in the stream and these were usually backed-up by other crews. Any or all of the marker-crews could be assigned to drop the original route-markers. Land-markers were a type of route-marker dropped a short distance from the target (between 15 and 20 miles). If the Main Force crews did a timed run from this point they could never bomb dummy TIs by mistake because the time factor would be wrong.

(ii) *Windowers* dropped strips of tin foil which produced echoes on the German ground controller's radar screens and also jammed radar-controlled flak guns. *Window* made it difficult to estimate the number of planes and impossible to identify individual ones. PFF sent *Windowers* ahead of the marker crews to try to buy a little peace for them to do a good bombing run. As the LSNF grew in strength, it gradually took over the role. Then it had a two-pronged effect because, when the Mosquitoes carried out actual raids they dropped *Window* to give the impression it was going to be a big raid, and the Germans were kept in doubt whether it was a main attack or a spoof.

(iii) Supporters[4] were usually inexperienced Pathfinder crews being blooded. They arrived in the target area with the first wave of Illuminators to help saturate the defences. The essential point for a Supporter was to be on time. His bombs could be dropped blindly, using special equipment, visually on markers or, if detailed, on flak defences.

---

2. This was usually an Emergency *Wanganui* but sometimes Blind Markers dropped both sky and groundmarkers.

3. The titles describe the aircraft's role; it was the crews who personalized them.

4. The word Supporter does not appear on the Battle Order until late 1943, but Air Vice-Marshal Bennett assured me they were used from the beginning.

Like *Windowers* they helped to take some of the pressure off marker crews.

(iv) Blind Illuminators dropped flares to help Visual Markers on *Newhaven* attacks. They used H2S to find the target and then dropped their flares blindly using one of the methods already described[5].

(v) Blind Markers dropped TIs and skymarkers using only their special equipment; if it was unserviceable they brought their markers back. H2S crews used one of the same methods as the Blind Illuminators. After August 17, 1944, they did not drop their TIs if the target had been marked visually. *Oboe* crews dropped on a release signal sent from a ground station.

Visual Markers used the Mk XIV bombsight to aim their TIs.

(vi) Primary Visual Markers only dropped their TIs if they could identify the aiming point visually. They were selected from the most expert and experienced Visual Markers.

(vii) Backers-up or Visual Centerers had to estimate the MPI of all the Primary Markers and drop their TIs on this point.[6] Their TIs were usually of a different colour from those of the primaries to help the Main Force distinguish between primary and secondary markers. They operated on all large scale attacks for it was their job to see that the target was illuminated at all times.

(viii) Recenterers had to keep the attack on the aiming point. Most attacks had a tendency to creep back from the target as the raid progressed and so the Visual Centerers overshot the A/P with their markers. It was hoped that the Main Force, seeing the TIs some distance away, would wait a second or two longer before dropping their load, bringing the weight of the attack back to the centre.

Owing to the uncertainty of the weather in the target area some crews always carried *Wanganui* flares in case the target was cloud-covered. They also dropped them if the Germans were using an effective smoke screen. When a Master Bomber was in attendance they were dropped only on an order from him.

PFF's role was not merely blazing the trail and finding the target: with the advent of better navigational aids, failure to do this was extremely rare. That concentration was the keynote to a successful raid has been stressed. PFF found this problem difficult to solve. Where the Main Force dropped their bombs was the responsibility of individual crews and a few fringe merchants could draw the MPI away from the aiming point.

(ix) To try to obviate this, a Master Bomber was detailed to control the more important raids. The idea was not a new one; it was first proposed by

---

5. See Mk XIV Bombsight and GPI.

6. The exception to this rule was when they were backing *Oboe* markers, then they bombed the *Oboe* TIs.

F/Lt E.W. Anderson in 1942 when he was at BCHQ, but the 'powers that be' considered it too risky. In early 1943, S/Ldr S.P. Daniels was given permission to control an attack on Munich but, owing to icing, failed to reach the target. W/Cdr G.P. Gibson was therefore the first to use it operationally when 617 Squadron attacked the Dams. W/Cdr J.H. Searby was the first to use it in conjunction with the Main Force. After a dress rehearsal at Turin on August 7-8, 1943, he led the attack on Peenemunde on the 17th-18th.

The duty of the Master Bomber was simplicity itself. He merely instructed the Main Force how to aim their bombs to achieve the greatest concentration. The role was not so simple, and that is why 'only men of proven ability possessing the qualities of leadership, flexibility of outlook, clear judgment and capable of immediate reaction to changed circumstances were selected for the job.'[7] The description is flattering and certainly men with lesser qualifications could have performed the task satisfactorily, but it was because the Main Force knew that the Master Bomber possessed these qualities that it obeyed his instructions without demur.

The requirements were different for large attacks over well defended targets from those on small strategic ones. On the former, his importance was mainly psychological. There were usually sufficient Markers, Backers-up and Recenterers to keep the A/P illuminated throughout the attack. Although in greater personal danger from flak and fighters on these targets, he had to impart a quiet confidence and coolness to the Main Force crews, keeping his voice calm and assured to help new crews conquer their 'butterflies'. As an Aussie skipper said after a raid on Leipzig: 'It's not always so much the instructions you notice, but the relief at hearing a good English voice getting things organised ahead of you after that long slog through flak and dirty weather.'[8]

The Germans used imitation TIs, decoy fires and smoke screens to cause as much confusion as possible for the bombers. If briefing instructions were carried out, then dummy TIs could never be mistaken for the real thing, but in the heat of the fray, when every gun seemed to be aiming at you and every searchlight searching for you, it was difficult for mere mortals to remember precisely what some officer had said hours before in the quiet of the briefing room. If there were fires round the dummy TIs it was more confusing, and as the Germans still tried to blow you out of the sky even when you were bombing their decoys, it gave the scene even more realism. So, the Main Force welcomed the Master Bomber as it had previously welcomed PFF: he relieved crews of the responsibility of decision, and their inadequacies and inexperience were not exposed. This

---

7. *Flight*, March 9, 1946.
8. David Irving, *The Destruction of Dresden*.

applied particularly to new crews who needed the help and encouragement while they were finding their feet.

On smaller targets, the Master Bomber's duty was the same, but the role was more intimate. The target area was smaller and so obviously was the margin of error. Smaller targets and fewer bombers required maximum concentration to achieve a successful raid. As the number of bombers was often as low as 50, the bombs of each aircraft were of relatively greater importance. The targets were in many cases vital strategically, so, if there were 10/10ths cloud, the Master Bomber had to dive through it to find the base, and then he had to decide whether it was safe to bring the Main Force down to attack. The heavy PFF contingent on these raids rarely numbered more than five, and often only three; Master, Deputy and Backer-up. *Oboe* Mosquitoes usually dropped the initial markers and the Master Bomber used them to pinpoint the aiming point. If he considered that the *Musical* markers were insufficiently accurate, he either marked the aiming point himself or instructed his Deputy to do so. The Master, Deputy and Backer-up had to be ready to reinforce the markers before they burnt out, or to re-mark if they were obliterated.

(x) The Deputy was the Master Bomber's 'Man Friday'. If for any reason the Master Bomber was unable to control the sortie, then the Deputy took over his full responsibility. His duties included those of a Primary Visual Marker.

(xi) 'Keep 'em flying' was a wartime slogan and an operational station had 2,000 airmen and WAAF whose primary job was to do this. Harris tried to get recognition for the work done by ground personnel and asked the Government to give them a special campaign medal, which they richly deserved, but all to no avail. Was it too much to ask of a Government to realize that their oft-quoted citation 'devotion above and beyond the call of duty . . .' applied to the daily task of the ground crews? Whilst not implying it was a nightly occurrence an incident at Oakington in November 1944 illustrates their dedication. Cpl Williams, an armourer with 7 Squadron broke his wrist during the usual flap to get the aircraft bombed-up. Nevertheless he continued with his duties for two hours until the worst of the rush was over.

Airframe fitters and engineers had to work in the open in every kind of weather and often against the clock. Electricians, working in ridiculously confined spaces, had to check all lights and power supplies. Armourers reloaded the ammunition and checked the guns and, the most dangerous job in the Air Force, they armed the bombs. The 'chop rate' among armourers was second only to that of aircrew. It was a trade where there was no second chance. There was no funeral, just a memorial service.

An accident at Gravely in July 1943, believed to have been caused by a No. 37 Arming Pistol, resulted in the deaths of seven airmen. Again, on

September 9, 1944, after an abortive sortie to Le Havre, at Upwood the five 156 Squadron Lancasters were being de-bombed when suddenly the bombs on one of the trailers exploded and seven airmen were killed; no trace was ever found of four of them; many other ground crew working on the aircraft were injured, three of them dangerously.

The success or failure of every attack depended on the serviceability of the special equipment. Radar mechanics specialized in one type of equipment – Gee, H2S or *Oboe* and, as these were all in or near the navigator's small compartment, they constantly found themselves baulking each other trying to reach their particular boxes. The API and the GPI were also in the navigator's funk hole and, in addition, a compass and the intercom had to be checked. The competition to get into the Wop's compartment was scarcely less hectic. He had even less space than the navigator and was virtually hemmed in by equipment.

The photographic department having loaded the cameras and set them so that the shutter would open when the photoflash ignited – this varied with the bombing height and the type of flash being used – fitted them on to the aircraft and checked the electrical connections. PPI cameras were fitted after the H2S sets had been tested because the focusing tube varied with each Mark of H2S. The initial assessment of the attack was based on photographs. From the moment the first plane landed, it was a mad rush developing and printing, so that the results could be on the AOC's desk at the earliest possible moment.

Each section had to co-operate in making it a team effort because everyone was working against the clock to get the aircraft ready in time, yet the work had to be done conscientiously. Faulty controls, unserviceable hydraulics, a sick engine, could heighten the tension on a sortie. Carelessness by the electrician could cause a hang-up or a wrong TI being dropped and might ruin an attack. A faulty instrument would create at least anxiety to a crew working under stress and might occasion disaster. That bombsights, compasses and the whole paraphernalia of gauges and rev-counters were working correctly was vital and not only for peace of mind. Countless small items, probably never used or only in emergency, like fire extinguishers, had to be checked daily. A jammed gun or the wrong type of ammunition could cause the death of the gunner and even of the whole crew.

They grumbled, that is part of the Englishman's heritage, but they still did their jobs, working all hours for poor pay and little credit. The overtime they put in out of necessity brought them no financial reward and no favours. Civilians, even in wartime, would have come out on strike for better pay and conditions, but pride in themselves, their aircraft and their squadrons kept the early returns, due to mechanical failure, down to a minimum.

Of the ground personnel who did not work on the aircraft equipment, perhaps the WAAF in the parachute section had the most responsible job. The only way to test a parachute was to use it and, as the humorists used to say the section never received any complaints. The WAAF MT drivers played an important role. They were the last women the crew saw before take-off and their smiles and 'Good luck' (not sentimentality but a fervent wish) eased the tension and most aircrew managed to smile back and say 'Thank you'.

The staff in Flying Control were in charge of two of the most dangerous manoeuvres of a sortie, take-off and landing. There were many others like administration and catering staffs: the sports officer and the padre; the non-Service personnel in the NAAFI and the 'Sally Ann' (Salvation Army). Specialized histories could be written about them all. If an ungrateful country did not appreciate them, the aircrew did, and so did men like Harris and Bennett. For, as sure as the army would never have got on to the Continent without the air forces so aircrews would never have got into the air without the diligence of their faithful friends on the ground.

Appendix XI
8 Group Squadrons

Squadron	*Code*		*Equipped*	*Re-equipped*
7	MG	Transferred from 3 Group August 1942	Stirlings	Lancasters July 1943
35	TL	Transferred from 4 Group August 1942	Halifaxes	Lancasters March 1944
83	OL	Transferred from 5 Group August 1942	Lancasters	
97	OF	Transferred from 5 Group April 1943	Lancasters	
105	GB	Transferred from 2 Group June 1943	Mosquitoes	
109	HS	Transferred from WIDU August 1942	Wellingtons	Mosquitoes August 1942
128	M5	Re-formed at Wyton September 1944	Mosquitoes	
139	XD	Transferred from 2 Group June 1943	Mosquitoes	
142	4H	Re-formed at Gransden Lodge October 1944	Mosquitoes	
156	GT	Transferred from 1 Group August 1942	Wellingtons	Lancasters January 1943
162	CR	Re-formed at Bourn December 1944	Mosquitoes	
163		Re-formed at Wyton January 1945	Mosquitoes	
405	LQ	Transferred from 6 Group April 1943	Halifaxes	Lancasters August 1943
571	8K	Formed at Downham Market November 1943	Mosquitoes	
582	60	Formed at Little Staughton April 1944	Lancasters	

The Pathfinder Force

Squadron	*Code*		*Equipped*
608	6T	Re-formed at Downham Market August 1944	Mosquitoes
627	A2	Formed at Oakington November 1943	Mosquitoes
635	F2	Formed at Downham Market March 1944	Lancasters
692	P3	Formed at Graveley January 1944	Mosquitoes

Map 25.

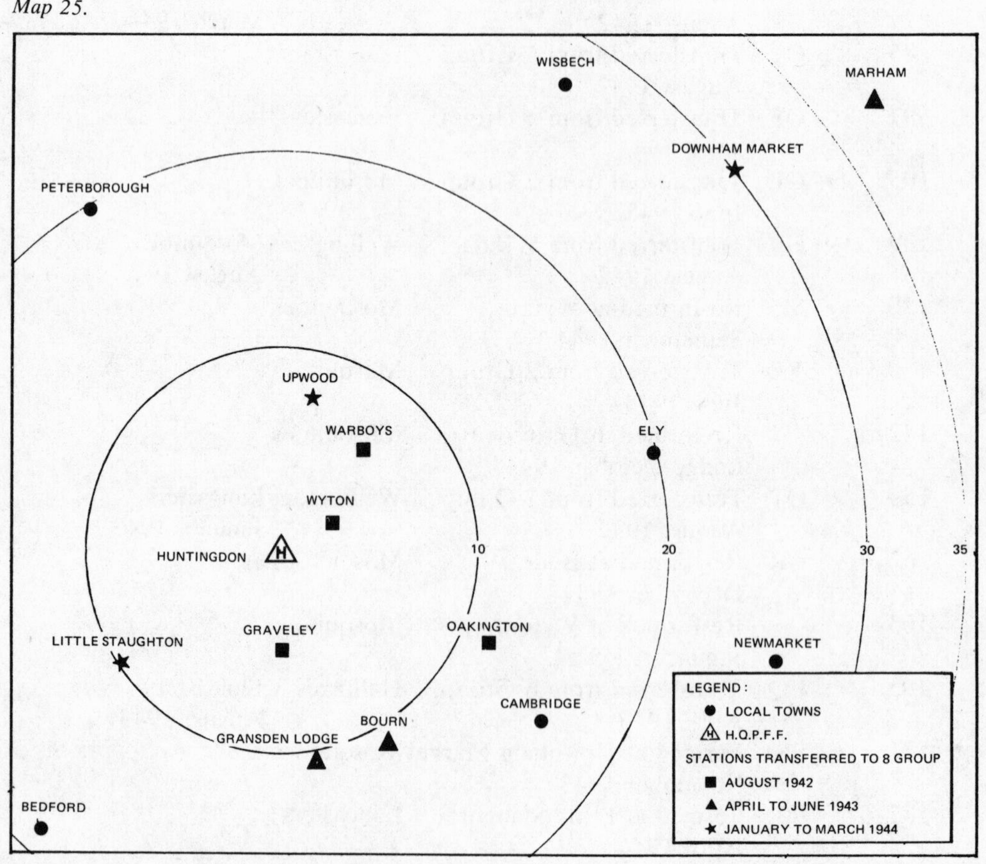

PFF Stations

Station	*Squadron*	*From*		*To*		*Posted to*
Bourn	97	April	1943	April	1944	5 Group (on loan)
	105	April	1944	May	1945	
	162	December	1944	May	1945	
Downham	635	March	1944	May	1945	
Market	571	April 7th	1944	April 12th	1944	Graveley
	608	August	1944	May	1945	
Graveley	35	August	1942	May	1945	
	692	January	1944	May	1945	
	571	April 12th	1944	April 22nd	1944	Oakington
Gransden	405	April	1943	May	1945	
Lodge	142	October	1944	May	1945	
Huntingdon	HQPFF	June	1943	May	1945	
Little	582	April	1944	May	1945	
Staughton	109	April	1944	May	1945	
Marham	105	June	1943	April	1944	Bourn
	139	June	1943	July	1943	Wyton
	109	July	1943	April	1944	Little Staughton
	1655 MCU	July	1943	March	1944	Warboys
Oakington	7	August	1942	May	1945	
	1409 Flight	April	1943	January	1944	Wyton
	627	November	1943	April	1944	5 Group (on loan)
	571	April 22nd	1944	May	1945	
Upwood	156	March	1944	May	1945	
	139	February	1944	May	1945	
Warboys	156	August	1942	March	1944	Upwood
	PFFTU	March	1944	May	1945	
	1655 MCU	March	1944	December	1944	
	became					
	16 OTU	December	1944	May	1945	
Wyton	PFFHQ	August	1942	June	1943	Huntingdon
	83	August	1942	April	1944	5 Group (on loan)
	139	July	1943	February	1944	Upwood
	1409 Flight	January	1944	May	1945	
	128	September	1944	May	1945	
	163	January	1945	May	1945	

Appendix XII
The effect of area bombing on production

Map 26.

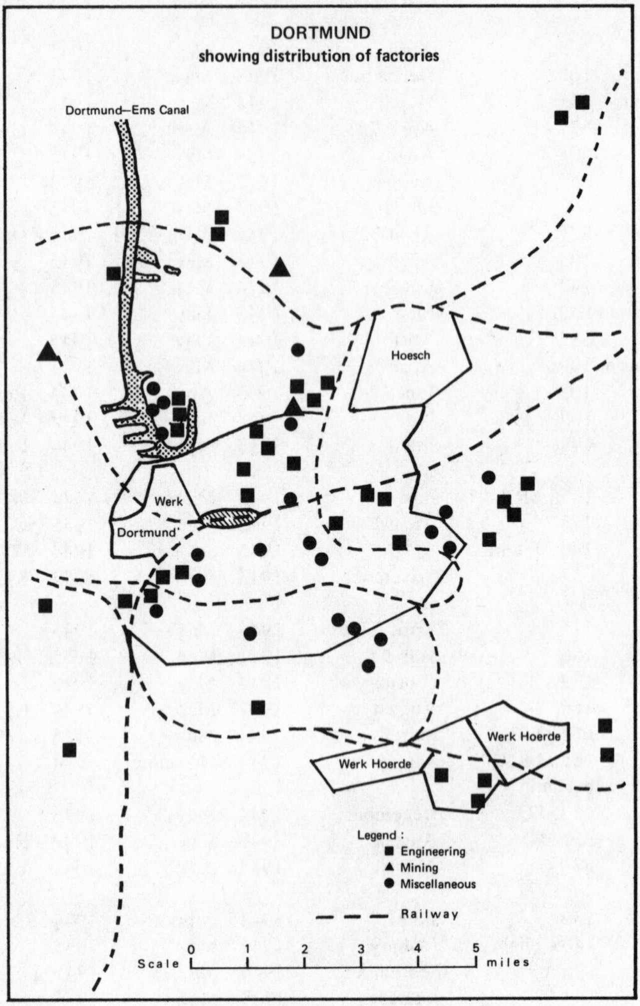

DORTMUND
showing distribution of factories

Dortmund–Ems Canal
Hoesch
Werk
Dortmund'
Werk Hoerde
Werk Hoerde

Legend :
Engineering
Mining
Miscellaneous
Railway

Scale 0 1 2 3 4 5 miles

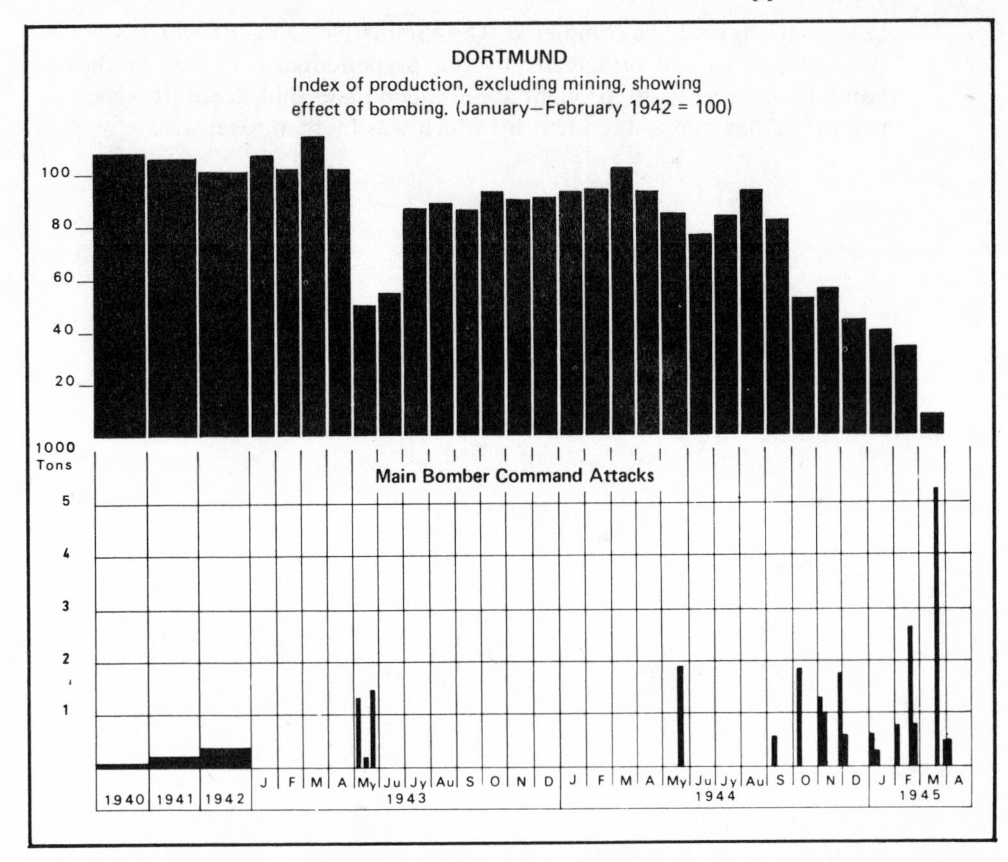

Fig 15 The small raid in May, 1943 was the Dams raid. The breaching of the Mohne dam caused flooding in the pumping stations and the coal mines. There was a serious temporary shortage of water, and production in the mines was affected for several weeks.
The small attacks from September 1944 were all against the towns oil plants. The attack of November 11, 1944 from above cloud on the Hoesch Benzine plant caused serious damage in the main complex. Loss of production in the three main plants was almost entirely due to the damage of the main services. Not until the saturation raid of March 1945 did its recovery become hopeless, although only under conditions of peace could it have reached its 1942 level.

To illustrate the effect of area bombing on production Dortmund was selected because its main factories were on the outskirts of the town. The immediate effect, clearly indicated in the graph (Fig 15), was due to the disruption of the services (gas, electricity and water) and damage to the small industries scattered through the town.

Production loss in the three main factories was only small until the autumn of 1944 when systematic attacks caused additional damage before repairs could be completed. The cumulative damage to the essential services, caused principally by the preponderance of HE in the bomb-loads, eventually brought about a complete shut-down irrespective of the damage to the factories which was by then extensive.

Abbreviations

AA	Anti-aircraft
ABC	Airborne Cigar
AI	Air Interception
AMOs	Air Ministry Orders
AOC	Air Officer Commanding
AOC-in-C	Air Officer Commanding-in-Chief
A/P	Aiming Point
ASI	Airspeed Indicator
ASV	Air-to-Surface Vessel (radar device)
AVM	Air Vice-Marshal
BAT	Blind Approach Technique
BCH	Bomber Command Headquarters
CAS	Chief of the Air Staff
CHL	Chain Home Low
CIU	Central Interpretation Unit (Stationed at Medmenham)
CO	Commanding Officer
CSBS	Course Setting Bombsight
Do	Dornier
DR	Dead Reckoning (Navigation)
ETA	Estimated Time of Arrival (Navigation)
F/Lt	Flight Lieutenant
FNSF	Fast Night Striking Force (See LNSF)
F/O	Flying Officer
Fw	Focke-Wulf
GAF	German Air Force
GCI	Ground Controlled Interception
G/Capt	Group Captain
GP	General Purpose (bomb)
HC	High Capacity (bomb)
HCU	Heavy Conversion Unit
HE	High Explosive
He	Heinkel

HQ	Headquarters
IAS	Indicated Airspeed
IBs	Incendiary Bombs
IFF	Identification Friend of Foe
Ju	Junkers
LBTI	Long-Burning Target Indicator
LNSF	Light Night Striking Force (8 Group Mosquito bombing force) also known as FNSF
MAN	*Maschinenfabrik Augsburg-Nurnberg*, AG
MAP	Ministry of Aircraft Production
MC	Medium-Capacity (bomb)
MCU	Mosquito Conversion Unit
Me	Messerschmitt
Met	Meterological
MEW	Ministry of Economic Warfare
MPI	Mean Point of Impact
MT	Motor Transport
MTU	Mosquito Training Unit
NJG	*Nachtjagdgeschwader*
ORB	Operations Record Book
ORS	Operational Research Section
OTU	Operational Training Unit
PD	Precision Device
PFF	Pathfinder Force
P/O	Pilot Officer
PoW	Prisoner of War
PPI	Plan Position Indicator (H2S)
PRU	Photographic Reconnaissance Unit
RAAF	Royal Australian Air Force
RAE	Royal Aircraft Establishment
RAF	Royal Air Force
RCAF	Royal Canadian Air Force
RDF	Radio Direction Finding
RNZAF	Royal New Zealand Air Force
SAAF	South African Air Force
SAP	Semi-Armour Piercing (bomb)
S/E	Single-engined
SIS	Special Intelligence Service
S/Ldr	Squadron Leader
TAF	Tactical Air Force
T/E	Twin-engined
TI	Target Indicator
TRE	Telecommunications Research Establishment
USAAF	United States Army Air Force

U/T	Under Training
VHF	Very High Frequency (radio)
VLBTI	Very Long Burning Target Indicator
W/Cdr	Wing Commander
WIDU	Wireless Intelligence Development Unit
W/T	Wireless Telegraphy

Glossary

Bailie Beam	A superior (narrower) Lorenz beam.
Berlin Method	The policy of dropping both skymarkers and groundmarkers irrespective of cloud conditions over the target.
Big City	Berlin.
Boffins	Technical scientists – 'back-room boys'.
Boozer	The code name for a detector which warned crews that enemy radar was holding the bomber. A yellow light lit up if the bomber was held in an AI beam and a red light when it was held by a Wurzburg.
Bullseyes	Cross-country flights made by crews of Training Command in conjunction with British ground defences to enable crews to obtain experience of conditions over German targets. U/T Pathfinder crews dropped marker bombs and flares.
Butt Report	Mr Butt collated information on the accuracy of British bombing under various weather conditions, states of the moon and types of target. The report stated that only one in five aircraft got within 75 square miles of the target. Its conclusions were a contributory factor in the lowering of crew morale in the autumn of 1941.
Caterpillar Club	To become a member an airman had to have made a compulsory parachute descent.
Cat's-eyes fighters	See *Wild Boars*.
Chop rate	The loss rate of aircraft on operations.
Cigar	The code name for British jamming of German VHF telephonic communications.
Coned	Being caught and held by searchlights.
Controlled	At attack when a Master Bomber was in attendance.

Cookies	4,000-pound bombs.
Cope	A successful *Oboe* sortie.
Corkscrew	Dive and climb manoeuvre in which bomber's path resembled a corkscrew. The most successful of the evasive-action techniques.
Corona	Spurious orders to German fighters.
Creepback	The drift further and further back along the line of approach.
Ditching	Forced landing of an aircraft on water.
FIDO	Fog investigation and dispersal operation. Burners placed at intervals on each side of the runway; the heat helped to disperse the fog and the burners provided a flare path.
Gaggle	Loose formation formed by British bombers on daylight operation.
Gardening	Minelaying in enemy waters. The mines were called vegetables: the areas were given terms like Forget-me-not and Artichoke.
Gee	Radar aid to navigation employing three ground stations.
Gomorrah	Name given to the successive attacks on Hamburg from July 24-25 to August 2-3 1943.
GH (AR5525)	Blind-bombing radar device. *Oboe* in reverse.
Grand slam	22,000-pound bomb.
Graviner	Fire extinguisher placed near the aircraft engines; detonated either automatically by thermostatic control or manually by button or switch.
H2S	A radar aid to navigation and target identification.
H2X	American version of H2S.
Happy Valley	The Ruhr Valley.
Jostle	A device for jamming German radar especially AA barrage.
Knickebein	A German navigation and bombing aid.
Long Stop	A groundmarker bomb(usually yellow) dropped to mark the limit of bombing or cancel stray TIs. Later the term was personalized when a special crew was detailed for the purpose.
Mandrel	Radio swamping of the German early-warning system.
Manna	Code name for sorties to Holland, April-May 1945, when supplies and food were dropped for the starving Dutch.

Millenium	First '1,000-bomber' raid, Cologne, May 30-31, 1942.
Monica	Tail warning device. See Appendix VIII.
Musical	Prefix added to marking techniques when *Oboe* Mosquitoes did the primary marking.
Naxos	German radar device enabling fighters to home on to transmissions from British bombers using H2S, *Fishpond* and *Monica*.
Neptune	Code word for the amphibious operations within *Overlord*, June 5-6, 1944.
Newhaven	Visual Groundmarking.
Oboe	Blind bombing radar device. See Appendix I.
Overlord	Code name for Allied invasion of France, 1944.
Overture	Code name for Oboe HE sorties.
Pampas	Code name for Met Flight sorties.
Pan	Concrete dispersal points for aircraft, usually circular.
Parramatta	Blind Groundmarking using radar.
Pickwick	Code name for instruction to bomb the upwind edge of the smoke.
Random Error	The MPI of all bombs aimed at a target.
Sampson	Blind Gee bombing attack.
Scrub	RAF slang for cancel.
Shaker	Method of illuminating and marking a target with the aid of Gee-equipped aircraft.
Siren Tours	Mosquito H2S training flights when a 500-pound bomb was dropped on each of four different targets.
Spoof	A subsidiary attack designed to draw the enemy fighters away from the Main Force.
Systematic Error	When crews were ordered to bomb Target Indicators and not attempt to identify the target for themselves the random error decreased dramatically but a new error was introduced, 'the displacement of the markers from the A/P'; this was known as the Systematic Error.
Take to the silk	Bale out.
Tallboy	12,000-pound penetrating (earthquake) bomb.
Tame Boars	Ground-controlled German nightfighters.
Tinsel	Code name for British jamming of radio telephonic communication between German nightfighters and ground controllers.
Wanganui	Blind skymarking
Wild Boars	'Freelance' German nightfighters also known as Cat's-eyes fighters.

Window	Tinfoil strips dropped by British bombers to jam German radar.
'Y' Aircraft	Aircraft equipped with H2S.
Zephyrs	Averaged winds from selected crews broadcast to all bombers.

Index

Photo Credits

Air Ministry: 55, 58b, 58d, 58e,
Author: 20, 21, 22, 24, 25, 28, 40, 56, 57, 58a, 58c, 59, 60, 63, 64
S. Baker – Garbett/Goulding Collection: 7, 41, 42
Mrs Bazalgette: 43, 49
Air Commodore G.W. Benington: 47
S.P. Daniels – Garbett/Goulding Collection: 9, 13
H.J. Davies – Garbett/Goulding Collection: 2, 10
William Green: 3
Imperial War Museum: 17, 18, 19, 45, 52, 53, 54
Howard Lees: 1, 5, 6, 8, 12, 15, 16, 23, 26, 29, 30, 33, 37, 38, 48, 50, 51, 61, 62
Sir Bernard Lovell: 35, 36
'Hamish' Mahaddie: 11
Mrs L.A. Palmer: 44
RRE Malvern: 14, 27, 34
Ald. H.H. Sandford: 4
Mike Symons: 31, 32, 39, 46